cises that are suitable for both manual and computer solution.

In addition, there is a complete review of the literature of the field and extensive bibliographies have been included.

Simulation in Business and Economics will be of special interest as a reference book for management scientists, operations researchers, systems analysts, industrial engineers, and computer programmers.

It can be read and used profitably by those who do not have computer training or access to a computer.

SIMULATION
IN BUSINESS
AND ECONOMICS

Robert C. Meier

University of Washington

William T. Newell

University of Washington

Harold L. Pazer

State University of New York at Albany

SIMULATION
IN BUSINESS
AND ECONOMICS

PRENTICE-HALL, INC., Englewood Cliffs, New Jersey

© 1969
by PRENTICE-HALL, Inc.
Englewood Cliffs, New Jersey

LIBRARY OF CONGRESS
CATALOG CARD NUMBER 69-10302

CURRENT PRINTING (last digit)
10 9 8 7 6 5 4 3 2

Prentice-Hall International, Inc., *London*
Prentice-Hall of Australia Pty. Ltd., *Sydney*
Prentice-Hall of Canada, Ltd., *Toronto*
Prentice-Hall of India Private Ltd., *New Delhi*
Prentice-Hall of Japan, Inc., *Tokyo*

Printed in the United States of America

Preface

This book is an introduction to simulation techniques as they apply to business and economics. It presents the basic concepts involved in simulation, describes applications of simulation to business and economic analysis, and discusses technical problems associated with the use of simulation. Heuristic and gaming methods are included since they are related techniques and are often termed simulations. Because most simulation studies in practice are conducted with the aid of a digital computer, emphasis is on the design and operation of computer models.

Exercises suitable for both manual and machine computation are provided at the end of each chapter. Those exercises most suited to hand-computation appear first, followed by exercises most appropriately done with the aid of a computer. With the exception of exercises in Chap. 7 which deal specifically with certain specialized computer simulation languages, any general programing language such as FORTRAN can be used for writing programs to work the exercises.

Mathematical and statistical aspects of simulation are introduced with the assumption that the reader has some knowledge of algebra, statistics, and optimizing techniques. Many references to basic sources are given in the text to assist in reviewing these concepts. Though mathematical, statistical, and computer aspects of simulation are treated extensively, the reader will also find much material of a less technical nature.

The order in which topics are presented in the book is the intended sequence for study, but the chapters can be read somewhat independently of each other. Chapter 7 might well be read between Chaps. 1 and 2 by those persons with particular interest in computer considerations in model construction. For the reader who desires to explore further in the field of simulation, extensive bibliographies have been provided at the end of each chapter. Additional references may be found in the following sources:

Malcolm, D.G., "Bibliography on the Use of Simulation in Management Analysis," *Operations Research*, Vol. 8, No. 2, (March–April, 1960).

Shubik, Martin, "Bibliography on Simulation, Gaming, and Allied Topics," *Journal of the American Statistical Association*, Vol. 55, No. 292 (December, 1960).

Simulation and Gaming: A Symposium. AMA Management Report Number 55. New York: American Management Association, Inc., 1961, pp. 113–131.

Morgenthaler, George W., "The Theory and Application of Simulation in Operations Research," in *Progress in Operations Research*, Vol. I, Russell L. Ackoff, ed.. New York: John Wiley & Sons, Inc., 1961, pp. 413–19.

Teichroew, Daniel, "A History of Distribution Sampling Prior to the Era of the Computer and Its Relevance To Simulation," *Journal of the American Statistical Association*, Vol. 60, No. 309, (March, 1965), pp. 44–49.

Bibliography on Simulation. White Plains, New York: International Business Machines Corporation, 1966.

Naylor, Thomas H., *Bibliography on Simulation and Gaming*. (The Institute of Management Sciences College on Simulation and Gaming), Durham, North Carolina: Duke University, June 1, 1968.

We are indebted to our families, our students, and the secretarial staff of the Graduate School of Business Administration of the University of Washington for their contributions to this book. Professor Rocco Carzo, Jr. of Pennsylvania State University, Professor Malcolm M. Jones of the Massachusetts Institute of Technology, and Mr. John M. Kohlmeier, formerly of the University of Chicago and now with Arthur Andersen & Co., provided helpful comments on the draft of the manuscript.

ROBERT C. MEIER

WILLIAM T. NEWELL

HAROLD L. PAZER

Contents

3 INDUSTRIAL DYNAMICS
AND LARGE SYSTEM SIMULATION

4 SIMULATION
IN ECONOMIC ANALYSIS

Basic Concepts
in Simulation

1 Simulation of business and economic systems has evolved as one of the most interesting and potentially powerful tools available for analyzing business and economic problems. Through simulation techniques the business analyst, operations researcher, or economist has the means for observation and experimentation which have long been the essence of the approach of the physical scientist. Building and running a simulation model permits observation of the dynamic behavior of a system under controlled conditions, and experiments may be run to test hypotheses about the system under study. In other words, simulation provides a laboratory for analysis of problems that often cannot be solved by other means.

Early uses of the simulation technique usually involved experimentation with physical models representing the phenomena under investigation. As such, simulation was widely employed in engineering and scientific studies. Since administrative and economic processes are not easily represented by physical models, simulation by this method has been little used by social scientists and managers. However, simulation by means of digital computers has found wide acceptance in both engineering and scientific work and in the analysis of administrative and economic problems.

As the term is used in business, economics, and other social sciences, simulation refers to the operation of a numerical model that represents the structure of a dynamic process. Given the values of initial conditions, parameters, and exogenous variables, a simulation is run to represent the behavior of the process over time. This simulation run may be considered to be an experiment on the model. A set of variables describes the state of the system at a beginning point in time. These variables are used in the model together with any exogenous inputs to generate the behavior of the system during a time interval. The results are values of the variables that describe the state of the system at the end of the time interval. This process is repeated until the desired length of time has been represented. As an example, in a model representing an inventory system, values of the beginning inventory and receipts and disbursements during a time interval are used to generate the value of the inventory at the end of the time interval.

Experimentation by means of computer simulation can overcome some of the restrictions that exist when other forms of analysis are used. It opens up the possibility of dealing with the dynamics of processes too complex to be represented by more rigid mathematical models such as linear programming and calculus maximization and minimization models. Simulation may make possible experiments to validate theoretical predictions of behavior in cases where experimentation on the system under study would be impossible, prohibitively expensive, or complicated by the effects of interaction of the observer with the system under study.

Some Definitions

One of the characteristics of the field of simulation, which is often typical of an emergent field, is a lack of uniform terminology. The terms *simulation*, *Monte Carlo*, *gaming*, *model sampling*, and various combinations thereof have been used interchangeably at times, whereas at other times they have been given specific meanings. There remains some disagreement, but in this book we will use the following definitions, which follow closely those given by Thomas and Deemer[1] and Morgenthaler.[2] Our definitions are more restrictive than the definitions implied by some writers.

To *simulate*, according to Morgenthaler's definition, is "to duplicate the essence of the system or activity without actually attaining reality itself."[3] Thus, *simulation* may be said to be the use of a model to represent over time essential characteristics of a system or process under study. The model may be manipulated in ways impossible or impractical to perform on the system being represented. The dynamics of the behavior of the system represented may be inferred by the operation of the model.

In this book we deal almost exclusively with simulation models which are, or can be, programed for computation on a digital computer. Analog models, as opposed to digital simulation models, will be mentioned where appropriate, but little work has been done with them in business and economics. A universal characteristic of the models that we would call simulation models is that time is an essential element of the model. If a distinction is to be drawn between simulation and the use of other mathematical or symbolic analytic techniques, it is the emphasis on description of the behavior of the system or phenomena over time and the ability to observe this behavior

---

[1]Clayton J. Thomas and Walter L. Deemer, Jr., "The Role of Operational Gaming in Operations Research," *Operations Research*, Vol. 5, No. 1 (February, 1957), pp. 4–7.

[2]George W. Morgenthaler, "The Theory and Application of Simulation in Operations Research," in *Progress in Operations Research*, Vol. I, Russell L. Ackoff, ed. (New York: John Wiley & Sons, Inc., 1961), pp. 366–372.

[3]*Ibid.*, p. 367.

that most clearly distinguishes simulation as a separate technique. Thus, analytical models such as linear programming models are excluded from this restricted definition.

Monte Carlo is the technique of selecting numbers randomly from one or more probability distributions for use in a particular trial or run in a simulation study. Although Monte Carlo methods have been known for some time, the application of the term "Monte Carlo" and popularization of the use of the method in scientific studies are attributed to von Neumann and Ulam, who used it to study neutron diffusion problems.[4] The method was also quickly adapted to the solution of difficult nonprobabilistic problems such as evaluating multiple integrals.[5] We will give a simple illustration of the evaluation of an integral by a Monte Carlo method in Chap. 8. Some authors have suggested restricting the use of the term "Monte Carlo" to apply only to studies in which variance reduction techniques are applied to the sampling process. However, in current usage the term refers generally to the selection of values at random from probability distributions.

Simulating customer arrivals at a service facility by randomly selecting the interval between arrivals from a probability distribution will illustrate the Monte Carlo method. The first two columns of Table 1.1 define a proba-

Table 1.1 PROBABILITY DISTRIBUTION OF ARRIVAL INTERVALS

Interval Between Arrivals (minutes)	Probability of Occurrence	Corresponding 2-Digit Numbers
1	0.10	00–09
2	0.25	10–34
3	0.40	35–74
4	0.20	75–94
5	0.05	95–99

bility distribution of arrival intervals. In the third column, sets of two-digit numbers are assigned to each of the arrival intervals. Ten numbers (00–09) are assigned to the arrival interval of one minute, since its probability of occurrence is 0.10; twenty-five numbers (10–34) are assigned to an interval of two minutes, since the probability of occurrence is 0.25; and so forth. We now obtain two-digit random numbers from a table of uniformly distributed ran-

---

[4]Daniel D. McCracken, "The Monte Carlo Method," *Scientific American*, Vol. 192, No. 5 (May, 1955).

[5]A much earlier example of the use of a Monte Carlo technique to solve a deterministic problem is the well-known needle experiment to determine the value of π, which is attributed to the Frenchman Buffon. In this experiment a needle (or stick) of length D was thrown at random onto a flat surface ruled with parallel lines separated by a distance of $2D$. The experimental value of π is the number of throws divided by the number of times the needle intersects a line.

dom numbers[6] and use the third column of Table 1.1 to select an arrival interval. If the two-digit random number were 27, for instance, the time until the next arrival would be selected as two minutes, since 27 falls into the 10–34 set of numbers in column 3. Following this procedure repeatedly in effect converts a sequence of uniformly distributed random numbers, which can be obtained from a table or generated easily, into a sequence of arrival intervals with the desired frequency of occurrence.

Table 1.2 shows the results of simulating the first five arrivals at the service facility. Random numbers were obtained from the first column of the table of uniformly distributed random numbers in Appendix A and matched against the numbers in the last column of Table 1.1. The first number obtained from the table of random numbers was 53, which is included in the interval 35–74, corresponding to an arrival interval of three minutes. The procedure was repeated for the other arrivals. The first arrival occurred three minutes after the simulation began at time zero, the second three minutes later, or at time six minutes, and so on. If the table were extended for a sufficient number of samples, it would be expected that the arrival intervals from one to five minutes would appear with the relative frequencies shown in the second column of Table 1.1.

Table 1.2   SIMULATED ARRIVAL TIME OF FIVE CUSTOMERS

Sample Number	Random Number	Arrival Interval (minutes)	Arrival Time (minutes)
1	53	3	3
2	67	3	6
3	11	2	8
4	80	4	12
5	18	2	14

Gaming is the use of a game model to permit players to make decisions and observe the behavior of a model as a result of their actions. The literature on gaming often does not distinguish between games and simulation, but they may be differentiated by the concept of play. A game model simulates a dynamic environment in which human beings make decisions at various stages of the simulation. Games are primarily used for training, but they have important research applications as well. When gaming is used seriously to determine optimal solutions for strategies and to determine optimal structures for systems, it may be termed *operational gaming*. Thomas and Deemer define *operational gaming* as the "serious use of *playing* as a primary device to formulate a *game*, to solve a *game*, or to impart something of the

---

[6]The first table of Appendix A contains uniformly distributed random numbers. A discussion of the generation and properties of uniformly distributed random numbers appears in Chap. 8.

solution of a *game*."[7] These are fine distinctions and not always clear-cut in each situation. Note that gaming does not imply the use of the mathematical theory of games. Game theory is a mathematical approach to the analysis of strategies and the determination of optimal strategies for opponents in conflict situations. Although both games and game theory involve elements of competition or conflict, game theory has been rarely applied to the play of business games.

Model sampling is a technique of sampling from a stochastic process to determine through multiple trials the nature of a probability distribution that would be difficult or impossible to determine by standard statistical procedures. From these trials the shape of the probability distribution and the moments of the distribution may be estimated. Model sampling utilizes the Monte Carlo method—random sampling from a probability distribution—but model sampling does not include observation of the behavior of a process through time. Consequently it does not quite fit the narrower definition of simulation which we have suggested. Model sampling, or distribution sampling as it is also called, has a long history of use by statisticians to derive empirically distributions that are difficult or impossible to derive by other means. One of the earliest examples of this use of model sampling is the derivation of the *t* distribution by Student in 1908.[8] Illustrations of the application of model sampling are given in the analysis of PERT networks in Chap. 2 and evaluation of parameter estimation techniques in Chap. 4.

Heuristic methods, or at least some forms of them, have been called simulations since they appear in certain ways to simulate human decision-making or problem-solving processes. Because heuristic techniques are quite different from the concept of simulation as we have defined it, we would not include heuristics under our definition of simulation. However, since heuristic approaches have often been termed simulations, we include in Chap. 5 a definition of heuristics and a description of the various types of models to which this term has been applied.

Engineering and Scientific Precedents

Simulation methods in engineering and scientific studies have been in use well over 50 years, substantially predating the use of simulation in business and economics. Table 1.3 outlines the chronological development of analog simulation methods that came into use long before digital methods. An analogy, according to Webster, is "a relation of likeness between two things

---

[7]Clayton J. Thomas and Walter L. Deemer, Jr., "The Role of Operational Gaming in Operations Research," *Operations Research*, Vol. 5, No. 1 (February, 1957), p. 6

[8]For a complete discussion of early uses of model sampling by statisticians see: Daniel Teichroew, "History of Distribution Sampling Prior to the Era of the Computer and Its Relevance to Simulation," *American Statistical Association Journal*, Vol. 60, No. 309 (March, 1965).

or of one thing to or with another, consisting in the resemblance not of the things themselves but of two or more attributes, circumstances, or effects."[9] Analog simulations, as this definition suggests, are simulations in which one physical system is used, for purposes of analysis, to represent another system that it resembles in certain essential ways.

Table 1.3 CHRONOLOGICAL DEVELOPMENT OF ANALOG SIMULATIONS

Time Period	Development
Late 19th and early 20th century	Use of fluid flow and soap film models in engineering work
	Use of direct current analogs to solve electric-power distribution problems
Late 1920's	First large-scale attempt to employ indirect analog-computation techniques —the Busch mechanical differential analyzer
1930's	Wide interest in the application of mechanical methods of solving algebraic and ordinary differential equations
1940–45	Introduction of electronic differential analyzers resulting from development of electronic technique for military applications
1945 to present	Rapid expansion of applications of the electronic differential analyzers

Source: Based upon information presented in: Walter J. Karplus and Walter W. Soroka, *Analog Methods: Computation and Simulation* (New York: McGraw-Hill Book Company, Inc., 1959).

The electrical analogy to a vibrating spring system is comparatively straightforward, yet demonstrates the basic concepts of analog simulation.[10] Figure 1.1 is a diagrammatic representation of the suspension system of an automobile. Figure 1.2 is an electrical analogy for the same suspension system. Although the analogy is not immediately apparent, consider the following equations:

$$F - k \int_0^t v \, dt - sv - m \frac{dv}{dt} = 0 \qquad (1.1)$$

$$E - \frac{1}{c} \int_0^t i \, dt - Ri - L \frac{di}{dt} = 0 \qquad (1.2)$$

Equation (1.1) is the equilibrium equation for the spring system in Fig. 1.1,

---

[9]*Webster's New International Dictionary*, 2nd ed. (Springfield, Mass.: G. & C. Merriam Co.).

[10]For a more complete discussion of spring systems and other physical analogs see: Walter J. Karplus and Walter W. Soroka, *Analog Methods: Computation and Simulation* (New York: McGraw-Hill Book Company, Inc., 1959).

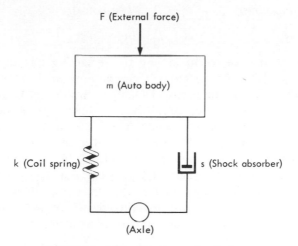

FIGURE 1.1. Automobile Suspension System

while (1.2) is the equilibrium equation for the electrical circuit in Fig. 1.2. In this electrical analog, voltage represents the applied external force,[11] the reciprocal of the capacitance corresponds to the stiffness of the spring, the resistance represents the damping effect of the shock absorber, and the inductance of the coil in the electrical circuit is equivalent to the mass of the auto supported by the spring. Symbolically, the following quantities are analogous in Eqs. (1.1) and (1.2).

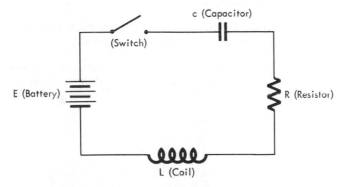

FIGURE 1.2. Electrical Analog of Suspension System

(Force) $\qquad F = E$ (Voltage)

(Spring constant) $\qquad k = \dfrac{1}{c}$ (Reciprocal of capacitance)

---

[11]The force can be viewed as being applied downwards on the auto body or upwards on the axle. In either case, the effect is to compress the coil spring and shock absorber.

(Dampening) $s = R$ (Resistance)

(Mass) $m = L$ (Inductance)

Time t appears in both equations and the remaining quantity v, vertical velocity, in Eq. (1.1) is represented by i, current flow, in (1.2).

When the switch in the electrical analog shown in Fig. 1.2 is closed, the behavior of the electrical system over time is analogous (after allowances are made for differences in scaling between the two systems) to the behavior of the suspension system when a force F is applied to the system. If a designer were interested in the effect upon the amount of vibration resulting from a change of shock absorber "stiffness," the problem could be solved by varying the resistance R and observing the effect upon the current flow i. By varying the parameters of the electrical system (i.e., resistance, inductance, capacitance, and voltage) characteristics of various suspension systems can be simulated quickly and cheaply.

Digital simulation, as we have noted, is quite different from analog simulation in that it involves manipulations of numerical, rather than physical models of the process under study. As an illustration of a digital simulation of a physical process in which the Monte Carlo method is useful, consider the simulation of the movement of a particle of matter in a plane. The particle moves in a random direction until it collides with another particle, at which time it moves in a new random direction until it collides with another particle. Let us assume that all directions of movement in a single plane are equally likely and that the distance moved between collisions can be described by the probability distribution in Table 1.4.[12]

Table 1.4 PROBABILITY DISTRIBUTION OF DISTANCE MOVED AND CORRESPONDING RANDOM NUMBERS

Distance Moved between Collisions	Probability of Occurrence	Corresponding 2-Digit Random Numbers
1	0.01	00
2	0.03	01–03
3	0.08	04–11
4	0.18	12–29
5	0.30	30–59
6	0.20	60–79
7	0.12	80–91
8	0.05	92–96
9	0.02	97–98
10	0.01	99
	1.00	

---

[12]An example of the use of Monte Carlo to study an actual problem similar to the one we have given as an illustration may be found in: N. Metropolis, "Phase Shifts—Middle Squares—Wave Equation," in *Symposium on Monte Carlo Methods*, Herbert A. Meyer, ed. (New York: John Wiley & Sons, Inc., 1956), pp. 35–36.

Movement of the particle over time can be simulated by randomly selecting a direction and distance of movement and repeating the process over and over again. We use a table of random numbers to determine the direction by selecting from it three-digit random numbers between 000 and 359. If the number is 360 or greater, it is ignored and another is chosen; if it is less than 360, the direction of movement is the number of degrees shown by the random number, measured from some arbitrary 0 degree line. Similarly, the distance moved can be selected from the distribution of distances in Table 1.4, two-digit random numbers being used. A single five-digit random number can be used to select both the direction and distance if we let the first three digits determine the direction and the last two the distance (if it is assumed that any random number will be discarded when the first three numbers are greater than 359). Table 1.5 shows the selection of the direction and distance of successive movements of the particle, using the first table of Appendix A as a source of random numbers.

Table 1.5 SELECTION OF DIRECTION AND DISTANCE
OF MOVEMENT USING RANDOM NUMBERS

Random Number	Angle (deg.)	Distance
11682	116	7
18002	180	2
10332	103	5
32280	322	7
06359	63	5
24285	242	7
19215	192	4
20823	208	4
18203	182	2
32030	320	5

The simulated movement of the particle is illustrated in Fig. 1.3. The net distance moved from the origin after the ten movements is represented by the distance d_{10}. Repeating the experiment a large number of times would provide an estimate of the expected value of d_{10}. Patterns of movement similar to those that were simulated in this illustration appear fairly frequently in scientific studies and have been given the general name of "random walk." This illustration has been greatly simplified, but the basic simulation technique used here is applicable to the analysis of more complex phenomena.[13]

[13]See, for instance, Martin J. Berger, "An Application of the Monte Carlo Method to a Problem in Gamma Ray Diffusion," in *Symposium on Monte Carlo Methods*, Herbert A. Meyer, ed. (New York: John Wiley and Sons, Inc., 1956). Or see Don L. Bunker, "Computer Experiments in Chemistry," *Scientific American*, Vol. 211, No. 1 (July, 1964).

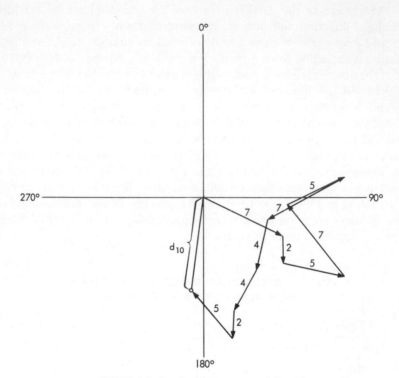

FIGURE 1.3. Simulated Movement of Particle

Development of Simulation in Business and Economic Analysis

The use of simulation in business and economic analysis, in contrast to the relatively long history of its application in engineering and scientific studies, is a fairly recent development. The technique emerged as a major tool of analysis in business and economics as digital computers started to become widely available in the mid-1950's, and since that time there has been a continuous rapid growth of interest in digital simulation methods. An indication of the newness of the field is the fact that very little of the current large body of literature dealing with business and economic simulation was published before 1955. Prior to the introduction of the digital computer, digital simulation techniques were little used in business and economic analyses. The techniques were not well known, and the volume of computations usually required by simulation models of practical interest made manual computations too cumbersome and expensive. Occasionally, analog devices had been used in simulation studies,[14] but the difficulty of finding suitable analogs precluded any widespread use of analog methods.

Because of programing difficulties, slow speed, and limited memory capacity of the first digital computers, and lack of familiarity with the technique, early simulation studies generally involved uncomplicated phenomena such as simple inventory systems, simple waiting line problems, and small econometric models. As digital computation techniques have matured with the development of computers with greatly increased capacity and sophisticated software packages, simulation models of more complex processes and larger systems have become practical. In addition, some programing problems have been alleviated by the development of computer programs and languages designed particularly for digital simulation of the types of systems likely to be encountered in business and economic studies. Specialized languages and programs such as GPSS (General Purpose Systems Simulator), SIMSCRIPT, and DYNAMO in many cases substantially reduce the time and cost of writing simulation programs. Improvements in both hardware and software which have taken place in recent years now make it feasible to simulate systems of greater complexity than could have been dealt with in the past. Consequently, the range of problems for which digital simulation is a practical tool of analysis has been increased manyfold.

There is also an increasing awareness that business and economic problems must be looked at in terms of the total system with all of the interactions between the parts, and simulation is a tool that offers excellent opportunities for adopting this point of view. The behavior of a system is a result of the combined effect of actions and reactions through all parts of the system. Decisions and policies must be evaluated on the basis of their impact on the immediate local behavior of the system and on their long-run consequences for more remote parts of the system as well. Thus, it is necessary to consider not only the actions in one part of the system, but also reactions of other components and their continuing interactions.

Many practical limitations exist on our ability to construct dynamic large-scale business and economic models. Gathering appropriate data is a task of great magnitude; realistic dynamic models using mathematical methods are difficult to construct, and the capability has been lacking to perform calculations required for analysis of complex systems. Simulation techniques that make use of the capacity of modern digital computers and new concepts in software can be of material assistance in removing some of

---

[14]Irving Fisher, for instance, used a hydraulic model to simulate economic phenomena in the late nineteenth century. Later electrical analogs were suggested for use in economic analysis. See N. F. Morehouse, R. H. Strotz, and S. J. Horwitz, "An Electro-Analog Method for Investigating Problems in Economic Dynamics: Inventory Oscillations," *Econometrica*, Vol. 18, No. 4 (October, 1950).

these barriers to understanding and effectively controlling the behavior of large business and economic systems.

Analysis and Simulation of an Inventory Problem

To illustrate how a common phenomenon encountered in logistics, distribution, and materials management systems can be simulated, let us consider an elementary inventory problem. A single item of inventory is to be replenished under an order point-order quantity system. Average demand is ten units per day and lead time between placing a replenishment order and receiving the quantity ordered is four days. The item costs $5 per unit to purchase and is sold for $10 per unit. Inventory holding costs of 20 per cent per year are computed on the value (purchase price) of average inventory. Cost of placing and receiving each order to replenish the stock is $20, regardless of the size of the order.

Analytical solution

The objective is to find the order point and order quantity that will minimize the total annual cost of maintaining this item of inventory. We will first find an optimum solution mathematically and then compare the analytic solution with a simulation approach.

The order point is found by multiplying usage per day by the lead time, the number of days which elapse between placement and receipt of an order. Since demand and lead time are fixed quantities in this example, no safety stock is necessary to protect against uncertainties. Therefore, the order point is simply 4×10, or 40 units.

The optimum order quantity is the quantity that minimizes total cost of handling the item for some period of time such as a year. If we assume that there are 250 working days in a year, total cost TC is given by

$$TC = (250)(10)(5) + \frac{(250)(10)}{x}(20) + \frac{x}{2}(5)(0.20)$$

$$= 12{,}500 + \frac{50{,}000}{x} + 0.5x \qquad\qquad (1.3)$$

where

$$x = \text{order quantity}$$

The first term on the right-hand side of Eq. (1.3) is the purchase cost, the second is ordering and receiving cost, and the third is inventory carrying cost. Following the usual calculus techniques for finding maximum or minimum points, we take the first derivative of the total cost expression and set it equal to zero.

$$\frac{dTC}{dx} = -\frac{50,000}{x^2} + 0.5 = 0 \tag{1.4}$$

Solving for x, we find that the minimum cost order quantity is

$$x = \sqrt{\frac{50,000}{0.5}} = 316 \tag{1.5}$$

By substitution in Eq. (1.3) the total cost per year is found to be

$$TC = 12,500 + \frac{(250)(10)}{316}(20) + \frac{316}{2}(5)(0.20)$$

$$= 12,816 \tag{1.6}$$

Of the yearly total cost, \$12,500 is the purchase cost, which is unaffected by the order quantity, and \$316 is the sum of ordering cost and carrying cost, which is affected by the order quantity.

Simulation of the problem

We observed earlier that analog simulations are rarely practical in analyzing business and economic problems due in part to the difficulty of finding suitable physical systems to represent the process under study. The inventory problem is a possible exception, since we could devise several relatively simple physical analogs of this elementary inventory system. One that might be used is a hydraulic model—a reservoir of water with a drain pipe at the bottom, a valve for regulating flow out of the drain pipe, and a container of suitable size for replenishing the water supply in the reservoir from some other source. By appropriately adjusting the rate of flow through the drain, the size of container used to replenish the reservoir, and timing of replenishments, this physical system could be made to simulate the inventory system. As a practical matter, such an analog simulator would be cumbersome and subject to error in measurement, and could not easily be expanded to accommodate more realistic systems.

A much more practical approach, and the only one which would be seriously considered, is to simulate the system digitally. Since the system is quite simple and involves no probabilistic elements, simulation of its behavior is almost a trivial matter and could easily be done by hand. We will illustrate simulation of the system using a digital computer, as it demonstrates the basic simulation approach. The computer program used is designed to simulate more complex probabilistic systems, but it can simulate the deterministic system analyzed in the preceding section by properly specifying the nature of the system and parameters to be used.[15]

Figure 1.4 shows output from a simulation run of the system for 50 periods or days. Data used in the run are shown in the first part of the printout. In the computer run the number of periods was set at 50, stock level was reviewed every period to see whether the order point was reached, price was set at $5 per unit, inventory was given an initial value of 100 units, an order point of 40 units and order quantity of 316 as calculated in the previous section were used, cost of placing and receiving a replenishment order was set at $20, and an interest rate or carrying cost of 0.20/250 or 0.0008 per time period was used. With these data the program simulated operation of the system for 50 periods and listed each transaction as it occurred. Finally, the program summarized the results and printed them out in the run summary.

Total cost for 50 periods as shown in the run summary includes only the variable cost that is affected by order quantity and does not include purchase price which, in this case, is independent of order quantity. This total cost corresponds to the sum of the last two terms of Eq. (1.6), which is $316. We would expect that total cost for the simulated operation of the system for $\frac{50}{250}$ of a year would be $\frac{1}{5}$ of $316, or $63. However, there is a difference of approximately $9 which occurs because the summarized costs from the simulation run are costs of running the system for 50 periods beginning with an initial inventory of 100 units, whereas the results of the analytic solution represent the long-term average cost of running the system. If the simulation were run for a larger number of periods, total cost per year would be closer to that determined by the analytic approach. The difference observed in this case is indicative of a fundamental problem in the interpretation of results of any simulation run and will be discussed further in Chap. 9.

As a final comment on this example, we should note that the simulation model did not locate the optimum value of the order quantity. Rather, we calculated the optimum value analytically and used this value in a run of the model. Simulation models in most cases have no capacity to optimize; they simply represent what will happen if a system is set up to operate in a certain way with whatever values are chosen for the decision variables. As a consequence, when optimum values are unknown and the objective of a simulation study is to locate optimum values of one or more decision variables in a system, a simulation model is used essentially as a vehicle for search. A simulation model does not in itself produce optimum values of decision variables in the sense that a linear programming model, for example, produces optimum values. In Chap. 9 we will discuss techniques for searching for optimum values in conjunction with simulation models.

---

[15]See Appendix B for a listing of the program and instructions for its use.

RUN INPUT DATA

NUMBER OF TIME PERIODS = 50
INTERVAL BETWEEN REVIEWS = 1
PRICE OF ITEM = 5.00 PER UNIT
BEGINNING INVENTORY = 100 UNITS
ORDER POINT = 40 UNITS
ORDER QUANTITY = 316 UNITS
COST OF PLACING REPLENISHMENT ORDER = 10.00
COST OF RECEIVING REPLENISHMENT ORDER = 10.00
COST OF LOST DEMAND = 0.00 PER UNIT
INTEREST COST PER TIME PERIOD = 0.000800

TRANSACTIONS

PERIOD	ON HAND	ON ORDER	ORDERED	DUE IN	RECEIVED	DEMANDED	LOST	COST
1	90	0				10		
2	80	0				10		
3	70	0				10		
4	60	0				10		
5	50	0				10		
6	40	0				10		
6	40	316	316	10				10.00
7	30	316				10		
8	20	316				10		
9	10	316				10		
10	326	0			316			10.00
10	316	0				10		
11	306	0				10		
12	296	0				10		
13	286	0				10		
14	276	0				10		
15	266	0				10		
16	256	0				10		
17	246	0				10		
18	236	0				10		
19	226	0				10		
20	216	0				10		
21	206	0				10		
22	196	0				10		
23	186	0				10		
24	176	0				10		
25	166	0				10		
26	156	0				10		
27	146	0				10		
28	136	0				10		
29	126	0				10		
30	116	0				10		
31	106	0				10		
32	96	0				10		
33	86	0				10		
34	76	0				10		
35	66	0				10		
36	56	0				10		
37	46	0				10		
38	36	0				10		
38	36	316	316	42				10.00
39	26	316				10		
40	16	316				10		
41	6	316				10		
42	322	0			316			10.00
42	312	0				10		
43	302	0				10		
44	292	0				10		
45	282	0				10		
46	272	0				10		
47	262	0				10		
48	252	0				10		
49	242	0				10		
50	232	0				10		

RUN SUMMARY

TOTAL DEMAND = 500.
AVERAGE INVENTORY = 161.00
NUMBER OF ORDERS = 2
NUMBER OF RECEIPTS = 2
DEMAND LOST = 0
SERVICE FACTOR = 1.00

CARRYING COST =	32.20
ORDERING COST =	20.00
RECEIVING COST =	20.00
LOST DEMAND COST =	0.00
TOTAL COST =	72.20

FIGURE 1.4. Computer Simulation of Deterministic Inventory Problem

Simulation of a more complex inventory problem

To illustrate a stochastic digital simulation, let us expand the original problem and assume that demand and lead time vary according to certain probability distributions. We will assume that only one demand for the item occurs each day, although the number of units demanded varies randomly according to the distribution in Table 1.6. Lead time varies according to the distribution in Table 1.7. We will also suppose that there is a certain probability, as shown by Table 1.8, of losing orders that are backordered because of a shortage of inventory. The table is interpreted to mean that there is a 30

Table 1.6 PROBABILITY DISTRIBUTION OF DAILY DEMAND

Number of Units Demanded	Probability of Occurrence
5	0.01
6	0.03
7	0.06
8	0.11
9	0.19
10	0.31
11	0.17
12	0.07
13	0.03
14	0.02
	1.00

Average demand = 9.72 units/day

Table 1.7 LEAD TIME DISTRIBUTION

Lead Time	Probability of Occurrence
2	0.15
3	0.20
4	0.30
5	0.20
6	0.15
	1.00

Average lead time = 4.0 days

Table 1.8 PROBABILITY OF LOSING BACKORDERS

Number of Periods Backordered	Probability of Loss
0	0.30
1	0.40
2	0.55
3	0.75
4	1.00

per cent probability of losing an order by cancellation on the day it is received if inventory is not available, there is a 40 per cent chance of losing an order that is held over to the next day, and so on up to the fifth day, when there is a 100 per cent chance that an order not filled by that day is lost. Let us also assume that it costs $10 to enter a backorder when demand cannot be filled and that the cost of losing orders because of unavailability of stock is the $5 per unit profit margin.

Mathematical analysis of this more complex (and more realistic) inventory problem to determine the optimum order point and order quantity is not an easy task because of interaction between the demand, lead time, and backorder loss distributions. Since this is not a treatise on inventory theory, the analysis will not be carried further.[16] Rather, we will demonstrate a simulation of the problem using the same computer program employed earlier to simulate the deterministic inventory problem.

A printout of results of simulated operation of the probabilistic system for 100 periods is reproduced in Fig. 1.5. The first section of the printout is a summary of run input data. Note that the cumulative distributions of lead time and demand derived from Tables 1.6 and 1.7 and the backorder loss probability from Table 1.8 were given to the program as data. Two numbers arbitrarily called X and Y were entered to be used in generating random numbers. The program uses these two numbers as a starting point for generating a sequence of uniformly distributed random numbers between 0 and 1 which are used to select demand and lead times, and to determine when backorders are lost during the simulation run. The first of the sequence of random numbers generated internally by the program is printed out in the third line of the run input section.

Figure 1.6 illustrates the Monte Carlo process through which the program uses random numbers and the cumulative demand distribution to select the number of units demanded in any period. As an example, if the random number generated is 0.52981, the program in effect reads across to the cumulative distribution of demand, determines that 0.52981 falls above the cumulative probability of 9 units and below the cumulative probability of 10 units, and selects 10 as demand for that period. It may be seen from Fig. 1.6 that this procedure, when carried out over and over again, will result in selection of various demands from 5 to 14 with frequencies proportional to the vertical distances corresponding to each level of demand. The net result is that the technique generates a sequence of demands with the same statistical characteristics as the distribution of demand in Table 1.6.[17]

---

[16]An excellent discussion of the analysis of inventory models similar in structure to this problem is contained in: Robert B. Fetter and Winston C. Dalleck, *Decision Models for Inventory Management* (Homewood, Illinois: Richard D. Irwin, Inc., 1961), Chaps. 1 and 2 and Appendix E.

[17]This statement should be qualified somewhat, since on any single run the demands generated may not have exactly the distribution desired. The problem is one of sample size and length of run and will be discussed in Chap. 9.

```
                              INVENTORY SIMULATION
                                 DEMONSTRATION

                                RUN INPUT DATA

X =  107.00
Y =   97.00
INITIAL RANDOM NUMBER =  0.338383
NUMBER OF TIME PERIODS = 100
INTERVAL BETWEEN REVIEWS =   1
PRICE OF ITEM =     5.00   PER UNIT
BEGINNING INVENTORY =    100   UNITS
ORDER POINT =     40   UNITS
ORDER QUANTITY =    316   UNITS
COST OF PLACING REPLENISHMENT ORDER =    10.00
COST OF RECEIVING REPLENISHMENT ORDER =    10.00
COST OF ENTERING BACKORDER =    10.00
COST OF LOST DEMAND =     5.00   PER UNIT
INTEREST COST PER TIME PERIOD = 0.000800
```

	LEAD TIME	CUMULATIVE FREQUENCY
	2	0.1500
	3	0.3500
	4	0.6500
	5	0.8500
	6	1.0000

	DEMAND	CUMULATIVE FREQUENCY
	5	0.0100
	6	0.0400
	7	0.1000
	8	0.2100
	9	0.4000
	10	0.7100
	11	0.8800
	12	0.9500
	13	0.9800
	14	1.0000

PERIODS BACKORDERED	PROBABILITY OF LOSS
0	0.3000
1	0.4000
2	0.5500
3	0.7500
4	1.0000

TRANSACTIONS

PERIOD	ON HAND	ON ORDER	ORDERED	DUE IN	RECEIVED	DEMANDED	ON BACKORDER	BACKORDERED	LOST	COST
1	91	0				9	0			
2	82	0				9	0			
3	74	0				8	0			
4	64	0				10	0			
5	51	0				13	0			
6	41	0				10	0			
7	36	0				5	0			
7	36	316	316	9			0			10.00
8	26	316				10	0			10.00
9	342	0			316		0			
9	332	0				10	0			
10	319	0				13	0			
11	310	0				9	0			
12	301	0				9	0			
13	291	0				10	0			
14	282	0				9	0			
15	271	0				11	0			
16	261	0				10	0			
17	254	0				7	0			
18	246	0				8	0			
19	237	0				9	0			
20	224	0				13	0			
21	213	0				11	0			
22	199	0				14	0			
23	189	0				10	0			
24	182	0				7	0			
25	170	0				12	0			
26	160	0				10	0			
27	154	0				6	0			
28	144	0				10	0			
29	138	0				6	0			
30	131	0				7	0			
31	122	0				9	0			
32	112	0				10	0			
33	102	0				10	0			
34	90	0				12	0			
35	80	0				10	0			
36	70	0				10	0			
37	60	0				10	0			

FIGURE 1.5. Computer Simulation of Probabilistic Inventory Problem

TRANSACTIONS

PERIOD	ON HAND	ON ORDER	ORDERED	DUE IN	RECEIVED	DEMANDED	ON BACKORDER	BACKORDERED	LOST	COST
38	49	0				11	0			
39	43	0				6	0			
40	32	0				11	0			
40	32	316	316	44						10.00
41	20	316				12	0			
42	9	316				11	0			
43	0	315				10	1		1	10.30
44	316	0			316		1			10.00
44	315	0					0			
44	306	0				9	0			
45	300	0				6	0			
46	288	0				12	0			
47	277	0				11	0			
48	270	0				7	0			
49	261	0				9	0			
50	254	0				7	0			
51	242	0				12	0			
52	235	0				7	0			
53	228	0				7	0			
54	215	0				13	0			
55	201	0				14	0			
56	192	0				9	0			
57	184	0				8	0			
58	173	0				11	0			
59	163	0				10	0			
60	153	0				10	0			
61	142	0				11	0			
62	134	0				8	0			
63	123	0				11	0			
64	113	0				10	0			
65	106	0				7	0			
66	96	0				10	0			
67	88	0				8	0			
68	78	0				10	0			
69	68	0				10	0			
70	58	0				10	0			
71	51	0				7	0			
72	43	0				8	0			
73	35	0				8	0			
73	35	316	316	79						10.00
74	26	315				9	0			
75	15	316				11	0			
76	4	315				11	0			
77	0	316				10	0		6	30.00
78	0	316				10	10	10		10.00
79	316	0			316		10			10.00
79	306	0					0			
79	295	0				11	0			
80	284	0				11	0			
81	273	0				11	0			
82	264	0				9	0			
83	253	0				11	0			
84	243	0				10	0			
85	234	0				9	0			
86	223	0				11	0			
87	213	0				10	0			
88	201	0				12	0			
89	190	0				11	0			
90	181	0				9	0			
91	174	0				7	0			
92	165	0				9	0			
93	156	0				9	0			
94	147	0				9	0			
95	137	0				10	0			
96	130	0				7	0			
97	118	0				12	0			
98	110	0				8	0			
99	99	0				11	0			
100	94	0				5	0			

RUN SUMMARY

TOTAL DEMAND = 960.
AVERAGE INVENTORY = 155.68
NUMBER OF ORDERS = 3
NUMBER OF RECEIPTS = 3
DEMAND LOST = 6
SERVICE FACTOR = 0.99
NUMBER OF BACKORDERS = 2
AVERAGE NUMBER OF PERIODS TO FILL BACKORDERS = 1.00
AVERAGE NUMBER OF PERIODS TO FILL ALL ORDERS = 0.01

CARRYING COST =	62.27
ORDERING COST =	30.00
RECEIVING COST =	30.00
LOST DEMAND COST =	30.00
BACKORDERING COST =	20.00
TOTAL COST =	172.27

FIGURE 1.5. (Continued)

19

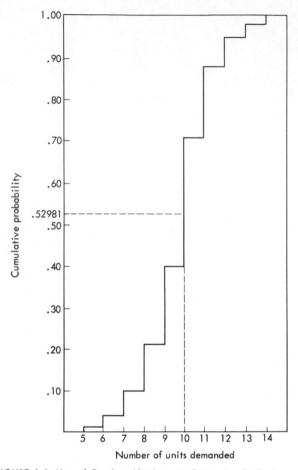

FIGURE 1.6. Use of Random Numbers to Determine Daily Demand

The transactions section of Fig. 1.5 traces behavior of the system when both demand and lead time are random variables rather than fixed quantities and when the loss of backorders is governed by a probability distribution. Unlike the transactions section of Fig. 1.4, in which demand and lead time are regular quantities and there are no backorders, the events in Fig. 1.5 exhibit random characteristics governed by the underlying probabilities, and there are occasional shortages.

Results of the 100-period simulation run are listed in the run summary section of Fig. 1.5. Although the order point and order quantity used in the probabilistic case are the same as those used in the earlier deterministic case, and although mean values of the demand rate and lead time used in both runs are approximately equal, the results are quite different. Cost of operation of the stochastic system for 100 periods is much more than double the cost of operating the deterministic system for 50 periods. One of the major reasons for this difference is that there are additional cost elements present in the second simulation, since it is possible to have backorders and to lose orders. In addition, the cost of operating the probabilistic system is subject to random fluctuations from run to run because of the way in which probabilistic elements of the system happen to interact during the run. Consequently, it is possible to obtain different costs of operation on different runs of the same system.

Simulation of the stochastic problem made it possible to observe the interaction of three probabilistic elements in the system and see effects of this interaction in terms of total cost, service level, and length of time to fill orders. Additional runs of longer duration would be required to establish confidence in the results of the simulation. In actual practice, a simulation of this nature could be used to search for optimum values of the order point and order quantity by experimenting with pairs of values other than the one pair used in the demonstration run.[18] In Chap. 9 we will use a similar inventory problem to illustrate an approach to optimization with simulation models. A simulation run such as we have shown could also serve the purpose of checking results of theoretical calculations regarding optimum operation of the system if the theoretical calculations required significant simplifications or approximations.

Justification for Simulation

There are a number of reasons for using simulation to analyze business and economic problems, some of which we have already mentioned. Simulation offers a unique opportunity to observe the dynamic behavior of complex interactive systems. A carefully constructed, realistic simulation model provides a laboratory environment in which to make observations under controlled conditions. Simulation provides an experimental environment for testing hypotheses, decision rules, and alternate systems of operation under a variety of assumed conditions.

Simulation may be used in situations where there are no practical analytic approaches available and where it is too costly or impossible to experiment with the actual system under study. Many processes, such as the decision process in an organization or the interaction of a firm with its environment, are too complex to be represented by more formal mathematical structures. Even those processes that can be formulated mathematically, such as large multichannel, multistage queuing problems and complex scheduling problems, may defy attempts at solution by mathematical procedures that

---

[18]The reader should, perhaps, be reminded that the order point and order quantity used in the demonstration run are *not* optimum values for the stochastic problem. They are values which were optimum for the deterministic problem, but are not necessarily optimum for the more complex problem.

are currently available. It is in these cases that simulation may prove to be the only practical method of analysis.

Although simulation is often thought of as a technique to be turned to only after all other approaches have been examined and found wanting, simulation has certain unique characteristics that may justify its use in preference to other techniques. Simulation permits direct and complete observation of the dynamic behavior of processes. Time can be compressed or expanded in a simulation run to provide observations in any desired degree of detail. Each run of a simulation model may be viewed as an experiment from which observations of a variety of system characteristics may be obtained. When simple criteria for evaluating policies in a complex system do not exist, or when performance measures are not evaluated in the same way by all observers, the ability of simulation to provide a total picture of system operating characteristics is a significant advantage over mathematical procedures that produce only single, static answers.

Simulation also has an important role in training and in the development of actual operating policies and procedures. Operational gaming models are designed specifically for training, but other simulation models can serve as training devices by demonstrating the operation of systems under different conditions and permitting observation of simulated results of applications of analytic methods to such problems as manpower planning, scheduling, and economic policy determination. Since simulation models are often close replicas of actual operating systems, the model can often be used to develop and test operating policies and procedures before they are implemented in the actual system.

Problems and Future Prospects

Validation of models and interpretation of experimental results present practical and theoretical questions in the use of simulation techniques that are not completely resolved. How are we to know that a model represents the process under study? How are we to understand what is going on in a model of a complex system? How are we to test the results to yield predictions that are empirically accurate? Analogies between wind tunnel models and chemical pilot plants and simulation models are frequently drawn, but these analogies break down when we consider the underlying structures. The same fundamental laws of nature govern the behavior of an airplane model in a wind tunnel or a chemical pilot plant as govern the full-scale airplane or chemical plant. But a simulation model is a numerical representation of a system and is not governed by any physical laws that make it similar in operation to the system being modeled. A valid simulation model should behave in a manner similar to the underlying phenomena. This is a necessary validation criterion, but alone may not be sufficient to permit us to rely on its predictive abilities. Theoretical insights into the underlying phenomena that govern the behavior of business, economic, and social systems being simulated are critical to the construction of a valid model. There is no consensus on methods to validate simulation models; some approaches are discussed in Chap. 9.

Development of appropriate experimental procedures is another area often given insufficient attention when simulation techniques are used. In contrast to analytic methods that yield solutions to problems, simulation experiments yield results that must be treated as experimental data. Procedures for inferring relationships from data obtained from simulation runs are much the same as those employed in any experimental situation, although the inclusion of time as a principal feature of simulation models raises some particular problems with regard to length of run, starting conditions, and so forth. The comparison that was made earlier in the chapter between results of the simulation of an inventory system and results obtained by theoretical analysis suggests some of the care that must be exercised in interpreting data obtained from a simulation model. The question of design of simulation experiments is discussed in Chap. 9.

Because simulation models are deceptively easy to conceptualize and because fewer abstractions need be made in constructing simulation models, simulation may be chosen over other methods of analysis. However, the costs of designing, programing, accumulating data for, and running a simulation model are often much higher than anticipated. Simulation would not, in many cases, be selected as the technique for analysis if these costs were estimated correctly. Experience and skills accumulated in building simulation models, development of specialized computer languages, and lower unit cost of processsing information on computers are contributing to reducing the cost of simulation, but it still remains an expensive tool of analysis.

Developments in digital simulation techniques have been constrained by limitations on computer size, difficulties in communicating with computers, and restrictions of computer accessibility. These constraints have been relaxed somewhat with the appearance of larger, faster computers and more natural programing languages. Relative to early machine language coding methods, current languages have evolved to a high level, although they do not yet duplicate the natural language of the analyst. Simulation will develop even more rapidly as communication is facilitated by new problem-oriented languages and more convenient input-output devices such as graphic display terminals.

Computer accessibility is significantly enhanced by remote terminals for input and output and time-sharing computer systems. Remote time-sharing systems remove a primary communication-accessibility bottleneck imposed by batch-processing systems. In a batch-processing system an analyst writes a program, delivers it to a computer installation, and waits for his output for several hours or more even under the best circumstances. To write a program, debug it, and obtain meaningful output is a lengthy process. In a time-sharing system, the computer may work sequentially for a short time on each of a number of problems submitted to it. As a result, response to the user at a remote terminal is almost immediate, and the time taken both to write and to run programs is substantially reduced. Remote terminals using graphic devices that display output on a screen electronically further speed the process. The development of time-shared computers coupled with remote terminals, problem-oriented languages, and graphic display input-output devices will greatly multiply the power of simulation techniques. Applications of these types of technological advances which have already been made in the field of engineering design indicate something of what may be expected in the future in the field of simulation.[19]

Taken on balance, simulation as a practical tool of analysis has developed enormously. With growing understanding of the basic structure of business and economic problems and continued expansion of computing capability, an increasing number of proposed procedures for dealing with business and economic problems will be tested by simulation before they are applied to the real world. Further, it is not entirely fanciful to envision the day when many managers of business and economic affairs leave a significant portion of the day-to-day work of making routine decisions to computer programs while they occupy themselves with devising new strategies, systems, and decision rules for the computer. These new systems and decision rules in turn will be tested through simulation before they are integrated into operating procedures.

If this, in fact, becomes the *modus operandi* of the future, we can expect to see significant changes in the character and function of management, particularly at the intermediate levels. There will be a considerable reduction in the amount of routine decision making, data processing, and data transmission actually done by the manager; these routine tasks will be accomplished automatically by the computer. Many managers, instead of carrying line operating responsibilities, will occupy their time with the much more creative and challenging tasks of developing new computer information systems and decision rules and testing their ideas through simulation. Unquestionably this will require somewhat different skills and training than are presently required of middle managers. It will be necessary that they be familiar with computer hardware and software, be able to analyze information and decision systems, be capable of suggesting methods suitable to the computer for routinely analyzing and processing information, and be able to develop workable computer algorithms, both mathematical and non-mathematical, for making decisions automatically. Persons with the requisite breadth of knowledge and skills, both theoretical and practical, are

[19]R. A. Siders, *et al.*, *Computer Graphics: A Revolution in Design* (New York: American Management Association, 1966).

difficult to find in most organizations. It will be necessary to develop persons with these capabilities if full use is to be made of these new developments.

The preceding conjectures about the character of management in the future are not, of course, a consequence of the impact of simulation alone. Simulation is just one part, although an important part, of the developments that are taking place on the broad front of quantitative and computer methods and their application to business and economic problems. There has been a continued growth of the use of more sophisticated methods, and there is no indication that the pace of change is slackening. On the contrary, there is every indication that we are only in the early stages of a technological revolution in the way in which we analyze and manage our business and economic affairs. One technique, such as simulation, cannot be said to have the primary effect on the course of this revolution. However, simulation, together with other techniques and concepts, and the computing capacity of modern electronic digital computers are likely to bring about changes which were thought impossible as recently as 10 or 15 years ago, and which, even today, may seem far removed from reality.

EXERCISES

1.1 Generate a sequence of 50 arrivals with the times between arrivals selected at random according to the probability distribution shown in Table 1.1.
   a. What is the mean time between arrivals?
   b. Group the arrivals into five sequences of 10 arrivals and find the mean time between arrivals for each of the five sequences.
   c. Compute the theoretical mean time between arrivals mathematically and compare it to your results in parts a. and b. above.

1.2 The following is approximately a unit normal probability distribution that has been converted to a discrete distribution.

Value of variable	−3	−2	−1	0	1	2	3
Probability of occurrence	0.01	0.06	0.24	0.38	0.24	0.06	0.01

   a. Use the method shown in Fig. 1.6 to select a sample of 50 from the distribution.
   b. Find the mean of the sample you have drawn.
   c. Compare the frequencies of occurrence in the sample of each of the values from −3 to +3 with the frequencies in the original distribution.

1.3 Repeat the simulation shown in Fig. 1.4, using the distribution of demand shown in Table 1.6 instead of a constant demand. If demand cannot be met, a cost of $5 per unit of lost demand is incurred. Compare the cost of operation that you obtain with the costs shown in Fig. 1.4.

1.4   Design a method to determine the distribution of demand during
      lead time when the demand and lead time distributions are known.
      a. Find the distribution of demand during lead time, using the distri-
         butions in Tables 1.6 and 1.7.
      b. Based on your results, what is the inventory level at which a re-
         plenishment order would have to be placed if 95 per cent pro-
         tection against runout during replenishment were desired?
      c. Is your procedure a simulation model or a case of model sampling?

1.5   An auto club maintains four emergency vehicles at stations in four
      areas of the city. When calls for service are received, the time taken for
      a vehicle to answer the call and return to its station varies randomly
      according to the distribution shown below.

Service time	40	60	80	100	120	140	160
Probability of occurrence	0.05	0.15	0.30	0.20	0.15	0.10	0.05

The time between calls for service at each of the four stations averages
120 minutes, but it is equally likely that the interval is 90, 100, 110,
130, 140, or 150 minutes. Currently an emergency vehicle answers a
call, returns to its station, and either waits for another call in its area or
goes out immediately if another call in its area has already been received.
It has been proposed that emergency vehicles from one area answer
calls in the other areas if they are not out. Driving time between areas
is 10 minutes each way. Construct a simulation model that will
permit a comparison of the alternative methods of operation and
evaluate the merits of the proposed method of operation.

BIBLIOGRAPHY

Hammersley, J. M., and D. C. Handscomb, *Monte Carlo Methods*. New York:
      John Wiley & Sons, Inc., 1964, Chap. 1.

Metropolis, Nicholas, and S. Ulam, "The Monte Carlo Method," *Journal of the
      American Statistical Association*, Vol. 44, No. 247 (September, 1949).

Meyer, Herbert A., ed., *Symposium on Monte Carlo Methods*. New York: John
      Wiley & Sons, Inc., 1956.

Morgenthaler, George W., "The Theory and Application of Simulation in Oper-
      ations Research," in *Progress in Operations Research*, Vol. I, Russell L.
      Ackoff, ed. New York: John Wiley & Sons, Inc., 1961.

Teichroew, Daniel, "History of Distribution Sampling Prior to the Era of the
      Computer and Its Relevance to Simulation," *American Statistical Associa-
      tion Journal*, Vol. 60, No. 309 (March, 1965).

Thomas, Clayton J. and Walter L. Deemer, Jr., "The Role of Operational Gaming
      in Operations Research, *Operations Research*, Vol. 5, No. 1 (February, 1957).

Tocher, K. D., *The Art of Simulation*. London: The English Universities Press,
      Ltd., 1963.

Ulam, S., "On the Monte Carlo Method," in *Proceedings of a Second Symposium
      on Large-Scale Digital Calculating Machinery*. Cambridge, Massachusetts:
      Harvard University Press, 1951.

Simulation in Business

2 Simulation models have been constructed of production control systems, inventory control systems, logistics systems, transportation facilities, service facilities, maintenance operations, quality control systems, and customer behavior—to mention just a few of the many business applications. A glance through the bibliography at the end of the chapter will confirm that simulation is a technique that has been widely used and which has received much attention in the literature. Although it is impossible to give an exhaustive treatment because of the number and variety of studies that have been done, in this chapter we give illustrations of several different types of simulation studies. Our discussion is directed primarily toward simulation in business, but much of the material in the chapter is equally applicable to similar types of systems in government and the military. In some areas, such as the simulation of inventory and logistics systems, the most extensive uses of simulation have been in the analysis of military problems. The discussion in this chapter will serve to introduce the reader to the principal uses of simulation for analyzing problems found in businesses and similar organizations.

Inventory Systems

Inventory control was one of the first areas in business to be examined mathematically. In 1931 Raymond published a book which dealt in great detail with lot size problems,[1] and following World War II operations researchers, mathematicians, statisticians, and economists all contributed to

---

[1] F. E. Raymond, *Quantity and Economy in Manufacture* (New York: McGraw-Hill Book Company, Inc., 1931).

the growing literature dealing with theoretical aspects of inventory control.[2] As a consequence, it is not unusual that inventory is one of the first areas in which simulation was utilized. Not only has the large body of theoretical work assisted in clearly conceptualizing inventory problems, but inventory problems inherently involve relatively well-defined flows over time which lend themselves to simulation. The justification for using simulation is readily apparent upon examination of the theoretical literature, since analysis of one-item inventory problems can be a challenging mathematical task even when simplifying assumptions are made regarding the characteristics of customer demand, characteristics of lead time, and cost behavior.

An early instance of the use of simulation to analyze an inventory system was reported by Robinson of Imperial Oil Limited at the first system simulation symposium held in 1957.[3] One application of simulation discussed by Robinson was to determine the feasibility of using central warehousing in conjunction with field warehouses. The problem was to investigate working characteristics of a proposed central warehouse and to ensure that no bottlenecks would occur in its operation. A simulation was performed on a digital computer using a program written especially for the project. The program was capable of accepting data regarding initial inventory levels of items stocked at the central warehouse and simulating operation of the system when recapitulations of actual daily orders from field warehouse were given as input data. The computer printed out periodic reports of stock levels and also provided information on shortages and waiting lines for facilities. A flow diagram of the program for filling requisitions is shown in Fig. 2.1.

Robinson reports the following conclusions from the simulation studies.

> ... It is clear that in many cases where complex relationships, both of predictable and random natures, occur, it is easier to set up and run through a simulated situation than it is to develop and use a mathematical model representing the entire process under study. In many cases an activity can be affected by numerous random influences. The probabilities involved for each type of influence can be separately examined. However, the calculation of the probability of the combined sequence of activities spilling over into each other and interacting, in what is sometimes referred to as a cascading effect, leads into very deep mathematical waters in the field of Stochastic Processes.
>
> To avoid an impossible or unprofitable attempt to solve a complex operation using equations to seek so-called optimal answers,

---

[2]See, for instance:

K. Arrow, T. Harris, and J. Marschak, "Optimal Inventory Policy," *Econometrica*, Vol. 19, No. 3 (July, 1951).

A. Dvoretzky, J. Kiefer, and J. Wolfowitz, "The Inventory Problem," *Econometrica*, Vol. 20, No. 2 (April, 1952) and No. 3 (July, 1952).

Thomas M. Whitin, *The Theory of Inventory Management* (Princeton, N. J.: Princeton University Press, 1953).

[3]*Report of the System Simulation Symposium.* Sponsored by the American Institute of Industrial Engineers, The Institute of Management Sciences, and Operations Research Society of America (New York, May, 1957), pp. 47–58.

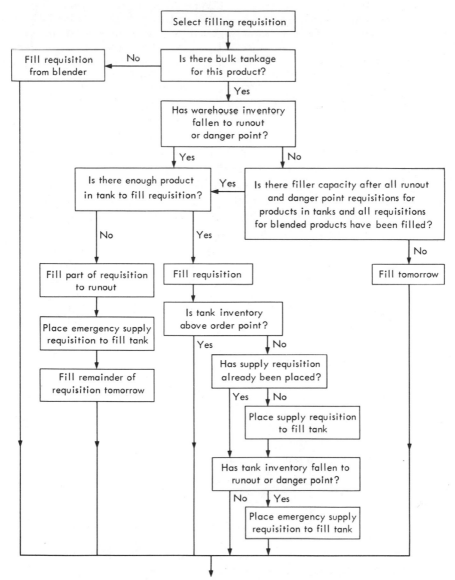

FIGURE 2.1. Flow Diagram for Filling Requisition to Replenish Warehouse Stocks (by permission from *Report of the System Simulation Symposium*, sponsored by A.I.I.E., T.I.M.S., and O.R.S.A., New York, May, 1957)

we turn to a simulation of a system such that we may repeatedly experiment and obtain statistically reliable empirical results. . . .

Where no analytic solution is available, the search for an ever-improving answer through the sequential solution of alternate trials,

until finally running and rerunning additional cases doesn't produce any material improvement, brings us near to what we can, with confidence, rely on as being something approximating an optimal solution
. . . .

Summing up, you may agree that through simulating reality on a modest scale, we can do some research that might not be feasible otherwise; while at the same time we may provide management with a dramatic demonstration piece to help appraise situations and make profitable decisions.[4]

Since Robinson did not report on the computer program itself, let us look at some of the characteristics of the inventory simulation program that is documented in Appendix B to see how a typical inventory simulation program operates. This program is designed to simulate one item of inventory at one stock point, but the basic concepts are applicable to more complex systems. In this program certain basic calculations are carried out in each time period. The length of the time period is usually assumed to be one day, but the user can assume any length of period as long as input data regarding demand rates, lead times, cost parameters, and so forth are appropriately scaled. As outlined in Appendix B, the program offers a number of options concerning the type of system to be simulated and the way in which results are presented; we will discuss the operation of the program in producing the results shown previously in Fig. 1.5.

Data regarding the program options to be used for the run and data describing the characteristics of the inventory system to be simulated are first punched on cards according to the instructions shown in Appendix B. The program uses this data in printing out the "Run Input Data" section and then uses the data to run through a simulation of the system for 100 periods. Events occurring during the simulated operation of the system are shown in the "Transactions" section of Fig. 1.5.

Each time period the program goes through the following basic steps:

1. The file of inventory replenishment orders previously placed is checked to see whether any orders are due in; if so, the inventory level is increased to reflect these receipts.

2. The file of unfilled customer backorders is checked to determine whether any orders can now be filled from inventory.

3. Demand for the period is generated from the probability distribution of demand, the technique described in Chap. 1[5] being used.

4. The inventory level is reduced by an amount equal to the number of units demanded. If the inventory is exhausted as a result, any excess demand is placed on backorder.

---

[4]*Report of the System Simulation Symposium.* Sponsored by the American Institute of Industrial Engineers, The Institute of Management Sciences, and Operations Research Society of America (New York, 1957), p. 57f.
[5]See Fig. 1.6.

5. Each order in the backorder file, if there is any, is examined in sequence and the backorder loss probability distribution is used to determine randomly whether the backorder remains in the file or whether it is lost.

6. The number of periods since the last review of inventory level is compared with the number of periods between reviews selected for the run. If the proper number of periods have elapsed, the sum of the inventory level and outstanding replenishment orders is compared with the order point, and a replenishment order is placed, if necessary. The amount of the replenishment order is equal to the order quantity specified for the run, and the time at which the order will be received is selected randomly from the lead time distribution. The replenishment order is then placed in the replenishment order file.

After step 6 is completed, the "clock" in the program is incremented by one time period and the cycle is repeated for the next time period. This continues until the number of time periods specified for the run has been reached, after which summary statistics for the run are printed out in a "Run Summary," as illustrated in Fig. 1.5.

In the program a fixed cycle is repeated for each time period, since it is likely that one or more transactions will take place in an inventory system during each period, and a fixed cycle lends itself to a simple program structure in which the computer program merely loops repetitively through the same program steps. Although the program does not permit modification of order point and order quantity during a run, automatic computation of order points and order quantities and other features could easily be added by inserting additional routines in the repetitive cycle. Also, it should be noted that some of the output options and other features of this particular simulation program were designed to facilitate use of the program as an educational device rather than as an analytical tool.[6]

A more powerful production-inventory-distribution simulator has been written in SIMSCRIPT by two of the authors.[7] This program is capable of simulating an entire system rather than one item of inventory at one stock point. Figure 2.2 is a schematic diagram of the type of system that can be simulated with the program. The number of products, branches, and plants that can be included in a simulated system is limited only by the memory capacity of the computer on which the program is run. Since the program is written in SIMSCRIPT, a programing language designed especially for simu-

---

[6]Extensive use has been made of the program in the classroom and in businessmen's seminars to illustrate the operation of inventory systems with random elements and to experiment with the application of theoretical concepts to the optimization of inventory systems. Most frequently it has been used in conjunction with a case study, "Southern Hydraulic Supplies Company," which appears in: A. N. Schrieber, R. A. Johnson, R. C. Meier, W. T. Newell, and H. C. Fischer, *Cases in Manufacturing Management* (New York: McGraw-Hill Book Company, 1965).

[7]The SIMSCRIPT program was developed by Robert C. Meier and William T. Newell in the course of a research project supported by the Western Management Science Institute.

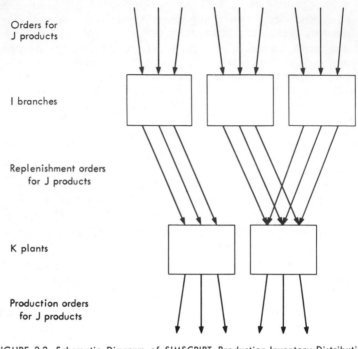

Orders for
J products

I branches

Replenishment orders
for J products

K plants

Production orders
for J products

FIGURE 2.2. Schematic Diagram of SIMSCRIPT Production-Inventory-Distribution
Simulator

lation projects, further discussion will be delayed until Chap. 7, which deals
with simulation languages.

Job Shop Scheduling

A job shop consists of a collection of machines, some of them similar and
some with differing characteristics, each of which operates independently
of the others. A job is a unit of product or group of units that must be
processed by certain of the machines in the shop. Each job is routed in
sequence through a set of machines that must perform operations on the job.
Because of the characteristics of the job and/or machines in the shop, alternate
routes may be available for some jobs. Time taken at each machine for a job
is a function of setup time, run time, and number of units in a job, and it may
also be affected by other factors such as machine breakdowns and operator
delays. In scheduling jobs through a shop with these characteristics, the
objective is to ensure that operations are done in proper sequence and that
jobs are scheduled on machines without conflict between jobs while attempting to meet criteria such as minimizing late deliveries, or minimizing in-process
inventories, or maximizing utilization of equipment. Scheduling is further
complicated by the fact that breakdowns and other delays occur and changes

are made in jobs after processing has begun. Because these characteristics are found in situations other than machine shops, job shop scheduling has come to be considered a general type of scheduling problem.

Henry Gantt, a pioneer in the scientific management movement of the early 1900's, invented the Gantt chart as a device to assist in maintaining control of job-shop-type operations.[8] Although Gantt charts and similar devices are useful in developing feasible schedules and preventing conflicts between jobs, they do not resolve the question of *how* jobs should be scheduled to meet one or more of the criteria mentioned above.

Theoretical work on the question of optimal control of job shop operations has been of fairly recent origin, utilizing in many cases newly developed operations research techniques. Efforts to produce analytical solutions that take into consideration sequencing restrictions on operations within jobs and noninterference restrictions between jobs, while minimizing a criterion such as total time taken to complete all jobs, have resulted in the development of theoretical models using techniques such as combinatorial analysis and integer linear programming.[9] The principal difficulty with analytical approaches along these lines, however, has been that even with a relatively small number of jobs and machines and with simplifying assumptions as to the operating characteristics of the shop, computational problems can easily grow beyond the capacity of modern high-speed digital computers. As a consequence of these inherent theoretical and computational difficulties, interest in the use of simulation as an alternative approach to job shop problems developed at an early date, and discussions of job shop simulation are among the earliest applications of simulation found in the literature.[10]

Theoretical approaches to the job shop problem have generally been based on assumptions that the number of jobs, the sequence of operations on them, the operation times, and the available facilities are known and fixed. The objective, then, has been to find by theoretical methods specific times at which operations should be performed which will optimize some criterion. In contrast, simulation approaches are oriented toward representing dynamic behavior of the shop as jobs pass through the shop in such a way that various

---

[8]A discussion of the basic Gantt chart and some modern versions is contained in: Franklin G. Moore, *Production Control*, 2nd ed. (New York: McGraw-Hill Book Company, Inc., 1959), pp. 483–496.

[9]An excellent review of theoretical work on job shop scheduling is found in: Roger L. Sisson, "Sequencing Theory," in *Progress in Operations Research, Vol. I*, Russell L. Ackoff, ed. (New York: John Wiley & Sons, Inc., 1961). See also: Alan S. Manne, "On the Job Shop Scheduling Problem," Ralph E. Gomory, "An All-Integer Programming Algorithm," and Alfred E. Story and Harvey M. Wagner, "Computational Experience with Integer Programming for Job-Shop Scheduling" in *Industrial Scheduling*, John F. Muth and Gerald L. Thompson, eds. (Englewood Cliffs, N. J.: Prentice-Hall, Inc., 1963).

[10]See Alan J. Rowe, "Computer Simulation Applied to Job Shop Scheduling," in *Report of the System Simulation Symposium*. Sponsored by the American Institute of Industrial Engineers, The Institute of Management Sciences, and Operations Research Society of America, (New York, 1957). Also James R. Jackson, "Simulation Research on Job Shop Production," *Naval Research Logistics Quarterly*, Vol. 4, No. 4 (December, 1957).

operating policies can be tested under reasonably realistic conditions and without the gross simplifications that are usually necessary to make mathematical formulations tractable. The basic scheme in job shop simulation is to release jobs to the shop over time and follow them as they wait for machines to become available, are processed, and finally are completed by the shop. By gathering appropriate statistics about queue length, waiting times, equipment utilization, labor utilization, and so forth, behavior of the shop may be evaluated with regard to alternative operating policies. For instance, rules for timing the release of jobs, rules for determining which job is processed first when two or more jobs require processing on the same machine at the same time, and the desirability of providing alternative routes for jobs may be evaluated through simulation. In addition, effects of different load conditions can be observed together with effects of machine breakdowns, probabilitistic processing times, rush orders, and the like. Because of the complexity of job shop operations and interactions between the many parts of the system, analytical approaches have been successful in dealing only with portions of the total system, and then usually with very restrictive assumptions. In contrast, Fig. 2.3 shows the characteristics of a job shop simulator and the wealth of realistic detail that can be included.[11]

Of the many aspects of job shop operations which could be investigated through simulation, the one that has been examined most extensively is the proper rule to use in assigning priorities to jobs as they arrive at machines for processing. These rules, called dispatch rules, determine which job will be placed on the machine when it become available. Some dispatch rules that have been suggested are:

1. Choose the job with shortest processing time on the machine.
2. Choose the job that has the smallest amount of slack time, i.e., scheduled completion date minus the sum of remaining processing times.
3. First come, first served.
4. Choose the job with earliest scheduled date for the current operation.
5. Choose the job with earliest scheduled completion date.
6. Choose a job at random from jobs waiting to be processed.

Evaluation of these and other rules and combinations of the rules has frequently been a primary objective of job shop simulation.

Results of one evaluation through simulation of the six rules mentioned above are summarized in Table 2.1. They were obtained by using data from the fabrication shop of the El Segundo Division of the Hughes Aircraft

---

[11]The program was developed jointly by IBM and General Electric Company personnel and resulted from pioneering work in this field at General Electric. It was later released in revised form by IBM and is described in: *The Job Simulator*. (M&A-1) IBM Mathematics and Applications Department, 1271 Avenue of the Americas, New York 27, New York, 1960.

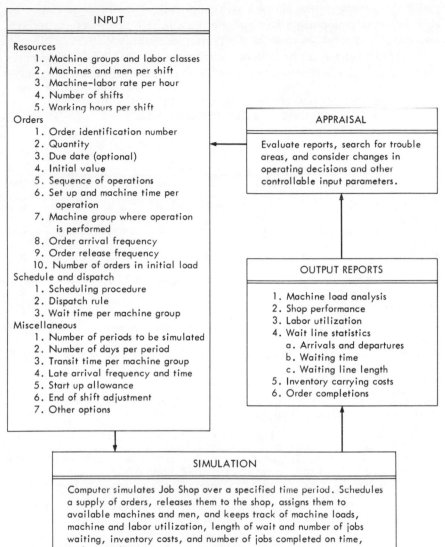

FIGURE 2.3. Characteristics of Job Shop Simulator (by permission from Earl Le-
Grande, "The Development of a Factory Simulation Using Actual
Operating Data," *Management Technology*, Vol. 3, No. 1, May, 1963)

Company.[12] As such, they are indicative of the relative merit of the dispatch
rules under conditions in existence at this particular plant and not of the

---

[12]Earl LeGrande, "The Development of a Factory Simulation Using Actual Operating Data," *Management Technology*, Vol. 3, No. 1 (May 1963).

merit of the rules in general.[13] A direct outgrowth of job shop simulation in this case was development of a simulation scheduler which was incorporated into the actual control system of the fabrication facility.[14]

Table 2.1 shows the breadth of data that are obtainable by using simulation to approach the job shop problem. These results were obtained by vary-

Table 2.1   SUMMARY OF RESULTS OF JOB SHOP SIMULATION USING VARIOUS DISPATCH RULES[a]

Criteria	Dispatch rule[b]					
	1	2	3	4	5	6
Number of orders completed	1446	1044	1115	1078	1323	1030
Percentage of orders completed late	24.5	20.4	37.8	42.0	33.0	30.1
Mean of completion distribution[c]	−6.56	−4.16	−3.57	−3.04	−4.20	−5.20
Standard deviation of completion distribution	9.9	2.0	10.0	9.2	8.2	10.4
Average number of orders waiting in the shop	961.4	1313.4	1320.4	1416.9	1148.9	1432.1
Average wait time of orders	0.360	0.697	0.949	1.003	0.710	0.544
Yearly cost of carrying orders in queue	128,909	102,800	117,836	108,903	98,502	122,372
Ratio of inventory carrying cost while waiting to inventory cost while on machine	13.292	12.136	12.391	12.092	12.239	13.024
Percentage of labor utilized	0.632	0.580	0.587	0.574	0.548	0.579
Percentage of machine capacity utilized	0.268	0.246	0.249	0.243	0.232	0.245
Total relative rank[d]	8.70	8.54	6.93	6.77	7.52	7.40

[a]Source: Earl LeGrande, "The Development of a Factory Simulation Using Actual Operating Data," *Management Technology*, Vol. 3, No. 1, May, 1963.
[b]Numbers correspond to numbers of rules discussed in text.
[c]Negative values are days early.
[d]Based on the performance of each rule with respect to the best rule for each criteria and with equal weighting of the criteria. Highest total is the best rule.

---

[13]Some efforts have been made to evaluate dispatch rules and combinations of them independent of any particular job shop setting. For a description of this work, the reader is referred to: Morton Allen, "The Efficient Utilization of Labor Under Conditions of Fluctuating Demand," and H. C. Fischer and G. L. Thompson, "Probabilistic Learning Combinations of Local Job-Shop Scheduling Rules," in *Industrial Scheduling*, John F. Muth and Gerald L. Thompson, eds. (Englewood Cliffs, N.J.: Prentice-Hall, Inc., 1963). J. Heller, "Some Numerical Experiments for an $M \times J$ Flow Shop and Its Decision-Theoretical Aspects," *Operations Research*, Vol. 8, No. 2 (March–April, 1960).
[14]A description of the control system is given in: Harry W. Steinhoff, Jr., "Daily System for Sequencing Orders in a Large-Scale Job Shop," in *Readings in Production and Operations Management*, Elwood S. Buffa, ed. (New York: John Wiley & Sons, Inc., 1966); and Michael H. Bulkin, John L. Colley, and Harry W. Steinhoff, Jr., "Load Forecasting, Priority Sequencing, and Simulation in a Job Shop Control System," *Management Science*, Vol. 13, No. 2 (October, 1966).

ing only the dispatch rules from simulation run to simulation run and without changing any other factors or data. Similar data could be obtained to analyze, for instance, effects of varying the quantity of equipment in the shops, while all other factors were kept unchanged. In fact, countless experiments could be performed to explore effects of changing various factors or even combinations of factors. This aspect of job shop simulation points up what is frequently a significant difference between strictly theoretical and simulation approaches to problems. In theoretical approaches we often find that a portion of the problem is treated in the abstract and often with significant simplifying assumptions. The results, however, of such theoretical calculations are generally fairly compact and interpretable. In simulation many more factors and dynamic interactions between them are usually included in the model, and a variety of statistics regarding operation of the system may be obtained. However, the quantity of data, of which Table 2.1 is an example, places an additional burden of interpretation on the experimenter, since selection of appropriate criteria for evaluating operation of the system is often not much easier in the case of a simulation than it is in the real world.

As a final comment on job shop simulation, it should be noted that early work in this field led directly to development of SIMSCRIPT, one of the major simulation programing languages currently in use. Although SIMSCRIPT is a general language and not specifically designed for job shop simulation, features that are incorporated in it are such that job shop simulation is readily accomplished with SIMSCRIPT. A job shop simulation model is one of the major illustrations in the SIMSCRIPT manual.[15] We will discuss SIMSCRIPT in detail in Chap. 7.

Pert Networks

Since their development in the late 1950's, critical path and PERT methods for control of projects consisting of many interrelated activities have achieved widespread publicity and acceptance.[16] The basic concept in an analysis of the PERT or critical path type is to view a project as a series of activities which must be accomplished according to certain precedence relationships. These relationships may be represented by an arrow diagram or network, as shown in Fig. 2.4, in which arrows represent activities that take time while circles represent events that are points in time. Precedence relationships in a network are indicated by establishing the convention that all activities leading into

---

[15]H. M. Markowitz, B. Hausner, and H. W. Karr, *SIMSCRIPT: A Simulation Programming Language.* Memorandum RM-3310-PR, Santa Monica, Calif.: The RAND Corporation, November, 1962 (Englewood Cliffs, N.J.: Prentice-Hall Inc., 1963), Chap. 3.

[16]Two of the earliest published descriptions of these methods are: J. E. Kelley, Jr. and M. R. Walker, "Critical Path Planning and Scheduling," Mauchley Associates, Inc. in *Proceedings of the Eastern Joint Computer Conference*, 1959; and *Program Evaluation Research Task, Summary Report, Phase 2* (Washington, D.C., September, 1958), Special Projects Office, Bureau of Naval Weapons, Department of the Navy.

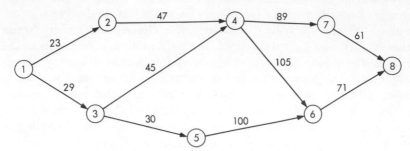

FIGURE 2.4. Project Network with Activity Times

an event must be completed before activities leading out of an event can begin.

Estimates are made of the time required for each activity, and these are the numbers shown above the arrows in Fig. 2.4. By numbering events so that all activities lead from lower to higher numbered events, we can represent each activity time estimate by t_{ij} ,were i is the preceding event number, j is the succeeding event number, and $i < j$. If we denote the earliest time at which event j can occur by E_j, the earliest times for the n events in a network can be computed by letting $E_1 = 0$ and using the relationship

$$E_j = \max_i (E_i + t_{ij}) \qquad (2.1)$$

to determine successively E_2, E_3, . . . , E_n.[17] Having found E_n, the earliest time at which the end event can occur, we now let L_j denote the latest time for an event j and compute the latest event times by letting $L_n = E_n$ and using the relationship

$$L_i = \min_j (L_j - t_{ij}) \qquad (2.2)$$

to find L_{n-1}, L_{n-2}, . . . , L_1. L_1, of course, will be found to equal 0.

The procedure locates one or more paths through the network on which $E_i = L_i$ for all events on the path. This path (or paths) is known as the *critical path*(s), since it is activities on this path that effectively determine the shortest time in which the project can be completed. On all other non-critical paths $E_i < L_i$ and the difference, which we will call S_i, is known as event slack for event i. For the network and activity times shown in Fig. 2.4, we calculate earliest and latest event times and slack times with the results shown in Table 2.2. The critical path passes through events 1-3-4-6-8, since there is no slack in these events.

---

[17]Note that only the events i connected to event j by activities i, j are used in calculating E_j.

Table 2.2 CALCULATION OF EVENT TIMES

	Earliest time	Latest time	Event slack
Event	E_i	L_i	S_i
1	0	0	0
2	23	27	4
3	29	29	0
4	74	74	0
5	59	79	20
6	179	179	0
7	163	189	26
8	250	250	0

The PERT technique elaborates on this basic critical path procedure by requiring an activity time estimate in the form of a probability distribution that represents the likelihood of completing an activity in various lengths of time. To simplify making the probabilistic estimates and data processing requirements, PERT procedures require only an estimate of optimistic time a, pessimistic time b, and most likely time m for each activity. A beta distribution is assumed for each activity i, j whose mean μ_{ij} and variance σ_{ij}^2 can be approximated by

$$\mu_{ij} = \frac{a + 4m + b}{6} \tag{2.3}$$

$$\sigma_{ij}^2 = \left(\frac{b - a}{6}\right)^2 \tag{2.4}$$

The PERT system then uses the mean activity times in computing the critical path by the procedure outlined earlier. No use is made of the probabilistic element in the activity time estimates until *after* the critical path is found, and at that time variances of activities *on the critical path only* are used to compute the variance of the distribution of completion time for the end event. In the PERT system, the mean μ_n of the distribution of completion time for the end event is the sum of the means of activities on the critical path

$$\mu_n = \Sigma\mu_{ij} \quad \text{(for all activities } i, j \text{ on the critical path)} \tag{2.5}$$

and the variance σ_n^2 of the distribution of completion time for the end event is the sum of the variances of activities on the critical path,

$$\sigma_n^2 = \Sigma\sigma_{ij}^2 \quad \text{(for all activities } i, j \text{ on the critical path)} \tag{2.6}$$

The assumption is also made that, because of the central limit theorem, the sum of the times on the critical path is normally distributed so that μ_n and

σ_n^2 completely specify the distribution of completion time of the end event (i.e., the project completion time).

A bias in the PERT procedure for obtaining the distribution of project completion time can be demonstrated by using the network in Fig. 2.4.[18] We replace the deterministic time estimates for the network in Fig. 2.4 with probabilistic estimates required by the PERT system, as shown in Table 2.3. For convenience of comparison, times in Table 2.3 have been chosen so that mean activity times as calculated by Eq. (2.3) are identical to the time estimates shown in Fig. 2.4. Under these circumstances calculations for finding the critical path using the PERT procedure are identical to those shown in Table 2.2, and the critical path is the same as was found previously.

Table 2.3   PERT ACTIVITY TIME ESTIMATES

Activity	Time estimates			Mean	Variance
	a	m	b		
1, 2	10	25	28	23	9.0
1, 3	20	25	54	29	32.1
2, 4	41	47	53	47	4.0
3, 4	31	42	71	45	44.5
3, 5	11	33	37	30	18.7
4, 6	70	110	120	105	69.4
4, 7	79	89	99	89	11.1
5, 6	80	100	120	100	44.5
6, 8	59	70	87	71	21.8
7, 8	42	63	72	61	25.0

Table 2.3 also shows the variances of the activites as calculated by Eq. (2.4). To find the variance of the end event by the PERT method, we use Eq. (2.6) so that

$$\sigma_8^2 = \sigma_{1,3}^2 + \sigma_{3,4}^2 + \sigma_{4,6}^2 + \sigma_{6,8}^2$$
$$= 32.1 + 44.5 + 69.4 + 21.8$$
$$= 167.8 \tag{2.7}$$

and

$$\sigma_8 = 13.0$$

Under the PERT assumptions, then, the project completion time is normally distributed with a mean of 250 and a standard deviation of 13.0.

---

[18]This bias in the PERT procedure has been discussed on a number of occasions in the literature. One of the most complete and lucid discussions, and one which we will refer to again, is: K. R. MacCrimmon and C. A. Ryavec, *An Analytical Study of the PERT Assumptions*, Memorandum RM-3408-PR (Santa Monica, Calif.: The RAND Corporation December, 1962).

Since the network is small, it would be legitimate to argue that the central limit theorem does not hold and that the final distribution will not be approximately normal. However, in large networks this is probably not a serious source of error in the PERT calculations. More serious is the fact that the PERT calculations consistently bias the mean of the completion time toward values which are too small. This occurs because PERT does not consider the time distributions of activities that are off the critical path in computing parameters of the project completion time distribution. As an example of how bias occurs, suppose that all activities on the critical path through events 1-3-4-6-8 were accomplished in the optimistic time a, as shown in Table 2.3. Also, suppose that all activities on the path through events 1-2-4-7-8 were accomplished in the pessimistic time b, as shown in Table 2.3. Then the length of the "critical path" 1-3-4-6-8 would be 180, whereas the length of the "noncritical path" 1-2-4-7-8 would be 252.

Obviously, interaction of the various activity time distributions both on and off the critical path can produce situations where noncritical paths can become critical and the critical path can become noncritical. As a result the PERT-calculated project completion time distribution is biased on the low side. The degree of bias is dependent upon whether there are any paths that are close to the PERT-calculated critical path in length and upon the variability of activity times both on and off the critical path.

Various methods for determining approximately the amount of bias and some methods for analytically determining the exact distribution have been suggested.[19] Simulation affords a straightforward method of determining, to any degree of accuracy required, the distribution of the project completion time.[20] The simulation procedure consists of selection of one time at random from each of the activity time distributions in the network, and calculation of the critical path and project completion time based on this sample of activity times. The process is repeated over and over and results in the generation of the project completion time distribution. In addition, the frequency with which different activities appear on the critical path can be determined, if desired.

To demonstrate the use of simulation as outlined above, a computer program was written as a seminar project at the University of Washington.[21] The program was used to compare simulation results with analytical results

---

[19]An approximate method is given by D. R. Fulkerson, "Expected Critical Path Lengths in PERT Networks," *Operations Research*, Vol. 10, No. 6 (1962).

An exact method is given by J. J. Martin, "Distribution of Time through a Directed, Acyclic Network," *Operations Research*, Vol. 13, No. 1 (January–February, 1965).

[20]Whether simulation is faster computationally than other methods is not known, since no comparisons have as yet been published of the results of tests of different methods on typical networks.

[21]Several different programs were developed at the University of Washington in the spring of 1963. The results discussed here were obtained by Messrs. Ahlers, Daniels, Plotke, and Tinius with a program which they developed.

Table 2.4   ACTIVITY TIME DISTRIBUTIONS

Activity time distribution for activities 1, 2; 2, 3; 3, 4; 4, 5.

Activity time	1	2	3
Probability	$\frac{1}{5}$	$\frac{3}{5}$	$\frac{1}{5}$

Activity time distribution for activities 1, 3; 2, 4.

Activity time	1	3	5
Probability	$\frac{1}{5}$	$\frac{3}{5}$	$\frac{1}{5}$

Activity time distribution for activity 2, 5.

Activity time	2	5	8
Probability	$\frac{1}{5}$	$\frac{3}{5}$	$\frac{1}{5}$

Activity time distribution for activity 1, 5.

Activity time	3	7	11
Probability	$\frac{1}{5}$	$\frac{3}{5}$	$\frac{1}{5}$

Source: K. R. MacCrimmon and C. A. Ryavec, *An Analytical Study of the PERT Assumptions*, Memorandum RM-3408-PR (Santa Monica, Calif.: The RAND Corporation, December, 1962), pp. 30ff.

obtained by MacCrimmon and Ryavec.[22] Figure 2.5 shows one of the networks analyzed by MacCrimmon and Ryavec. Times shown on the activities in Fig. 2.5 are the means of the activity time distributions. The discrete activity time distributions used by MacCrimmon and Ryavec to obtain analytically the true project completion time distribution are shown in Table 2.4. Results of the simulation are compared with the PERT-calculated mean and analytically calculated mean in Table 2.5. After 90 samples the simulation results are very close to the actual values of μ and σ and are much better than the PERT-calculated results. In addition to the results shown in Table 2.5, the program computes the standard error of the mean. A useful addition to the program would be a check after each run (or after each five or ten runs) to determine whether the standard error of the mean has been reduced to some predetermined level and instructions to terminate the run whenever this level is reached.

In the preceding discussion we have referred to the procedure as a simulation of the network. Although this terminology is not incorrect in terms of popular usage of the word *simulation*, it should be noted that the approach does not quite fit within the definition of simulation in Chap. 1. The Monte Carlo method, of course, is used to select times from the probability distributions of activity times, but the technique does not involve observing the operation of the network through time in quite the same sense that behavior of systems such as inventory systems are observed through time by simulation. Rather, times are selected by the Monte Carlo method for each of the activi-

---

[22]K. R. MacCrimmon and C. A. Ryavec, *An Analytical Study of the PERT Assumptions*, Memorandum RM-3408-PR (Santa Monica, Calif.: The RAND Corporation, December, 1962).

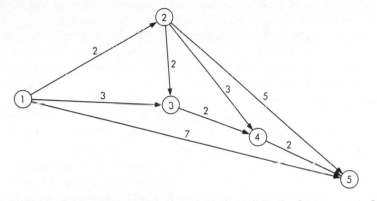

FIGURE 2.5. Project Network (by permission from K.R. MacCrimmon and C.A. Ryavec, *An Analytical Study* of the PERT Assumptions, Memorandum RM-3408-PR, The RAND Corporation, Santa Monica, California, December, 1962)

ties, and calculation of the project completion time is then a straightforward arithmetic computation. This use of the Monte Carlo method to determine through multiple trials a probability distribution that would be difficult or impossible to get by analytical methods is more properly termed *model sampling*.

Table 2.5   COMPARISON OF PERT, ANALYTICAL, AND
SIMULATION RESULTS

	Project Completion Time	
Method of computation	μ	σ
PERT	8.00	1.26
Analytically	9.23	1.39
Simulation		
40 samples	9.67	1.27
50 samples	9.12	1.55
90 samples	9.36	1.41

Waiting Lines

Waiting line or queuing problems arise in processes and systems in which customers or transactions arrive at a service facility where they must wait in line until served. In systems of this nature it is often of interest to determine the effects of such things as number of servers, service time distribution, arrival distribution, and queue discipline[23] on the distribution of queue

---

[23]Queue discipline is the particular rule governing the operation of the queue. For example, queues may operate on a first-in, first-out basis, or the customers may have various priorities which govern the order of service.

length, distribution of time in queue, total transit time through the facility, utilization of the facility, and so forth. Queuing problems are of significant interest in the design of service facilities in the telephone industry, in the operation of toll collecting and checkout facilities, in the design of data processing facilities, and in the determination of repair facility requirements— to name a few major applications.

Waiting line problems have been investigated analytically since the early 1900's, and Erlang's work "The Theory of Probabilities and Telephone Conversations" published in 1909 is the pioneering work in the field. In the 1920's T.C. Fry and E.C. Molina made significant contributions to the field which have been followed, particularly since the Second World War, by many further theoretical advances. The general direction of this work has been toward extending theoretical results to a wider variety of systems and arrival and service characteristics.[24] In spite of the fact that much analytical progress has been made, however, it is not difficult to propose system configurations, operating procedures, and input characteristics that are not susceptible to analysis by the mathematical methods that have been developed. Consequently, simulation has been found to be a very powerful and useful tool for analyzing systems in which queues are a significant feature to be investigated. Besides making tractable problems which could not otherwise be investigated, simulation also permits observation of the dynamic behavior of the system under study, permits tracing of movement of individual customers or transactions through the system, and can include the use of complex logical decisions in directing and regulating the flow of traffic through the system. No similar flexibility of analysis is possible with a strictly theoretical approach, and this is a principal reason for the extensive application of simulation to such problems in recent years.

The general procedure in simulating these systems is to generate customer arrivals or transactions at intervals corresponding to the actual arrival distributions in the system under study. These transactions are then entered into the system, and statistics regarding their progress in time through the system are tabulated together with statistics regarding queue lengths and utilization of facilities within the system. Transactions, for instance, may be customers arriving at a service facility such as a checkout stand, or units of product moving through a manufacturing process, or customer orders flowing through an order processing system.

As a specific example, consider the simulation of an elementary system composed of a single server; let us assume that the server is an order taker for a wholesaler. The order taker can service an average of 15 customers per hour,

---

[24]For an excellent review of theoretical work in the field and an extensive bibliography, see: Thomas L. Saaty, *Elements of Queueing Theory With Applications* (New York: McGraw-Hill Book Company, Inc., 1961).

and service times are exponentially distributed.[25] Following the conventional notation used in the queuing literature, we let μ = mean service rate, or $\mu = 15$. If the service times are exponentially distributed, then the frequency function of service times $f(t_s)$ is given by

$$f(t_s) = \mu e^{-\mu t}$$
$$= 15e^{-15t} \tag{2.8}$$

Customers arrive to place orders with the order taker at an average rate λ of 10 per hour, and the number of arrivals follows a Poisson distribution.[26] The resulting interarrival time distribution is an exponential with frequency function $f(t_a)$ given by

$$f(t_a) = \lambda e^{-\lambda t}$$
$$= 10e^{-10t} \tag{2.9}$$

Some properties of the system which might be of interest can be determined analytically by queuing theory as follows.[27]
The utilization factor ρ of the facility is

$$\rho = \frac{\lambda}{\mu} = \frac{2}{3} \tag{2.10}$$

The average number of customers in the system (including the customer being serviced) is

$$\frac{\rho}{(1 - \rho)} = \frac{2/3}{1 - 2/3} = 2 \tag{2.11}$$

The average length of the waiting line is

$$\left[\frac{\rho}{(1 - \rho)}\right] - \rho = 2 - \frac{2}{3} = 1\frac{1}{3} \tag{2.12}$$

To simulate this system, we generate customer arrivals, using the

---

[25]This particular form of service distribution is used because it is one distribution which can be analyzed by theoretical queuing formulas. For a complete discussion of the distribution and its relationship to the Poisson process, see: Thomas L. Saaty, *Mathematical Methods of Operations Research* (New York: McGraw-Hill Book Company, Inc., 1959), p. 336.

[26]For a discussion of the Poisson input, see: Thomas L. Saaty, *Mathematical Methods of Operations Research* (New York: McGraw-Hill Book Company, Inc., 1959), pp. 335f.

[27]The derivation of these and other queuing formulas can be found in any of the standard works on queuing theory, such as the works by Saaty referenced previously.

cumulative customer arrival distribution $F(t_a)$, which can be derived from Eq. (2.9).

$$F(t_a) = 1 - e^{-\lambda t}$$
$$= 1 - e^{-10t} \tag{2.13}$$

The process of determining the time between arrivals from $F(t_a)$ is the same as was described in connection with the inventory example in Chap. 1 and is shown in Fig. 2.6. We generate a random number between 0 and 1, 0.79810, for example, read horizontally across to the cumulative distribution, and down to the time axis.[28] If it is assumed that the simulation is just starting, the first customer would arrive at 0.16 hours, as shown in Fig. 2.6, and the time between arrivals of succeeding customers would be determined by repeated application of the same procedure.

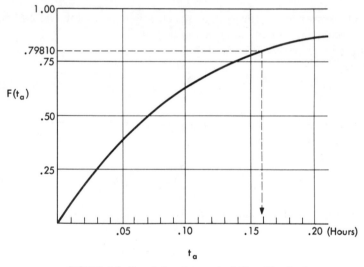

FIGURE 2.6. Cumulative Interarrival Time Distribution

The cumulative service time distribution $F(t_s)$, which may be derived from Eq. (2.8), is

$$F(t_s) = 1 - e^{-\mu t}$$
$$= 1 - e^{-15t} \tag{2.14}$$

This distribution is shown in Fig. 2.7. Service times are selected from the distribution, the technique demonstrated in Fig. 2.6 being used. When the

---

[28]The derivation of Eq. (2.13) together with a mathematical method for selecting times from a negative exponential distribution is discussed in Chap. 8.

first simulated customer arrives at the order taker, the first service time is selected, and the simulation continues with successive generation of arrival and service times. When customers arrive while the order taker is occupied, they are held in queue until the order taker is free and their turn comes for service. As simulated time advances, statistics could be kept on the utilization of the order taker, length of queue, and number of customers in the system. These statistics would converge on the analytical results shown in Eqs. (2.10), (2.11), and (2.12) after a sufficiently long period of time. Other statistics could, of course be collected as desired. In this particular illustration, the statistics would be useful in determining whether additional order takers are required to provide a reasonable level of service.

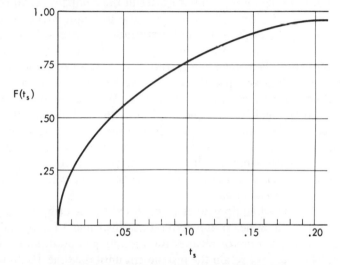

FIGURE 2.7. Cumulative Service Time Distribution

It is apparent that a good deal of record keeping is necessary to create customer arrivals, move customers at the proper time and in proper sequence past the order taker, and keep desired statistics. Since queuing formulas are available to determine statistics of interest in this simple system, they would probably be used in preference to simulation. In dealing with more complicated systems of this nature, queuing formulas may not be available, and it is in these circumstances that simulation would be the proper tool of analysis. As noted previously, however, simulation of even a small system demands a substantial amount of computation and record keeping, and larger systems would be impractical, if not impossible, to simulate without a digital computer.

Using a computer eliminates the need for hand computation and recording but requires preparation of a program, which can be a formidable task and, fortunately, is not always necessary. A program called the General

Purpose Systems Simulator (GPSS) has been developed which is capable of simulating a wide variety of systems in which the principal feature of interest is the flow of transactions through a system. Queuing problems fit quite well the structure of GPSS, and in Chap. 7 we will use the simple order taker system to illustrate the structure and capabilities of GPSS.

A system, more complex than the one just described, that has been analyzed through simulation is an instrument calibration system in a large manufacturing organization.[29] Movement of instruments through the system, waiting lines and times that develop, and utilization of calibration technicians were of principal interest in the study. Because of the complexity of the system and desire to explore a variety of aspects of the system, simulation using GPSS was chosen as the tool for analysis.

There are four calibration laboratories in the company, each of which has several thousand pieces of general purpose test equipment assigned to it for periodic repair, calibration, and certification. When an instrument is sent to the calibration laboratory, it is logged in and cleaned by a receiving clerk and put on a shelf until a calibration technician is available. Technicians and work areas are specialized as to the type of instruments they can calibrate, although there is an overlap in skills. When a technician who can calibrate the instrument is available, he begins the calibration. If he completes the calibration, the instrument is returned to the receiving clerk, who logs it out and sends it to a storage crib if it is delay-dated, or directly to a user if it is nondelay-dated.[30] If the calibration is not complete at the end of the shift, a technician on the next shift completes the work and sends the instrument to the receiving clerk.

After delay-dated equipment is transported to the crib, it is logged in and placed on a shelf. When a user requests an instrument for the first time, the date that it will be due for recalibration is stamped on it, and it is given to the user. The user may retain the instrument until the time a calibration is due or he may return it, and another user may check it out until the calibration due date. Nondelay-dated instruments usually remain in the original user's area until they are due for recalibration. If an instrument fails in use,

---

[29]The study of the system was conducted by Mr. Charles E. Carpenter and Mr. Gary W. Dickson. The description of the simulation which follows is adapted from: Charles E. Carpenter, "Use of General Purpose Systems Simulator II in Systems Analysis," unpublished MBA research report (Seattle: University of Washington, 1964). See also: Stephen K. Didis and Charles E. Carpenter, "Simulation Study of a Test Equipment Calibration and Certification System," *The Journal of Industrial Engineering*, Vol. 27, No. 8 (August, 1966).

[30]Delay-dated instruments are sent to a crib from the laboratory. When a user requests the instrument from the crib for the first time, the specified cycle in days is added to the current date, and the result is the date the instrument must be returned for calibration. Nondelay-dated instruments are sent directly to a user from the calibration laboratory. The specified cycle in days is added to the date the instrument leaves the calibration laboratory, and the result is the date the instrument must be returned for calibration.

it is immediately sent to the calibration laboratory for repair and re-calibration.

The model has three basic parts: the instrument flow, a loading routine, and a shift clock. The instrument flow represents the calibration system itself and is a closed loop of all processes that instruments can go through. Transactions move through this loop, shown in Fig. 2.8, in simulated time just as instruments move in the calibration system in real time. The loading routine is utilized when a simulation run is to begin and the total number of instruments to be simulated must be realistically distributed through the system.[31] Since the calibration system operates on two shifts with differing numbers of technicians on each shift, the shift clock is necessary to keep track of the shift and when it is due to end. In addition, the shift clock is used to tabulate daily statistics about operation of the system. While transactions are moving in the instrument flow, a single transaction is moving in another closed loop called the shift clock. The movement of this transaction is similar

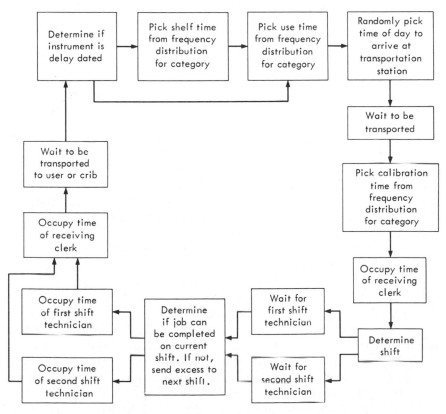

FIGURE 2.8. Flow Chart of Calibration System Simulation

[31] A complete discussion of loading the model appears in Chap. 9.

in concept to the movement of the hour hand on a clock. At the beginning of each shift, the time that the shift will end is computed and stored for reference when checking whether or not a calibration can be completed in the current shift. During each shift and at the end of the day, the shift clock transaction is used to tabulate certain statistics about the instrument flow.

The following is a list of information which the model can provide on any run.

1. A history of each run giving the daily value of each of the following:
   a. Quantity of instruments in the calibration laboratory at the end of each day.
   b. Average flow time of calibrations completed during the day.
   c. Average utilization of calibration technicians during the day.
   d. Quantity of instruments arriving at the calibration laboratory.
   e. Quantity of instruments leaving the calibration laboratory.

2. A frequency distribution with mean and standard deviation of each of the following:
   a. Quantity of instruments in the laboratory at the end of the day and at the end of the first shift.
   b. Flow time of instruments through the laboratory.
   c. Utilization of technicians each day.
   d. Total quantity calibrated in each category and the total work load in hours in each category.
   e. Total time between calibrations for each instrument.
   f. Time between removals of instruments from the shelf.

A use of the model was to study effects of a proposed combination of two laboratories, one of which calibrated about three times as many instruments as the other. The proposed combination entailed routing all work through the large laboratory and setting up a transportation system to carry instruments to and from the smaller laboratory. The procedure used was to simulate the operation of the two laboratories separately and then to simulate the combined operation with the same total number of technicians and with the same work load.

In the simulation of the combined operation average flow time for equipment calibrated in the larger laboratory was decreased by six hours from 38 to 32 hours, but transportation added an average of 29 hours to flow time for equipment from the smaller laboratory. Since the larger laboratory calibrated three times as much equipment as the smaller, average increase in flow time for all equipment was one hour, from 38 to 39 hours. The simulation showed that in the combined laboratory average quantity of equipment in calibration or waiting for calibration would decrease from 154 to 121 instruments. This saving plus savings in administration cost, facilities, and better management control were felt to more than offset the one-hour increase in average flow time, especially since users serviced by the smaller laboratory said that the increase in flow time would not seriously affect their operations. The combination of the two laboratories was then implemented.

This illustration provides a good example of the type of system analysis for which simulation is well suited and the range of possible management decisions that may be investigated through simulation. Because of the availability of a computer simulation language that could readily handle the particular type of system to be simulated, computer programing costs were not excessive. From the standpoint of flexibility, accuracy, and cost, analysis through simulation was particularly attractive in this case.

Forecasting

A relatively simple direct application of simulation is in the evaluation of various statistical forecasting schemes. Such schemes are used to make forecasts, say of sales, for future time periods based on sales data from past time periods. Moving averages and exponential smoothing are two of the more widely used methods. One problem in determining whether a statistical forecasting method may be useful is that there are a large number of alternatives. Even if other methods are ignored, moving averages and exponential smoothing alone offer many possibilities since moving averages of different lengths may be tried and, in the case of exponential smoothing, different values of the smoothing constant[32] can be tested. In addition, the effects of including seasonal and cyclical factors may be investigated.

One of the principal ways of validating any statistical forecasting method is to try the method on past data and observe the amount of forecast error. In other words, a simulation is performed in which a forecast is made for each time period using only the past data that would have been available had the forecasting method actually been in use. Then the simulated forecast is compared with actual data for the time period, and the procedure is repeated for succeeding time periods. By comparing distributions of forecast error for different forecasting methods, i.e., various lengths of moving averages, different values of α, etc., some evidence is obtained relative to expected performance of the methods. Although simulated performance of a method on past data is no guarantee of future performance, it is one of the best tests that is available.

Table 2.6 is a tabulation of the results of simulating two forecasting methods, a twelve-month moving average and exponential smoothing with $\alpha = 0.10$, on sales data for 60 time periods. Seventy-two periods of data

---

[39]In the exponential smoothing method, the smoothing constant α is any number between 0 and 1 which is used in making the forecast as follows.

$$\text{new forecast} = \alpha(\text{actual from last period})$$
$$+ (1 - \alpha)(\text{previous forecast})$$

A complete explanation of exponential smoothing is found in: R. G. Brown, *Smoothing, Forecasting and Prediction of Discrete Times Series* (Englewood Cliffs, N.J.: Prentice-Hall, Inc., 1963). A further discussion of exponential smoothing also appears in Chap. 3.

were used in the simulation. However, to eliminate effects of starting conditions on the simulation, 12 periods previous to the start of the table have been deleted from the analysis. The distributions of forecast errors are shown in Figs. 2.9 and 2.10.

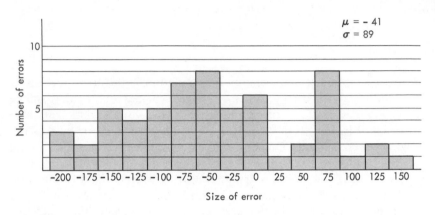

FIGURE 2.9. Frequency Distribution of Forecast Errors Using Twelve-Month Moving Average

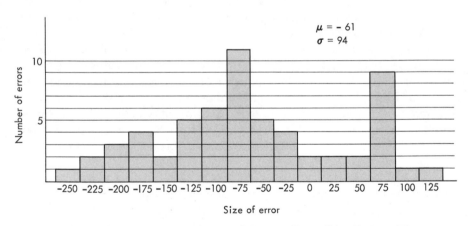

FIGURE 2.10. Frequency Distribution of Forecast Errors Using Exponential Smoothing, $\alpha = .10$

As the distributions of forecast errors suggest, neither of the forecasting methods is very good, since the errors are probably unacceptably severe. The tabulation of forecast errors indicates that correction for a short-term cycle, perhaps a seasonal cycle, would be appropriate, since the forecast errors tend to swing periodically from plus to minus. As we look at the error distributions, the bias of the mean for both methods suggests that correction for an upward trend would be in order. In addition, different lengths of moving average and different values of alpha should, of course, be tested in conjunction with the cycle and trend corrections. Simulating these and other possibilities would be quite burdensome if the calculations were done by hand, but with a digital computer there is no particular difficulty in this respect. The simulation programs that performed the calculations for Table 2.6 were written in FORTRAN in about an hour and actual running of each program for 72 time periods of data took only a few seconds. A fore-

Table 2.6 RESULTS OF SIMULATION OF TWO FORECASTING METHODS

Period	Sales	Moving Average (12 month)		Exponential Smoothing ($\alpha = 0.10$)	
		Forecast	Error[a]	Forecast	Error[a]
1	381	496	115	461	80
2	372	500	128	453	81
3	494	503	9	445	−49
4	526	510	−16	450	−76
5	564	516	−48	458	−106
6	547	520	−27	468	−79
7	544	519	−25	476	−68
8	612	516	−96	483	−129
9	610	515	−95	496	−114
10	579	515	−64	507	−72
11	435	517	82	514	79
12	441	514	73	506	65
13	403	509	106	500	97
14	358	511	153	490	132
15	442	509	67	477	35
16	485	505	20	473	−12
17	541	502	−39	475	−66
18	590	500	−90	481	−109
19	562	503	−59	492	−70
20	571	505	−66	499	−72
21	551	501	−50	506	−45
22	536	496	−40	511	−25
23	454	493	39	513	59
24	488	494	6	507	19
25	430	498	68	505	75
26	432	501	69	498	66
27	534	507	−27	491	−43
28	578	514	−64	496	−82
29	608	522	−86	504	−104
30	677	528	−149	514	−163
31	641	535	−106	531	−110
32	627	542	−85	542	−85
33	634	546	−88	550	−84
34	609	553	−56	558	−51
35	505	559	54	564	59
36	478	564	86	558	80
37	481	563	82	550	69

Table 2.6 (Continued)

Period	Sales	Moving Average (12 month)		Exponential Smoothing ($\alpha = 0.10$)	
		Forecast	Error	Forecast	Error
38	480	567	87	543	63
39	568	571	3	537	−31
40	636	574	−62	540	−96
41	685	579	−106	549	−136
42	785	585	−200	563	−222
43	746	594	−152	585	−161
44	775	603	−172	601	−174
45	742	615	−127	619	−123
46	758	624	−134	631	−127
47	640	637	−3	644	4
48	706	648	−58	643	−63
49	743	667	−76	650	−93
50	683	689	6	659	−24
51	861	706	−155	661	−200
52	861	730	−131	681	−180
53	888	749	−139	699	−189
54	959	766	−193	718	−241
55	949	780	−169	742	−207
56	995	797	−198	763	−232
57	967	815	−152	786	−181
58	952	834	−118	804	−148
59	841	850	9	819	−22
60	880	867	−13	821	−59

[a]Forecasts that are too high are considered to have positive errors; those that are too low have negative errors.

casting method which gives much better results than those in Table 2.6 is suggested in Exercise 2.17.

If analyses of this nature were undertaken frequently, the development of more elaborate programs would be appropriate. One such program reported in the literature has the capability of simulating the following forecasting schemes:

1. Single moving average.
2. Single moving average with least squares trend.
3. Double moving average.
4. Single moving average with least squares trend and exponential seasonals.
5. Single exponential smoothing.
6. Single exponential smoothing with trend and seasonals.
7. Second order exponential smoothing.
8. Double exponential smoothing.
9. Triple exponential smoothing.[33]

---

[33]Donald Gross and Jack L. Ray, "A General Purpose Forecast Simulator," *Management Science*, Vol. 11, No. 6 (April, 1965).

Quality Control Systems

A general purpose quality control system simulator has been developed for use in analyzing operating characteristics of alternative configurations of inspection stages.[34] It is necessary to simulate not only the inspection activity but also those operation and assembly activities that change the quality of the product as it flows through the system. The quality control simulation program accomplishes this system representation by means of a number of generalized block types and interconnecting flows.

The simulator allows consideration of up to three defined levels of quality. These levels could represent good items, items with major defects, and items with critical defects—or any other combination of three quality levels which the analyst considers pertinent. The flow at any point in the system is described by a quantity vector representing the amount of product at each quality level and a cost vector representing the per-unit value of items at each of the three quality levels. The actual activities in the simulated system are represented by making use of three generalized types of blocks; operation, inspection, and assembly blocks, and the interconnections between them. By judicious choice of descriptive parameters these blocks can represent an extremely wide range of production activities.

Activities of a straight line nature, i.e., those using a one-to-one ratio between inputs and outputs, are described by means of an *operation block*. From a quality control viewpoint the important aspects of this type of process are changes in the quality and value of inputs. Consequently, the operation block makes use of a matrix of defect generation probabilities and a value-added vector, which are given as input data at the beginning of a simulation run. The matrix shows for each incoming quality level, let us say, good items, items with major defects, and items with critical defects, the proportion of items which will exit at each of these three levels.

The sample matrix in Fig. 2.11 would result in the following average changes in quality. (Any *individual* unit, however, is changed in quality level by randomly selecting its outgoing condition by using the probability distribution in the row of the matrix corresponding to its incoming level.) (1) Of those items entering the operation as good, 95 per cent leave as good, 4 per cent leave with major defects, and 1 per cent leave with critical defects. (2) Of those items entering with major defects, none leave as good, 90 per cent leave with major defects, and 10 per cent leave with critical defects. (3) Of those entering with critical defects, 100 per cent leave with critical defects. Upgrading of quality can be represented by having nonzero entries in the lower left portion of the matrix.

---

[34]The quality control system simulator was developed and programmed by one of the authors, Harold L. Pazer,

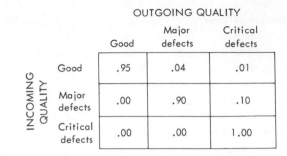

FIGURE 2.11. Matrix of Defect-Generation Probabilities for Operation Block

A value-added vector represents the cost of the operation for each quality level. If cost is not dependent upon quality, all elements of this vector for an operation block are the same. The operation block, in effect, updates the description of the flow to reflect the impact of a production activity.

Inspection blocks perform the function of selectively dividing the input flow on the basis of quality standards. Perfect efficiency at this point would result in all good items continuing in the flow to the next production activity, while all defective items would be diverted from the system into a reject flow. The unit cost of the inspection activity must also be included. Since perfect efficiency at inspection stations is not a likely occurrence, the inspection activity is represented by a vector of rejection probabilities such as (0.01, 0.70, 0.98). This vector describes an inspection station that rejects 1 per cent of the good items submitted to it (a type I error), 70 per cent of the items with major defects, and 98 per cent of the items with critical defects (corresponding to type II errors of 0.30 and 0.02, respectively). The performance of the block on any individual item is determined at random using these probabilities. A value-added vector represents the unit cost of inspection for each of the three quality levels. The effect of the inspection block, therefore, is to divide the input flow in accordance with the efficiency of the inspection station and to update the value of the output flows to reflect the cost of inspection.

Assembly blocks are used to simulate operations of a convergent nature, that is, those in which a number of flows are combined to form a single output flow of assembled units. The assembly block of the quality control simulator can combine four primary flows and four secondary flows into a single assembled unit. Primary flows are defined as those that are of sufficient importance to be analyzed in detail by the simulation. They are generally the output of an operation block or an inspection block. However, in the case of cascading they may also represent the output of another assembly block. Secondary flows represent inexpensive parts (of the nuts and bolts variety) that do not merit detailed analysis. These secondary flows are generated within the assembly block, and their quality is represented by the dichotomous classification of good or defective.

Assembly ratios given as input data at the start of the simulation are used to specify the number of units of each primary and secondary flow required to produce a single assembled unit. Since it is unlikely that the amounts in each of the primary flows will be exactly proportional to the assembly ratios, it is necessary to determine which of the primary flows will determine the maximum amount to be assembled and to determine the excess amount for the other flows. Secondary flows, by definition, are items in abundant supply which do not limit the number of assemblies.

A vector of assembly ratios might be as follows: (2, 4, 3, 0, 8, 12, 0, 0). This vector is interpreted in the following manner by the assembly block. Two units of primary flow 1 are joined with four units of primary flow 2 and three units of primary flow 3. The assembly requires eight units of secondary flow 1 and twelve units of secondary flow 2. Primary flow 4 and secondary flows 3 and 4 are not used by this assembly block. This vector, in effect, directs the assembly block to combine 29 separate parts into a single assembled unit. Assemblies of considerably greater complexity than this example can be simulated easily. Since the assembly unit is a combination of a number of units from primary and secondary flows, it is necessary to re-define the quality standards to allow the output to be described in terms of the three quality levels of the simulation. For example, it could be stated that an assembly containing two components with major defects would still be classified as one with a major defect, whereas an assembly with three or more major defects would be classified as one with a critical defect. Decision rules such as this are part of the data input to the assembly block. A value-added vector provides the cost of the assembly operation, which is added to the value of the component parts to obtain updated values for the outgoing flow. In summary, the assembly block combines primary and secondary flows, records excess parts, defines the quality levels for assembled units, and determines their value.

To represent a complex production system the number of operation, inspection, and assembly blocks and the interconnections between them are defined by inputs to the simulation program. In addition, matrices and vectors that provide necessary quality and cost information to describe the specific characteristics of each of the blocks are given to the program as input data.

When a system is modeled, inspection blocks are inserted at potential locations in the system and any desired number of simulated items of production are run through the system. A summary block provides statistical measures for evaluating the configuration, the most important of these being the cost of each unit passing through the system as well as the mean and standard deviation for all units passing through a specific configuration.

Markov Processes

A Markov process is a model of a probabilistic system that is characterized by a sequence of trials or experiments in which the results of a trial are dependent upon the immediately preceding trial. Fundamental concepts of a Markov process are the state of a system at a point in time and the transition from one state to another, and a fundamental assumption is that there are a finite number of mutually exclusive states. The process reveals the behavior of the system as it moves from one time period to another and the conditions under which the system stabilizes, if it does stabilize. The behavior of Markov processes has been analyzed chiefly by algebraic and matrix methods, but they can also be simulated using the Monte Carlo technique.

The probabilistic nature of the transition from one state to another in a Markov process may be represented by a matrix of transition probabilities. Letting S represent the state of a system, and $S_i(n)$ represent the state of a system after the nth trial, we specify the probability of a transition from state i to state j after the next trial as p_{ij}. In a Markov process the transition probability p_{ij} is a function only of the states S_i and S_j, and not of any previous history and may be written as a conditional probability

$$p_{ij} = P[S_j(n)|S_i(n-1)] \tag{2.15}$$

The transition probability p_{ij} is the probability that the system which is now in state i will be in state j after the next trial, or the probability that the system will be in state S_j after the nth trial, given that the system was in state S_i after the $(n-1)$th trial. A system which behaves according to this process is a discrete-state, discrete-transition Markov process.

An elementary example will illustrate the process. A customer has a choice of two brands of a product, brand A and brand B. There is a probability of 0.8 that if his previous purchase is brand A, his next purchase will be brand A. That is, $p_{aa} = 0.8$. Similarly, $p_{ab} = 0.2$. When his previous purchase is brand B, $p_{ba} = 0.3$ and $p_{bb} = 0.7$. These probabilities do not change with subsequent purchases. This is an example of a discrete-state, discrete-transition Markov process, because the probability of purchasing a given brand on his next purchase is dependent only upon his immediate prior purchase and is independent of earlier purchases. We would like to study the behavior of this system through time, and to answer some questions about the likelihood of buying brand A or B after a given number of purchases, given that the first purchase was brand A or B.

The transition probabilities are shown graphically in a transition diagram in Figure 2.12. In the transition diagram the states of the system are circles and the transition probabilities are represented by arrows. The transition probabilities may also be written in the form of a matrix.

$$\mathbf{P} = \begin{bmatrix} p_{aa} & p_{ab} \\ p_{ba} & p_{bb} \end{bmatrix} = \begin{matrix} & A & B \\ A & \begin{bmatrix} 0.8 & 0.2 \\ B & 0.3 & 0.7 \end{bmatrix} \end{matrix} \tag{2.16}$$

The sum of the elements in each row of the transition matrix P is 1, because

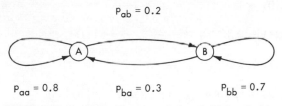

FIGURE 2.12. Transition Diagram of Brand Choice Problem

the entries in each row represent the probabilities for all possible transitions from the state represented by that row.

The behavior of this process may be simulated using the Monte Carlo technique by assigning random numbers from 0 through 7 to p_{aa}, 8 and 9 to p_{ab}, 0 through 2 to p_{ba}, and 3 through 9 to p_{bb}. Table 2.7 shows the results of simulating 10 trials, given that the initial purchase was brand A. Note that brand A was purchased 6 times and brand B 4 times and that the tenth purchase was brand B. To determine the relative frequency of occurrence of each state, a larger number of trials would be used; and to determine the relative frequency of occurrence of each state on the nth trial, the simulation would be repeated several times. If a sufficient number of trials and simulations were made, the relative frequencies will approach the calculated probabilities of occurrence of each state.

Table 2.7   SIMULATION OF BRAND CHOICE MARKOV PROCESS
GIVEN THAT THE INITIAL PURCHASE IS BRAND A

Trial number	Random number	Brand purchased
1	5	A
2	6	A
3	1	A
4	8	B
5	1	A
6	7	A
7	1	A
8	8	B
9	4	B
10	7	B

In this example there is a limiting-state probability distribution which is independent of the initial purchase. Limiting-state probabilities are the state probabilities which are approached after a large number of trials and which do not change with further trials. Consider the calculated state probabilities of buying brands A and B on the second purchase following the initial purchase given that the initial purchase was brand A. Let $p_{ij}(n)$ be the conditional probability of buying brand j after n more purchases, given that the initial purchase was brand i. Since we specified that the initial purchase was brand A, the state probabilities are calculated as follows:

$$\mathbf{p}_{aa}(0) = 1 \tag{2.17}$$

$$\mathbf{p}_{aa}(1) = 0.8 \tag{2.18}$$

$$\mathbf{p}_{ab}(1) = 0.2 \tag{2.19}$$

$$\mathbf{p}_{aa}(2) = (p_{aa})(p_{aa}) + (p_{ab})(p_{ba}) = (0.8)(0.8)$$
$$+ (0.2)(0.3) = 0.7 \tag{2.20}$$

$$\mathbf{p}_{ab}(2) = (p_{aa})(p_{ab}) + (p_{ab})(p_{bb}) = (0.8)(0.2)$$
$$+ (0.2)(0.7) = 0.3 \tag{2.21}$$

There is a probability of 0.7 that the system will be in state A after two trials and 0.3 that it will be in state B, given that the initial state was A. If we carried this further we would find find that as n becomes very large, the state probabilities approach limits which are independent of the initial state of the system, as shown in the limiting-state probability matrix.

$$\mathbf{P}^{\infty} = \begin{array}{c} \\ A \\ B \end{array} \begin{array}{cc} A & B \\ \begin{bmatrix} 0.6 & 0.4 \\ 0.6 & 0.4 \end{bmatrix} \end{array} \tag{2.22}$$

The probabilities of buying brands A and B are 0.6 and 0.4 regardless of the initial purchase. A Markov process which exhibits this property is called an ergodic process. A discussion of methods for calculating these probabilities is beyond the scope of this book, but they are covered in the references at the end of the chapter.

Total Firm

The preceding discussion of the use of simulation in analysis of various business problems naturally gives rise to the question of whether it is feasible to simulate operation of the total firm rather than just portions of it at a time. If such a total firm simulator could be constructed, observation and analysis of the interactions of the subsystems within a firm would be possible and problems of suboptimization, which arise inevitably when parts of the firm are examined individually, would be avoided.

The possibility of such a total firm simulator is dependent on the level of aggregation which the analyst is willing to accept. As shown by several of the preceding illustrations in this chapter, it is quite possible with existing techniques and data processing equipment to simulate in fairly minute detail the events that occur in a limited area. However, it is not possible, even with the very powerful computing equipment that is becoming available, to simulate *all* of the activities in detail in *all* of the subsystems of a firm. Even if no technological constraints were present, the desirability of constructing an all-encompassing microscopic simulator of the total firm would be open to question, since the analyst would be faced with an impossible task of determining what experiments to perform, what data to collect, and how to interpret the results. In other words, a model that is not a significant abstraction from the real world suffers from many of the same difficulties of interpretation and analysis which are found in the real world. As a consequence any meaningful approach to total firm simulation involves a considerable amount of abstraction and aggregation, and just how this is done is a function of the point of view and objectives of the model builder.

It should be noted that the necessity for abstracting and aggregating and the necessity for emphasizing certain phenomena and ignoring others make it impossible to draw a clear line between total firm simulations and simulations of subsystems. In a sense, all models are only representations of portions of the total activities of the firm. But some of the models tend to be oriented much more than others to the total firm point of view, and we will discuss several in this section. Two types of models that may be regarded as total firm simulation models, those incorporating Forrester's industrial dynamics concepts and those used in business games, will be discussed in later chapters.

Functional model

This type of model is exemplified by the simulation of the hypothetical Task Manufacturing Corporation.[35] The philosophy underlying this simulator, designed by Sprowls and Asimow at the University of California at Los Angeles is to create models of the subsystems or functional areas that comprise the total firm and its environment. Fig. 2.13 shows the various subsystems which comprise the total model. Models of each of the subsystems are designed to describe the behavior of individual units within that subsystem. In other words, the Task Manufacturing Corporation simulator is a collection of micromodels of the various functions of the business and its surroundings. To provide a specific basis for construction of the various models, it is assumed that Task is a small manufacturing firm employing 400 persons and manufacturing five related products in the building hardware line. Sales are in the range of $3 to $3.5 million annually. The manufacturing facility

---

[35]The model is described in: R. C. Sprowls and M. Asimow, "A Computer Simulated Business Firm," in *Management Control Systems*, Donald G. Malcolm and Alan J. Rowe, eds. (New York: John Wiley & Sons, Inc., 1960). See also: R. C. Sprowls, "Business Simulation" in *Computer Applications in the Social Sciences*, Harold Borko, ed. (Englewood Cliffs, N. J.: Prentice-Hall, Inc., 1962).

Another total firm simulation model utilizing the functional approach is of the hypothetical Mark I Corporation. This simulator, developed at Systems Development Corporation is described in: John Kagdis and Michael R. Lackner, "A Management Control Systems Simulation Model," *Management Technology*, Vol. 3, No. 2 (December, 1963).

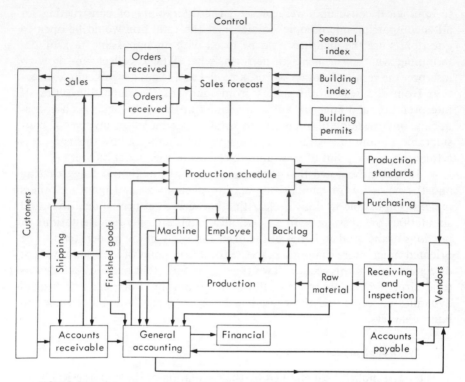

FIGURE 2.13. Subsystems of Task Manufacturing Company (by permission from R. Clay Sprowls and Morris Asimow, "A Computer Simulated Business Firm" in *Management Control Systems*, edited by Donald G. Malcolm and Alan J. Rowe, New York: John Wiley & Sons, Inc., 1960)

is made up of seven departments, and raw materials consisting of castings, steel strip, and steel bars are assumed to be available locally.

Sprowls and Asimow have described the simulator as follows:

... Each of the subsystems is sufficiently general, self-contained, and complete that it can be dealt with as an entity. In a sense, each model of a subsystem is analogous to a "black box" and if certain inputs are specified, outputs will appear. Some of the outputs are uniquely determined and some are determined only in a stochastic sense.

Just as a collection of subsystems does not comprise a business firm, neither does a collection of models comprise a representation of a business firm. The subsystems must be coupled together to permit inputs and outputs to come from and exit to both the external world and other subsystems. Formal policies, managerial decisions, and informal policies which have developed from customs and traditions determine the ways in which these couplings are allowed to occur. The set of human and material subsystems and the couplings conditioned by formal and informal policies comprise the business firm. Correspondingly, the set of separately programmable models of subsystems coupled by interconnecting programs comprises a representation of a business firm—a simulated firm which can be manipulated on a computer. Some of these interconnections—but by no means all of them—are shown in [Fig. 2.13].[36]

Information and decision model

Bonini's model of the firm, although it deals with functional areas, as does the Task model, emphasizes the information and decision system within the firm.[37] Like the Task model, Bonini's model is designed to simulate a manufacturing firm. The firm produces four products, has five manufacturing departments, and sells through seven district sales offices with a total of forty salesmen.

One of the distinguishing features of Bonini's model is the inclusion in the model of behavioral factors, notably indexes of pressure on individuals within the organization which affect their performance and decisions within the model. For instance, the index of pressure on a salesman for a certain month is the average of five factors with weights as shown:

a. Index of pressure of his superior (25%)
b. His quota relative to his sales in the past month (40%)
c. Sales of the "average" salesman in his district relative to his sales (10%)
d. Seventy-five one hundredths plus the fraction of his products less than 75 per cent of quota (10%)
e. His total quota for the past quarter relative to his total sales for the last quarter (15%)

The index, in turn, determines whether any changes are made in the mean and standard deviation of the sales distribution from which the salesman's sales rate for the month is drawn at random. Bonini includes four types of salesmen in his model, for each type there is a schedule showing the effects that various levels of the index of pressure have on the mean and standard deviation of the sales distribution, which is used to determine the salesman's performance during the month. Similar procedures are used to affect the behavior or performance of the foremen, district sales managers, general sales manager, and vice-president of manufacturing.

The simulation model is organized around the three major activities of planning, control, and operations. Plans are made quarterly, or every three periods, since the month is the basic time increment in the model, and involve the preparation of a sales forecast, sales administration budget, manufacturing administration budget, manufacturing cost estimate, and finally an over-all company plan. The sales forecast, sales and manufacturing administrative

---

[36]R. C. Sprowls and M. Asimow, "A Computer Simulated Business Firm," in *Management Control Systems*, Donald G. Malcolm and Alan J. Rowe, eds. (Englewood Cliffs, N. J.: Prentice-Hall, Inc., 1960), pp. 323 ff.

[37]Charles P. Bonini, *Simulation of Information and Decision Systems in the Firm* (Englewood Cliffs, N.J., Prentice-Hall, Inc., 1963).

budgets, and the manufacturing cost estimates are functions[38] of performance in previous periods. The over-all company plan for the next quarter is determined by combining the cost and sales estimates with the product price estimates (assumed to be the prices from the previous period) to give an estimate of the expected profit. This profit is then compared with the profit goal (the average of profits from the preceding ten quarters), and if the goal is not attained by the plan an iterative procedure is followed to adjust the cost, sales, and price estimates until the profit goal is reached. This adjusted plan is then used to determine the target level of production operations for the next quarter.

Control in the firm is exerted through the establishment of sales quotas and manufacturing standard costs and through the use of the indexes of felt pressure. As mentioned previously, various indexes of felt pressure affect the simulated behavior and performance of the components of the firm. In each index of pressure there is a contagion factor reflecting the pressure from the immediate level above in the organization and other factors that relate information about performance of an individual or in a specific area to the index of pressure. The various indexes of pressure then indirectly control the firm's operations by their inclusion in the computer programs that simulate the operations of the firm.

Actual operations of the firm are simulated on a period-by-period basis by computing for each period actual production, manufacturing costs, actual sales, and administrative expenses. In these calculations, the indexes of felt pressure have an effect on manufacturing costs, administrative expenses, and performance of the salesmen through alteration of the means and standard deviations of distributions from which the actual period values are chosen. The level of sales is also influenced by an assumed long-term upward trend and three-year cycle in the market for the firm's product and by certain assumed price elasticities for each of the products.

To provide the opportunity for experimentation, provision was made for altering certain portions of the model between simulation runs. The areas in which changes were made for purposes of experimentation with the model are:

    a. Inventory valuation
    b. Amount of contagious pressure
    c. Sensitivity to pressure
    d. Sales force knowledge of inventory
    e. Variability of sales and cost distributions
    f. Amount of market growth trend
    g. Tightness of industrial engineering department
    h. Utilization of past vs. present information on control

To determine the effects of changes in these eight areas on the model and

---

[38]That is, they are related to the results of operations from previous periods through computer programs that Bonini describes in some detail.

their interaction, Bonini used a fractional factorial experimental design involving 64 simulation runs, each of which was for 108 periods, or nine years.[39] Of the many variables that could have been traced during the simulation runs, Bonini chose to record and analyze time series for six variables; price, cost, inventory, sales, profit, and index of pressure.

Although the specific results of Bonini's experimentation are not of particular interest here, this simulation study does illustrate quite well the amount of detail that must be included in any total firm simulation model. And it also illustrates how the interests of the analyst have much to do with the construction of the model. In Bonini's model, the treatment of the functional areas and the firm's information and decision system is greatly influenced by his emphasis on the behavioral spects of decision making.

Budget model

Mattessich has developed still another approach to total firm simulation using a budget model of the firm.[40] This model uses the conventional accounting structure of a firm as its framework, and the output from the model is in the form of various period-by-period budgets and projected financial statements. Mattessich calls models such as the Task Manufacturing Company and Bonini's model "control models," whereas he considers his own approach to be very close to conventional budgeting systems. The argument for this approach is that the control models that have been developed are too cumbersome and expensive for practical application in most firms, whereas the budget model is sufficiently similar to present accounting systems and practices to offer the promise of some practical application with relatively little reorientation of thinking within the firm.

Like the two models described previously, the budget model is designed to simulate a manufacturing firm. The model is so constructed that the dimensions, i.e., number of products, number of raw materials, number of departments, etc., are variable and determined by the input data. Mattessich's model does not simulate the behavior or flow of individual entities or transactions within the firm. Rather, the behavior of the system is determined in an aggregate way through sets of coefficients, such as standard labor hours, operating expense rates, and overhead rates, which are inputs into the simulation program. Other data inputs determine the period-by-period levels of sales and production for the simulated firm. Outputs from the computer program are rather complete sets of period-by-period sales, production, material, labor, overhead, expense, and cash budgets, together with income statements and balance sheets. Since the model contains no stochastic elements, the outputs from the computer program are uniquely determined

---

[39]The use of experimental designs in simulation studies will be discussed in Chapter 9.

[40]Richard Mattessich, *Simulation of the Firm Through a Budget Computer Program* (Homewood, Ill.: Richard D. Irwin, Inc., 1964).

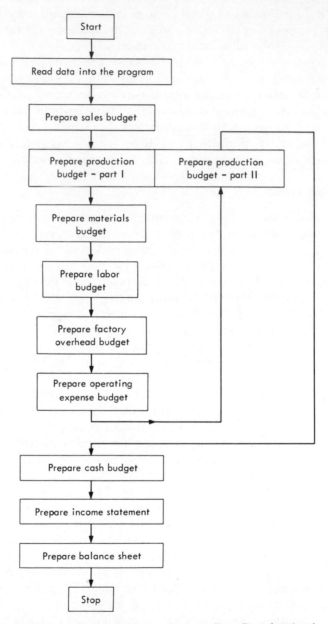

FIGURE 2.14. Budget Simulation Program Flow Chart (reprinted by permission from Richard Mattessich, *Simulation of the Firm Through a Budget Computer Program*, Homewood, Illinois : Richard D. Irwin, Inc., 1964)

by whatever input data and coefficients are given to the program. A flow chart of the program is shown in Fig. 2.14.

Summary

In addition to the illustrations given here, there are many other examples of applications of simulation in business, as the references at the end of this chapter indicate. As these examples suggest, many early applications have been related to production and inventory problems. These are two areas in which much theoretical work of a mathematical and statistical nature has been done previously, work which on one hand has provided a clear understanding of the structure of the problems and on the other hand has revealed that there are certain processes inherently difficult to attack by mathematical analysis which are amenable to analysis by simulation. As simulation techniques become more widely known and as problems in other areas, such as long-range planning, marketing, and distribution, are formulated and understood more precisely, applications of simulation in those areas will expand substantially.

Several aspects of long-range planning are well suited to simulation. Formulations of long-range strategies are hampered by difficulties in predicting outcomes of alternatives and in examining the wide range of alternative strategies available. Simulation models can facilitate this evaluation because they can accept management's forecasts and assumptions about a firm's environment and growth capabilities, can process the necessary data, and can reveal dynamic interactions over the desired time span. If restraints on enterprise growth, such as available financial resources, technical and managerial manpower, and physical facilities, are built into a simulation model, projected growth rates can be evaluated. Alternately, if growth targets and goals are built into a model, the resources required to achieve them can be determined. In short, simulation can be used to pretest long-range strategies and plans. In the marketing area anticipated competitor's reactions to marketing strategies, customer response to marketing programs, consumer behavior patterns, and sales forecasting methods are examples of situations that can and are being analyzed by simulation.

Another area is analysis of the structure and behavior of complex distribution systems. It has become apparent that decisions on plant location warehouse location, transportation methods, inventory policies, and customer service policies interact to such an extent that decisions on each must be evaluated on the basis of their impact on the other components in the system. The dynamics of this type of problem are such that they can be investigated only by simulating alternative system configurations.

An example of an approach to simulating a quality control system different from that presented in this chapter is Bowman and Fetter's model of a statistical quality control process which examines one control station and is designed to investigate the costs associated with alternative statistical control chart plans. It accepts empirical probability distributions describing a production and a sampling process, product specifications, and costs of inspection, looking for nonexistent defects and failure to discover defects. The program simulates operation of the production process under a specified control plan and may be used to observe the operation of the control plan and the effect on cost of varying sample size and control chart limits.

There are few applications that have been repeated frequently enough so that they could be called standard applications. In fact "one of a kind" simulations that do not closely resemble any preceding work either in subject matter or structure are perhaps more the rule than the exception. Of the areas in which simulation has been used, the analysis of inventory problems, job shop scheduling problems, and various types of waiting line phenomena are those in which the greatest amount of experience has been gained. In most other areas the investigator who chooses to use simulation is likely to find few precedents for his work.

EXERCISES

2.1   Simulate the servicing of 50 customers through the order taker system described in the section of this chapter which deals with waiting lines. Use the interarrival time distribution shown in Fig. 2.6 and the service time distribution shown in Fig. 2.7.

  a. From your simulation determine the percentage utilization of the order taker, average number of customers in the system, and average length of waiting line.

  b. Compare the results obtained by simulation with the theoretical values given by Eqs. (2.10), (2.11), and (2.12).

2.2   The frequency distribution of demand for a product on any day is shown below. The distribution is a Poisson distribution with mean of 2. The lead time distribution (time between placement and receipt of a replenishment order) is also shown.

Demand		Lead Time	
Units	Probability	Days	Probability
0	0.135	2	0.30
1	0.271	3	0.40
2	0.271	4	0.30
3	0.180		
4	0.090		
5	0.036		
6	0.012		
7	0.004		
8	0.001		

Demand that cannot be filled is lost. Orders to replenish inventory are placed at the end of the day and are received in the morning several days later as determined from the lead time distribution. Two alternative replenishment policies are being considered:

Policy 1: Whenever the inventory level drops below 7 units, place an order for 10 units.

Policy 2: Whenever the inventory level drops below 11 units, place an order for 10 units.

a. Simulate the system for 30 days for each policy starting with an inventory of 10 units. Compare the policies in terms of: number of orders, average inventory, and number of units of lost demand.

b. What cost information would be necessary to determine the optimal policy?

2.3 A firm is attempting to decide if one or two service facilities should be built. The following information is available.

Arrivals per Time Period		Distribution of Service Times	
Number	Probability	Time	Probability
0	0.6	1	0.2
1	0.3	2	0.6
2	0.1	3	0.2

Assume that all customers arrive at the beginning of a time period. Service time includes the time required to exit from the facility.

a. Simulate the one-facility and two-facility systems for 25 time periods each and obtain the following statistics.
   i. Average length of queue.
   ii. Maximum length of queue.
   iii. Percentage utilization of service facilities.
   iv. Average time in queue.
   v. Maximum time in queue.

b. Discuss the importance of each of these statistics. What is the impact on these statistics of starting with the system empty and not clearing it at the end?

2.4 A newsboy buys papers in bundles of 20 for six cents each and sells them for ten cents each. Unsold papers have no value. In analyzing past sales it is found that three demand distributions exist, depending on news events in the paper. A "good" news day results in headlines of interest to many potential customers; "typical" and "poor" days yield headlines of less interest. Historically 20 per cent of the days have been "good," 50 per cent "typical," and 30 per cent "poor." The demand distributions are summarized below.

PROBABILITY DISTRIBUTIONS OF DEMAND

Demand	Poor	Type of News Day Typical	Good
40	0.05		
50	0.20	0.03	
60	0.41	0.07	
70	0.26	0.28	
80	0.08	0.30	0.02
90		0.25	0.15
100		0.07	0.28
110			0.24
120			0.12
130			0.09
140			0.06
150			0.04

Simulate a 30 day period and compare mean daily profit, maximum profit, and minimum profit for the following three strategies: buy 60 papers each day, buy 80 papers each day, buy 100 papers each day.

2.5   A job shop has four work areas: A, B, C, and D. Orders flow through the work areas in different sequences depending on the nature of the order. Work areas process only one order at a time, and an order is never interrupted in a work area once processing begins. The orders shown below are received by the shop.

Order number	Date rec'd*	Delivery date*	Work area sequence and processing times**
101	001	008	D-5, B-1
102	001	009	A-4, D-2, C-2
103	002	012	C-4, B-4
104	003	012	A-6, C-2
105	005	008	C-1, D-1
106	007	015	D-3, C-1
107	007	016	B-3, D-1, C-1, A-2
108	008	013	B-2 C-3
109	009	023	C-2, D-8, A-1, B-1
110	011	026	C-2, B-4, A-8
111	011	022	B-2, A-3, C-3
112	012	019	D-1, C-3
113	015	024	A-2, B-5
114	018	025	B-6, C-1
115	020	030	A-1, D-9

*Dates shown are manufacturing day numbers
**Data shown are work area followed by number of days of processing in that area. Work must be done in sequence shown.

Simulate the processing of these orders, using the following decision rules to determine priority, and compare the rules in terms of average days late and average waiting time of orders.

a. First come, first served.

b. Shortest processing time.

    c. Earliest completion date.

2.6   The following questions refer to the project network in Fig. 2.5 and the activity time distributions for the network in Table 2.4.

    a. Randomly select 20 sets of activity times for the network and find the critical path for each set.

    b. Based upon the 20 replications in part *a*. above, construct an empirical distribution of completion time for the network.

    c. Calculate the mean and standard deviation for the distribution in part *b*. above and compare these with the analytically calculated results in Table 2.5.

2.7   The arrow diagram for a PERT network is shown below. Estimates of the optimistic, pessimistic, and most likely times are as follows:

	Time Estimates		
Activity	*a*	*m*	*b*
1, 2	7	10	13
1, 3	9	14	19
2, 3	2	5	8
2, 4	14	20	26
3, 4	13	19	25

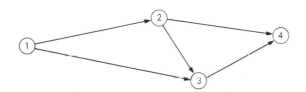

    a. Use the usual PERT procedure to find the mean of the distribution of completion time.

    b. Use model sampling with a sample size of 15 to determine the distribution of completion time for the end event in the network. Assume that activity times are uniformly distributed between the optimistic and pessimistic times. Compute the mean of the distribution of completion times and find the relative frequency with which different paths in the network are critical.

2.8   A new law requires the inspection of all passenger vehicles at state inspection stations. The designer of the stations plans to have two inspection positions on a lane, each performing about half of the inspections. Tests indicate that the times for inspections in the first position are uniformly distributed between 2.00 and 3.00 minutes, whereas times for the second position are uniformly distributed between 1.50 and 3.50 minutes. Simulate the operation of a lane for one hour in each case to determine the following:

    a. Expected capacity of an inspection lane if there is no space between the inspection positions.

b. Capacity if the lane is designed to accommodate one car between the positions.

Ignore transit times for the vehicles between the inspections points in your calculations.

2.9   An educational laboratory has 15 teaching machines. Students using these machines find that they periodically need the laboratory supervisor to answer questions, make minor adjustments on the machines, etc. Times between requests for assistance from each student follow an exponential distribution with a mean of 30 minutes. Times taken by the supervisor to answer the requests also follow an exponential distribution with a mean of two minutes.

a. Simulate the operation of the laboratory to determine the total waiting time of the students during a one-hour study period.

b. Determine the effect of hiring an assistant who could answer the requests as well as the laboratory supervisor.

2.10   Generate a time series of Y for 25 periods, using the following equation:

$$Y = 100 + 2t + 5Z$$

where t is the number of the time period and Z is a normally distributed random variable with zero mean and unit variance.

a. Forecast the value of Y for each period, using exponential smoothing with $\alpha = 0.20$.

b. For the last 20 periods obtain the following:
   i. The distribution of forecast errors.
   ii. Mean error.
   iii. Maximum positive and negative errors.

2.11   Brown (see footnote 32) suggests that the following variation on the basic exponential smoothing system will correct forecasts for trend.

New forecast $= \alpha$(actual data last period)

$+2(1 - \alpha)$(last period forecast)

$-(1 - \alpha)$(forecast two periods previous)

a. Use this forecasting equation with $\alpha = 0.20$ to forecast the value of Y, using the time series for Y generated in Exercise 2.10.

b. For the last 20 periods obtain the following:
   i. The distribution of forecast errors.
   ii. Mean error.
   iii. Maximum positive and negative errors.

c. Compare the results obtained in part b. above with those obtained in Exercise 2.10.

2.12   Data on breakdowns of cabs collected by a taxi company suggests that the mileage between failures of three major systems—carburetor, electrical, and cooling—is uniformly distributed with the following means and ranges:

System	Mean mileage	Range
Carburetor	23,000	+10,000
Electrical	20,000	± 7,000
Cooling	40,000	±20,000

Determine by simulation the cost of repairs and maintenance over a cab life of 250,000 miles when the following maintenance policies are used:

Policy 1: Wait for failure, repair all systems to original condition.

Policy 2: Inspect every 15,000 miles and repair all systems to original conditions; if failure occurs, repair all systems.

Policy 3: Same as policy 2 except inspect every 20,000 miles.

Policy 4: Wait for failure and repair only failure.

Policy 5: Inspect and repair every 20,000 miles; if failure occurs, repair only failure.

The cost of inspecting and repairing all systems to original condition is $100; cost of repairing a failure is $80; cost of repairing a failure and restoring other systems to original condition at the same time is $175.

2.13 Central Car Wash has an excellent location at a busy downtown intersection. Customers fall into two categories; 75 per cent are wash only customers and 25 per cent come for a wash and quick wax. Revenue from a wash and wax customer is twice that of a wash only customer. The service time distribution is normal for both categories with a mean of 7 minutes and standard deviation of 1 minute for wash customers and a mean of 11 minutes and standard deviation of 2 minutes for wash and wax customers. Currently there are two wash and wax booths and a waiting area that will accommodate two additional cars. The owner is considering adding another wash only booth at the expense of one of the waiting spaces. Eight per cent of the arriving customers leave if they cannot be serviced immediately, while 92 per cent will wait if a parking space is available. Because of traffic in the area, customers go to a competitor if a waiting space is not available. The establishment is open 12 hours per day (any cars in the waiting area at closing time are processed). The interarrival time distribution is exponential with a mean of six minutes during the first four hours of operation and a mean of four minutes during the remaining hours.

a. Simulate the operation of the car wash for 10 days both with and without the new booth. For the two arrangements of facilities, determine:

i. Percentage utilization of the booths.

ii. Number of customers of each type serviced and number lost.

      iii. Average number of customers waiting.

      iv. Average time spent by customers both in waiting and being serviced.

    b. Compare the relative amount of revenue obtained from the present booths with that obtained with the addition of a new booth.

2.14 A small research firm is confronted at the beginning of each month with two alternatives for the investment of $10,000. Project A is equally likely to yield a payoff of either $0 or $30,000. Alternative B will yield an end-of-month payoff of $0 with probability 0.10, $10,000 with probability 0.60, and $20,000 with probability 0.30. The firm currently has only $10,000 and a poor credit rating. If its cash balance becomes zero at any time, it will become bankrupt and go out of business.

    a. Simulate each of the following strategies for 25 one-year periods and calculate the firm's cash balance at the end of each one-year period. Assume that the firm starts each of the 25 simulated years with a balance of $10,000 and that alternatives A and B are available at the beginning of each month.

      i. Choose alternative A each month.

      ii. Choose alternative B each month.

      iii. Choose alternative A whenever the cash balance is greater than $10,000 at the beginning of the month; choose B if the balance is $10,000 or less.

    b. Construct a frequency distribution for the year-end cash balances under each strategy and find the mean year-end cash balance for each strategy. What is the empirical probability of bankruptcy. under each strategy?

2.15 Five items of inventory at a single stock point in a logistics system are obtained from the same source. Demand for item A is independent of demand for item B, but both have the demand distribution shown in Exercise 2.2. Similarly, demand for items C, D, and E is independent, but all three have the demand distribution shown below. The distribution is a Poisson distribution with mean of 3.

Daily demand (Items C, D, and E)

Units	Probability
0	0.050
1	0.149
2	0.224
3	0.224
4	0.168
5	0.101
6	0.050
7	0.022
8	0.008
9	0.003
10	0.001

The lead time distribution is identical for all five items since they are obtained from one source, and it is the same as shown in Exercise 2.2. Demand that cannot be filled is lost. Two different methods of replenishing the inventory of these five items are being considered.

Method 1: Order items separately as the inventory of each item reaches its order point. For items A and B the order point for each is 10 units and the order quantity for each is 20 units. For items C, D, and E the order point for each is 15 and the order quantity for each is 30 units.

Method 2: Whenever *any one* of the five items reaches its order point, place an order for *all five* items at once. In this case, the order quantity for each item is the difference between the inventory level and a target quantity. For items A and B, the target quantity is 30, and for items C, D, and E this quantity is 45.

a. Simulate the system for 250 days of operation for each of the methods. Compare the methods by the following criteria:
  i. Number of orders.
  ii. Average inventory of each item.
  iii. Units of lost demand for each item.
b. What cost information would be necessary to evaluate the two methods?

2.16 Work Exercise 2.7, assuming that the activity times are normally distributed with mean equal to m and the 3σ points indicated by a and b. Use a sample size of 100.

2.17 Brown (see footnote 32) suggests the following forecasting procedure to take into account both trend and cycles.

Ratio = actual last period/base series

Average ratio = α(ratio) + $(1 - \alpha)$(old average ratio)

Trend in ratio = average ratio − old average ratio

Average trend = α(trend) + $(1 - \alpha)$(old average trend)

Expected ratio = average ratio + $\dfrac{1 - \alpha}{\alpha}$(average trend)

Forecast = (expected ratio)(base series)

a. Use this forecasting method with a base series consisting of the average of the surrounding quarter from the previous year to find the best value of α for forecasting sales in Table 2.6.
b. Compare the distribution of forecast errors for the best value of

α obtained in part *a.* above with the error distributions of the two forecasting methods illustrated in Table 2.6.

2.18 A machine is either running (in state R) or shut down for repairs (in state D). Assume that changes in state may occur only between days and that these changes behave according to a Markov process; that is, the probability of being either in state R or D depends only upon the state the machine was in on the previous day. Transition probabilities are given in the following transition matrix:

$$P = \begin{array}{c} \\ R \\ D \end{array} \begin{array}{cc} R & D \\ \begin{bmatrix} 0.75 & 0.25 \\ 0.50 & 0.50 \end{bmatrix} \end{array}$$

a. Draw a transition diagram representing the system. Given that the machine was in state R initially, simulate the next 10 days, using the Monte Carlo technique. Repeat the simulation 20 times and compute the relative frequency of occurrence of states R and D on the tenth day. Compare the results of the simulation with the theoretical limiting-state probabilities for R and D of 0.667 and 0.333, respectively.

b. If the machine is running (state R) it generates a value of $100 per day; if it is shut down (state D) there is a value of $-\$10$ per day. Estimate the long-run expected value for the process based upon the results obtained from the simulation.

c. A preventive maintenance expenditure of $10 per day will result in an increase in the probability of remaining in state R to 0.90, but will not affect the probability of remaining in state D. The transition matrix for this case is

$$P = \begin{array}{c} \\ R \\ D \end{array} \begin{array}{cc} R & D \\ \begin{bmatrix} 0.90 & 0.10 \\ 0.50 & 0.50 \end{bmatrix} \end{array}$$

Repeat the simulation and analysis of parts *a.* and *b.* above, using the revised transition probabilities, and make a recommendation on whether the preventive maintenance policy should be followed.

2.19 A customer has a choice of three brands of a product A, B, and C, Assume that his purchases are made according to a Markov process with the transition probabilities given in the following transition matrix:

$$P = \begin{array}{c} \\ A \\ B \\ C \end{array} \begin{array}{ccc} A & B & C \\ \begin{bmatrix} 0.6 & 0.2 & 0.2 \\ 0.2 & 0.7 & 0.1 \\ 0.3 & 0.2 & 0.5 \end{bmatrix} \end{array}$$

Draw a transition diagram representing the process. Simulate 20 consecutive purchases, given each of the initial conditions listed below. Repeat each simulation 20 times and compute the relative frequency of occurrence of each state on the twentieth purchase.

  a. Given that the initial purchase is brand A.
  b. Given that the initial purchase is brand B.
  c. Given that the initial purchase is brand C.
  d. Given that on his initial purchase he is equally likely to choose A, B, or C.

BIBLIOGRAPHY

Ackerman, Sanford S., "Even-Flow, A Scheduling Method for Reducing Lateness in Job Shops," *Management Technology*, Vol. 3, No. 1 (May, 1963).

Ackoff, Russell L., ed., *Progress in Operations Research, Vol. I.* New York: John Wiley & Sons, Inc., 1961, pp. 311–326, 366–374, 392–419.

Allen, Morton, "The Efficient Utilization of Labor Under Conditions of Fluctuating Demand," in *Industrial Scheduling*, John F. Muth and Gerald L. Thompson, eds. Englewood Cliffs, N. J.: Prentice-Hall, Inc., 1963.

Amstutz, Arnold E., *Computer Simulation of Competitive Market Response.* Cambridge: The Massachusetts Institute of Technology Press, 1967.

Baker, C. T., and B. P. Dzielinski, "Simulation of a Simplified Job Shop," *Management Science*, Vol. 6, No. 3 (April, 1960).

Berman, Edward B., "Monte Carlo Determination of Stock Redistribution," *Operations Research*, Vol. 10, No. 4 (July-August, 1962).

Bonini, Charles P., *Simulation of Information and Decision Systems in the Firm.* Englewood Cliffs, New Jersey: Prentice-Hall, Inc., 1963.

Bowman, Edward H., and Robert B. Fetter, *Analysis for Production and Operations Management*, 3rd ed. Homewood, Ill.: Richard D. Irwin, Inc., 1967, Chaps. 5 and 11.

Boyd, D. Franklin, "Enterprise Models: A New Management Technique," *Industrial Management Review*, Vol. 8, No. 1 (Fall, 1966).

Brooks, Richard M., "A Sugar Refinery Simulation Model," *Management Technology*, Vol. 2, No. 2 (December, 1962).

Bulkin, Michael H., John L. Colley, and Harry W. Steinhoff, "Load Forecasting, Priority Sequencing, and Simulation in a Job Shop Control System," *Management Science*, Vol. 13, No. 2 (October, 1966).

Carpenter, Charles E., "Use of General Purpose Systems Simulator II in System Analysis." Unpublished MBA research report. Seattle: University of Washington, 1964.

Carter, Eugene, and Kalman J. Cohen, "The Use of Simulation in Selecting Branch Banks," *Industrial Management Review*, Vol. 8, No. 2 (Spring, 1967).

Cyert, R. E., E. A. Feigenbaum, and J. G. March, "Models in a Behavioral Theory of the Firm," *Behavioral Science*, Vol. 4, (April, 1959).

Datz, I. M., "Simulated Shipping," *Datamation*, Vol. 12, No. 2 (February, 1966).

Davis, Gordon B., Howard Ambill, and Herbert Whitecraft, "Simulation of Finance Company Operations for Decision Making," *Management Technology*, Vol. 2, No. 2 (December, 1962).

Didis, Stephen K., and Charles E. Carpenter, "Simulation Study of a Test Equipment Calibration and Certification System," *The Journal of Industrial Engineering*, Vol. 17, No. 8 (August, 1966).

Drake, Alvin W., *Fundamentals of Applied Probability Theory*. New York: McGraw-Hill Book Company, 1967, Chapter 5.

Dzielinski, B. P., C. T. Baker, and A. S. Manne, "Simulation Tests of Lot Size Programming," *Management Science*, Vol. 9, No. 2 (January, 1963).

Dzielinski, B. P., and A. S. Manne, "Simulation of a Hypothetical Multi-Item Production and Inventory System," *The Journal of Industrial Engineering*, Vol. 12, No. 6, (November-December, 1961).

Emery, James C., "Simulation Techniques in Inventory Control and Distribution," in *Operations Research Reconsidered*. A.M.A. Report No. 10, 1958.

Fetter, R. B., and J. D. Thompson, "The Simulation of Hospital Systems," *Operations Research*, Vol. 13, No. 5 (September-October, 1965).

Gerson, Martin L., and Richard B. Maffei, "Technical Characteristics of Distribution Simulators," *Management Science*, Vol. 10, No. 1 (October, 1963).

Gessford, John E., "Computer Simulation Yields Evaluation of Procurement Policies," *Management Technology*, Vol. 2, No. 2 (December, 1962).

Gunn, William A., "Airline System Simulation," *Operations Research*, Vol. 12, No. 2 (March-April, 1964).

Heller, J., "Some Numerical Experiments for an $M \times J$ Flow Shop and Its Decision-Theoretical Aspects," *Operations Research*, Vol. 8, No. 2 (March-April, 1960).

Hespos, Richard F., "Simulation as an Aid to Staffing a Customer Service Function," *Management Technology*, Vol. 3, No. 2 (December, 1963).

Hespos, Richard F. and Paul F. Strassmann, "Stochastic Decision Trees for the Analysis of Investment Decisions," *Management Science*, Vol. 11, No. 10 (August, 1965).

Hoggatt, Austin C., and Frederick E. Balderston, eds., *Symposium on Simulation Models: Methodology and Applications to the Behavioral Sciences*. Cincinnati: Southwestern Publishing Co., 1963.

Jackson, James R., "Simulation Research on Job Shop Production," *Naval Research Logistics Quarterly*, Vol. 4, No. 4 (December, 1957).

Jennings, Norman H., and Justin H. Dickens, "Computer Simulation of Peak Hour Operations in a Bus Terminal," *Management Science*, Vol. 5, No. 1 (October, 1958).

Kemeny, John G., Arthur Schleifer, Jr., J. Laurie Snell, and Gerald Thompson, *Finite Mathematics with Business Applications*. Englewood Cliffs, N.J.: Prentice-Hall, Inc., 1962, Chapter 4.

Klingel, A. R., "Bias in PERT Project Completion Time Calculations for a Real Network," *Management Science*, Vol. 13, No. 4 (December, 1966).

Koomanoff, Frederick A., and James A. Bontadelli, "Computer Simulation of Railroad Freight Transport Operations," *The Journal of Industrial Engineering*, Vol. 18, No. 1 (January, 1967).

Lathrop, John B., and John E. Walsh, "Some Practical Simulations of Operations," *The Journal of Industrial Engineering*, Vol. 9, No. 5 (September-October, 1958).

LeGrande, Earl, "The Development of a Factory Simulation System Using Actual Operating Data," *Management Technology*, Vol. 3, No. 1 (May, 1963).

Mattessich, Richard, "Budgeting Models and System Simulation," *Accounting Review*, Vol. 36, No. 3 (July, 1961).

——— *Simulation of the Firm Through a Budget Computer Program*. Homewood, Ill.: Richard D. Irwin, Inc., 1964.

Mayer, Charles S., "Pretesting Field Interviewing Costs Through Simulation," *Journal of Marketing*, Vol. 28 (April, 1964).

McKenney, James L., "A Clinical Study of the Use of a Simulation Model," *The Journal of Industrial Engineering*, Vol. 18, No. 1 (January, 1967).

Mitchner, Morton, and Raymond P. Peterson, "An Operations-Research Study of the Collection of Defaulted Loans," *Operations Research*, Vol. 5, No. 4 (August, 1957).

Packer, A. H., "Simulation and Adaptive Forecasting as Applied to Inventory Control," *Operations Research*, Vol. 15, No. 4 (July–August, 1967).

Pritsker, A. B., "Monte Carlo Approach to Setting Maintenance Tolerance Limits," *The Journal of Industrial Engineering*, Vol. 14, No. 3 (May–June, 1963).

Report of the System Simulation Symposium. Sponsored by the American Institute, of Industrial Engineers, The Institute of Management Sciences, and Operations Research Society of America, New York, May, 1957.

Report of the Second System Simulation Symposium. Sponsored by the American Institute of Industrial Engineers, The Institute of Management Sciences, and Operations Research Society of America, Evanston, Illinois, February, 1959.

Shubik, Martin, "Simulation of the Industry and the Firm," *The American Economic Review*, Vol. 50, No. 5 (December, 1960).

Smith, Wayland P., and Jasvantrai C. Shah, "Design and Development of a Manufacturing Systems Simulator," *The Journal of Industrial Engineering*, Vol. 15, No. 4 (July–August, 1964).

Sprowls, R. C., and M. Asimow, "A Computer Simulated Business Firm," in *Management Control Systems*, Donald G. Malcolm and Alan J. Rowe, eds. Englewood Cliffs, N.J.: Prentice-Hall, Inc., 1960.

Starr, Martin K., and David W. Miller, *Inventory Control: Theory and Practice*. Englewood Cliffs, N.J.: Prentice-Hall, Inc., 1962, pp. 221–258.

Steinhoff, Harry W., "Daily System for Sequencing Orders in a Large-Scale Job Shop," in *Readings in Production and Operations Management*, Elwood S. Buffa, ed., New York: John Wiley & Sons, Inc., 1966.

Trilling, Donald R., "The Use of a Job Shop Simulator in the Generation of Production Schedules," *Production and Inventory Management*, Vol. 7, No. 3 (July, 1966).

Van Slyke, Richard M., "Monte Carlo Methods and the PERT Problem," *Operations Research*, Vol. 11, No. 5 (September–October, 1963).

Vergin, R. C., "Scheduling Maintenance and Determining Crew Size for Stochastically Failing Equipment," *Management Science*, Vol. 13, No. 2 (October, 1966).

Wells, William D., "Computer Simulation of Consumer Behavior," *Harvard Business Review*, Vol. 41, No. 3 (May–June, 1963).

Industrial Dynamics and Large System Simulation

3 Industrial dynamics is one approach to analyzing the behavior of large-scale systems suggested by Forrester of the Massachusetts Institute of Technology.[1] Analysis of the decision processes of the manager and his role as a decision maker in an interacting environment under dynamic conditions is the central focus of industrial dynamics.[2] Industrial dynamics represents something of a departure from the types of models used for small-scale systems. The difference is largely one of perspective which dictates a change in the level of abstraction of the model. A primary tool for analysis is system simulation in which events are considered in the aggregate. To facilitate construction of these types of models, the DYNAMO computer simulation language was developed.[3] Note that there is a distinction between industrial dynamics and computer simulation through the use of DYNAMO. Simulation is a technique for constructing and operating dynamic models, whereas industrial dynamics is primarily a philosophy, a way of looking at organizations and systems, and a methodology for study of the behavior of industrial systems.

Industrial Dynamics Perspective

The industrial dynamics philosophy proposes that effective management of an organization should recognize the character of the organization as a series of interconnected feedback networks with dynamic interactions among the components of the organization. As Forrester has defined it:

---

[1] Jay W. Forrester, *Industrial Dynamics* (Cambridge, Mass.: The Massachusetts Institute of Technology Press, 1961).

[2] Jay W. Forrester, "Managerial Decision Making," *Management and The Computer of the Future*, Martin Greenberger, ed. (Cambridge, Mass.: The Massachusetts Institute of Technology Press, 1962), Chap. 2.

[3] Alexander L. Pugh, III, *DYNAMO User's Manual*, 2nd ed. (Cambridge, Mass.: The Massachusetts, Institute of Technology Press, 1963). The language is also discussed in detail in Chap. 7.

Industrial dynamics is the study of the information-feedback characteristics of industrial activity to show how organizational structure, amplification (in policies), and time delays (in decisions and actions) interact to influence the success of the enterprise. It treats the interactions between the flows of information, money, orders, materials, personnel, and capital equipment in a company, an industry, or a national economy.

Industrial dynamics provides a single framework for integrating the functional areas of management —marketing, production, accounting, research and development, and capital investment. It is a quantitative and experimental approach for relating organizational structure and corporate policy to industrial growth and stability.[4]

Because of the close relationship between the type of simulation model developed and the framework within which the industrial dynamics perspective is structured, it is necessary to delve into this framework in some detail in order to understand the nature and implications of the model. Forrester has not proposed a single model to represent industrial activity; rather, he has proposed the development of particular models to represent specific systems (companies, industries, or economies). In other words, he has suggested an approach to the construction of models.

There are two basic components of the structure of a system viewed from the industrial dynamics perspective. These are the varying *rates of flow* and the resultant changes in *levels of variables* in the system. Levels represent accumulations of resources in the system being modeled. They may be inventories of goods, amounts of information or ideas, cash balances, number of orders on hand, number of people in the work force, or the amount of equipment on hand. Levels may exist in the information flows as well as in the physical flows in the organization. They may take the form of information about past events or the past behavior of rates of flow, as, for example, the average production rate for last week or last month. Levels may also represent ideas or feelings, such as a level of satisfaction or a degree of confidence. Rates of flow represent the activities and decision functions in the system and may be the movement of goods, payments of money, expenditure of effort, arrival or departure of people, or acquisition of equipment. Decision functions regulate these flow rates.

In an industrial dynamics model, the rates of flow, the flow paths of the components of the system, and the states of the system represented by accumulated levels of the components are meant to involve all the resources of the organization. These would include materials, orders, money, manpower, capital equipment, the interconnecting information networks, and the decision processes governing the rates of flow.

Typically, individual events are considered in an aggregate sense in order that they may be treated as continuous flows. This permits concentrat-

---

[4]Jay W. Forrester, *Industrial Dynamics* (Cambridge, Mass.: The Massachusetts Institute of Technology Press, 1961), p. 13.

ing on the continuity of the system. Because we are dealing here with models of large-scale systems, this aggregation permits us to examine the over-all behavior of systems and their components and is similar to a top-level manager's view of his organization. Individual sales are made, individual items are produced, and individual orders are shipped, but he is primarily concerned with the rates of flow of orders, production, and shipments. As Forrester pointed out, this perspective is not close enough to consider individual thought processes, nor is it far enough to be concerned only with results and not to consider the nature of the decision process.[5] The manager is concerned with how goals are set by subordinates, what information sources are utilized in making decisions, and what will be the nature of various subordinates' responses to economic and social pressures. Discrete events are not ruled out of the model, however. Where appropriate, particularly significant events may be singled out for consideration, or discontinuities and noise may be treated as random disturbances generated from a probability distribution.

As an illustration of the industrial dynamics point of view, let us consider the structure of the closed-loop feedback control system of Fig. 3.1. There are three primary functions: The decision activity, which may be human or mechanical, the action resulting from the decision, and the information feedback, which reports on the action. The process of control is continuous.

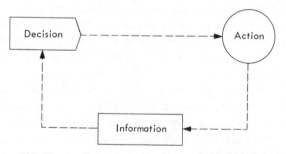

FIGURE 3.1. Closed-Loop Feedback Control System

Such a control system may be considered in more detail, as in Fig. 3.2. In this system decisions go through an implementation process that transforms them into actual achievements. The implementation process is complicated by complex structural relationships in the organization. The process may be further complicated by time delays between a decision and its implementation and noise or random behavior in the organization.

In addition, note the distinction between actual and apparent achievements. Apparent achievements will be more or less representative of actual achievements, depending upon the quality of information received through

[5]Jay W. Forrester, *Industrial Dynamics* (Cambridge, Mass.: The Massachusetts Institute of Technology Press, 1961), p. 96.

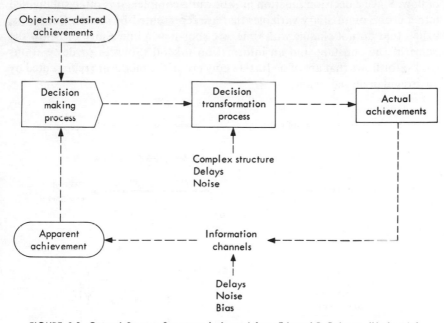

FIGURE 3.2. Control System Structure (adapted from Edward B. Roberts, "Industrial Dynamics and Design of Management Control Systems," *Management Technology*, Vol. 2, No. 3, December, 1963)

the feedback process. This information is affected by delays, noise, and bias in the information channels. The decision process itself is characterized as goal-seeking behavior which responds to any difference between the organization's objectives and its apparent achievements. It is the industrial dynamics point of view that managers can operate most effectively if they recognize that this control system structure permeates each organization and its components.

The Decision Process as Viewed and Modeled by Industrial Dynamics

The Industrial Dynamics Research Group at the Massachusetts Institute of Technology Sloan School of Management has developed a flow diagramming technique that has been found useful in developing the system of mathematical equations in a model.[6] Fig. 3.3 shows the symbols that are used. The six types of flows are identified by different types of lines used to connect portions of the system. Levels are shown as a block with the contents indicated inside the block. Decision functions are shown as valves that control the rates

[6]Jay W. Forrester, *Industrial Dynamics* (Cambridge, Mass.: The Massachusetts Institute of Technology Press, 1961), Chap. 8.

of flow. Since a decision function may be quite complex, it is often subdivided into a group of auxiliary variables that are represented by circles. Constants, values that do not change with time, are shown as a line above or below the name of the constant and an information takeoff. Sources or destinations (sinks) for flows that are of no further concern in the model are represented by an irregular closed shape.

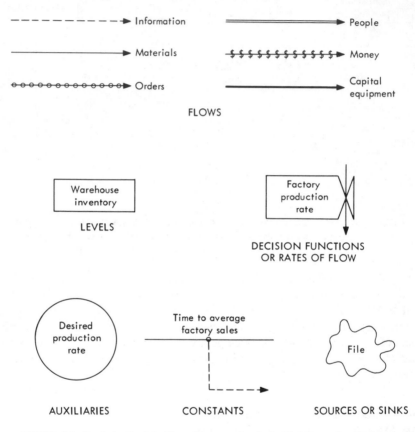

FIGURE 3.3. Symbols Used in Flow Diagramming Industrial Dynamics Models

The decision process is based upon information about levels in the system, and results in control of rates of flow between levels. These rates determine subsequent changes in levels or system states. The process is illustrated in Fig. 3.4. Decisions, as used in this context, may be overt decisions of people in the system, or they may be implicit decisions that result from the condition of the system. As an example, the warehouse shipping rate in Fig. 3.4 may result from the number of unfilled orders and amount of material in inventory.

One test that may be applied to distinguish between rates and levels is

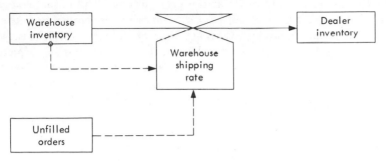

FIGURE 3.1. Flow Diagram of Decision Process

whether the value in question would exist independently of the passage of time. Rates represent activity; there would be no activity (and consequently no rate of flow) if time in the system were brought to a halt. On the other hand, accumulated quantities in levels would continue to exist. As an example, instantaneous rates of sales in a model would cease, but average rates of sales for the day or week would remain. Thus, an average is a form of level.

An industrial dynamics model is made up of two primary types of equations which represent levels and rates. The mathematics is not complex, consisting mostly of simple algebraic and first order difference equations. The equations have been designed to facilitate the construction of models of the types of organizations and decision processes discussed above. These equation types are readily handled by the DYNAMO computer language. As DYNAMO permits names with five alphabetic and numeric characters, most of the equations which follow will use five letters, chosen for their mnemonic significance, for the variable names. In addition to the identifying characters, each variable name carries a notation that signifies the time period involved. These time notations are used in the same manner as the subscripts used in difference equation notation.

Equation (3.1) is an example of a level equation.

$$\text{DINV.K} = \text{DINV.J} + (\text{DT})(\text{WSHPR.JK} - \text{DSHPR.JK}) \qquad \textbf{(3.1)}$$

where

DINV = Dealer INVentory (units)

DT = Delta Time, the time interval between solutions of the equations (weeks)

WSHPR = Warehouse SHiPping Rate (units per week)

DSHPR = Dealer SHiPping Rate (units per week)

The equation states that the present amount of units in inventory at time K equals the amount in inventory at the previous time J plus the change in inventory over the time interval J to K.[7] Change in inventory over the JK time interval is the summation over that time interval of the difference between the rate of receipts, represented by WSHPR, and the rate of shipments, represented by DSHPR. Multiplying the difference in rates by DT effects this summation. If DT, the solution interval for the model, were one week, then the change in inventory during that week would be the difference between the amounts received and shipped in that week. If, as is usually the case, DT is some fraction of a week, say 0.1 week, the equation would express the change over one tenth of a week as represented by the difference between one tenth of a week's receipts and shipments. In calculus terminology an expression analogous to Eq. (3.1) is the following integral:

$$DINV_t = DINV_{t-1} + \int_{t-1}^{t} (WSHPR - DSHPR)dt \qquad (3.2)$$

where $DINV_{t-1}$ is the beginning inventory. Industrial dynamics models use difference equations since they are easily solved on a digital computer.

Equation (3.3) is an example of a rate equation.

$$WSHPR.KL = \frac{WUNOR.K}{DFWOR} \qquad (3.3)$$

where   WSHPR = Warehouse SHiPping Rate (units per week)

WUNOR = Warehouse UNfilled ORders (units)

DFWOR = Delay in Filling Warehouse ORders (weeks)

The equation states that the warehouse shipping rate over the next time interval KL is equal to the amount of unfilled orders at the present time K divided by the delay in filling orders at the warehouse. In other words, the rate is equal to the value of a level divided by a delay. In this instance the delay is the average length of delay and may be expressed as a constant. If the delay is a constant and is taken to equal one week, then the denominator on the right-hand side of the equation may be omitted and the equation would become

$$WSHPR.KL = WUNOR.K \qquad (3.4)$$

The delay might also be a variable, in which case the denominator of Eq. (3.3) would be DFWOR.K.

---

[7]In difference equation notation the times represented by J, K, and L would correspond to $t - 1$, t, and $t + 1$.

A shipping rate may depend not only on the number of unfilled orders but also on the amount of inventory on hand, as indicated in the flow diagram of Fig. 3.4. The decision function represented in this figure might be formulated as follows:

$$\text{WSHPR.KL} = \begin{cases} \dfrac{\text{WUNOR.K}}{\text{DFWOR}}, & \text{WUNOR.K} \leq \text{WINV.K} \\[2ex] \dfrac{\text{WINV.K}}{\text{DFWOR}}, & \text{WUNOR.K} > \text{WINV.K} \end{cases} \tag{3.5}$$

This formulation would prevent negative inventories by restricting shipping rate to an amount that would not deplete inventory within a given time.

Conceptually, a model may be constructed entirely from equations for levels, rates, and constants. Rate equations, or decision functions, may be formulated entirely from levels and constants. However, if this were done, many rate equations would become so complex as to obscure their meaning. In order to more conveniently represent and understand these decision functions, auxiliary equations are introduced which break down decision functions into their component parts. This may be illustrated by the following series of equations:

$$\text{WDINV.K} = (\text{WWIND})(\text{AVWSL.K}) \tag{3.6}$$

$$\text{WINAJ.K} = (1/\text{TAWIN})(\text{WDINV.K} - \text{WINV.K}) \tag{3.7}$$

$$\text{WORDR.KL} = \text{AVWSL.K} + \text{WINAJ.K} \tag{3.8}$$

where

WDINV = Warehouse Desired INVentory (units)

WWIND = Warehouse Weeks INventory Desired (units)

AVWSL = AVerage Warehouse SaLes (units per week)

WINAJ = Warehouse INventory AdJustment (units per week)

TAWIN = Time to Adjust Warehouse INventory (weeks)

WINV = Warehouse INVentory (units)

WORDR = Warehouse ORDer Rate (units per week)

The relationships expressed by Eqs. (3.6), (3.7), and (3.8) could be expressed in a single rate equation,

$$\text{WORDR.KL} = \text{AVWSL.K} + \frac{(\text{AVWSL.K})(\text{WWIND}) - \text{WINV.K}}{\text{TAWIN}}$$

$$(3.9)$$

in which all terms are either levels or constants, but in which the meaning is not so clear as in three separate equations. These three equations define an order rate made up of average sales at a point in time, plus an amount to adjust inventory levels to some desired state, the desired state being a function of the average sales.

Delays and Smoothing

The importance of the effect of time lags on the behavior of dynamic systems is stressed in industrial dynamics because time lags determine many aspects of system behavior. Delays may be found in the flows of both physical quantities and information. In the former case, lags would represent delays in movements of goods, people, money, etc. In the latter instance, they would represent such things as information transmission delays and smoothing of time series of information. Smoothing of information flows is closely related to the concept of delaying the flow of physical quantities in a system. Smoothing delays the impact of transient fluctuations on the system and filters out higher frequency fluctuations, thereby altering the sensitivity of the system to them. Thus, in information smoothing there is a tradeoff to be evaluated between reducing the impact of noise and other short-term fluctuations and reducing time lags in recognizing significant changes in the data being received.

Two commonly used techniques for smoothing time series are the moving average and exponential smoothing that were mentioned previously in the discussion of forecasting in Chap. 2. These two methods have different operating characteristics in terms of the weight given to data in a time series. In the expression for the n-period moving average $\bar{x}_t$ in Eq. (3.10) we note that equal weight is given to each of the previous n periods of data.

$$\bar{x}_t = \frac{1}{n}(x_t + x_{t-1} + x_{t-2} + \cdots + x_n)$$

$$(3.10)$$

where

n = number of periods of data in the average

x_t = data for the most recent period

x_{t-1} = data for the next earlier period

.
.
.

x_n = data for n periods ago

As the moving average is recalculated each period, the value for the most recent period becomes x_t, the old x_t becomes x_{t-1}, and so forth, to x_n, which is dropped from the average. Until data for a period are finally dropped from the average their weight in the average is the same as when the data entered the average.

There are many times when older data should be given less weight than more recent data, and an exponential moving average does this.[8] When exponential smoothing is used, data for the latest period are weighted by α initially, and in each succeeding period the data are, in effect, further weighted by $(1 - \alpha)$. As a result, each period of data is carried along indefinitely, but with lower and lower weight. To illustrate this point, suppose that the exponential moving average for the previous period $\bar{x}_{t-1}$ is 100 and that an α of 0.20 is being used. If the value x_t for the latest period is 110, the new exponential moving average $\bar{x}_t$ would be calculated as follows.

$$\begin{aligned}\bar{x}_t &= \alpha x_t + (1 - \alpha)\bar{x}_{t-1} \\ &= (0.20)(110) + (1 - 0.20)(100) \\ &= 22 + 80 = 102 \end{aligned} \tag{3.11}$$

The latest value 110 is weighted by 0.20 and contributes 22 to the exponential moving average. When data are obtained for the next period, this 22 is now a part of the old average and is further weighted by $(1 - \alpha)$, in this case 0.80. In succeeding periods it is weighted in each period by 0.80 so that gradually its impact on the average diminishes.

Equation (3.11) can be rewritten in the following form:

$$\bar{x}_t = \bar{x}_{t-1} + \alpha(x_t - \bar{x}_{t-1}) \tag{3.12}$$

In this form the new smoothed moving average is the old average plus some fraction of the difference between the new data and the old average. In industrial dynamics models, we may think of the smoothing constant α in terms of a smoothing time constant of T time periods. Then α would be replaced by $1/T$.

$$\bar{x}_t = \bar{x}_{t-1} + \frac{1}{T}(x_t - \bar{x}_{t-1}) \tag{3.13}$$

Putting this in DYNAMO notation and generalizing to any solution interval DT gives the following expression for first order exponential smoothing:

$$\text{AVG.K} = \text{AVG.J} + \frac{\text{DT}}{\text{T}}(\text{DATA.JK} - \text{AVG.J}) \tag{3.14}$$

---

[8] A more complete explanation may be found in Robert G. Brown, *Smoothing, Forecasting, and Prediction of Discrete Time Series* (Englewood Cliffs, New Jersey: Prentice-Hall, Inc. 1963), Chap. 7.

The average at time K equals the old average at time J, plus a fraction of the difference between the values of the rate of flow over the time period J to K and the old average.

There are other advantages to using an exponential moving average. Since we are attempting to model decision processes, an exponential moving average may more appropriately reflect intuitive behavior than an arithmetic moving average, because it gives less and less weight to older information. The choice of smoothing time constant T determines the response of the average to changes in the flow of the series. Larger values of T give less weight to recent data and consequently more weight to the old average. Thus the average would respond more slowly to transients. In this sense exponential smoothing acts also to delay the effect of variations in information flow.

The treatment of exponential delays in the flow of physical quantities requires a slightly different set of equations than for smoothing information. This is so because often a variable delay is encountered in material flows and it is essential that no units be lost or created by variations in the delay period. Thus the following pair of equations is used to delay the flow of physical units.

$$LEVEL.K = LEVEL.J + (DT)(INFLW.JK - OUTFL.JK) \quad \textbf{(3.15)}$$

$$OUTFL.KL = \frac{LEVEL.K}{DELAY.K} \quad \textbf{(3.16)}$$

where

$$LEVEL = LEVEL \text{ (amount) of units in the delay}$$

$$INFLW = INFLoW \text{ rate}$$

$$OUTFL = OUTFLow \text{ rate}$$

$$DELAY = \text{average time of the DELAY}$$

Equation (3.16) indicates that the outflow rate over the coming time period is equal to the amount in the delay divided by the length of the average delay period, the amount in the delay having been determined by the difference between the inflow and outflow rates over the preceding time period [Eq. (3.15)].

When the dynamic behavior of systems is being evaluated, not only is the average delay important, but also the reaction of the delay to transients. One can shape the transient response of the model by cascading first order exponential delays into higher order delays or by selecting other delay functions, such as a discrete delay. Because the character and behavior of delays are fundamental to industrial dynamics analysis, we shall examine the transient response of several delay functions.

In Figs. 3.5 and 3.6 are shown output rates from first, second, and third order exponential delays in response to a unit step increase and a pulse input rate at time zero. Note that for the first order exponential delay there is a small increase in the output rate at once rising to approximately sixty per cent of the input rate at the time of the average delay. For the second order delay the output rate is zero at first, but it begins to rise immediately afterwards. In the case of the third order delay the output rate is also zero at first, but there is a delay before any output appears. The output rate increases slowly, rises to a maximum, and then declines.[9] Higher order exponential delays would prolong the rise in output rates still more. At the extreme is the discrete delay, in which there is no response to the input rate until the end of the delay period, when the output rate reflects the input rate.

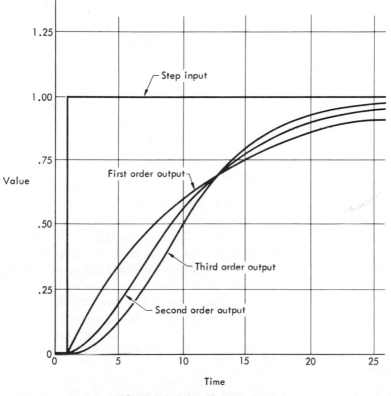

FIGURE 3.5. Delay Output—Step

[9]Because of the frequency with which third order delays are used, the DYNAMO compiler provides a function for them in which the user need only specify the inflow and outflow rates, and the average delay period.

$$\text{OUTFL.KL} = \text{DELAY3(INFLW.JK, DELAY)}$$

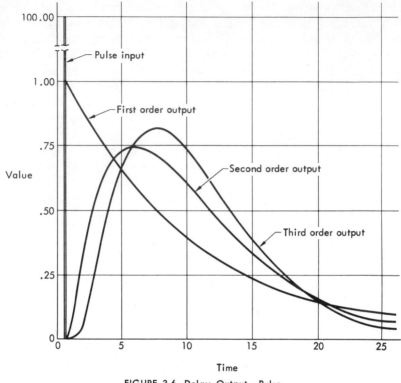

FIGURE 3.6. Delay Output—Pulse

It is important to select delay functions that adequately represent the system being modeled. As an example, a first order delay might represent response to an advertisement to which there is a small initial response, rising to a peak shortly thereafter. A third order delay might represent the response to a transportation system in which goods are being delivered to different destinations. In this case there is a delay before any goods arrive at their destination. A discrete delay might represent the flow between two points where all goods put into the system traverse it in the same time interval.

Model of a Production-Distribution System

In order better to visualize the decision processes discussed above, we will develop a model and illustrate the behavior of a simple production-distri-bution-inventory system. An analysis of such a basic model will reveal much about the construction of feedback models and their dynamic properties.

The purpose of this example is to illustrate the process by which such models may be constructed, not to develop a finished model of the nature and structure of a production-distribution system. This model contains a number of decision rules and policies which may be considered naive, shortsighted, and uninformed. The restriction of the model to a set of elementary decision rules was imposed in the interest of brevity and simplicity.

The configuration of such a system would include the rates of orders, production, and shipments; levels of inventories; ordering decisions; and delays in the flows of orders and shipments. The basic structure of the model is illustrated in Fig. 3.7. In this system the manufacturer's products are sold directly to dealers, and in turn to customers. The company maintains a factory warehouse that is adjacent to, but is managed more or less autonomously from, the factory production organization. Orders from dealers are received by the factory warehouse, and shipments are made to dealers from the factory warehouse. The warehouse places orders with the factory. The factory cannot respond instantly to changes in the rate of flow of incoming orders, but is restricted by an adjustment delay representing the time required to adjust production rates.

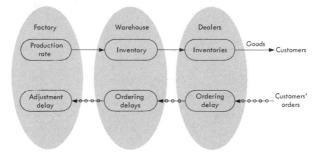

FIGURE 3.7. Basic Structure of Production-Distribution System

There are two major physical flows in this system. One is the flow of goods from the factory through the warehouse inventory through the dealers' inventories to the customer. The other is the flow of orders from customers to dealers, from dealers to the factory warehouse, and from the warehouse to the factory. Other physical flows might be included, such as money, personnel, and capital equipment, but they will be omitted from this example. Interconnecting these flows is a complex network of information flows. Delays in the adjustment of factory production rates, delays in the response of the dealer and warehouse sectors occasioned by their reordering decision rules, and delays in the transportation of goods from the factory warehouse to the dealers are included in the model.

Dealer Sector

Figure 3.8 is a detailed flow diagram of the dealer sector of the model.[10] There are two major parts to the dealer sector: that part affecting the flow of

---

[10]The complete set of equations in DYNAMO format which comprises this model is shown in Appendix C.

goods to the customer, and that part determining the dealers' order rate. Orders flow in from customers through the dealer sales rate.[11] Goods flow into the dealers' inventories through the goods received rate, and out through the dealers' shipping rate. The resulting dealer inventories DINV at any time are a function of the inventory at the preceding time and the difference between the rate of receipts GRECR and shipments DSHPR over the ensuing time interval. They are determined by the level equation:

$$\text{DINV.K} = \text{DINV.J} + (\text{DT})(\text{GRECR.JK} - \text{DSHPR.JK}) \qquad (3.17)$$

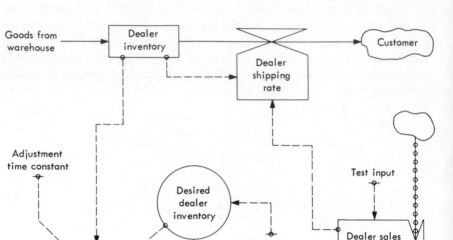

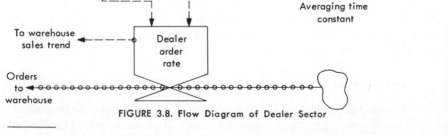

FIGURE 3.8. Flow Diagram of Dealer Sector

---

[11]Dealer sales rate is used as a test input to test the response of the system to varying patterns of customer demand.

The dealer shipping rate is normally a direct function of the dealer sales rate DSLSR under most conditions. However, to avoid the possibility of negative dealer inventories, the shipping rate is taken to be the sales rate only if there are sufficient goods in inventory to satisfy the sales rate. If not, then the shipping rate is limited by the amount of goods on hand divided by the delay in filling dealer orders DFDOR.[12]

$$
\text{DSHPR.KL} = \begin{cases} \text{DSLSR.JK}, \dfrac{\text{DINV.K}}{\text{DFDOR}} \geq \text{DSLSR.JK} \\[2mm] \dfrac{\text{DINV.K}}{\text{DFDOR}}, \dfrac{\text{DINV.K}}{\text{DFDOR}} < \text{DSLSR.JK} \end{cases} \tag{3.18}
$$

This model assumes that orders which cannot be filled from stock are lost, and that there is a very short delay between the time sales are made and goods are shipped.

The dealer reordering policy relates purchase orders to both the rate of sales and to the amount of goods on hand in inventory. They use a simple and some what naive, but not unrealistic, decision rule. Orders are placed for the purpose of meeting a sales forecast and bringing inventories to a desired level. The sales forecast is an extrapolation of the sales trend derived from a moving average. Thus, the dealer order rate DORDR is determined by the sum of the average sales rate AVDSL and the appropriate inventory adjustment DINAJ.

$$
\text{DORDR.KL} = \text{AVDSL.K} + \text{DINAJ.K} \tag{3.19}
$$

A first order exponentially smoothed moving average is used to compute the projected sales trend. The smoothing equation employs a time to average dealers' sales TAVDS which, in the demonstration run of this model shown later in the chapter, is 12 weeks.

$$
\text{AVDSL.K} = \text{AVDSL.J} + (\text{DT})(1/\text{TAVDS})(\text{DSLSR.JK} - \text{AVDSL.J})
$$
$$
\tag{3.20}
$$

Dealers try to maintain inventory levels commensurate with projected demand, in this instance a four-week supply. Hence, the dealer desired inventory DDINV is a product of average dealer sales (the forecast) and the number of weeks of inventory which it is desired to have on hand DWIND.

$$
\text{DDINV.K} = (\text{DWIND})(\text{AVDSL.K}) \tag{3.21}
$$

They adjust their inventories by finding the difference between the desired

---

[12]See Eq. (3.3) and the discussion following it for a further explanation of the use of a level and delay to determine a rate.

and actual levels of inventories. The entire magnitude of the adjustment is not applied at once, but is delayed by an adjustment time factor, time to adjust dealer inventory TADIN. Choice of this time constant determines the fraction of inventory adjustment applied each time period, and consequently the rapidity with which the attempt is made to bring inventory into line with the desired level. It will here be taken to be eight weeks.

$$DINAJ.K = (1/TADIN)(DDINV.K - DINV.K) \qquad (3.22)$$

Warehouse Sector

Basic decision rules in the warehouse sector, as illustrated in Fig. 3.9, are similar to those in the dealer sector with two important differences. First, orders that cannot be filled from warehouse inventory are not lost, as in the case of the dealer sector, but are retained in an unfilled order file until goods are available to fill them. The second difference is the set of three time constants that are important factors in the reordering decision rules. These are (1) averaging time constant used in the exponential smoothing equation to compute a sales forecast, (2) number of weeks inventory which it is desired to have on hand, and (3) fraction of inventory adjustment applied to each time period. They are taken to be twelve weeks, eight weeks, and sixteen weeks respectively.

Dealer orders flow directly into the warehouse unfilled order file, and are removed from this file when shipments are made from the warehouse inventory. The number of unfilled orders on hand WUNOR is defined by a level equation that accumulates the difference between dealer order rate DORDR and warehouse shipping rate WSHPR.

$$WUNOR.K = WUNOR.J + (DT)(DORDR.JK - WSHPR.JK)$$
$$(3.23)$$

The expression for warehouse shipping rate is similar to that used previously for dealer shipping rate [Eq. (3.18)], except that warehouse shipping rate relates to unfilled orders on hand rather than to incoming sales rate. Warehouse inventory is a function of goods flowing in from the factory and goods being shipped to dealers, and is determined by the same equation type as dealer inventories [Eq. (3.17)].

Note that goods do not flow immediately from warehouse inventory to dealer inventories, but there is a transit delay period TRNDL. A third order exponential function[13] was chosen to represent this delay because it seemed to approximate reasonably the characteristics of a physical transportation system as represented in this model. The following expression is used to represent this delay function:

$$GRECR.KL = DELAY3(WSHPR.JK, TRNDL) \qquad (3.24)$$

---

[13]See footnote 9.

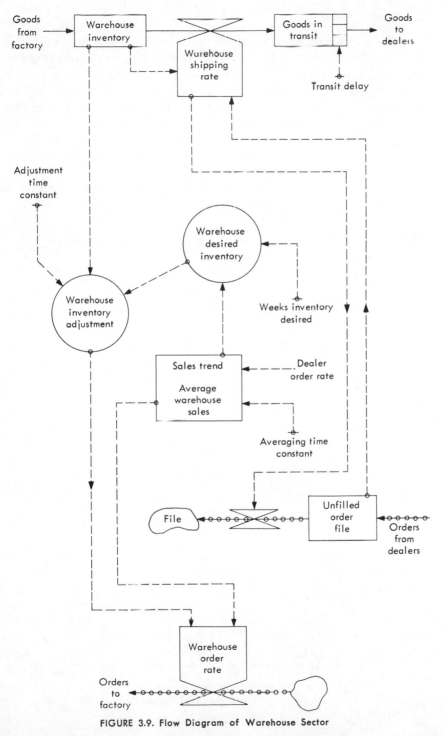

FIGURE 3.9. Flow Diagram of Warehouse Sector

Factory Sector

The components of the factory sector are shown in the flow diagram of Fig. 3.10. The two major segments are processing of incoming orders from the warehouse, and decision rules for determining factory production rate. As in the case of the warehouse sector, sales are not lost if orders cannot be filled immediately, but are kept on hand until deliveries can be made. Orders from the warehouse flow into a factory order backlog, and are removed when finished goods are delivered to the warehouse. The expression for this is a level equation similar to the expression for warehouse unfilled order file [Eq. (3.23)]. The factory production rate is a complex expression comprised of auxiliary variables, constants, and a level equation. The basic production

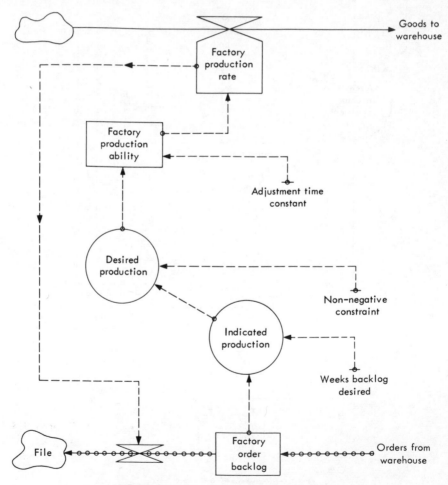

FIGURE 3.10. Flow Diagram of Factory Sector

rate policy is one which attempts to maintain an order backlog related to production rate. In this instance desired backlog is equal to four weeks of production. This policy is followed because the warehouse is adjacent to the factory that maintains inventories of the factory's finished goods output.

Since the factory's scheduling policy is one which attempts to maintain a four-week backlog of orders, adjustments must be made in production rate to maintain the relationship in the face of fluctuating levels of backlog. An indicated production rate INDPR is first determined which relates current level of order backlog FOBKL to weeks of backlog desired WBKLD, in this model four weeks.

$$INDPR.K = FOBKL.K/WBKLD \qquad (3.25)$$

Because of the simplicities of this particular system, situations may arise which indicate a negative factory production rate, which is clearly a meaningless concept. In a more realistic model decision rules and parameters of the system would be such that this would not occur. However, in this elementary system to prevent such a happening we insert a nonnegative restraint on desired production DEPR.

$$DEPR.K = \begin{cases} INDPR.K, & INDPR.K \geq 0 \\ 0, & INDPR.K < 0 \end{cases} \qquad (3.26)$$

This expediency is clearly not good modeling practice, since the model should not do what the system being modeled cannot do. It can generally be avoided by careful and more elaborate construction.

A first-order delay function is next introduced to account for the fact that factory production ability FPRAB cannot be immediately adjusted. It takes time to hire and train employees, notice may be required before they can be laid off, and it takes some time to adjust raw material inventories to accommodate new production levels. In this system we represent all these delays by one average time constant, time to adjust production TAJPR, here taken to be four weeks.

$$FPRAB.K = FPRAB.J + (DT)(1/TAJPR)(DEPR.J - FPRAB.J)$$
$$(3.27)$$

Simulation Results

Figure 3.11 is plotted output from a simulation of 52 weeks' operation of this system. The model was started in an equilibrium state with the rates (sales, ordering, shipping, and production) at 10,000 units per week and inventories at 40,000 units. A 2000 units per week increase in dealers' sales rate was injected at the eighth week in order to observe transient response of the system.

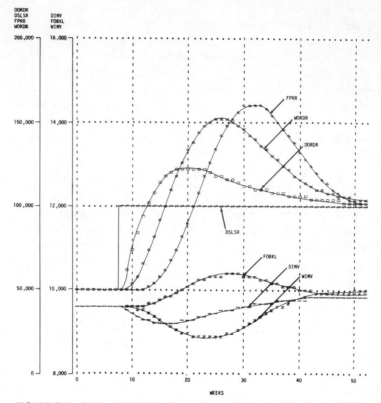

FIGURE 3.11. Plotted DYNAMO Output from Production-Distribution Model

The system responds with the type of amplification and time lags which we have come to associate with this type of system. Following a 20 per cent increase in sales, dealers' order rate increased 29 per cent by the twentieth week (a 12-week lag), warehouse order rate rose 40 per cent by the twenty-sixth week (an 18-week lag), and factory production rate was up 44 per cent by the thirty-first week (a 23-week lag). Dealer inventories fell 25 per cent by the sixteenth week, and warehouse inventory was down 49 per cent by the twenty-fourth week. Note also that it required nearly a year before the system approximated a new equilibrium position. Other behavior patterns would have resulted from the choice of different parameter values. An exploration of these variations is suggested in the exercises at the end of the chapter.

It should be noted that there is a limit to the amount of improvement of system performance that can be obtained by altering the constants in the model. Further changes would require altering the structure of the system itself, and might take the form of changes in decision rules and in information flows.

Other Industrial Dynamics Models

Most of the work done to date in industrial dynamics can be classified into three major areas: the dynamics of steady-state systems, the dynamics of growth systems, and the inclusion of intangible factors and organization policy.

Dynamics of Steady-State Systems

The production-distribution model examined earlier is an example of a steady-state system. The purpose of this class of model is generally to stabilize fluctuations in activities at steady-state levels. An important example of this type of analysis is the study by Forrester of the Sprague Electric

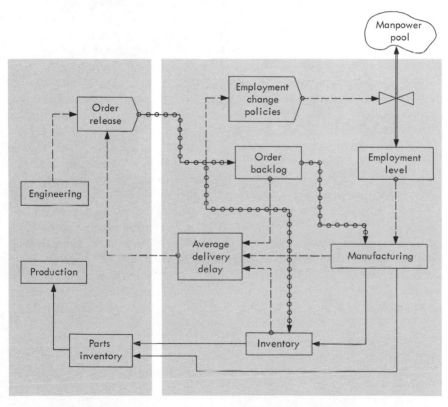

CUSTOMER SECTOR   COMPANY SECTOR

FIGURE 3.12. Basic Structure of Customer-Producer-Employment Model (adapted from Jay W. Forrester, *Industrial Dynamics*, Cambridge, Massachusetts: The Massachusetts Institute of Technology Press, 1961)

Company.[14] The flow diagram in Fig. 3.12 represents the basic structure of the manufacturing system in question. This project, the first to explore the application of industrial dynamics to an actual situation, was undertaken to evaluate the interaction of production, inventory, and employment policies for the purpose of reducing costly fluctuations. One product line was selected for detailed examination, and a simulation model was developed to test hypotheses about causes of aggregate system behavior patterns.

Insights into the system's behavior, new priority rules for scheduling incoming orders, and new inventory policies resulted from the project. In the flow diagram, a feedback loop is shown which relates the company's ability to fill orders, as represented by delivery delay, and the customers' ordering policy. It was felt at one time that this was one of the primary determinants of long-term instabilities in the company's incoming order rate.

Although the study and use of the simulation model did result in improved internal stability, it did not stabilize long-term fluctuations in the incoming order rate as originally predicted. Bruce R. Carlson, who supervised the company's participation in the program, has described these results in some detail.[15] This study demonstrated the fact that it is important to determine all relevant factors in the feedback loops affecting system performance. Carlson concluded, "the Sprague project does not, to date, support that part of [the] concept which implies that relatively easily descerible factors interact to form feedback loops which dominate the behavior of a given system."[16]

Extensions of this work to include similar applications to other companies have been reported in the literature. Schlager reported on the application to three companies in the Milwaukee area who were found to have systems and problems not unlike those of the Sprague Electric Company.[17] One company was a manufacturer of instruments for liquid flow measurement which was experiencing significant fluctuations in production and employment. It was found that some parts of the original Sprague model could be adapted, substantially reducing model construction time. A more extensive cost structure was added to the model and certain sectors were disaggregated, such as production-inventory control, personnel, and purchasing. Another company was encountered which produced high unit value industrial ma-

---

[14]Forrester, Jay W., *Industrial Dynamics* (Cambridge, Mass.: The Massachusetts Institute of Technology Press, 1961), Chaps. 17 and 18.

[15]Bruce R. Carlson, "An Industrialist Views Industrial Dynamics," *Industrial Management Review*, Vol. 5, No. 2 (Fall, 1964).

[16]*Ibid.*, p. 18. Forrester pointed out that this conclusion was drawn after about one year of operation when the system had a transient response of four years or more, and that there was a substantial decrease in employment due to a rise in productivity created by greater stability in work force assignments (personal correspondence).

[17]Kenneth J. Schlager, "How Managers Use Industrial Dynamics," *Industrial Management Review*, Vol. 5, No. 2 (Fall, 1964).

chinery. In that study it was found that neither product aggregation nor direct labor hours could be used as the basis for the aggregated physical flows in the model because of the unique characteristics of the system. As a result the study team turned to the concept of using (as the basis for the model) a flow of projects instead of a flow of goods through the system. A third study dealt with analyzing product life cycles.

An industrial dynamics simulation of the production and distribution systems of a tufted carpet mill has been conducted by the National Bureau of Standards.[18] It is of interest because it illustrates many of the problems encountered in aggregating into a continuous model varieties of product lines and manufacturing processes. The basic structure of this industry is represented in Fig. 3.13. It consists of five major sectors: yarn manufacturing, mill (where carpet is tufted), finishing (where undyed carpets are dyed and permanent backings are applied to both piece-dyed and stock-dyed carpets), wholesale, and retail. Of particular interest is the approach to aggregation developed in the mill stage. The varieties of products (colors, sizes, patterns, and materials) are represented by four product types, and manufacturing processes are represented by machine hours per plant. The simulated production manager plans work for the coming week on the basis of sampled requirements and average productivities of the work force. In executing this plan the mill is constrained by shortages of yarn, in which case work proceeds on other products for which yarn is available. This study illustrates some of the possibilities for simulating such discrete activities as weekly production scheduling, where qualitative measures of performance are needed.

Interesting applications of industrial dynamics models to economic-biological systems may be found in the extensive analyses that have been made of the management of commercial salmon fisheries along the western rim of North America by the College of Fisheries at the University of Washington.[19] Research has been directed at designing management systems for establishing fishing policies that will maximize long-run production of food and protect this resource from depletion. These studies have lent themselves to continuous-flow simulation models because the fisheries management functions as a regulator in a feedback control system. Mature salmon which escape fishermen's nets move in late summer to fresh water spawning grounds, spawn, and then die. The progeny which result eventually migrate to the ocean feeding grounds. When they mature, adult fish return to their

[18]Jerome A. Yurow, "Analysis and Computer Simulation of the Production and Distribution Systems of a Tufted Carpet Mill," *The Journal of Industrial Engineering*, Vol. 18, No. 1 (January, 1967).

[19]G. J. Paulik and J. W. Greenough, Jr., "Management Analysis for a Salmon Resource System," in *Systems Analysis in Ecology*, Kenneth E. F. Watt, ed. (New York: Academic Press, Inc., 1966), Chap. 9.

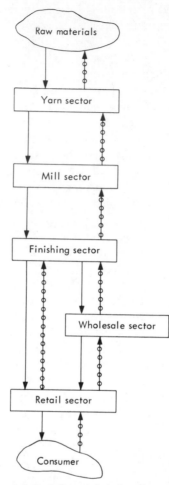

FIGURE 3.13. Structure of Tufted Carpet Industry (by permission from Jerome A. Yurow, "Analysis and Computer Simulation of the Production and Distribution System for a Tufted Carpet Mill," *The Journal of Industrial Engineering*, Vol. 18, No. 1, January, 1967)

fresh water spawning grounds and the cycle is repeated. There is each year an optimum number of returning adults (spawners) of each homogenous group (stock) of fish that should be allowed to spawn, because of the physical limitations of the fresh water spawning grounds. A run of a given species may consist of a heterogeneous mixture of several stocks.

Analysis may be subdivided into interseasonal and intraseasonal phases. The interseasonal analysis is concerned with determining optimum numbers of each species of fish which should be allowed to escape the fishery for the spawning grounds. A variety of population dynamics models, analytical techniques, and computer simulation techniques have been applied to this phase of the problem. Of interest to us here is a DYNAMO simulation model developed to aid in studying management decisions made during the fishing season. These decisions are designed to realize optimum escapement levels determined in the interseasonal analysis. Problems exist because it is not possible to regulate carefully the portion of each individual stock escaping the fishery.

The fishery management agency controls the flow of fish only by opening or closing the fishery in different fishing areas. Decisions are governed by a desire to satisfy a complex set of often incompatible objectives, and are hampered by time lags in obtaining information during the season and by time lags in getting decisions carried out. As an example of this incompatibility, if a fishery is working simultaneously on two species in an area, closing the fishery may allow the proper number of one species to escape to the spawning grounds, but too many of the other, whereas opening the fishery may allow the proper number of the latter group to escape, but not enough of the former. Determination of the optimum number of fish to be allowed to escape the fishery at any time depends on such factors as age and size composition of the group of returning fish, weather conditions, intensity of placement and efficiency of fishing gear, and density of fish in the fresh water nursery areas.

The model, the basic structure of which is illustrated in Fig. 3.14, consists of five interrelated sectors: (1) fish migration sector, (2) fixed fishing gear sector, (3) mobile fishing gear decision-making sector, (4) fishing sector, and (5) fishery management sector.

In the fish migration sector two species of fish move through three fishing areas, which comprise the fishery. Whereas all fish pass through area one, they afterwards diverge into either area two or three. The two species differ as to whether they pass completely through the fishing area before escaping for the spawning grounds (the target species) or escape continuously as they move through the fishing area (the diffusion species). Fishing by either mobile fishing gear or fixed fishing gear is done in each area, although only one area is shown in Fig. 3.14. Operation of the fixed gear is dependent only on its location and management permission to fish, because fixed gear fishes whenever it is permitted to do so.

Fishermen operating mobile gear decide whether to fish and at what location in each area. Their decision is based on several major factors, as depicted in the model: permission to fish granted by the fishery management agency, forecast of the expected value of the future catch for each species, operating costs, and present locations of both fixed and mobile gear. The expected catch forecast is determined from information from each area about the previous day's catch, an estimate of fish abundance, and the preseason forecast. The fishery management agency's decision as to whether to open or close the fishery depends upon a comparison of actual escapement

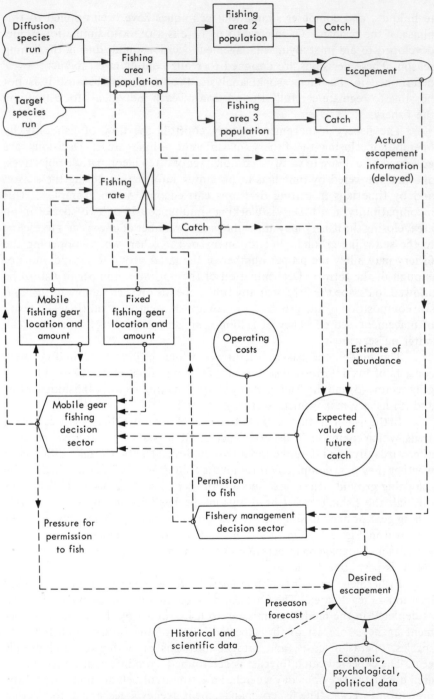

FIGURE 3.14. Model of Salmon Fishery System

from each area with desired escapement. Information on actual escapement is delayed a few days by time lags involved in collecting data in the field, and transmitting and analyzing it. Desired escapement levels are determined from the preseason forecast. Note that there is also pressure from fishermen for permission to fish, which is taken into account by the management agency.

This model has proved most useful in providing a precise way of describing these ecological systems and discovering and demonstrating the mechanisms at work which account for actual observations of the system. It is felt that simulation models may aid significantly in acquiring some understanding of behavioral causes in complex biological systems. In particular they may prove helpful in studying the impact of different policies for management of natural resources and in planning research programs. Other models are being constructed of Pacific salmon, halibut, and tuna fisheries.

Dynamics of Growth Systems

In contrast to steady-state systems, growth systems exhibit long-term trends over time. Characteristic of this type of system are the growth of product markets, enterprises, industries, and economies, as well as systems dealing with projects having discernible life cycles, such as research and development projects.

Certain aspects of growth patterns of small firms were investigated in a study by Packer in which the impact of two sets of basic policies on growth of the firm were examined.[20] These policies governed the acquisition of professional manpower, both technical and managerial, and acquisition of productive capacity. An outline of the basic model is shown in Fig. 3.15.

Growth of the system occurs through the action of two primary positive feedback loops. The first relates the positive effect of productive capacity expansion on increases in customer order rate. An increase in order rate raises the order backlog and lowers inventory. This creates pressure for expansion of capacity, which, when realized, reduces the firm's delivery delay, which is one factor working to increase the order rate.

The second positive feedback loop relates the effect of acquisition of professional manpower and the firm's ability to absorb additional manpower on the customer order rate. As in the first feedback loop, increases in customer order rate cause order backlog to rise and inventory to fall, thus creating pressure for expansion of the firm's professional effort. Acquisition of professional manpower results in an increase in the firm's professional capabilities, but this increase is restrained by its ability to absorb additional professional effort. The expanded professional capability expended on activities

[20]David W. Packer, *Resource Acquisition in Corporate Growth* (Cambridge, Mass.: The Massachusetts Institute of Technology Press, 1964).

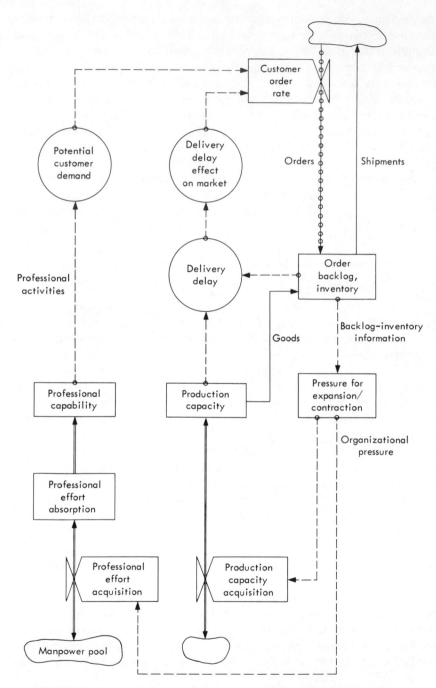

FIGURE 3.15. Model of Corporate Growth System (by permission from David W. Packer, *Resource Acquisition in Corporate Growth*, Cambridge, Massachussetts : The Massachusetts Institute of Technology Press, 1963)

affecting the firm's market has a positive effect on potential demand which is another factor working to increase the order rate.

Several other feedback loops interact with these to produce the fluctuating growth behavior indicated in Fig. 3.16. According to the study, this behavior resulted from the firm's inability rapidly to absorb professional employees into the organization. Attention devoted to training and fitting in newcomers detracted from activities necessary to create demand for the firm. As productive capacity grew faster than demand, cutbacks were necessary. These interactions resulted in cycles of expansion and contraction.

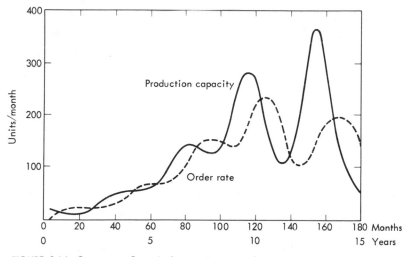

FIGURE 3.16. Corporate Growth System Behavior (by permission from David W. Packer, *Resource Acquisition in Corporate Growth*, Cambridge, Massachusetts: The Massachusetts Institute of Technology Press, 1963)

The dynamics of the life cycles of research and development projects undertaken by research and development firms were analyzed in a study by Edward B. Roberts.[21] The basic feedback system underlying such projects is depicted in Fig. 3.17. Note that the research and development process has been aggregated to consider continuous flows of interrelated activities rather than separate discrete events, and that the model focuses on the entire project life cycle rather than on segregated problems of the phases of projects.

A research and development project's life cycle begins with exogenous events referred to as the changing world situation. As a result of such changes, potential customers and producers of new products are continually engaged in activities leading to the perception of the need for and value of new products. From this they attempt to determine the magnitude of effort and costs required to develop such products. At this point a research and develop-

[21]Edward B. Roberts, *The Dynamics of Research and Development*. (New York: Harper & Row, Publishers, 1964).

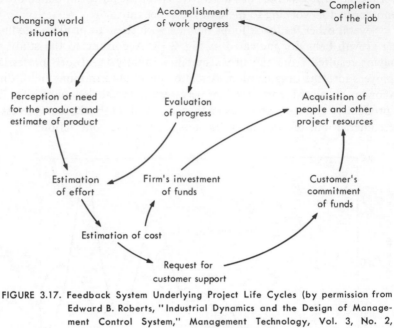

FIGURE 3.17. Feedback System Underlying Project Life Cycles (by permission from Edward B. Roberts, "Industrial Dynamics and the Design of Management Control System," Management Technology, Vol. 3, No. 2, December, 1963)

ment firm has two alternatives. It can either request customer support or invest its own money in the project. A favorable reaction from the customer or a positive analysis of risks involved in committing the firm's own funds results in a flow of funds into the project which permits acquisition of people and other resources necessary to carry out the project. The rate at which progress on the project is accomplished depends upon a number of factors, such as the technologies involved, the magnitude of the effort, managerial influences, and organizational factors affecting efficiency of work. Both the customer and the research and development firm attempt to assess progress by comparing their interpretations of results achieved with their perception of desired results. These evaluations are fed back into the process and may lead to modification of the program and the support required for its completion. This process continues until the project is completed or cancelled. As a result of analyzing the behavior of the simulation model, Roberts concluded that two policies critical to the success of such projects are willingness of the firm to undertake risks, and its integrity in bidding on cost reimbursement contracts.

Intangible Factors and Organization Policy

More recent research in industrial dynamics has been directed toward simulation of factors other than tangible and physical flows such as those of inventories and people. The level of aggregation considered in industrial dynamics models permits inclusion of many intangible factors of managerial decisions and organizational behavior. Problems associated with modeling these factors are even more difficult than the aggregation problems related above. Such factors are nearly impossible to measure accurately, but considerable progress has been made in representing some of the important influences on organizational behavior in simulation models. This has been possible because no attempt is made to predict individual behavior, but rather to treat aggregate behavior. Inclusion of such factors permits giving attention to much higher level management problems than would be possible if the model's structure were restricted to tangible flows in the system. Several areas of research are under study. These include modeling the dynamics of a power structure in an organization, the incentive environment in an organization's system, and implementation of organization change.[22]

An example of an approach that might be used in modeling certain intangible factors is the adjustment to pressure. Both the growth system model and the project life cycle model discussed earlier included factors creating pressure for change, such as pressure for expansion. The modeling problem is to develop a function that relates these factors. Although we may not know at the outset just what the nature of such a function ought to be, we might be able after observation and study of the system to approximate extreme points and the general shape of the relationship.

As we have noted earlier, it is possible to use the simulation model itself to determine when more precise data is required by testing the sensitivity of over-all behavior of the model to changes in response patterns of individual components. If for these components response at extreme points and the general shape of the response pattern can be approximated—a situation that often holds—then an experiment may be designed in which a range of values is tried on succeeding runs of the simulation model. If over-all response of the system to such changes over this range is insignificant, then there may be little need for more precise data. On the other hand, if the system response is significant the system is said to be sensitive, and the need for more precise data may be readily recognized.

Summary

Industrial dynamics simulation models share many of the advantages and limitations of other types of simulation models. But since industrial dynamics models represent something of a departure from the structure of other models, they present unique problems and offer the possibility of unique contributions. An important difference between industrial dynamics models and most of the models considered in other chapters is in their perspective as reflected in the treatment of individual events. Where industrial dynamics

---

[22]See: Edward B. Roberts, "New Direction in Industrial Dynamics," *Industrial Management Review*, Vol. 5, No. 2 (Fall, 1964), p. 10; and L. Fillmore McPherson, III, "Organizational Change," *Industrial Management Review*, Vol. 6, No. 3 (Spring, 1965).

models focus on continuous flows in feedback systems, others usually focus on discrete events and transactions. Industrial dynamics models typically deal with large, complex systems and are often similar to models that would be run on analog computers. To assist in programming industrial dynamics models for digital computers, the DYNAMO language has been developed.

The orientation of industrial dynamics is toward simulating high level decision processes and interaction among components in large systems. However, the rationality of decision functions in such systems may be difficult to determine, and it is not an easy task to represent these decision processes in the equation structure of a simulation model. Validation of a model dealing with such high level decision processes is not easy if the user requires evidence of validity beyond mere superficial similarity of the model with the real world.

A problem confronting the analyst is finding appropriate measures for improved performance of the system. Control systems may be designed to improve the stability of behavior, but stability is not necessarily the most appropriate criterion in economic systems. Cost or profit considerations often dictate a certain amount of instability. Industrial dynamics models have not generally included cost and profit functions; neither have they included formal optimizing techniques.[23] In part, this is due to the fact that DYNAMO has a closed structure that does not lend itself to experimentation with optimizing techniques in the decision functions.

Applications cited in this chapter suggest the value of industrial dynamics as a method for simulating a wide variety of systems. In any particular case, choice of an industrial dynamics model over more conventional simulation models rests principally on the degree to which the phenomena under investigation can realistically be represented within the industrial dynamics philosophy. Although much can be gained from insights obtained through the use of such concepts as feedback loops and control of rates of flow by decision functions, there are many problems which cannot profitably be structured in these terms. A major advantage of using the industrial dynamics philosophy when applicable is the ease of programing industrial dynamics models using DYNAMO.

EXERCISES

3.1   Suppose that in Eqs. (3.17) and (3.18) the shipping rate DSHPR is dependent only upon the amount of goods on hand DINV and the order filling delay DFDOR.

---

[23]For more detailed comments on these problems, see: Charles C. Holt and Ronald A. Howard, discussants of "Managerial Decision Making," by Jay W. Forrester in *Management and the Computer of the Future*, Martin Greenberger, ed. (Cambridge, Mass.: The Massachusetts Institute of Technology Press, 1962), Chap. 2; and Harvey M. Wagner, "Review of Industrial Dynamics," *Management Science*, Vol. 10, No. 1 (October, 1963), pp. 184–186.

$$DSHPR.KL = DINV.K/DFDOR$$

Inventory is increased by the goods received rate GRECR and depleted by the shipping rate.

$$DINV.K = DINV.J + (DT)(GRECR.JK - DSHPR.JK)$$

The initial inventory is 100 units, order filling delay is 10 weeks, shipping rate is 10 units/week, and the computation interval DT is 1 week. The goods received rate is initially 10 units/week and increases to 100 units/week in the third week. Simulate the system for 30 weeks and explain the behavior of the system.

3.2 Simulate the system in Exercise 3.1 for 30 weeks, but assume that the goods received rate is initially 10 units/week and beginning in the third week it increases at the rate of 5 units/week/week (15 units/week the third week, 20 units/week the fourth week, etc.). Plot the results and explain the behavior of the system.

3.3 Simulate the system in Exercise 3.1 for 22 weeks. Assume that the goods received rate is initially 10 units/week and beginning in the third week it increases at the rate of 5 units/week/week for 5 weeks. It then decreases at the rate of 5 units/week/week for 5 weeks, but, beginning in the thirteenth week, it again increases at the rate of 5 units/week/week for 5 weeks. It then decreases at the same rate for 5 weeks. Plot the results and explain the behavior of the system.

3.4 Consider a simplified version of the dealer sector of Fig. 3.8. Inventory DINV is increased by the goods received rate GRECR and depleted by the shipping rate DSHPR.

$$DINV.K = DINV.J + (DT)(GRECR.JK - DSHPR.JK)$$

The goods received rate is dependent on unfilled orders WUNOR and the transit delay or delay in filling and delivering orders TRNDL.

$$GRECR.KL = WUNOR.K/TRNDL$$

The level of unfilled orders is increased by the ordering rate DORDR and decreased by the goods received rate.

$$WUNOR.K = WUNOR.J + (DT)(DORDR.JK - GRECR.JK)$$

The ordering rate is a function of the shipping rate and the difference between desired inventory DDINV and actual inventory and an adjustment time factor TAJIN.

$$DORDR.KL = (1/TAJIN)(DDINV - DINV.K) + DSHPR.JK$$

Beginning and desired inventories are each 100 units, unfilled orders are 40 units, transit delay and inventory adjustment time factor are each 4 weeks, and the computation interval DT is 1 week. The shipping rate is initially 10 units/week and increases to 15 units/week in the third week. Sketch the flow diagram for this system, using the symbols in Fig. 3.3. Simulate the system for 20 weeks, plot the results, and explain the behavior of the system.

3.5   Simulate the system in Exercise 3.4 for 20 weeks but change the transit delay to 10 weeks and unfilled orders to 100 units. Plot the results and explain the behavior of the system.

3.6   Simulate the system in Exercise 3.4 for 20 weeks but change the inventory adjustment time factor to 10 weeks. Plot the results and explain the behavior of the system.

3.7   Simulate for 21 days a moving average from a first order exponential smoothing function of the form shown in Eq. (3.14). Let DT be 1 day, the smoothing time constant be 6 days, and the initial value of the moving average be 100 units/day. Input to the smoothing function is a time series which starts at 100 units/day, increases at the rate of 6 units/day/day (106 units/day the second day, 112 units/day the third day, etc.) for 5 days, then decreases at the rate of 6 units/day/day for 10 days, and then increases again at the same rate through the twenty-first day. Plot the results and explain the characteristics of this average.

3.8   Simulate for 21 days a moving average from a third order exponential smoothing function, using the same total delay (smoothing time constant) and input data series as in Exercise 3.7. Note that a third order delay is comprised of three first order delays cascaded or arranged in series so that the output of the first is input to the second and output of the second is input to the third. To maintain the total delay of 6 days it is necessary to assign one-third of that delay to each first order smoothing function. Plot the results and compare the behavior of the third order delay with the first order delay in Exercise 3.7.

3.9   Run the production-distribution simulation model described in the text of the chapter (see Appendix C for a complete listing of the model) for 10 weeks. Let DT be 1 week and assume that the step increase in dealer sales DSLSR occurs in the second week. Plot the results.

3.10 Investigate the operating characteristics of the production-distribution system described in the text of the chapter (see Appendix C for a complete listing of the model) by making a series of runs with the following changes in delay parameters.
   a. Reduce time to average dealers' sales TAVDS to 6 weeks and time to adjust dealer inventory TADIN to 4 weeks.
   b. Reduce time to average warehouse sales TAVWS to 4 weeks and time to adjust warehouse inventory TAWIN to 8 weeks (return parameters changed in part a to their original values).

c. Increase time to adjust production TAJPR to 12 weeks (return parameters changed in parts *a.* and *b.* above to their original values).

3.11 Construct a simulation model of the interaction of a firm and its market to demonstrate the impact of a firm's advertising policies and its ability to deliver goods on sales. Months backlog desired is 3 months and time to adjust production is 24 months. Sales are generated by advertising expenditures with the sales rate (units per month) the product of advertising expenditures (dollars per month) and advertising effectiveness. The firm's advertising policy is to spend $1.00 per unit of average sales. First order exponential smoothing with an averaging time constant of 12 months is used to find average sales. Advertising effectiveness in terms of units of sales generated by each dollar of advertising expenditures is a function of the firm's ability to deliver goods as perceived by customers. The table below shows the relationship between advertising effectiveness and average delivery delay. Average delivery

Average delivery delay (months)	0	1	2	3	4	5	6
Advertising effectiveness (units/$)	2.0	1.9	1.7	1.5	1.3	.7	.5

delay is a first order exponentially smoothed moving average of delivery delay with an averaging time constant of 6 months. It represents the time delay for customers to recognize a change in delivery delay. The firm's delivery delay is the ratio of order backlog to current production rate.

a. Develop a flow diagram illustrating the relationships in the model and identify the positive and negative feedback loops.

b. Simulate the behavior of the system for 100 months, using the following initial conditions.

Order backlog = 3000 units

Production rate = production ability

Production ability = desired production

Average sales = 1000 units/month

Average delivery delay = current delivery delay

c. Explain the dynamic behavior of the system.

3.12 Use the model developed in Exercise 3.11 to determine behavior resulting from the following changes.

a. Reduce production time constant to 12 months.

b. Increase delivery delay averaging time constant to 12 months.

c. Decrease sales averaging time constant to 6 months.

    d. Alter advertising effectiveness by developing a new table of your own choosing.

    e. Change parameter values to attempt to smooth the growth rate.

BIBLIOGRAPHY

Ansoff, H. Igor, and Dennis P. Slevin, "An Appreciation of Industrial Dynamics," *Management Science*, Vol. 14, No. 7 (March, 1968).

————, "Comments on Professor Forrester's Industrial Dynamics—After the First Decade," *Management Science*, Vol. 14, No. 9 (May, 1968).

Carlson, Bruce R., "An Industrialist Views Industrial Dynamics," *Industrial Management Review*, Vol. 5, No. 2 (Fall, 1964).

Carlson, Bruce R., "Industrial Dynamics," *Management Services*, Vol. 1, No. 2 (May–June, 1964).

Fey, Willard R., "An Industrial Dynamics Case Study," *Industrial Management Review*, Vol. 4, No. 1 (Fall, 1962).

Forrester, Jay W., "Advertising: A Problem in Industrial Dynamics," *Harvard Business Review*, Vol. 37, No. 2 (March–April, 1959).

————, *Industrial Dynamics*, Cambridge, Massachusetts: The Massachusetts Institute of Technology Press, 1961.

————, "Industrial Dynamics," in *The Encyclopedia of Management*, Carl Heyel, ed. New York: Reinhold Publishing Company, 1963.

————, "Industrial Dynamics: A Major Breakthrough for Decision Makers," *Harvard Business Review*, Vol. 36, No. 4 (July–August, 1958).

————, "Industrial Dynamics—After the First Decade," *Management Science*, Vol. 14, No. 7 (March, 1968).

————, "Industrial Dynamics—A Reply to Ansoff and Slevin," *Management Science*, Vol. 14, No. 9 (May, 1968).

————, "Managerial Decision Making," in *Management and the Computer of the Future*, Martin Greenberger, ed. Cambridge, Massachusetts: The Massachusetts Institute of Technology Press, 1962.

————, "Market Growth as Influenced by Capital Investment," *Industrial Management Review*, Vol. 9, No. 2 (Winter, 1968).

————, "New Opportunities for Instrumentation and Control in Management Systems," *Journal of Engineering Education* (June, 1963).

Jarmain, W. Edwin, ed., *Problems in Industrial Dynamics*, Cambridge, Massachusetts: The Massachusetts Institute of Technology Press, 1963.

Mathews, Stephen B., "The Economic Consequences of Forecasting Sockeye Salmon Runs to Bristol Bay, Alaska: A Simulation Study." Unpublished Ph. D. thesis. Seattle: University of Washington, 1967.

Newell, William T., "Teaching the Industrial Management Concept," *Teaching Trends in Business*. Proceedings of the 1965 Northwestern Universities of Business Administration Conference. Tacoma, Washington: Pacific Lutheran University, 1966.

Nord, Ole C., *Growth of a New Product: Effects of Capacity-Acquisition Policies*, Cambridge, Massachusetts: The Massachusetts Institute of Technology Press, 1963.

Packer, David W., *Resource Acquisition in Corporate Growth*. Cambridge, Massachusetts: The Massachusetts Institute of Technology Press, 1964.

Paulik, G. J., and J. W. Greenough, Jr., "Management Analysis for a Salmon Resource System," *Systems Analysis in Ecology*, Kenneth E. F. Watt, ed. New York: Academic Press, Inc., 1966, Chap. 9.

Pugh, Alexander L., III, *DYNAMO User's Manual*, 2nd ed. Cambridge, Massachusetts: The Massachusetts Institute of Technology Press, 1963.

Roberts, Edward B., *The Dynamics of Research and Development*. New York: Harper and Row, Publishers, Inc., 1964.

————, "Industrial Dynamics and the Design of Management Control Systems," *Management Technology*, Vol. 3, No. 2 (December, 1963) and a chapter in *Management Controls: New Directions in Basic Research*, C. Bonini, R. Jaedicke, and M. Wagner, eds. New York: McGraw-Hill Book Company, 1964.

————, "New Directions in Industrial Dynamics," *Industrial Management Review*, Vol. 6, No. 1 (Fall, 1964).

————, "Toward a New Theory for Research and Development," *Industrial Management Review*, Vol. 4, No. 1 (Fall, 1962).

Schlager, Kenneth J., "How Managers Use Industrial Dynamics," *Instrument Society of America Journal* (March, 1964) and reprinted in *Industrial Management Review*, Vol. 5, No. 1 (Fall, 1964).

Southward, Glenn M., "A Simulation Study of Management Regulatory Policies in the Pacific Halibut Fishery." Unpublished Ph. D. thesis. Seattle: University of Washington, 1966.

Sprague, Robert C., "Industrial Dynamics: Case Example," in Carl Heyel, *The Encyclopedia of Management*. New York: Reinhold Publishing Company, 1963.

Weymar, F. Helmut, "Industrial Dynamics: Interaction between the Firm and Its Market," in Wroe Alderson and Stanley Shapiro, *Marketing and the Computer*. Englewood-Cliffs, New Jersey: Prentice-Hall, Inc., 1963.

Wismer, David A. "On the Uses of Industrial Dynamics Models," *Operations Research*, Vol. 15, No. 4 (July–August, 1967).

Yurow, Jerome A., "Analysis and Computer Simulation of the Production and Distribution Systems for a Tufted Carpet Mill," *The Journal of Industrial Engineering*, Vol. 18, No. 1 (January, 1967).

Simulation in
Economic Analysis

4 The distinction between business and economic simulations is not a clear one, and we will not attempt to draw any strict line of demarcation. We include in this chapter a discussion of simulation models that are more closely allied with the work of economists rather than business analysts.

Economists have long been interested in quantification and the development of analytical economic models. This interest has led to construction of a large number of mathematical models used to explain and analyze economic phenomena. Some models are static in nature, whereas others have attempted to deal with the dynamic behavior of economic systems. Investigation of the question of equilibrium states of economic systems has long been prominent in the literature.

Simulation as a tool of economic analysis and model building is particularly useful in dealing with the dynamic behavior of economic systems over time. In contrast to some mathematical approaches to analysis of dynamic systems, simulation enables the investigator to determine not only the long-run state of the system, but also the time path through which the system travels to reach its final state. Simulation may also be useful in extending the range of problems that may be dealt with analytically when the complexity of the phenomena under investigation makes mathematical modeling difficult or impossible.

In economics it is useful to distinguish between macro models, dealing with aggregate behavior and relationships, and micro models, which deal with the behavior of individual units. Simulation techniques may be used in both macro and micro analyses, with the simulation structure appropriately adjusted to fit the circumstances. Macro models deal with determinants and behavior of gross national product, input-output analysis, and similar areas in which aggregate behavior is the subject of study. Models used for analysis include aggregate variables such as government expenditures, total personal consumption, industry expenditures, total supply and demand,

and so forth. Simulations of macro-economic phenomena similarly deal in the same aggregate variables and trace their behavior through time. In contrast, micro models deal with individual economic units, typically the individual household or consumer or individual firms, and simulations of micro-economic phenomena trace behavior of individual units through time. To be sure, the sum of behavior of individual economic units determines aggregate economic behavior, but the basic structure of a simulation model is quite different depending on whether the modeling process begins with the individual unit or with aggregate relationships. In later sections of this chapter we will discuss examples of both macro and micro simulation models, and the differences will be apparent.

In Chap. 1 we referred to the use of analog devices in simulation, but indicated that they were seldom practical for business and economic studies because of the difficulty of finding suitable analogs. Perhaps the most important exception is the use of electrical analogs to simulate economic phenomena that can be expressed with difference or differential equation structures. Models with these structures may be such that mechanical and electrical analogs can be constructed.[1] To make use of analog computations methods, however, the model must be constructed in terms of continuous functions or converted from a difference equation model to a system of continuous functions.[2] Although the necessity of using continuous functions may cause some difficulties, it is not as serious as the lack of flexibility of electrical analog computers, their unavailability to economists, and unfamiliarity with them on the part of economic analysts. As a consequence, although it is possible in certain cases to use analog simulation, an analog computer would rarely be used instead of a digital machine.[3]

In Chap. 1 we defined simulation and model sampling as somewhat different techniques. The distinction is that simulation involves a model that moves dynamically through time, whereas model sampling essentially consists of sampling repetitively from probability distributions to determine certain characteristics of the model which would be difficult or impossible

---

[1]An extensive discussion of aggregate economic models in engineering terms is found in: Arnold Tustin, *The Mechanism of Economic Systems*. 2nd ed. (London: William Heinemann, Ltd., 1957). See also: N. F. Morehouse, R. H. Strotz, and S. J. Horwitz, "An Electro-Analog Method for Investigating Problems in Economic Dynamics: Inventory Oscillations," *Econometrica*, Vol. 18, No. 4 (October, 1950); and Manuel Zymelman, "A Stabilization Policy for the Cotton Textile Industry," *Management Science*, Vol. 11, No. 5 (March, 1965).

[2]For a complete discussion of the relationship between difference and differential equations, see: Samuel Goldberg, *Introduction to Difference Equations* (New York: John Wiley and Sons, Inc., 1958), Secs. 1.7 and 2.12. This reference also contains many illustrations of dynamic economic models.

[3]A number of digital computer programs and languages have been developed which are specifically designed to permit solution on digital computers of problems which would normally be run on analog computers. Examples of such programs are DSL/90, a program for the 7090 series of IBM machines, and 1130 CSMP and CSMP/360, two programs currently maintained by IBM.

to obtain by conventional mathematical or statistical methods. Both simulation and model sampling may involve Monte Carlo techniques; however, dynamic movement of the model through time is not a strong feature of model sampling experiments.

In economics the most important use of model sampling has been as an approach to the investigation of various techniques of parameter estimation in econometric models. We will include a discussion of some of this work later in the chapter, since model sampling and simulation are closely related and model sampling experiments are often termed simulations.

Econometric Models

A major activity of economists in recent years has been construction of systems of mathematical equations, called econometric models, which describe in aggregate terms the economic process. A very simple econometric model is defined by the following six equations.[4]

$$C_t = \alpha_0 + \alpha_1 Y_t + \alpha_2 C_{t-1} \qquad (4.1)$$

$$I_t = \beta_0 + \beta_1 P_t + \beta_2 K_{t-1} \qquad (4.2)$$

$$W_t = \gamma_0 + \gamma_1 Y_t + \gamma_2 t \qquad (4.3)$$

$$Y_t = C_t + I_t + G_t \qquad (4.4)$$

$$P_t = Y_t - W_t \qquad (4.5)$$

$$K_t = K_{t-1} + I_t \qquad (4.6)$$

where

$$C = \text{consumption}$$

$$Y = \text{income}$$

$$W = \text{wage income}$$

$$P = \text{nonwage income}$$

$$I = \text{net investment}$$

---

[4]The model is a slightly modified version of one discussed in Maurice Liebenberg, Albert A. Hirsch, and Joel Popkin, "A Quarterly Econometric Model of the United States: A Progress Report," *Survey of Current Business*, Vol. 46, No. 5 (May, 1966). This article also contains a good basic introduction to econometric models and their uses. The model defined by Eqs. (4.1) through (4.6) will be discussed again in Chap. 8 to illustrate the concept of nonrecursive model structures, and results of a simulation run of the model with hypothetical data will be shown.

$$K = \text{net capital stock at end of period}$$

$$t = \text{time}$$

$$G = \text{government expenditures}$$

Equations (4.1), (4.2), and (4.3) describe the determinants of consumption, investment, and wages; Eqs. (4.4), (4.5), and (4.6) are definitional in nature. The α's, β's, and γ's in the first three equations are coefficients or parameters of the model which must be estimated from actual economic data.[5] Selection of the form of the equations and other details of the construction of econometric models will not be discussed here, as we are primarily interested in the use of the model for simulation purposes.

In this model, we regard C_t, Y_t, I_t, W_t, P_t, and K_t as endogenous variables, or those whose values are determined by the model. The quantity G is an exogenous variable, or one which is determined outside the system. At any point in time t, C_{t-1} and K_{t-1} may also be regarded as exogenous variables, since they are not determined by the system of equations at that point in time.

Once parameter values have been estimated, the model may be used to make predictions about the values of endogenous variables at time t by inserting values of G_t, K_{t-1}, and C_{t-1} in the system of equations and solving for the values of the endogenous variables. Alternatively, the model can be used to simulate behavior of the endogenous economic variables over time by solving the model for time t, $t + 1$, $t + 2$, and so forth. Under these circumstances, after initial solution of the model values of K_{t-1} and C_{t-1} are generated by the model itself, but values of the exogenous variable G must be given for the number of periods the simulation is to run. By using the econometric model as a simulator, effects of such things as changes in the level of government expenditures or changes in consumption habits can be observed dynamically as the model moves through successive time periods. To investigate effects of an increase in government expenditures, for instance, the value of the exogenous variable G might be held constant at a certain level for a number of time periods and then raised to a new higher level for succeeding time periods. One could observe effects on the endogenous variables resulting from this step increase in G. In the case of consumption, effects of changes in consumer habits could be observed by changing the values of some of the parameters in Eq. (4.1) and observing what happens to the endogenous variables in succeeding time periods.

Figure 4.1 is a hypothetical econometric model developed to illustrate the use of simulation for analysis of behavior of gross national product. The model is composed of three major sectors: consumption, government,

---

[5]A number of different methods have been developed for estimating these parameters. For a discussion of various methods and some of the problems encountered, see: J. Johnston, *Econometric Methods* (New York: McGraw-Hill Book Co., Inc., 1963).

and business. These sectors are represented by four, three, and eight equations respectively, plus one equation for gross national product and nine equations defining constants used in the sector equations. Two of the constants, government purchases from business GPB and wage payments by government WPG, are exogenous variables. Values of all other variables are endogenous, being determined within the model.

```
        GROSS NATIONAL PRODUCT DEFINITION

        GNP=CON+GOV+INV                           GROSS NATIONAL PRODUCT


        CONSUMPTION SECTOR

        CON=(APCON) (DIN)                         CONSUMPTION
        DIN=WPB+WPG+TRN+DIV-PTX                    DISPOSABLE INCOME
        PTX=(PTXRT) (WPB+WPG+DIV)                  PERSONAL TAXES
        SAV=DIN-CON                                SAVINGS


        GOVERNMENT SECTOR

        GOV=TRN+WPG+GPB                            GOVERNMENT EXPENDITURES
        TAX=PTX+BTX                                TAX RECEIPTS
        DBT=DBT+(DT) (GOV-TAX)                     ACCUMULATED DEBT


        BUSINESS SECTOR

        INV=SAV+RET                                BUSINESS INVESTMENT
        BUS=CON+GPB+BPB                            TOTAL BUSINESS ACTIVITY
        BPB=INV+(PRPCT) (BUS)                      BUSINESS PURCH. FROM BUS.
        WPB=(WGPCT) (BUS)                          WAGE PAYMENTS BY BUSINESS
        BPR=(BUS) (1-PRPCT-WGPCT)                  BUSINESS PROFITS
        BTX=(BTXRT) (BPR)                          BUSINESS TAXES
        DIV=(DIVRT) (BPR-BTX)                      DIVIDENDS
        RET=BPR-BTX-DIV                            RETAINED EARNINGS


        CONSTANTS

        APCON=.95                                  AVG. PROPENSITY TO CONSUME
        PTXRT=.25                                  PERSONAL TAX RATE
        BTXRT=.50                                  BUSINESS TAX RATE
        PRPCT=.72                                  BUSINESS PURCHASES PERCENT
        WGPCT=.25                                  BUSINESS WAGES PERCENT
        DIVRT=.50                                  DIVIDEND RATE
        TRN=25                                     GOVERNMENT TRANSFER PAYMENTS
        WPG=50                                     WAGE PAYMENTS BY GOVT
        GPB=100                                    GOVT PURCH. FROM BUS.
```

FIGURE 4.1. Hypothetical Econometric Simulation Model

The model was structured to be run on a digital computer using the DYNAMO simulation language. For simplicity, time subscripts and certain other details required by DYNAMO have been deleted from the model in Fig. 4.1.[6] Constants and functional relationships are intended to be plausible

---

[6]The structure of the DYNAMO language will be discussed in Chap. 7, at which point the model in Fig. 4.1 will be shown complete with time subscripts and equation form number and type designations as required by DYNAMO.

but not necessarily those that would be contained in a model used for analytical or predictive purposes.

When the model is run, the equations are evaluated once for each simulated time increment. The time interval Δt between times at which the equations are evaluated can be as large or small as desired. The smaller the simulated time increment, the more similar the operation of the model becomes to a continuous rather than a discrete system, but the cost of computation to simulate any given length of time rises. Since DYNAMO does not permit simultaneous solution of equations, the model equations are evaluated sequentially, although not in the sequence shown in Fig. 4.1. Values of the variables at simulated time t are used by the program to evaluate the model at $t + \Delta t$. The process continues until the desired total number of simulated time periods have elapsed. At the conclusion of a simulation run, tables and graphs of the behavior of the variables are printed out.

Structuring of the model shown in Fig. 4.1 for sequential solution of the equations at each time interval rather than simultaneous solution is an important difference between it and the model defined by Eqs. (4.1) through (4.6). With regard to sequential versus simultaneous models, Liebenberg, Hirsch, and Popkin make the following comment.

> It would be possible by different specifications of equations to remove the simultaneous character of the simple model. We could, for example, substitute Y_{t-1} for Y_t in [Eq. (4.1)]. Consumption would then depend exclusively on lagged variables. In that case, the equation could be solved in isolation from the others since all values on the right would be known.
>
> If the time period t is short enough, say a week, the substitution of lagged income for current income is not unreasonable; decisions to spend this week may well depend on last week's income and not on the current week's. When the time period is much longer—a quarter or more, as it is in almost all models—unidirectional causality becomes doubtful. That is, income earned within the quarter can clearly affect expenditures within the same period, so that causation runs in both directions. Such interdependence also applies to other variables and points up the importance of simultaneity in a realistic characterization of economic behavior.[7]

The model in Fig. 4.1 can be used to simulate effects of changes in government expenditures, taxes, consumption and savings habits, and so forth. Any changes of this nature are simulated by altering the necessary equations in the model. The basic model could also be expanded greatly in the three sectors and additional sectors could be added. An attractive feature of a simulation model is that it permits the investigator to examine with

---

[7] Maurice Liebenberg, Albert A. Hirsch, and Joel Popkin, "A Quarterly Econometric Model of the United States: A Progress Report," *Survey of Current Business*, Vol. 46, No. 5 (May, 1966), pp. 15–16.

Table 4.1 TABULATED RESULTS OF SIMULATION RUN OF HYPOTHETICAL ECONOMETRIC MODEL

TIME	GNP	CON	GOV	INV	DIN	BUS
.000	648.78	435.49	175.00	38.781	458.41	2049.8
.250	648.70	435.41	175.00	38.240	458.32	2049.4
.500	648.59	435.30	175.00	38.254	458.19	2048.8
.750	648.48	435.21	175.00	38.253	458.10	2048.3
1.000	648.41	435.14	175.00	38.251	458.03	2048.0
1.250	648.36	435.10	175.00	38.250	457.99	2047.8
1.500	648.32	435.06	175.00	38.250	457.96	2047.6
1.750	648.29	435.04	175.00	38.249	457.93	2047.5
2.000	648.27	435.02	175.00	38.249	457.92	2047.4
2.250	648.26	435.01	175.00	38.249	457.90	2047.4
2.500	648.25	435.00	175.00	38.248	457.89	2047.3
2.750	648.24	435.00	175.00	38.248	457.89	2047.3
3.000	648.24	434.99	175.00	38.248	457.88	2047.3
3.250	648.24	434.99	175.00	38.248	457.88	2047.3
3.500	648.23	434.99	175.00	38.248	457.88	2047.3
3.750	648.23	434.98	175.00	38.248	457.88	2047.3
4.000	648.23	434.98	190.00	38.248	461.63	2057.3
4.250	675.33	445.71	190.00	40.871	470.66	2103.0
4.500	682.39	452.72	190.00	41.085	477.77	2135.6
4.750	688.04	457.78	190.00	41.140	482.74	2160.8
5.000	691.97	461.39	190.00	41.223	486.29	2177.9
5.250	694.77	463.96	190.00	41.276	488.81	2190.2
5.500	696.78	465.79	190.00	41.314	490.61	2198.9
5.750	698.20	467.09	190.00	41.341	491.90	2205.1
6.000	699.22	468.02	190.00	41.360	492.81	2209.5
6.250	699.94	468.68	190.00	41.374	493.46	2212.7
6.500	700.45	469.16	190.00	41.383	493.93	2214.9
6.750	700.82	469.49	190.00	41.390	494.26	2216.5
7.000	701.08	469.73	190.00	41.395	494.49	2217.6
7.250	701.27	469.90	190.00	41.399	494.66	2218.5
7.500	701.40	470.02	190.00	41.401	494.78	2219.0
7.750	701.50	470.11	190.00	41.403	494.87	2219.4
8.000	701.57	470.17	190.00	41.404	494.93	2219.7
8.250	701.61	470.22	190.00	41.405	494.97	2220.0
8.500	701.65	470.25	190.00	41.406	495.00	2220.1
8.750	701.67	470.27	190.00	41.406	495.02	2220.2
9.000	701.69	470.29	190.00	41.407	495.04	2220.3
9.250	701.70	470.30	190.00	41.407	495.05	2220.3
9.500	701.71	470.30	190.00	41.407	495.06	2220.4
9.750	701.72	470.31	190.00	41.407	495.06	2220.4
10.000	701.72	470.31	190.00	41.407	495.07	2220.4

relative ease effects of parameter, policy, or structural changes. Since time paths of all variables are generated, simulation obtains more information than could be obtained by solving a set of equations once to obtain equilibrium values.

Table 4.1 shows tabulated results of a demonstration run of a slight variation of the model in Fig. 4.1. In this demonstration run the following initial values were used; consumption CON = 435, business activity BUS = 2050, and accumulated debt DBT = 250. Government purchases from business were changed from a constant value of 100 (millions of dollars) in Fig. 4.1 to a step function with a value of 100 up to year 4 and 110 thereafter. Similarly, wage payments by government increase from 50 to 55 at year 4. The run simulates the consequences of these exogenous increases in government expenditures.

Table 4.1 reveals that initial values were such that the model was not quite in equilibrium, but it quickly reaches equilibrium in year 3. The increase in government expenditures occurs at year 4, and the consequence is a rise in gross national product to a new equilibrium level in year 9. The increase in gross national product is more than three times the increase in government expenditures, demonstrating the multiplier effect due to the structure and parameters of the model. One might postulate other structural relationships or parameter values (such as lower or higher average propensity to consume) and observe effects of the same exogenous increase.

A more complicated aggregate model similar in structure to the one just discussed was developed by Holland and Gillespie to investigate problems of economic growth.[8] Their model, also programmed in DYNAMO, was used to explore the impact of planning, policy, and parameter variations on an underdeveloped economy.

Several econometric models have been developed with the objective of forecasting and analyzing economic conditions. The most ambitious of these is the Brookings-SSRC model, which contains over 300 equations (see Figure 4.2.).[9] The Brookings model uses a quarter of a year as its unit of time and includes error terms to represent uncertainties and random processes. The model can be used either as a one-period forecasting device or as a simulator, as described below.

> Suppose we are interested in the implications of the model for time period t. The reduced form equations contain lagged values of exogenous and endogenous variables for several time periods $t - 1$, $t - 2$, etc. These are taken as historically given. The set of lagged values relevant for the reduced form equations for period t is called the set of initial conditions.

---

[8]Edward P. Holland and Robert W. Gillespie, *Experiments on a Simulated Underdeveloped Economy: Development Plans and Balance-of-Payments Policies.* (Cambridge, Mass.: The Massachusetts Institute of Technology Press, 1963).

[9]*The Brookings Quarterly Econometric Model of the United States*, James S. Duesenberry, Gary Fromm, Lawrence R. Klein, and Edwin Kuh, eds. (Chicago: Rand McNally and Company, 1965).

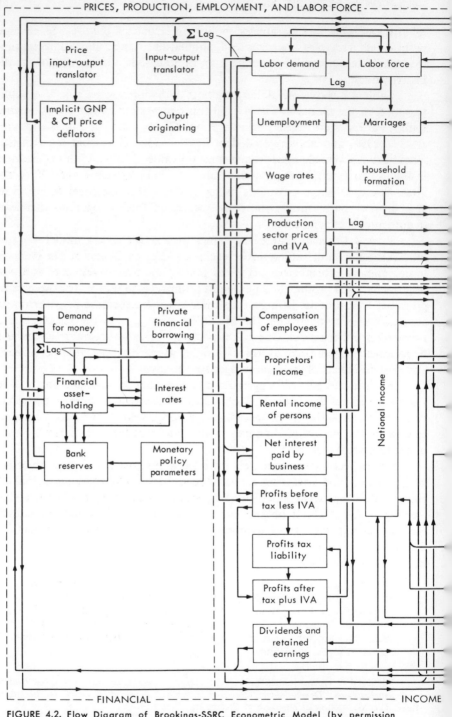

FIGURE 4.2. Flow Diagram of Brookings-SSRC Econometric Model (by permission from *The Brookings Quarterly Econometric Model of the United States,* James S. Duesenberry, Gary Fromm, Lawrence W. Klein and Edwin Kuh, Editors, Chicago: Rand McNally and Company, 1965)

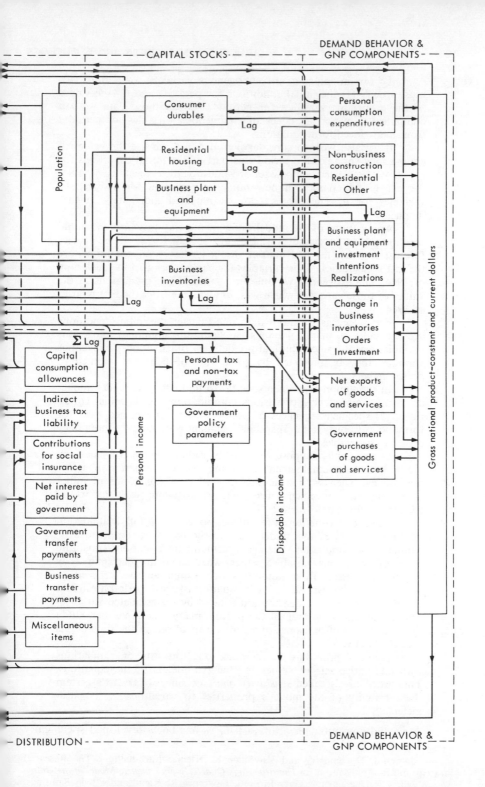

To obtain values of the endogenous variables for period t we must specify (1) the initial conditions for period t and (2) the values of the exogenous variables for period t. Given those data we can compute the numerical values of endogenous variables for period t from the reduced form equations.

If we also wish to consider period $t + 1$, we use the values of endogenous variables for period t as part of the initial conditions for $t + 1$. We must specify a new set of values for the exogenous variables for $t + 1$ and compute a new numerical solution for endogenous variables for it. The process can be repeated indefinitely in that manner.

Applications of the model differ in the way in which the initial conditions and exogenous variables are specified. For a one-quarter forecast for, say, the first quarter of 1964, the initial conditions are the historical values of the variables for periods prior to the beginning of 1964. The exogenous variables are independent predictions of the values of those variables which will, in fact, rule from the first quarter of 1964.

For a forecast of more than one quarter the initial conditions are the same as in the previous case and the nonpolicy exogenous variables are also unconditional predictions. But the policy exogenous variables may be predicted by some rule of behavior imputed to policy makers.

In simulation experiments we try to find what the model implies as to the consequences of various combinations of (1) initial conditions, (2) specified sequences of policy actions or specified rules for formation of policy, and (3) specified sequences of values of nonpolicy exogenous variables.

For example, suppose we were to follow the rule of balancing the budget at full employment and some rule for formation of monetary policy. Then we can ask: Under what combinations of initial conditions and movement of nonpolicy exogenous variables would we achieve full employment?

Since our equations are subject to error, a full examination of the properties of the model requires the use of random shock or Monte Carlo simulation. The error terms in the equations constitute a set of exogenous variables which we assume are determined by random processes. In a random shock simulation we proceed as before except that we add to each equation for each period a random variable drawn from a distribution defined by the estimated variance-covariance matrix. We repeat the process many times. We then study the distribution of outcomes of a forecast or of one of the simulations described above.

Another procedure is to work out forecasts or simulations with alternative sets of values for the parameters of the equations. This procedure is called *sensitivity analysis*, since we try to ascertain the sensitivity of the model's properties to variations of its parameters.[10]

A special computer program SIMULATE has been developed specifically

---

[10]James S. Duesenberry and Lawrence R. Klein, "Introduction: The Research Strategy and Its Application," in *The Brookings Quarterly Econometric Model of the United States*, James S. Duesenberry, Gary Fromm, Lawrence R. Klein, and Edwin Kuh, eds. (Chicago: Rand McNally and Company, 1965). pp. 10–11.

to run the Brookings model.[11] The reasons given for developing the program and using simulation as the basic technique for analysis are compelling.

> ... Verbal analysis supplemented with geometry have been the traditional tools for obtaining such insight, but increasingly economists have resorted to advanced calculus and matrix algebra for deepening their comprehension of complex systems. Unfortunately no body of mathematics exists for adequately treating large systems of assorted nonlinear dynamic relationships, but our recently increased ability to make numerical calculations with electronic computers opens the way for the experimental study of such systems.

> Equations that cannot be solved explicitly by mathematical operations to obtain an exact analytic solution often can be solved by numerical operations to obtain particular numerical solutions. This is the essence of simulation and the source of its power. However, the blind brute force search for the properties of a complex system offers us no panacea in the form of a self-sufficient methodology. . . . In a large simulation model the parameters are too many, the relationships too complex and the variables too numerous for generalizations to arise readily from the numerical exploration of a few points in a multi-dimensional space.

> Parallel mathematical analysis will be needed to aid in abstracting the essential behavior of such complex systems, and essentially mathematical insights will be needed to guide experimentation on simulation models.

> Complex nonlinear models will not, in general, be amenable to analytic solution in the foreseeable future. To obtain a mathematical problem that can be solved will require extensive simplifications. By sensitivity studies of the simulation model a great deal can be learned about simplifications that can be made without critically affecting the behavior of the system. In this way simulation studies can guide the search for mathematical formulations that can be *both* significant and analytically solvable. The insights gained from these solutions in turn should help in guiding the experimentation on and validation of complete simulation models. . . .

> ... The problem of controlling a complex dynamic economy may prove to be sufficiently difficult that statistical decision theory is needed to formulate policies that improve stability. In many industrial operations research analyses, finding a good decision strategy has required quite subtle and powerful tools. However, at the present time such analyses are not available for decision problems occurring in really complex systems, and it is likely for quite some time that we will have available approximate analyses that do not take into account the full complexity of the decision. These approximate methods can be evaluated by making simulation studies of the policies which they suggest, using the full complex nonlinear model.[12]

---

[11]Charles C. Holt, Robert Shirey, Donald V. Stewart, Joseph L. Midler, and Arthur H. Strand, *Program SIMULATE, a User's and Programmer's Manual.* University of Wisconsin, Social Science Research Institute, May, 1964. (Mimeographed.)

[12]Charles C. Holt, "Validation and Application of Macroeconomic Models Using Computer Simulation," in *The Brookings Quarterly Econometric Model of the United States*, James S. Duesenberry, Gary Fromm, Lawrence R. Klein, and Edwin S. Kuh, eds. (Chicago: Rand McNally and Company, 1965), pp. 640, 641, and 644.

Socioeconomic Systems

The econometric models discussed in the previous section dealt with aggregate variables, their interrelationship, and their behavior through time. In contrast, Orcutt and his associates have developed an approach to the analysis of economic systems which attacks the problem from the opposite direction, that of building up aggregate behavior through the simulation of individual units in the system.[13] The approach is justified as follows:

> Predictions about aggregates are needed, but they should be obtained by aggregating behavior of elemental units rather than by attempting to aggregate behavioral relationships of these elemental units. That is, aggregates should be obtained from a simulation of the real system in a fashion analogous to the way a census or survey obtains aggregates relating to real socioeconomic systems. Given a satisfactory simulation of the socioeconomic system developed in terms of the elemental decision-making units, aggregation of relationships would become more nearly feasible. Such aggregation would be interesting and useful, but it would no longer be a necessity.[14]

Although Orcutt's study had the long-range goal of simulating an entire socioeconomic system, the major work reported is on one portion of the system, the population sector. The basic structure of the simulation of this sector is to trace behavior of individual units of a model population made up of about 10,000 persons in approximately 4500 family units or households. In the computer simulation runs that were reported, the model population was initially given the same characteristics as the United States population in April, 1950 so that the model population approximated 1/15,000 of the United States population.

A simulation run consists of taking the initial population and moving it through successive increments of time, with the increment chosen to be one month as a matter of balance between computing time and accuracy. To accomplish this, data concerning the population were written on magnetic tape, and changes that take place in the population during a month were determined by making a single pass through the computer. On this pass the simulation program causes births, deaths, divorces, and marriages to occur in the population as it considers each household unit in turn. Probability distributions given to the program govern the occurrence of these basic events. The way in which the program operates is described below.

> ... suppose the simulation started with the month of January, 1960, and the first unit considered is an individual with the following characteristics (among others): male, white, age 34. We have already estimated the probability that an individual with these characteristics

---

[13]Guy H. Orcutt, Martin Greenberger, John Korbel, and Alice M. Rivlin, *Microanalysis of Socioeconomic Systems: A Simulation Study* (New York: Harper and Row, 1961).

[14]From p. 12 *Microanalysis of Socioeconomic Systems* by Guy H. Orcutt, *et al*. Copyright © 1961 by Harper & Row, Publishers, Incorporated. Used by permission of the publishers.

will die in this month at, say, 0.0002; i.e., this is the probability of death specified by the relevant operating characteristic. Now we make a random drawing from this distribution using random numbers generated by the machine for the purpose. There are two chances in 10,000 that the outcome of the draw will indicate *death* for this unit and 9998 that it will not. Depending on the outcome of the draw, the man either dies and is eliminated from the population (and from the household or other larger unit of which he may be a member) or he lives through the month.

In considering other aspects of a unit, there may, of course, be more than two possible outcomes. If the unit were a household, for example, the output *amount spent on durables* might have several possible values—$0, $1–100, $101–200, and so forth.

When each possible output for each unit has been considered in this way, the first pass, or month, is complete. We enter the second month with a population of units that is slightly different in both size and composition from the initial one. . . . The whole procedure is then repeated for the second month and for as many more as desired. To find out what has happened to the system at the end of, say, twelve months, we take a census and actually count the number of units with various characteristics or with combinations of characteristics.[15]

In addition to developing computer routines for performing the simulation, a great amount of effort was expended in getting accurate data to determine probabilities of births, deaths, marriages, and divorces. The reasonableness of the model was checked by making a trial run from April, 1950 to April, 1960 and comparing simulated behavior of the population with known actual behavior.[16] The model was then run experimentally to determine effects on the population of changing birth, death, marriage, and divorce probabilities.

Orcutt and his colleagues concluded that simulation is useful for determining aggregate behavior by simulating individual units. However, one cannot help but be impressed by the substantial effort necessary to simulate just births, deaths, marriages, and divorces. To extend the model to cover other sectors of a complete socioeconomic model in the same fashion will require many times the effort expended on the population sector.

Market Processes

There are two well-known simulation studies of market processes: Cohen's simulation of the shoe, leather, hide sequence[17] and Balderston and

---

[15]From pp. 29–30 *Microanalysis of Socioeconomic Systems* by Guy H. Orcutt, *et al.* Copyright © 1961 by Harper & Row, Publishers, Incorporated. Used by permission of the publishers. Details of specific mechanisms governing deaths, marriages, divorces, and births may be found in Chaps. 4, 5, 6, and 7 of this reference.

[16]An interesting feature of the structure of the simulation program is the provision of mechanisms for keeping the model "on the track" with respect to known data as the simulation proceeds. These mechanisms will be discussed in Chap. 8.

[17]Kalman J. Cohen, *Computer Models of the Shoe, Leather, Hide Sequence* (Englewood Cliffs, N.J.: Prentice-Hall, Inc., 1960).

Hoggatt's simulation of market processes based on the lumber industry.[18] Cohen's simulation resembles in some respects the econometric models discussed earlier in this chapter in that it deals with aggregate behavior of consumers, retailers, manufacturers, tanners, and hide dealers. Balderston and Hoggatt, on the other hand, deal with individual firms in the marketplace and their interactions with each other. Although both models attempt to explain and simulate market behavior, they offer an interesting contrast in model construction and data requirements. Cohen's model, like the econometric models described previously, relies heavily on the use of statistical methods such as regression and single equation least squares estimation to obtain values of parameters. On the other hand, Balderston and Hoggatt's model describes mechanisms by which individual firms in the marketplace interact with each other and no use is made of estimation procedures such as those used by Cohen. Emphasis, instead, is on a description of characteristics of firms in the market and decision rules used by them based on field studies of firms in the lumber market.

Cohen's model is composed of over 60 equations that relate in aggregate terms variables thought to be significant in the shoe, leather, hide sequence. These equations are similar in form to those in the econometric models discussed previously. That is, the equations generally relate values of variables for the current time period t to the values of other variables at the current time or to values of variables lagged one or more time periods in the past. To illustrate, in Cohen's model $Q(t)$, tanners' orders for all hides in month t, is found by[19]

$$Q(t) = C_{0,53} + C_{1,53} \, Hp(t-1) + C_{2,53} \, W(t) + C_{3,53} \, M_Q(t) \qquad \textbf{(4.7)}$$

where

$$Hp(t-1) = \text{average prices of hides in month } t-1$$

$$W(t) = \text{tanners' hide wettings in month } t$$

$$M_Q(t) = \text{average seasonal index in month } t \text{ for}$$
$$\text{tanners' orders for all hides}$$

and the C's are coefficients found by the use of the single equation least squares estimation technique[20] using historical data for the industry. The computer program written by Cohen determines values of the endogenous variables, such as $Q(t)$ above, for the current time period, writes these

---

[18]Frederick E. Balderston and Austin C. Hoggatt, *Simulation of Market Processes* (Berkeley: Institute of Business and Economic Research, University of California, 1962).

[19]Kalman J. Cohen, *Computer Models of the Shoe, Leather, Hide Sequence* (Englewood Cliffs, N.J.: Prentice-Hall, Inc., 1960), p. 47.

[20]See footnote 5.

values out on disk storage, and then repeats the computation for the next and succeeding time periods.

> In this manner, every "month" of the simulation generates the current values of each of the model's endogenous variables. These current values are transferred to the disks, where the endogenous variables are stored as time series. When the simulation has finished the final month, the time paths generated by the model for the entire period covered are punched out as complete time series, one variable at a time.[21]

Cohen actually produced two models which differ in the way in which values of the endogenous variables are handled during the simulation.

> ... One of these, Model II, is a process model. To the equations of Model II, the required past history, i.e., the actual values of some of the variables prior to 1930, and the observed time paths of the exogenous variables between 1930 and 1940 are adjoined. The resulting system is then used to generate time paths for all the endogenous variables between 1930 and 1940. Our other model, Model II E, is a one-period-change model, in which lagged values of the endogenous variables are replaced by their actually observed values.[22]

In effect, Model II E is constantly corrected for errors generated within the model, whereas Model II has no correction feature. After running both models and comparing values of eleven major endogenous variables obtained with actual observed values, Cohen concludes that his models "may incorporate some of the mechanisms which determine behavior in the shoe, leather, hide sequence."[23]

A complete comparison in chart form of the time series generated by the simulation model with actual observed values appears in Cohen's report of his work. These charts indicate that, although the model seems to simulate some aspects of the market process quite well, there are other aspects that are not well represented.

In contrast to Cohen's model, which relies heavily on statistical analysis of data regarding an industry, Balderston and Hoggatt's model is based on field studies of the way in which individual firms in the West Coast lumber market behave. Basic elements included in the simulation are three sets of participants in the market: manufacturers, wholesalers, and retailers linked together by flows of information, cash, and goods. Figure 4.3 illustrates this structure. In addition, there are demand functions for retailers which provide the driving force for the market process. For firms in the market, relatively simple asset and liability and cost structures are

---

[21]Kalman J. Cohen, *Computer Models of the Shoe, Leather, Hide Sequence* (Englewood Cliffs, N.J.: Prentice-Hall, Inc., 1960), p. 61.

[22]*Ibid.*, p. 16.

[23]*Ibid.*, p. 62.

specified, with parameter values selected to be consistent with observed characteristics of firms in the lumber market. To avoid biasing the results, each firm initially in the market at the three levels was made identical with other firms in that level. Initially, the market was set up with 20 manufacturers, 10 wholesalers, and 40 retailers with provision in the program for entry and exit of firms under specified conditions during the course of the simulation.

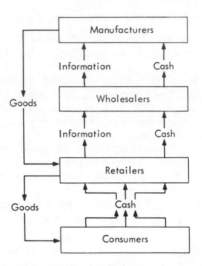

FIGURE 4.3. Structure of Lumber Market Simulation (by permission from Frederick E. Balderston and Austin C. Hoggatt, *Simulation of Market Processes,* Berkeley: Institute of Business and Economic Research, University of California, 1962)

Parameter values in the simulation were set to correspond to a basic market period of one month. Within this period, the program goes through a large number of market cycles, on the order of 50 to 100 per period, each of which is an attempt to arrange a transaction, all transactions are initiated by search messages from a wholesaler to retailers and manufacturers, since wholesalers are the only communication link. A flow chart of the method of generating transactions is shown in Fig. 4.4.

Since transactions are individual bargains among a wholesaler, a retailer, and a manufacturer and are dependent on the current characteristics of each, transactions may occur at different prices in the same market period. A market period is completed when the search for possible transactions is completed, a process that may result in differing numbers of market cycles per period. The unit cost of sending messages by wholesalers is an important parameter, and the total message cost is aggregated each time period.

In addition to creating transactions each period, decision rules in the simulation program make the following decisions each period.

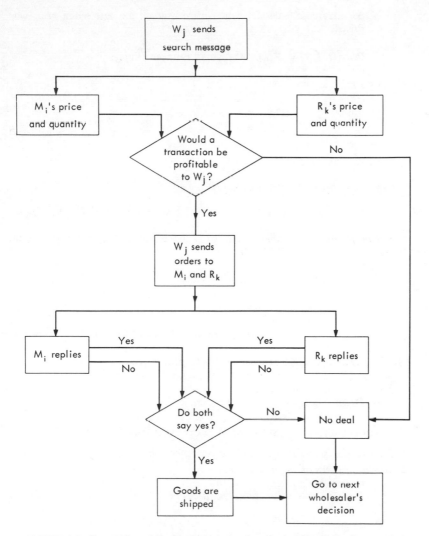

FIGURE 4.4. Generation of Transactions in Lumber Market Simulation (by permission from Frederick E. Balderston and Austin C. Hoggatt, *Simulation of Market Processes*, Berkeley: Institute of Business and Economic Research, University of California, 1962)

MANUFACTURERS' DECISIONS AT END OF EACH MARKET PERIOD

1. *Go out of business* if cash is negative, otherwise,
2. *Set offer price:*
   a. normal case (sales rose when price was cut, or fell when price was raised)

$$\text{Price } (t+1) = \text{Price } (t) + \frac{(\text{absolute change in price} \times \text{change in profit})}{\text{change in price} \times \text{scaling factor}}$$

   b. perverse case (sales fell when price was cut, or rose when price was
      raised)

   Price $(t + 1)$ = Price (t) + small random change

3. *Set output:*

   Output$(t + 1)$ = (Desired level of inventory)

   $$- \text{(actual level of inventory)}$$

4. *Set offer quantity:*

   Offer quantity $(t + 1)$ = (output $(t + 1)$

   $$+ \text{(inventory, end of } t)) \times \text{Buffer}$$

5. *Set preferences on wholesalers* (a or b chosen depending on experimental
   control parameter SWPREF):
   a. By experience:
       (1) compute, for each wholesaler

   $$H = \frac{\text{(number of transactions)}}{\text{(number of orders)}}$$
   $$\times \text{(total quantity shipped through this wholesaler)}$$

       (2) add small random factor to prevent ties
       (3) order wholesalers from highest value of H (best) to lowest
           value of H (worst)
   b. Order wholesalers by random choice

WHOLESALERS' DECISIONS AT END OF EACH MARKET PERIOD

1. *Go out of business if cash is negative,* otherwise,
2. *Set preferences on manufacturers*
   a. by past experience
       (same rule as for manufacturers)
       or
   b. by random choice
3. *Set preferences on retailers*
   a. by past experience
       (same rule as for manufacturers)
       or
   b. by random choice.

RETAILERS' DECISIONS AT END OF EACH MARKET PERIOD

1. *Pay wholesalers amount due for purchases in period (t).*
2. *Go out of business if cash is negative,* otherwise,
3. *Set quantity sold into final market,* to maximize expected profit.
4. *Set bid quantity:*

Quantity $(t + 1)$ = (Desired inventory in view of quantity sold into final market in period t) — (actual inventory)

5. *Set bid price:*

$P(t + 1) = P(t)$ + (difference between bid quantity for $(t + 1)$ and bid quantity for (t) × sensitivity parameter)

6. *Set preferences on wholesalers:*
   a. from past experience
      (same rule as for manufacturers)
      or
   b. by random choice.

OTHER DECISIONS, END OF EACH PERIOD

1. *Should there be new entry?*   Manufacturer
                                   Wholesaler
                                   Retailer
2. *Should there be another period?*   *Not* if this is the last period
                                        Not if market no longer has
                                           participants at some level
3. (On the average, every fifth period): *Expand or reduce* plant capacity.[24]

Balderston and Hoggatt report a series of eight computer runs, each 60 market periods in length. Each of the runs utilized a different combination of unit message cost and method of determining preferences of manufacturers, wholesalers, and retailers for doing business with each other. On the basis of these runs, they concluded that the simulation model is *viable* in that the market continued to operate during each run in a realistic way for the full 60 periods. They also found that the model appeared to reproduce market efficiency characteristics[25] and a size distribution of firms in the market as one would expect to find in the real world. Detailed charts of time paths of significant variables obtained during the eight runs are contained in the report of Balderston and Hoggatt. These charts suggest that the simulation is plausible in that output of the model is generally within the bounds of what one might expect to happen. Whether the model simulates the West Coast lumber industry is another matter, as no comparisons were made of the simulation model with behavior in the real world.

An interesting piece of information, not often contained in reports of research of this nature, is the summary of costs for constructing and

---

[24]Frederick E. Balderston and Austin C. Hoggatt, *Simulation of Market Processes* (Berkeley: Institute of Business and Economic Research, University of California, 1962), pp. 10–12.

[25]In the sense that profitable transactions were made up to the point of covering wholesale cost.

running the model. These costs amounted to over \$100,000 over a period of three years. Although modern computers and computer languages might reduce these costs somewhat, the costs incurred are indicative of the magnitude of effort and money that may be expended in the construction of simulation models, even of fairly modest scopes.

Estimation of Parameters in Econometric Models

In Chap. 2 a Monte Carlo approach to determining bias in the usual PERT calculations was discussed. Since the Monte Carlo approach did not involve analysis of behavior of a model through time, we termed the procedure model sampling rather than simulation. Model sampling has also been used to investigate the characteristics of techniques for estimating parameters of econometric models.[26]

To illustrate the nature of nature of the problem, let us rewrite the econometric model defined by Eqs. (4.1) through (4.6) in its complete form.[27]

$$C_t = \alpha_0 + \alpha_1 Y_t + \alpha_2 C_{t-1} + \mu_{1t} \tag{4.8}$$

$$I_t = \beta_0 + \beta_1 P_t + \beta_2 K_{t-1} + \mu_{2t} \tag{4.9}$$

$$W_t = \gamma_0 + \gamma_1 Y_t + \gamma_2 t + \mu_{3t} \tag{4.10}$$

$$Y_t = C_t + I_t + G_t \tag{4.11}$$

$$P_t = Y_t - W_t \tag{4.12}$$

$$K_t = K_{t-1} + I_t \tag{4.13}$$

Notice that the model in Eqs. (4.8) through (4.13) differs from the model in Eqs. (4.1) through (4.6) by the inclusion of μ_{1t}, μ_{2t}, and μ_{3t} in the first three equations.

> ... These terms, called disturbance terms, are included in explicit recognition of the fact that the other variables cannot fully explain movements of the dependent variables on the left-hand side. Assuming that no significant variables have been omitted, the disturbance terms can be regarded as reflecting random elements representing the net effect of a host of unknown and unpredictable factors. Ideally they are small so that the remaining ("systematic") part of each equation accounts for most of the movements in the dependent variable. The last three equations, because they hold by definition, contain no disturbance terms.[28]

---

[26]See footnote 5.

[27]This is the complete model discussed in the source referenced in footnote 4.

[28]Maurice Liebenberg, Albert A. Hirsch, and Joel Popkin, "A Quarterly Econometric Model of the United States: A Progress Report," *Survey of Current Business*, Vol. 46, No. 5 (May, 1966), p. 14.

As mentioned previously, statistical techniques have been developed for estimating values of parameters, the α's, β's, and γ's in Eqs. (4.8) through (4.10).[29] However, estimation techniques differ in their ability to yield parameter estimates with desirable properties, in particular, lack of bias and consistency. It is also difficult to ascertain the characteristics of different estimation techniques when small samples, typical of data actually available, are used. As a consequence, the Monte Carlo approach has been used to gain further information regarding properties of estimation techniques.

> ... The essence of the Monte Carlo approach is to postulate a model, and then to concentrate on one or more structures within the model by assigning specific numerical values to the parameters, including the elements of the variance-covariance matrix of the disturbances. For any such structure repeated samples of disturbances are drawn from the hypothesized disturbance distribution by using appropriate tables of random numbers. The sample size is usually chosen in the range 15 to 40, to reflect the small sample sizes with which econometricians typically have to work, at least in time-series analysis. In addition, arbitrary values are specified for the exogenous variables, and these are sometimes held constant from sample to sample and sometimes not. The exogenous variables are combined with the disturbance values for each sample to generate values for the endogenous variables. The estimating methods under study are then applied to each sample set of endogenous and exogenous values. This process is replicated a large number of times (typically 50, 100, or 200), and the resultant frequency distributions of estimates are studied in conjunction with the true values of the parameters in order to conjecture the small-sample properties of the estimators.[30]

An example of one such study of the properties of several estimation techniques is Schink's study of multicollinearity and autocorrelation in econometric models.[31] In this study, he postulated a simple two-equation hypothetical model similar to one used by Summers in a previous study.[32]

$$Y_1 - B_1 Y_2 + F_1 Z_1 + F_4 Z_4 + F_5 = U_1 \qquad \textbf{(4.14)}$$

$$-B_2 Y_1 + Y_2 - F_2 Z_2 + F_3 Z_3 + F_6 = U_2, \qquad \textbf{(4.15)}$$

---

[29]The development of a variety of methods, among them least squares, two-stage least squares, and limited-information single equation, has been prompted by such problems as the simultaneous equation nature of many econometric models, possibility of interdependence between observed values of a single variable, possibility of interrelatedness between the variables, and lack of independence of disturbance terms.

[30]J. Johnston, *Econometric Methods* (New York: McGraw-Hill Book Company, Inc., 1963), pp. 275–276.

[31]William A. Schink, "Effects of Multicollinearity and Autocorrelation on Estimates of Parameters," unpublished Master of Arts thesis (Seattle: University of Washington, 1965).

William A. Schink and John S. Y. Chiu, "Effects of Multicollinearity and Autocorrelation on Estimates of Parameters," *Journal of Financial and Quantitative Analysis*, Vol. 1, No. 2 (June, 1966).

[32]Robert Summers, "A Capital Intensive Approach to the Small Sample Properties of Various Simultaneous Equation Estimators," *Econometrica*, Vol. 33, No. 1, (January, 1965).

where the Y's are endogenous variables, the Z's are exogenous variables, U's are the disturbance terms, the B's are parameters of the endogenous variables, and the F's are parameters of the exogenous variables.[33] Values of the parameters were arbitrarily specified as follows: $B_1 = 1.75$, $B_2 = 1.50$, $F_1 = 0.25$, $F_2 = 0.30$, $F_3 = 0.15$, $F_4 = 0.20$, $F_5 = 1.51$, and $F_6 = 1.66$. Finally, the disturbance or error terms, the U's, were assumed to be independent.

Shink then generated fictitious time series data 25 periods in length for each of the Z's, the hypothetical exogenous variables. This was done in such a fashion that there was correlation between time series of the different variables, a property known as multicollinearity. Similarly, time series for the disturbance terms U_1 and U_2 were generated so that disturbances were auto-correlated; that is, a disturbance in one period affects that in the following period. This was accomplished through a Monte Carlo procedure using the relationship[34]

$$U_t = PU_{t-1} + e \qquad (4.16)$$

where

$U_t = $ disturbance term at time t

$U_{t-1} = $ disturbance term at time $t - 1$

$P = $ autocorrelation coefficient

$e = $ random quantity drawn by the Monte Carlo procedure from a normal distribution

By varying the value of P in Eq. (4.16) between 0 and 1, time series of disturbance terms can be generated, ranging from series with no correlation between successive values to series with very high correlation between successive values.

With time series for the Z's and U's thus specified and with assumed values of the B's and F's, time series for the Y's were obtained through the reduced form of the model specified by Eqs. (4.14) and (4.15).[35] This procedure generated time series for the exogenous and endogenous variables with

---

[33]William A. Schink and John S. Y. Chiu, "Effects of Multicollinearity and Auto-correlation on Estimates of Parameters," *Journal of Financial and Quantitative Analysis*, Vol. 1, No. 2 (June, 1966), pp. 44–45.

[34]*Ibid.*, p. 49.

[35]The reduced form of an econometric model is a system of equations which expresses the endogenous variables in terms of the exogeneous variables, parameters, and disturbance terms. An elementary explanation may be found in: Henri Theil, John C. G. Boot, and Teun Kloek, *Operations Research and Quantitative Economics: An Elementary Introduction* (New York: McGraw-Hill Book Company, 1965), pp. 75–77. A complete description of the method of generating the values of the endogenous variables is given in Appendix A of the previously referenced article by Schink and Chiu.

known autocorrelation and multicollinearity and with parameters and structure of the underlying model also known.[36]

Three parameter estimation procedures, least squares, limited information single equation, and two-stage least squares, were then applied to the artificially generated data to estimate parameters of the model. One application of the estimation procedure to one set of data would not necessarily yield "typical" results; therefore, the entire procedure for obtaining the time series of disturbance terms and endogenous variables and making parameter estimates was repeated to obtain representative samples. Since parameters of the model are known and the degree of multicollinearity and autocorrelation are controlled, conditions that would not be found in the real world, it is possible to compare the ability of the three estimation procedures to produce correct parameter estimates. On the basis of this model sampling procedure, Schink concluded that least squares was poorest of the three estimation procedures. The other two estimation procedures gave similar results when compared on the basis of mean square error or standard error. However, the limited information single equation technique was superior to two stages least squares in terms of amount of bias.

In summary, the study consisted of establishing a simple econometric model with known parameters, generating from the model artificial time series data including random disturbances, and applying the various estimation procedures to observe their ability to estimate correctly known parameters of the model. This technique enables the investigator to control completely the conditions of the study and, in effect, to create a setting in which results are not confounded by unknown or imprecisely known factors as they would be if actual economic data were used. Results, in a strict sense, apply only to the particular set of experiments performed, and it would be better to arrive at more general conclusions regarding characteristics of various estimating procedures by techniques which would ensure global applicability. But, in the absence of such methods, model sampling offers at least some basis for comparing estimating procedures.

Summary

Illustrations in this chapter have suggested uses of simulation in both micro and macro models of economic behavior and also for analyzing parameter estimation techniques. Of these applications probably the most immediately practical are those involving simulation to analyze the dynamic behavior of macro economic models and the use of model sampling to examine the efficiency of parameter estimation techniques. As our discussion has shown, simulation models dealing with individual units in an economic

---

[36]The procedure was repeated for conditions of "high," "medium," and "low" multicollinearity and "high," "medium," and "low" autocorrelation.

system are feasible as long as the number of units is kept relatively small or as long as the interactions are fairly simple. Programming complexities, lack of data regarding individual behavior, and computer hardware limitations, however, make it impossible at present to model large and complex economic systems in minute detail.

EXERCISES

4.1   A national income model based on savings and investment is defined by three equations

$$S_t = 0.05\,Y_{t-1}$$

$$I_t = 0.8(Y_t - Y_{t-1})$$

$$S_t = I_t$$

where Y is national income, S is savings, I is investment, and t is the time period. Simulate the behavior of this model for 10 periods, starting with an initial value for Y of 500.

4.2   A national income model is defined by the following equations

$$Y_t = C_t + I_t + G_t$$

$$C_t = 200 + 0.4\,Y_{t-1}$$

$$I_t = 75$$

where Y is national income, C is consumption, I is investment, G is government expenditures, and t is the time period. Initially government expenditures are 175 and national income is 750. In period 2 government expenditures increase to 190 and remain at that level. Simulate the behavior of the system through period 10 and trace the time paths of consumption and national income. (Note that what you have observed is the multiplier effect on national income due to the change in government expenditures.)

4.3   In the model in Exercise 4.2 substitute the following equation for I_t.

$$I_t = 75 + 1.5(C_{t-1} - C_{t-2})$$

Assume that government expenditures are initially 175, consumption is 500, and national income is 750. Government expenditures increase to 190 in period 2 and remain at that level. Simulate the behavior of the system through period 15 and trace the time paths of investment, consumption, and national income. Compare these results with the results obtained in Exercise 4.2. (Note that what you have observed is the multiplier-accelerator effect.)

4.4 Supply and demand for a commodity in a market are defined by

$$D_t = a - bP_t$$

$$S_{t+1} = cP_t$$

where D_t is quantity demanded, S_t is quantity supplied, P is price, t is the time period, and a, b, and c are parameters defining the supply and demand relationship for the commodity. Let us assume that the commodity is perishable so that the market price is the price at which all available supply can be sold, or that price for which

$$D_t = S_t$$

Simulate the market for 10 periods in each of the following cases, starting with an initial price of $7.50. Plot your results on a graph with quantity and price on the horizontal and vertical axes.

a. $a = 1000$, $b = 50$, $c = 40$

b. $a = 1000$, $b = 50$, $c = 50$

c. $a = 1000$, $b = 40$, $c = 50$

(Note that models of this type have been termed cobweb models for reasons which are apparent if the supply and demand curves are added to your plotted results.)

4.5 Simulate the behavior of the model in Exercise 4.1 for 10 periods when a disturbance term μ_t is added to the first equation. That is,

$$S_t = 0.05 Y_{t-1} + \mu_t$$

Assume that μ is uniformly distributed between -10 and $+10$. Compare your results with those obtained previously in Exercise 4.1.

4.6 Simulate the behavior of the model in Exercise 4.3 for 25 periods when the equation for C_t is replaced by

$$C_t = 200 + 0.4 Y_{t-1} + 25\mu_t$$

where μ_t is normally distributed with zero mean and unit variance.

4.7 Run the econometric model in Fig. 4.1 for 10 years, 40 quarters, using constants and initial values as shown in Fig. 4.1 and as described on p. 125 of the chapter. As in the demonstration run in the chapter, let government purchases from business increase to 110 and wage payments by government increase to 55 at year 4. However, change the model so that average propensity to consume APCON is a random quantity uniformly distributed between 0.91 and 0.99. Compare the results of your run, particularly the ending values, with those shown in Table 4.1.

4.8   In a population of 100 males at age 20, 80 per cent are employed and 20 per cent are unemployed. For those who are unemployed, the probability of finding a job in any year is 0.50. The probability that an employed individual loses his job in any year is 0.10. Yearly earnings of the employed males at age 20 are $5000. Yearly earnings of unemployed persons just becoming employed are $4500 regardless of any previous earning levels. The probability of a 10 per cent increase in earnings for an individual in any year is 0.20, the probability of a 5 per cent increase is 0.45, and the probability of no increase is 0.35. Simulate the changes that take place in this population over a period of 20 years, assuming that all changes in state for an individual occur just once at the end of each year. Trace the total income of the population and distribution of earnings level within the population over the 20 years.

4.9   Modify the model developed in Exercise 4.8 to include the following probabilities for becoming employed and unemployed.

Number of years unemployed	1	2	3	4	5 and over
Probability of becoming employed	0.50	0.40	0.30	0.20	0.10
Number of years employed	1	2	3	4 and over	
Probability of becoming unemployed	0.20	0.15	0.10	0.05	

Simulate the changes in the population over a period of 20 years, assuming that all changes take place for an individual just once at the end of each year. Trace the employment and income characteristics of the population over the 20 years.

BIBLIOGRAPHY

Adelman, Irma. "Long Cycles—A Simulation Experiment," *in Symposium on Simulation Models: Methodology and Applications in the Behavioral Sciences*, Austin C. Hoggatt and Frederick E. Balderston, eds. Cincinnati, Ohio: Southwestern Publishing Co., 1963.

Adelman, I. and F. Adelman, "The Dynamic Properties of the Klein-Goldberger Model," *Econometrica*, Vol. 27, No. 4 (October, 1959).

Balderston, F. E. and A. C. Hoggatt, *Simulation of Market Processes*. Berkeley: Institute of Business and Economic Research, University of California, 1962.

Baumol, William J. and Richard E. Quandt, "Rules of Thumb and Optimally Imperfect Decisions," *American Economic Review*, Vol. 54, No. 2, Part 1 (March, 1964).

Chu, Kong and Thomas H. Naylor, "A Dynamic Model of the Firm," *Management Science*, Vol. 11, No. 7 (May, 1965).

Clarkson, Geoffrey P. E. and Herbert A. Simon, "Simulation of Individual and Group Behavior," *American Economic Review*, Vol. 50, No. 5 (December, 1960).

Cohen, Kalman J., *Computer Models of the Shoe, Leather, Hide Sequence*. Englewood Cliffs, New Jersey: Prentice Hall, Inc., 1960.

Cohen, Kalman J., et al. "A General Model of Price and Output Determination," in *Symposium on Simulation Models: Methodology and Applications in the Behavioral Sciences*, Austin C. Hoggatt and Frederick E. Balderston, eds. Cincinnati, Ohio: Southwestern Publishing Co., 1963.

Cohen, Kalman J. and Richard M. Cyert, "Computer Models and Dynamic Economics," *Quarterly Journal of Economics*, Vol. 75, No. 1 (February, 1961).

de Leeuw, Frank, "Financial Markets in Business Cycles: A Simulation Study," *American Economic Review*, Vol. 54, No. 3 (May, 1964).

Duesenberry, James S., Otto Eckstein, and Gary Fromm, "A Simulation of the United States Economy in Recession," *Econometrica*, Vol. 28, No. 4 (October, 1960).

Duesenberry, James S., Gary Fromm, Lawrence R. Klein, and Edwin Kuh, eds., *The Brookings Quarterly Econometric Model*. Chicago: Rand McNally and Company, 1965.

Ferber, Robert E. and P. J. Verdoorn, *Research Methods in Economics and Business*. New York: The Macmillan Co., 1962, pp. 426–434.

Holland, Edward P., "Simulation of an Economy with Development and Trade Problems," *American Economic Review*, Vol. 52, No. 3 (June, 1962).

Holland, Edward P. and Robert W. Gillespie, *Experiments on a Simulated Underdeveloped Economy: Development Plans and Balance-of-Payments Policies*. Cambridge, Massachusetts: The Massachusetts Institute of Technology Press, 1963.

Holt, Charles C., "Linear Decision Rules for Economic Stabilization and Growth," *Quarterly Journal of Economics*, Vol. 76, No. 1 (February, 1962).

Holt, C. C., Robert Shirey, Donald Stewart, Joseph L. Midler, and Arthur H. Strand, *Program SIMULATE, A User's and Programmer's Manual*. University of Wisconsin, Social Science Research Institute, May, 1964. (Mimeographed.)

Johnston, J., *Econometric Methods*. New York: McGraw-Hill Book Company, Inc., 1963, Chap. 10.

Liebenberg, Maurice, Albert A. Hirsch, and Joel Popkin, "Quarterly Econometric Model of the United States: A Progress Report," *Survey of Current Business*, Vol. 46, No. 5 (May, 1966).

Morehouse, N. F., R. H. Strotz, and S. J. Horwitz, "An Electro-Analog Method for Investigating Problems in Economic Dynamics: Industry Oscillations," *Econometrica*, Vol. 18, No. 4 (October, 1950).

Morse, David C., "Evaluation of Industrial Dynamics for Simulation of the U. S. Economy." Unpublished MBA research report. Seattle: University of Washington, 1966.

Nagar, A. L., "A Monte Carlo Study of Alternative Simultaneous Equation Estimators," *Econometrica*, Vol. 28, No. 3 (July, 1960).

Neiswanger, W. A. and T. A. Yancey, "Parameter Estimates and Autonomous Growth," *Journal of American Statistical Association*, Vol. 54 (June, 1959).

Orcutt, Guy H., "Simulation of Economic Systems," *American Economic Review*, Vol. 50, No. 5 (December, 1960).

———— "Views on Simulation and Models of Social Systems," in *Symposium on Simulation Models: Methodology and Applications in the Behavioral Sciences*, Austin C. Hoggatt and Frederick E. Balderston, eds. Cincinnati, Ohio: Southwestern Publishing Co. 1963.

Orcutt, Guy H., Martin Greenberger, J. Korbel, and A. M. Rivlin, *Microanalysis of Socioeconomic Systems—A Simulation Study*. New York: Harper and Row, 1961.

Orr, Daniel, "Two Books on Simulation in Economics and Business," *Journal of Business*, Vol. 36, No. 1 (January, 1963.)

Preston, Lee E. and Norman R. Collins, *Studies in a Simulated Market*. Berkeley: Institute of Business and Economic Research, University of California, 1966.

Schink, William A., "Effects of Multicollinearity and Autocorrelation on Estimates of Parameters." Unpublished Master of Arts thesis. Seattle: University of Washington, 1965.

Schink, William A. and John S. Y. Chiu, "Effects of Multicollinearity and Autocorrelation on Estimates of Parameters," *Journal of Financial and Quantitative Analysis*, Vol. 1, No. 2 (June, 1966).

Shen, Stewart N. T., "A Simulation Study of the Effect of Errors in an Input-Output Model on Output Projections." Unpublished Master of Arts thesis. Seattle: University of Washington, 1966.

Summers, Robert, "A Capital Intensive Approach to the Small Sample Properties of Various Simultaneous Equation Estimators," *Econometrica*, Vol. 33, No. 1 (January, 1965).

Tustin, Arnold, *The Mechanism of Economic Systems*, 2nd ed. London: William Heinemann, Ltd., 1957.

Wagner, H. M., "A Monte Carlo Study of Estimates of Simultaneous Linear Structural Equations," *Econometrica*, Vol. 26, No. 1 (January, 1958).

Wolfe, Harry B., "Model of San Francisco Housing Market," *Socio-Economic Planning Sciences*, Vol. 1, No. 1 (September, 1967).

Yance, Joseph V., "A Model of Price Flexibility," *American Economic Reveiw*, Vol. 50, No. 3 (June, 1960).

Zymelman, Manuel, "A Stabilization Policy for the Cotton Textile Industry," *Management Science*, Vol. 11, No. 5 (March, 1965).

Heuristic Methods

5 The preceding chapters have dealt with simulation of processes that are principally physical or economic in nature, but it is also possible to simulate human decision and problem solving processes. In recent years increasing attention has been given to problem solving techniques and procedures, usually computerized, which are similar to, or which simulate, those that might be employed by intelligent problem solvers. The name "heuristic" has often been employed to describe methods of this type. Heuristic, however, is a broad term also used to describe methods that would probably not be thought of as simulations of human behavior or thought processes.

In this chapter we will discuss heuristic methods in general, including approaches that are clearly attempts to simulate thought and decision processes as well as some for which simulation is a less appropriate description. Regardless of where the line is drawn between heuristic methods that essentially simulate the decision maker's or problem solver's thought process and those that do not, the subject is an exciting one, since these methods offer possibilities for analysis and decision making in areas where formal mathematical structures or more traditional quantitative approaches are inadequate or computationally impractical.

Definition of Heuristics

The concept of heuristics is not new. The mathematician Polya credits the following men with important contributions.[1]

1. Pappus (lived around A.D. 300). He discussed an area of study which he termed analyomenous or "The Art of Solving Problems."
2. René Descartes (1596–1650). This famous mathematician and philosopher

---

[1]G. Polya, *How to Solve It* (Garden City, N.Y.: Doubleday & Company, Inc., 1957).

147

wrote *Discours de la Méthode* and left unfinished a manuscript, *Rules for the Direction of the Mind.*

3. Bernard Bolzano (1781–1848). The logician and mathematician included an extensive discussion of the rules and methodology of investigation in his book, *Wissenschaftslehre.*

According to Polya,

> Heuristic, or heuretic, or "ars inveniendi" was the name of a certain branch of study, not very clearly circumscribed, belonging to logic, or to philosophy or to psychology, often outlined, seldom presented in detail, and as good as forgotten today. The aim of heuristic is to study the methods and rules of discovery and invention. . . . Heuristic, as an adjective, means "serving to discover".[2]

Polya also describes what he terms the modern approach to heuristics.

> Modern heuristic endeavors to understand the process of solving problems, especially the mental operations typically useful in this process.[3]

Simon has made the following observations concerning heuristics and heuristic programing. Heuristics are

> . . . rules of thumb, that allow us to factor, approximately, the complex perceived world into highly simple components and to find, approximately and reasonably reliably, the correspondences that allow us to act on that world predictably.[4]

Heuristic programing is

> . . . a point of view in the design of programs for complex information processing tasks. This point of view is that the programs should not be limited to numerical processes, or even to orderly systematic nonnumerical algorithms of the kinds familiar from the more traditional uses of computers, but that ideas should be borrowed also from the less systematic, more selective, processes that humans use in handling those many problems that have not been reduced to algorithm.[5]

Clarkson provides an additional concept for consideration.

> When the rules or heuristics for processing information yield results consistent with those obtained by human subjects, the model is said to have 'simulated' the decision process—that is, the set of heuristics is sufficient to 'simulate' the behavior of the subject.[6]

---

[2]G. Polya, *How to Solve It* (Garden City, N.Y.: Doubleday & Company, Inc., 1957), pp. 112–3.

[3]*Ibid.,* pp. 129–30.

[4]Herbert A. Simon and Allen Newell, "Simulation of Human Thinking," in *Management and the Computer of the Future,* Martin Greenberger, ed. (New York: John Wiley & Sons, Inc., 1962), p. 113.

[5]Herbert A. Simon, *The New Science of Management Decision.* (New York: Harper & Row, Publishers, 1960), p. 30.

[6]Geoffrey P. E. Clarkson, *Portfolio Selection: A Simulation of Trust Investment* (Englewood Cliffs, N.J.: Prentice-Hall, Inc., 1962), p. 4.

Tonge defines heuristics as

> ... principles or devices that contribute, on the average, to the reduction of search in problem-solving activity.

and heuristic programing as

> ... the construction of problem-solving programs organized around such principles and devices.[7]

Finally, Kuehn and Hamburger provide still another definition.

> We prefer to look at heuristic programming as an approach to problem solving where the emphasis is on working towards optimum solution procedures rather than optimum solutions.[8]

The foregoing definitions are representative rather than exhaustive. Although these points of view are not directly contradictory, it is obvious that substantial differences exist. Differences in scope can be explained by the fact that the statements were tailored to the specific application of heuristics under consideration by the author.

Polya was emphasizing the usefulness of heuristics in the improvement of instruction in mathematics. Since his work predates the major advances in electronic data processing, his definitions are not computer oriented. Simon and Clarkson emphasize the use of computer programs to replicate rules of thumb utilized by human decision makers. Tonge requires that a reduction of search in problem solving be achieved. However, it is not required that the pattern of human problem solvers be followed. Kuehn and Hamburger incorporate the requirement that program improvement be accomplished in order to work toward optimum solution procedures.

For purposes of our discussion it is useful to think of heuristic methods as a master set containing three subsets as in Fig. 5.1. (Note that the subsets are shown to be overlapping, since they cannot be defined so that they are mutually exclusive.) We define the three subsets as follows:

Heuristic problem solving: Problem-oriented use of heuristics to achieve a reduction of search in the attainment of a satisfactory solution.

Artificial intelligence: The use of computer-oriented heuristics in programs that may accomplish one or more of the following:

1. Search—the systematic investigation of the solution space.
2. Pattern recognition—the acceptance of certain groupings of elementary units as identifiable entities.
3. Organization planning—the breaking down of a complex problem into subproblems, the sequencing of analysis according to priorities and recombination into a solution of the higher level problem.

---

[7]Fred M. Tonge, "The Use of Heuristic Programming in Management Science," *Management Science*, Vol. 7, No. 3 (April, 1961), p. 221.

[8]Alfred A. Kuehn and Michael J. Hamburger, "A Heuristic Program for Locating Warehouses," *Management Science*, Vol. 9, No. 4 (July, 1963), p. 644.

More sophisticated programs of this class may also include:

1. Learning—program modification resulting from experience.
2. Inductive inference—generalization for the purpose of prediction and decision making.

The orientation is toward efficient use of the computer to obtain apparently intelligent behavior rather than to attempt to reproduce the step-by-step thought process of a human decision maker.

Simulation of human thought: The use of a heuristic computer program to replicate thought process of a human decision maker. The major criterion is exactness of subject simulation rather than efficiency of problem soluton.

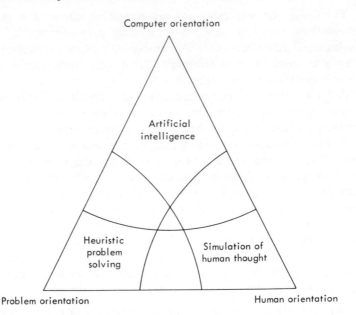

FIGURE 5.1. The Subsets of Heuristic Methods

Heuristic Problem Solving

Kuehn and Hamburger have developed a heuristic approach to solving the problem of locating warehouses where it is desired to equate the "marginal cost of warehouse operation with the transportation cost savings and incremental profits resulting from more rapid delivery."[9] A flow diagram of the heuristic program used to solve the problem is shown in Fig. 5.2.

The program utilizes three problem-oriented heuristics.

(1) Most geographical locations are not promising sites for a regional

---

[9]Alfred A. Kuehn and Michael J. Hamburger, "A Heuristic Program for Locating Warehouses," *Management Science*, Vol. 9, No. 4 (July, 1963), p. 643.

warehouse; locations with promise will be at or near concentration of demand.[10]

The problem is reduced by this rule from one with nearly an infinite number of possibilities to a problem which is finite. In fact it was found necessary in a trial problem to consider only 24 concentrations of demand as potential warehouse sites.

(2) Near optimum warehousing systems can be developed by locating warehouses one at a time, adding at each stage of the analysis that warehouse which produces the greatest cost savings for the entire system.[11]

The above heuristic permits analysis of the problem as one of step-wise minimization. Resulting from this heuristic is a reduction of the number of required cost evaluations from 2^M to M^2, where M is the number of potential warehouse sites being considered. For a problem with 24 warehouse sites the values are

$$2^{24} = 16,777,216$$

$$24^2 = 576$$

(3) Only a small subset of all possible warehouse locations need be evaluated in detail at each stage of the analysis to determine the next warehouse site to be added.[12]

An operational statement of this heuristic is: Evaluate the M potential warehouse locations, considering only the cost saving if *local* demand were supplied by that warehouse. Rank sites in order of potential local saving and select N of the locations that rank the highest. The N locations are called the intermediate buffer and are analyzed in detail to evaluate the cost savings which would accrue to the total system. A reduction in search is accomplished from M^2 combinations to $N \times M$. If the intermediate buffer were equal to five, only 120 (i.e., 5×24) evaluations would be required.

The second stage in the program is utilized after all M potential warehouse sites have either been assigned a warehouse or eliminated. This stage is called the bump-shift routine. Warehouses placed early in the procedure may become uneconomical as the result of later site selection. These warehouses are eliminated from the solution. A second function accomplished by the bump-shift routine is determining if a cost savings can be accomplished by moving a warehouse to another site within its territory (the territory is defined as those warehouse sites that are served by the warehouse being evaluated). If savings can be accomplished, the move is made.

---

[10]Alfred A. Kuehn and Michael J. Hamburger, "A Heuristic Program for Locating Warehouses," *Management Science*, Vol. 9, No. 4 (July, 1963), p. 645.

[11]*Ibid.*, p. 645.

[12]*Ibid.*, p. 645.

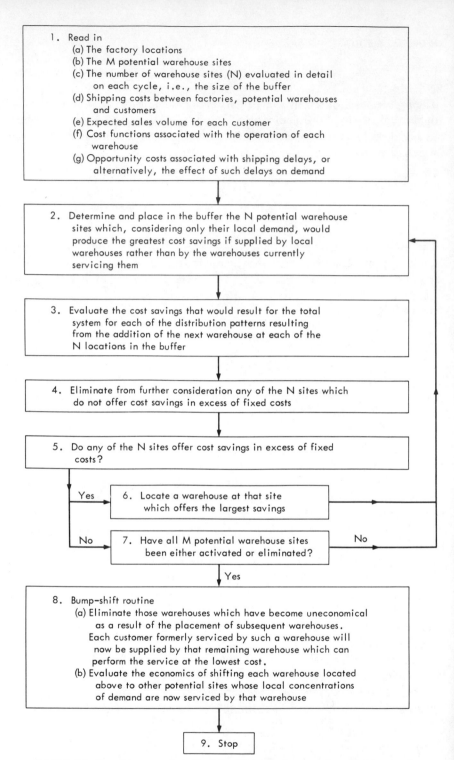

1. Read in
   (a) The factory locations
   (b) The M potential warehouse sites
   (c) The number of warehouse sites (N) evaluated in detail
       on each cycle, i.e., the size of the buffer
   (d) Shipping costs between factories, potential warehouses
       and customers
   (e) Expected sales volume for each customer
   (f) Cost functions associated with the operation of each
       warehouse
   (g) Opportunity costs associated with shipping delays, or
       alternatively, the effect of such delays on demand

2. Determine and place in the buffer the N potential warehouse
   sites which, considering only their local demand, would
   produce the greatest cost savings if supplied by local
   warehouses rather than by the warehouses currently
   servicing them

3. Evaluate the cost savings that would result for the total
   system for each of the distribution patterns resulting
   from the addition of the next warehouse at each of the
   N locations in the buffer

4. Eliminate from further consideration any of the N sites which
   do not offer cost savings in excess of fixed costs

5. Do any of the N sites offer cost savings in excess of fixed
   costs?

Yes

6. Locate a warehouse at that site
   which offers the largest savings

No

7. Have all M potential warehouse sites
   been either activated or eliminated?

No

Yes

8. Bump-shift routine
   (a) Eliminate those warehouses which have become uneconomical
       as a result of the placement of subsequent warehouses.
       Each customer formerly serviced by such a warehouse will
       now be supplied by that remaining warehouse which can
       perform the service at the lowest cost.
   (b) Evaluate the economics of shifting each warehouse located
       above to other potential sites whose local concentrations
       of demand are now serviced by that warehouse

9. Stop

FIGURE 5.2. Flow Diagram of a Heuristic Program for Locating Werehouses (by
permission from Alfred A. Kuehn and Michael J. Hamburger, "A
Heuristic Program for Locating Warehouses," *Management Science*,
Vol. 9, No. 4, July, 1963)

　　Kuehn and Hamburger tested their program on 12 sample problems involving location of warehouses in a distribution system with 50 markets, or concentrations of demand, and either one or two factories. In these test problems costs associated with the initial "no warehouses" configuration were lowered by adding or adding and deleting warehouses through application of the heuristics outlined above. Kuehn and Hamburger noted that in four of the test problems a minor adjustment in the final warehouse configuration would improve the solution slightly, but in the other eight cases no improvement on the solution could be found. Since computationally feasible optimizing techniques were not available, there was no way to determine whether better solutions were possible. Feldman, Lehrer, and Ray have since reported improving somewhat on Kuehn and Hamburger's solutions by using a different set of heuristics.[13] Recently a branch and bound algorithm has been used for the same general type of problem,[14] but no direct comparisons have been reported of the results and computer running time of a heuristic program versus the results and running time of the branch and bound algorithm.

　　Layout planning is another area in which heuristic problem solving methods have been developed. The layout planning problem, simply stated, is that of determining a configuration of activity areas which optimizes the location relationships between the activity areas. The complexity of the layout planning problem depends on the number of factors considered during the solution process. Some of these factors are the criteria to be used in evaluating layouts, restrictions on locations of certain activity areas, restrictions on the shape of the building, and restrictions on aisle and corridor locations. To arrive at a "best solution" to a layout planning problem, some comprehensive means of structuring the criteria and restrictions must be found. In practice, the layout planning problem has usually been solved by manual trial and error methods in which a number of alternative layouts are developed and evaluated on an intuitive basis. For a computerized layout planning procedure to improve on the intuitive method, the procedure must incorporate significant factors which influence the problem. Rigorous mathematical approaches to the layout planning problem have been difficult to apply, as the mathematical structures are often too rigid to accept the relevant factors and become too large to be computationally feasible.

　　One of the salient characteristics of the layout problem is that, in most cases, there are a large number of possible layouts to evaluate. As an example, consider the problem of locating n activity areas of equal size and shape in n locations of the same size and shape in a building. There are $n!$ different layouts that can be generated, since the first area could go into any one of n locations, the next area into any one of $n - 1$ locations, and so forth. Depending on the outside shape of the enclosed space, some of the $n!$

---

　　[13]E. Feldman, F. A. Lehrer, and T. L. Ray, "Warehouse Location under Continuous Economies of Scale," *Management Science*, Vol. 12, No. 9 (May, 1966), pp. 678–679.

　　[14]M. A. Efroymson and T. L. Ray, "A Branch-Bound Algorithm for Plant Location," *Operations Research*, Vol. 14, No. 3 (May–June, 1966).

configurations will have one or more activity areas that differ in their absolute locations when compared with another. There are a number of these configurations, however, which have identical distances between each activity area and every other activity area, that is, the same relative locations. For instance, in the case of $n!$ configurations having the same rectangular outside shape, the total number of different relative configurations is $n!/4$, since layouts can be rotated about their length and width, giving different absolute locations but the same relative locations. In the case of 16 areas of equal size located in a rectangular area, there are 2.0923×10^{13} absolutely different arrangements and 5.1857×10^{12} relatively different arrangements. It is apparent that regardless of whether the analyst in interested in absolutely or relatively different layouts, the problem is often beyond the capacity of even the largest digital computer if an exhaustive search is to be conducted for an optimum layout.

To illustrate a heuristic approach to the problem, we will discuss a program developed by Anderson.[15] The method used in this program to reduce the number of alternatives to be searched is similar to the method described by Armour and Buffa.[16] Essentially it consists of starting with a configuration and examining one at a time all possible exchanges of location between pairs of activity areas. If there are n activity areas in a configuration, then there are $n(n - 1)/2$ possible exchanges to consider. The exchange that produces the greatest improvement over the initial configuration is used to produce a new configuration. The exchange process is repeated for a series of configurations until one is found which cannot be improved by further exchanges. This heuristic approach drastically reduces the amount of search required but does not provide a provable optimum solution. The final solution is dependent, in part, on the initial configuration used to start the process.

The criterion used is that of total circulation cost, or cost of movement between activity areas. The number of trips between activity areas is input data (in the form of a matrix) to the heuristic program, as is cost of movement per unit distance. For any configuration, total circulation cost is the product of number of trips between areas, distance between areas (measured between the centers of the areas), and cost per unit distance. The program is based on the following assumptions about the characteristics of the problem:

1. Activity areas to be located have a given area.
2. The outside shape of the building is rectangular with dimensions given.
3. A single aisle of a given width runs the length of the building.

[15]Thomas R. Anderson, "Layout Planning for Minimum Circulation Cost," unpublished Master of Science thesis (Seattle: University of Washington, 1965).

[16]Gordon C. Armour and Elwood S. Buffa, "A Heuristic Algorithm and Simulation Approach to Relative Location of Facilities," *Management Science*, Vol. 9, No. 2 (January, 1963). The computer program, called CRAFT, is further described in Elwood S. Buffa, Gordon C. Armour, and Thomas E. Vollmann, "Allocating Facilities with 'CRAFT'," *Harvard Business Review* (March–April, 1964). CRAFT is available as a SHARE program for users of IBM computers.

4. The aisle can be moved across the width of the building to provide the proper amount of area on each side of the aisle as exchanges of location are made between activity areas of different size.

5. An activity area can be any rectangular shape which provides the required area and whose length-to-width ratio falls within specified limits.

6. Activity areas may be fixed in location, if desired.

The program has been tested on a problem solved manually by Reed.[17] Successive stages in the solution of the problem are shown in Fig. 5.3(a) through (e). The final solution in Fig. 5.3(e) is within 1.15 per cent of the solution obtained by Reed. Different input configurations may produce somewhat different results. Also, one slight difference between Reed's solution and the solution obtained by the heuristic program is that Reed placed one activity area across the end of the building. The heuristic program does not permit this possibility, since it was felt to be an undesirable configuration.

An interesting feature of the heuristic method, which can be seen in Fig. 5.3, is the way in which the aisle is shifted across the building as necessary to provide exactly the required amount of space on each side of the aisle. At the same time, the shapes of the activity areas are adjusted to compensate for movement of the aisle. Activity areas are always kept rectangular, and their length-to-width ratio is kept within given upper and lower limits to avoid unreasonably narrow shapes.

Besides the approaches which we have discussed, some other techniques proposed for the layout problem are a branch and bound method and a quadratic assignment algorithm.[18] An excellent evaluation of the comparative efficiency of the various techniques has been made by Nugent.[19] At present, there is no single approach to the layout problem which is best in terms of both quality of solution and computer running time. However, several methods are promising improvements over former manual methods, and they are computationally feasible.

Warehouse location and layout problems are good examples of the types of problems for which heuristic problem solving techniques have been suggested. In each case, there are many alternative solutions to be examined, in most instances too many to be completely enumerated even by a computer, and computationally feasible optimizing algorithms have been lacking. In this kind of situation heuristic programs have been found to be useful devices, since they provide reasonably good solutions at relatively low cost. Heuristic approaches are also usually more flexible than more rigorous algorithms,

---

[17]Ruddell Reed, *Plant Layout* (Homewood, Ill.: Richard D. Irwin, Inc., 1961), p. 216.

[18]See J. W. Gavett and Norman V. Plyter, "The Optimal Assignment of Facilities to Locations by Branch and Bound," *Operations Research*, Vol. 14, No. 2 (March–April, 1966); and Frederick S. Hillier and Michael M. Connors, "Quadratic Assignment Problem Algorithms and the Location of Indivisible Facilities," *Management Science*, Vol. 13, No. 1 (September, 1966).

[19]Christopher E. Nugent, Thomas E. Vollmann, and John Ruml, "An Experimental Comparison of Techniques for the Assignment of Facilities to Locations," *Operations Research*, Vol. 16, No. 1 (January-February, 1968).

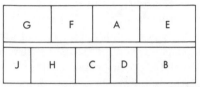

(a) Input configuration, total circulation cost: $91109.08

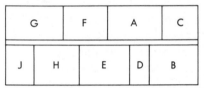

(b) First exchange. Total circulation cost: $81296.90

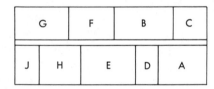

(c) Second exchange. Total circulation cost: $79629.99

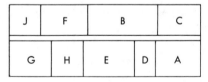

(d) Third exchange. Total circulation cost: $74746.98

(e) Fourth exchange. Total circulation cost: $74312.81

Minimum cost based on input configuration

FIGURE 5.3. Stages in Heuristic Solution of Layout Problem

since they do not require that the problem be formulated in any rigid mathematical structure.

Artificial Intelligence

Some computer approaches to assembly line balancing fall within our definition of artificial intelligence, particularly with respect to pattern recognition and organization planning. The line-balancing problem typically occurs in mass production industries where work elements must be performed on each unit processed by the line within a given set of sequencing limitations. The problem is to combine elements into a series of work stations capable of meeting a desired rate of production. The objectives are to create stations that do not exceed the maximum amount of time that may be taken at each station, to equalize the amount of work assigned to each station, and to minimize the number of work stations on the line.

As an illustration, consider the assembly of a small jewelry box. Parts to be assembled are the bottom, four sides, four leg brackets, four legs, two hinges, the top, and the two halves of a lock. Work elements, element times, and sequencing limitations for assembling the box are given in Table 5.1. Figure 5.4 is a diagram of the sequencing restrictions.

Table 5.1   ELEMENTS FOR ASSEMBLING JEWELRY BOX

Element	Description	Element Must Follow	Time (sec)
1	Screw leg brackets to bottom	—	36
2	Attach hinges to lid	—	26
3	Attach top half of lock to lid	—	5
4	Assemble four sides and bottom	—	15
5	Attach hinges and lid to back side	2, 3, 4	30
6	Screw four legs onto leg brackets	1, 4	9
7	Position bottom half of lock and attach to front side	5	7
		Total	128

If a production rate of one box per minute or one box per 60 seconds were required, then each work station could perform elements having a total time of not more than 60 seconds. Under these circumstances, at least three

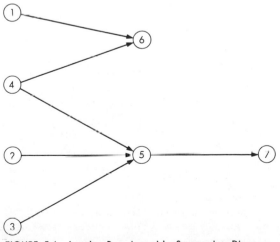

FIGURE 5.4. Jewelry Box Assembly Sequencing Diagram

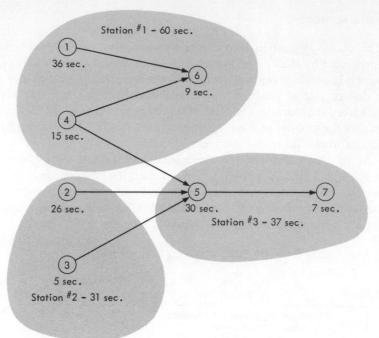

(a) Solution with considerable imbalance between stations.

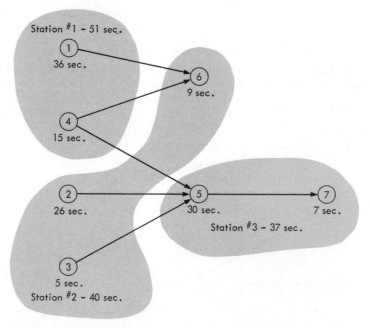

(b) Solution with improved balance between stations.
FIGURE 5.5. Assembly Line with Three Stations for 60-Second Cycle

work stations would be required, since it would be impossible for two stations to perform the required total of 128 seconds of work on each unit during a 60-second cycle. Figure 5.5(a) and (b) illustrate two possible methods of grouping the elements into three work stations. Of these, the second is preferable, since the total amount of work at each station is more evenly distributed.

A characteristic of the problem worth noting is that for a 60 second cycle, efficiency of the line (utilization of workers on the line) cannot be better than $128/3(60) = 71$ per cent. Figure 5.5(b) indicates that the line could just as well be run on a 51-second cycle with the same three men, in which case efficiency would rise to $128/3(51) = 84$ per cent.

Now let us look at another characteristic that is typical of line balancing problems. Theoretically, the minimum cycle time for a three-station jewelry box line should be $128/3 = 42.3$ seconds, and efficiency would then be 100 per cent. However, because of the indivisibility of basic work elements and sequencing restrictions, it is impossible to devise three work stations that would meet the requirements. A cycle time of 45 seconds can be obtained with three workers with the work stations shown in Fig. 5.6, and an efficiency of $128/3(45) = 95$ per cent is obtained. If a production rate is required which necessitates a cycle time of 44 seconds, four stations would be required with efficiency dropping to $128/4(44) = 73$ per cent.

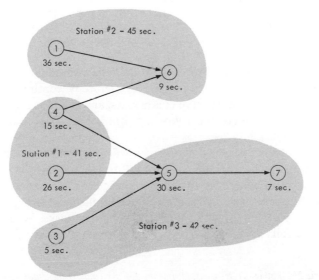

FIGURE 5.6. Assembly Line with Three Stations for 45-second Cycle

In practice, line-balancing problems are considerably more difficult to analyze than the preceding illustration because of the size of the problems and addition of zoning restraints which place restrictions on permissible combinations of elements. As a result, the person responsible for establishing work stations and their content may take hours to arrive at a reasonably balanced line. Procedures used in hand solutions of larger problems are similar to the trial and error method used in solving the preceding problem. As yet no computationally feasible mathematical algorithms have been developed for line balancing, nor are exhaustive search procedures possible in large problems, since there are usually too many possible combinations of elements that would have to be considered.

Tonge has developed a computer program for line balancing using heuristics which avoids the problem of searching all possible combinations of elements into work stations.[20] On the assumption that the sequencing limitations such as those shown in Table 5.1 or Fig. 5.4 have been established, the program operates in three major phases.[21]

In the first phase the program factors the heterogeneous environment of work elements into recognizable patterns. These patterns are:

1. Chain—"a group of adjacent elements whose relative order is completely determined, each except the first having a single direct predecessor and each except the last having a single direct follower."[22]
2. Set—"a group of elements whose relative order is completely unspecified, all having the same direct predecessors and followers."[23]
3. Z—"a group of four elements with the two front elements having common predecessors and the other two back elements having common followers. The single follower of one front element is one of the back elements; the two direct followers of the other front element are the back elements. The back elements have no other direct predecessors."[24]

The program attempts to develop a single compound chain that has chains, sets, and Z's as its elements. The hierarchy continues, since these elements may also be composed of chains, sets, and Z's. The number of levels is dependent upon the complexity of the problem. A flow chart of the first phase is shown in Fig. 5.7.

Output of the first phase serves as a starting point for activities of the second phase, which generates solutions through modification of the first phase output. Components of the second phase include an allocation routine and regrouping routines. Allocation is accomplished through a recursive procedure for matching work stations and groups of tasks. When the assignment routine fails, five regrouping procedures may be used by the program.

[20]Fred M. Tonge, *A Heuristic Program for Assembly-Line Balancing* (Englewood Cliffs, N.J.: Prentice-Hall, Inc., 1961).
[21]The program is written in IPL-IV, a language which will be discussed in Chap. 7.
[22]*Ibid.*, p. 20.
[23]*Ibid.*, p. 20.
[24]*Ibid.*, p. 21.

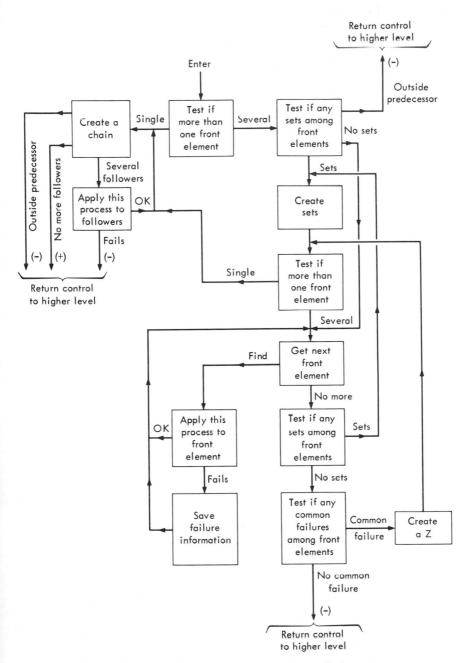

FIGURE 5.7. Flow Diagram of First Phase of Line Balancing Program (by permission from Fred M. Tonge, *A Heuristic Program for Assembly Line Balancing*, Englewood Cliffs, New Jersey: Prentice-Hall, Inc., 1961)

These are direct transfer, trading, sequential grouping, complete grouping, and exhaustive grouping. The program makes a choice of the regrouping routine (or routines) to be used, depending on the characteristics of the problem at that point. Figure 5.8 is a flow diagram of the second phase.

Once a satisfactory solution is obtained in the second phase, an attempt is made in the third phase to improve this solution by equalizing the work load between stations. This is accomplished by using transfer and trading

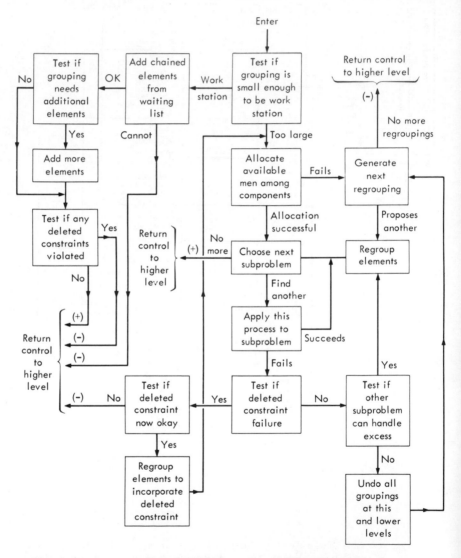

FIGURE 5.8. Flow Diagram of Second Phase of Line Balancing Program (by permission from Fred M. Tonge, *A Heuristic Program for Assembly Line Balancing*, Englewood Cliffs, New Jersey: Prentice-Hall, Inc., 1961)

heuristics described previously to reduce the time requirement of the largest work station. As reduction is accomplished, a new station will now become the largest and the procedure is repeated. The flow diagram for the third phase is shown in Fig. 5.9.

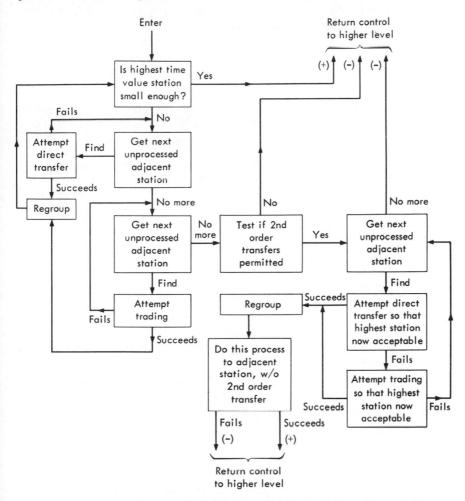

FIGURE 5.9. Flow Diagram of Third Phase of Line Balancing Program (by permission from Fred M. Tonge, *A Heuristic Program for Assembly Line Balancing*, Englewood Cliffs, New Jersey; Prentice-Hall, Inc., 1961)

Tonge solved three sample problems by the program, an eleven-element problem and a 21-element problem previously considered as examples by other authors and a 70-element problem representing actual applicance industry data. An industrial engineer's solution of the 70-element problem required 27 workmen, which exceeded by one the 26 determined by Tonge's program. Although learning was not included, Tonge comments that a learning routine could be incorporated to determine which heuristics tend to require less computing effort.[25]

Another example of work that falls under our definition of artificial intelligence is the study by Dickson of vendor selection by purchasing agents.[26] Dickson wrote a computer program designed to simulate decisions by particular purchasing agents regarding selection of vendors. We classify this study as an example of artificial intelligence rather than simulation of human thought, since there was no attempt to duplicate the thought process itself. Rather, emphasis was on producing the same decisions in given situations as the purchasing agents had made themselves.

The study was oriented around four hypothetical purchasing situations: purchase of paint, desks, a computer, and art work. For instance, in the case of paint, the hypothetical purchasing situation was as follows:

> A large company whose principal product is industrial chemicals has scheduled the repainting of the interior walls of its manufacturing plant. The painting is complicated due to the fact that all painted surfaces are subject to severe chemical fumes which tend to make paint deteriorate. Fortunately the surfaces to be painted are of a common substance, cement. It is estimated that 10 barrels of paint will be sufficient for the project. The necessary labor will be furnished under contract by a reliable painting firm.[27]

Dickson first determined the five factors, in addition to price, which a large group of purchasing agents considered to be most significant in the selection of a vendor for each of the four items. In the case of paint, delivery, procedural compliance, quality, technical capability, and guarantees were the significant factors other than price. Different sets of factors were significant for other purchased items.

Through trial and error, verbal descriptions of three different levels of significant factors for the four items were defined. Again with paint being used as an example, levels for the delivery factor were

Level i: Expected to be able to deliver within two days of the specified date at least 95 times out of 100.

Level j: Expected to be able to deliver within five days of the specified date at least 95 times out of 100.

Level k: Expected to be able to deliver within two weeks of the specified date at least 95 times out of 100.[28]

---

[25]For a discussion by Tonge of subsequent work on the utilization of learning in the selection of heuristics to be used, see: Fred M. Tonge, "Assembly Line Balancing Using Probabilistic Heuristics," *Management Science*, Vol. 11, No. 7 (May, 1965).

[26]Gary W. Dickson, "Decision-Making in Purchasing: A Simulation Model of Vendor Selection," unpublished DBA thesis (Seattle: University of Washington, 1965). The study is also discussed in Gary W. Dickson, "An Analysis of Vendor Selection Systems and Decisions," *Journal of Purchasing*, Vol. 2, No. 1 (February, 1966).

[27]Gary W. Dickson, "Decision-Making in Purchasing: A Simulation Model of Vendor Selection," unpublished DBA thesis (Seattle: University of Washington, 1965), p. 47.

[28]*Ibid.*, p. 227.

With this structuring of the decision problem, five purchasing agents were used as experimental subjects. Data first were gathered on each subject's evaluation in monetary terms of the differences between the levels of each of the factors associated with the hypothetical items to be purchased. To illustrate, for the delivery factor for paint, subject one evaluated the difference between levels i and j to be worth \$2.50 per barrel and the difference between j and k to be worth \$2.50 per barrel also. Similar data were gathered from the same subject for each factor and for each item.

Following determination of the subject's monetary evaluation of differences between levels of the factors for an item, the subject was given printed descriptions of characteristics of four potential vendors for the item together with bid prices. Vendor A for paint, for example, was described as follows.

VENDOR A

The most outstanding characteristics of Vendor A are his ability to meet delivery schedule and his compliance with this company's bidding and operating procedures. It is expected that A will be able to deliver on the specified date with no appreciable difficulty. In addition, it is expected that he will comply completely with all operating procedures. With regard to the technical capability, Vendor A is expected to be able to provide technical assistance if any problems arise regarding the paint; however, he will not be able to provide any basic research and development for new paint types.

Unfortunately, Vendor A is doubtful in regard to his ability to meet quality standards. The best knowledge available indicates that Vendor A will only have a fair chance of supplying paint that will last three years with no defects or only minor defects. If serious defects occur, it is expected that they may be major and will require re-painting of the wall or more. Making up somewhat for the quality difficulty is Vendor A's warranty policy. It is expected that he will refund 50 per cent of the cost of the paint and the associated labor if any major defects occur within two years of the application.

PRICE BID BY VENDOR A: \$175 PER BARREL[29]

After reading the descriptions and bid prices of vendors A,B,C, and D, the subject ranked the vendors in terms of his preferences for them, and the experimental session continued on to the next item. The same procedure was used for five subjects.

In preparing descriptions of the potential vendors, Dickson associated a particular level of each factor with the description. This information, of course, was not given to the subject. For paint vendor A, the delivery factor was at level i, and the level of other factors was similarly established. Vendor descriptions were written so that there was little question as to the level of the factors implied.

---

[29]Gary W. Dickson, "Decision-Making in Purchasing: A Simulation Model of Vendor Selection," unpublished DBA thesis (Seattle: University of Washington, 1965), p. 234.

Since the level of the factors suggested by the verbal descriptions of the vendor was predetermined and since the subjects' monetary evaluations of the differences between each level for each factor and each item had been established, it was then possible to use a computer program to predict each of the subject's preferences for the vendors for each item. The program makes paired comparisons of each of the vendors for each item to determine ranking of the vendors. In making paired comparisons of vendors, the preferred vendor is chosen by considering the difference between bid prices for the two vendors and the monetary value of the differences between levels of the factors for each vendor. As an example, hypothetical vendor A's bid price for paint is $175 per barrel. From the description of the vendors, vendor A's delivery is at level i and vendor B's delivery is at level k. Therefore, for subject one, who evaluated the difference between levels i and j to be worth $2.50 and the difference between j and k to be worth $2.50 for the delivery factor for paint, the $15 bid price advantage for A is reduced by $2.50 + $2.50, or $5.00. This process continues for the other four factors, and the preferred vendor is chosen depending on whether or not the $15 bid price advantage of A has been overcome by the net monetary value of differences between levels of the other five factors. Differences can result in the preference for the vendor with lower price increasing as well as decreasing, depending on whether factor levels are higher or lower for the low bidder as compared to the high bidder.

The computer program, in a sense, performs explicitly comparisons and evaluations that a purchasing agent makes implicitly in making a judgment as to his preference for vendors. Since the program uses as input the purchasing agent's own judgments as to the monetary value of differences between factor levels, the program also makes choices dictated by the particular value system of the purchasing agent. Results of this model were compared with the stated rankings of each of the five subject purchasing agents and were found to agree with the agents' rankings 85 per cent of the time. After comparing these results with a random vendor ranking and a number of less sophisticated ranking methods, Dickson concluded that the model performed quite well in simulating choices of the purchasing agents.

Simulation of Human Thought

An efficient solution to a problem is not necessarily the goal of simulating human thought. Rather, duplication of the thought process is the objective. Consequently, heuristics are oriented around the human thought process rather than being problem- or computer-oriented. An excellent example of the simulation of human thought processes is the work done by Clarkson on simulation of the decision making process of a trust investment officer.[30] In

---

[30]Geoffrey P. E. Clarkson, *Portfolio Selection: A Simulation of Trust Investment* (Englewood Cliffs, N.J.: Prentice-Hall, Inc., 1962).

his study, Clarkson noted in detail the processes through which the trust officer arrived at investment decisions. These processes, or protocols, were then translated into a computer program which simulated the trust officer's decision making process. The model of the trust investment process is shown diagrammatically in Fig. 5.10. Three major subdivisions exist in the model.

Selection of the current list of stocks

To provide the computer with background information equivalent to that accumulated by the decision maker through years of experience, a list of stocks, the "B" list, is introduced as input. These stocks are judged to be of investment quality and are included on this list if, and only if, they are held by leading trust institutions. The A list is a subset of the B list and includes those stocks that appear to be a good investment at this particular point in time. Selection of the A list is accomplished by a routine called the "scanner," which examines the economy expectation list and the industry expectation list. If the expectation lists indicate that conditions are favorable, a company which is below average for its industry may still be included on the A list. On the other hand, if the expectation lists indicate that environmental conditions are doubtful, some companies will not be included even though they are rated somewhat above average for their industry.

Choosing the investment policy

It was found from the protocol that a complex of information regarding characteristics of each client was factored by a set of heuristics into four types of investment goals, each with a different emphasis on growth and income.

> Information on the client is fed into the model in the form of a list which contains the following attributes: (i) the desired amount of growth, (ii) the desired amount of income, (iii) whether current income is sufficient for the client's needs, (iv) the desired amount of stability of income and principal, (v) income tax bracket, (vi) client's profession, (vii) client's place of legal residence, (viii) whether trust is revocable or not, and (ix) whether trust is legal or not.[31]

Of the above criteria, the first seven are used in this phase of the program. The last two are used by the portfolio selection process. Each client is placed into one of four accounts on the basis of the relative desire for appreciation as contrasted to dividends. The four classifications are:

1. Growth account

---

[31]Geoffrey P. E. Clarkson, *Portfolio Selection: A Simulation of Trust Investment* (Englewood Cliffs, N.J.: Prentice-Hall, Inc., 1962), p. 31.

STRUCTURE OF DECISION PROCESS

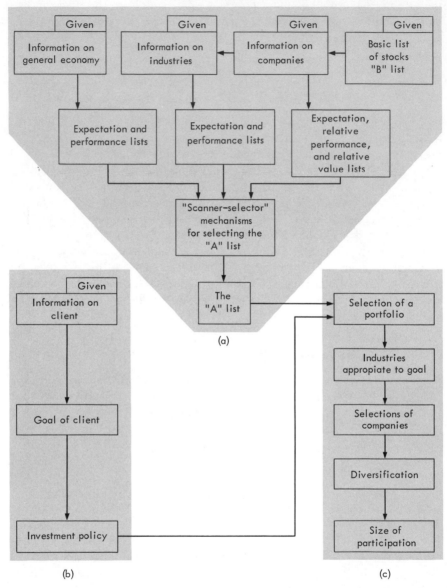

FIGURE 5.10. Model of the Trust Investment Process (by permission from Geoffrey P.E. Clarkson, *Portfolio Selection: A Simulation of Trust Investment,* Englewood Cliffs, New Jersey: Prentice-Hall, Inc., 1962)

2. Growth and income account
3. Income and growth account
4. Income account

Selecting the portfolio

The investment policy will determine the particular industries to be considered, since there is a set of industries associated with each investment goal. Appropriate industries are selected from the A list, and companies in other industries are excluded from further consideration. For example, the following group of industries are associated with an income-oriented account: auto and equipment, banks, container, food, insurance, metals—copper, oil—domestic, retail trade, railroad, and utilities.

After the appropriate list of industries has been selected, companies in each of the pertinent industries are ranked on the basis of the dominant attribute of the investment policy. If a portfolio were being selected for an income account, companies within each of the above industries would be ranked on the basis of yield. The selector then picks from an industry the company at the head of this list and applies a set of tests to determine if it is in line with the investment goal. Unless the value of some attribute is considerably out of line, the selection heuristic will pick that company and move to the next industry. If, however, that company is rejected, the next company on the list is subjected to the same tests and so on, until a selection has been made or until all companies in the industry have been evaluated. The next industry is then considered. If, after all of the industries have been processed, funds remain to be invested, the process is repeated with a relaxed criterion.

Figure 5.11 provides a comparison of output of the simulation with actual decisions made by the trust investment officer. One difference exists between the two portfolios. General Public Utilities was considered by the model to be overpriced and was not included in list A. The trust investment officer had not noticed this fact. Clarkson remarks that the model was at fault for not allowing for possible time lags in assimilation of information. In total, however, the program did very well in modeling both the results and the observable thought process of the decison maker.

A similar approach has been used by Corner to study and simulate thought processes of a person engaged in two-person, zero-sum games.[32] Although game theory could provide optimum mixed strategies for playing the games, the person used as the subject was unaware of the mathematical

---

[32]This research was conducted under direction of one of the authors and is described fully in: C. Richard Corner, "Simulation of Human Thought: A Study of Decision Making in a Structured, Competitive Environment," unpublished MBA thesis (Pullman, Washington: Washington State University, 1965).

1 GOAL OF ACCOUNT: HIGH INCOME AND PRINCIPAL SAFETY
2 FUNDS AVAILABLE FOR INVESTMENT AND IN COMMON STOCKS: $28,000

The TRUST INVESTMENT MODEL selected the following portfolio for Account 3

Number of Shares	Stock	Price	Total	Estimated Dividends
100	American Can Company	$38	$3,800	$200
100	Continental Insurance	53	5,300	200
100	Duquesne Light Company	24	2,400	116
100	Equitable Gas	37	3,700	185
100	Pennsylvania Power and Light	27	2,700	125
100	International Harvester	45	4,500	240
100	Libbey Owens Ford	50	5,000	250
100	Socony Mobil Oil Co.	38	3,800	200
			$31,200	$1,516

Estimated Yield 4.9 per cent

The TRUST INVESTMENT OFFICER selected the following portfolio for Account 3

Number of Shares	Stock	Price	Total	Estimated Dividends
100	American Can Company	$38	$3,800	$200
100	Continental Insurance	53	5,300	200
100	Duquesne Light Company	24	2,400	116
100	Equitable Gas	35	3,500	185
100	General Public Utilities	26	2,600	112
100	International Harvester	45	4,500	240
100	Libbey Owens Ford	50	5,000	250
100	Socony Mobil Oil Co.	37	3,700	200
			$30,800	$1,503

Estimated Yield 4.9 per cent

FIGURE 5.11. Comparison of Simulated and Actual Investment Decisions (by permission from Geoffrey P.E. Clarkson, *Portfolio Selection: A Simulation of Trust Investment*, Englewood Cliffs, New Jersey: Prentice-Hall, Inc., 1962)

solution of games. Unknown to the subject, his opponent was playing optimum mixed strategies determined by game theory.

Prior to the start of the experiment, the subject was given the following instructions:

1. You are playing an opponent. Whatever you lose, he will gain.
2. You will choose a strategy from those listed along the left edge of the matrix. Your opponent will choose his strategy from the top of the matrix.
3. The square at the intersection of your chosen row with your opponent's chosen column tells how much you win. A negative value means that you pay him the amount in the square.
4. Every time you make a choice, there will be a selection that is more advantageous to you than the other alternatives. The advantageous choice may not be the same when you are playing the same game additional times, because your opponent's strategy may vary.
5. You will play each game ten times.

The method of recording the subject's thought process was similar to that employed by Clarkson. The protocol was taken by means of a tape recorder, which the subject operated in a room separated from his opponent. Thus the subject was permitted to talk freely without fearing that the information would be used against him.

Ten game matrices were used to develop the protocol; each game was played ten times. Figure 5.12 shows one of the game matrices; the following are excerpts from the recording of the subject's thought processes in playing this game.

Opponent

	A	B	C	D
1	– 2	– 1	0	3
2	3	– 3	3	– 3
3	1	1	– 3	1
4	– 1	3	– 1	– 1
5	– 1	0	1	0

(Player, along the left edge)

FIGURE 5.12. Sample Game Payoff Matrix (by permission from C. Richard Corner, *Simulation of Human Thought: A Study of Decision Making in a Structured, Competitive Environment,* unpublished MBA thesis, Pullman, Washington: Washington State University, 1965)

Choice 4. That didn't work. He hasn't chosen A, but he probably figures that I expect an A, so he won't play it. I should switch to my relatively safe row 3, although it's not very profitable even if I do win. If I play row 3, I have a chance to win in 3 of the 4 categories in either A, B, or D. Okay, I choose 3.

Choice 5. Maybe he sees my preference for row 3. I'll take a chance that he does not, and I will choose 3 again.

Choice 6. I won one last time on 3. He's chosen C, D, B, C and A. He seems to be jumping all over the place as if he is trying to figure me out. I think I'll try row 2. It has not been good in the past. If he chooses either A or C, I win relatively big winnings.[33]

In total, one hundred choices were made by the subject. These were analyzed to construct the flow chart of the subject's thought processes shown in Fig. 5.13.

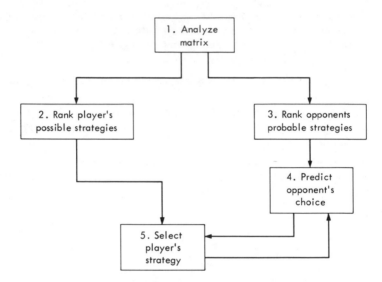

FIGURE 5.13. Flow Chart of Subject's Thought Process (by permission from C. Richard Corner, *Simulation of Human Thought : A Study of Decision Making in a Structured*, Competitive Environment, unpublished MBA thesis, Pullman, Washington : Washington State University, 1965)

The subject was keenly aware of the competitiveness of the situation and assumed that his opponent was likewise cognizant of this characteristic. As indicated by the flow chart, the subject first attempted to predict the opponent's choice and then chose the alternative that would be most profitable against the predicted action by the opponent. A further assumption was made by the subject that the opponent was analyzing the subject's past choices

---

[33]C. Richard Corner, "Simulation of Human Thought: A Study of Decision Making in a Structured, Competitive Environment," unpublished MBA thesis (Pullman, Washington: Washington State University, 1965), Appendix 5.

for patterns. For example, if the subject noted that his own last four choices were 1, 2, 1, 2, he assumed that the opponent would suspect a pattern and anticipate a 1 for the next choice. The subject would then ask. "If my opponent expects me to choose 1, which strategy would he select?" (Let us assume that choice C would be most beneficial to the opponent.) The subject would then reason, "I predict that he will choose C; therefore, I should select row 4 to obtain the maximum gain."

The computer program developed to simulate the subject's thought process as shown in Fig. 5.13 was written in IPL-V.[34] Flow charts of the program are included in Appendix D.

After developing the model of the subject's thought process and the computer program, Corner replayed nine of the ten games that had been used in developing the model. (One game could not be played because the program did not allow sufficient storage.) Choices for the model's opponent were the same as those of the subject's opponent. Although the program varied from matrix to matrix in its ability to replicate the subject's original choices, results were encouraging. After ten plays of each of the nine games, the computer model's net winnings were +5 as compared to the subject's net winnings of +51 when he initially played the games. The same games were also played by a naive computer routine making completely random choices—again playing against the same choices as the subject had originally faced—and the results were net winnings of −24 on one trial and −22 for a different set of random choices.

Although any claims, based on the work of Clarkson, Corner, and others, to having progressed toward the goal of simulating human thought must be modest indeed, it is apparent that the problem is not totally intractable. With the proper approach, and given the capacity of modern computers, these illustrations demonstrate that it is possible to simulate certain decision processes even though no mathematical model of the process can be constructed.

Summary

Heuristic approaches have often been termed simulations although heuristics tend to deal with such things as thought processes, intelligent behavior, and effective problem solving or search methods rather than with the physical and economic aspects of processes which were the focal point of simulation models discussed in previous chapters. Heuristic methods cannot be defined narrowly in terms of specific techniques. Instead, they are *ad hoc* methods designed to fit specific problems, and they are only loosely linked together by such

---

[34]IPL-V will be discussed in Chap. 7.

common characteristics as the emphasis on achieving results that are "good enough" rather than optimal and the emphasis on using procedures similar to those that human problem solvers or decision makers might use. Heuristic methods may be thought of as embracing a philosophy for approaching problems rather than constituting an organized and definable set of techniques.

Heuristic techniques have received considerable attention in the literature because they offer an approach to problems that cannot be solved by classic mathematical and statistical models such as linear programming, integer programming, and queuing theory. In addition to the illustrations given in this chapter, applications of heuristic techniques have recently been suggested in such varied areas as sales forecasting, project scheduling, accounts receivable management, personnel selection, and production planning. Experience has also shown that heuristic methods are, in fact, practical methods as evidenced by the use of the CRAFT[35] program to solve actual layout problems. With further research additional applications of heuristic methods will undoubtedly be forthcoming in areas where no use of these methods has yet been made.

EXERCISES

5.1   Develop a flow chart for a heuristic program that determines whether to hire applicants for a clerical position with a company. Define clearly the data inputs to the program and decision rules.

5.2   Develop a flow chart for a heuristic program that determines whether an applicant is accepted into the freshman class in a university. Define clearly the data inputs and decision rules.

5.3   Develop a flow chart for a computer program that would search for an optimal policy in the situation described in Exercise 2.2.

5.4   Develop a simple assembly line balancing program and test it on the data in Table 5.1.

5.5   A record of action taken upon the applications of 24 customers by a loan manager is shown below. The following code is used.
   a. Married (M), single (S).
   b. Income < $5000 (−5), $5000 ≤ Income ≤ $10,000 (5–10), Income > $10,000 (10+).
   c. Held present job mor than two years? (yes), (no).
   d. Owns his home? (yes), (no).
   e. Loan granted (L.G.), loan denied (D).

---

[35]See footnote 16.

01	a.	M	02	a.	S	03	a.	M
	b.	10+		b.	−5		b.	5–10
	c.	Yes		c.	No		c.	Yes
	d.	No		d.	Yes		d.	No
	e.	L.G.		e.	D		e.	L.G.
04	a.	M	05	a.	S	06	a.	S
	b.	5–10		b.	10+		b.	5–10
	c.	No		c.	Yes		c.	Yes
	d.	No		d.	Yes		d.	No
	e.	D		e.	L.G.		e.	L.G.
07	a.	S	08	a.	M	09	a.	S
	b.	10+		b.	10+		b.	−5
	c.	No		c.	No		c.	No
	d.	No		d.	Yes		d.	No
	e.	D		e.	L.G.		e.	D
10	a.	M	11	a.	S	12	a.	M
	b.	−5		b.	5–10		b.	−5
	c.	No		c.	No		c.	Yes
	d.	Yes		d.	No		d.	No
	e.	D		e.	D		e.	L.G.
13	a.	M	14	a.	S	15	a.	S
	b.	5–10		b.	10+		b.	5–10
	c.	Yes		c.	Yes		c.	Yes
	d.	Yes		d.	No		d.	Yes
	e.	L.G.		e.	L.G.		e.	L.G.
16	a.	S	17	a.	M	18	a.	M
	b.	−5		b.	10+		b.	−5
	c.	Yes		c.	Yes		c.	Yes
	d.	No		d.	Yes		d.	Yes
	e.	D		e.	L.G.		e.	L.G.
19	a.	M	20	a.	S	21	a.	S
	b.	10+		b.	−5		b.	10+
	c.	No		c.	Yes		c.	No
	d.	No		d.	Yes		d.	Yes
	e.	D		e.	L.G.		e.	L.G.
22	a.	M	23	a.	S	24	a.	M
	b.	5–10		b.	5–10		b.	−5
	c.	No		c.	No		c.	No
	d.	Yes		d.	Yes		d.	No
	e.	L.G.		e.	D		e.	D

Analyze the records to discover the decision rules employed by the loan manager and design a computer program to simulate the decision process. Validate your model by comparing the program's decisions to grant or deny a loan to those made by the manager in the cases shown above.

5.6   A player is involved in a game against nature in which there are three states of nature and three possible actions that can be chosen by the player. In this game nature selects a state randomly and the player makes his choice with full knowledge of nature's choice. The payoffs to the player are random quantities selected from normal distributions whose parameters are specified in the payoff matrix below. The information in the payoff matrix is not known to the player.

Player	Nature 1	2	3
1	$\mu = -1$ $\sigma = 2$	$\mu = +1$ $\sigma = 2$	$\mu = 0$ $\sigma = 2$
2	$\mu = 0$ $\sigma = 2$	$\mu = +2$ $\sigma = 2$	$\mu = -2$ $\sigma = 2$
3	$\mu = +1$ $\sigma = 2$	$\mu = -3$ $\sigma = 2$	$\mu = +2$ $\sigma = 2$

Design a computer program to play the game which allows the player to learn by experience as the game progresses.

a. Play the game for 100 plays and calculate for each 10 plays average winnings (or losses) of the player. On the basis of this information, plot a learning curve for the player.

b. Record for each 10 plays the number of times the player made the best choice for the state of nature he faced. Plot this learning curve.

c. Repeat parts *a.* and *b.* above with the standard deviation of the payoff in all cases changed to 5. Compare the learning curves with those obtained previously.

BIBLIOGRAPHY

Anderson, Thomas R., "Layout Planning for Minimum Circulation Cost." Unpublished Master of Science thesis. University of Washington, Seattle, Wash., 1965.

Armour, Gordon C. and Elwood S. Buffa, "A Heuristic Algorithm and Simulation Approach to Relative Location of Facilities," *Management Science*, Vol. 9, No. 2 (January, 1963).

Bowman, Edward H. and Robert B. Fetter, *Analysis for Production and Operations Management*, 3rd ed. Homewood, Ill.: Richard D. Irwin, Inc., 1967, Chap. 12.

Buffa, E. S., G. C. Armour, and T. E. Vollmann, "Allocating Facilities with Craft," *Harvard Business Review*, March–April, 1964.

Clarkson, Geoffrey P. E., *Portfolio Selection: A Simulation of Trust Investment.* Englewood Cliffs, N.J.: Prentice-Hall, Inc., 1962.

Clarkson, G. P., and A. H. Meltzer, "Portfolio Selection: A Heuristic Approach," *Journal of Finance*, Vol. 15, No. 4, (December, 1960).

Corner, C. Richard, "Simulation of Human Thought: A Study of Decision Making in a Structured, Competitive Environment." Unpublished MBA thesis. Pullman, Washington: Washington State University, 1965.

Crecine, John P., "A Computer Simulation Model of Municipal Budgeting," *Management Science*, Vol. 13, No. 11 (July, 1967).

Cyert, R. M., J. G. March, and C. G. Moore, "A Model of Retail Ordering and Pricing by a Department Store," in *Quantitative Techniques in Marketing Analysis*, Ronald E. Frank, Alfred A. Kuehn, and William F. Massey, eds., Homewood, Ill.: Richard D. Irwin, Inc., 1962.

Dickson, Gary W., "Decision Making in Purchasing: A Simulation Model of Vendor Selection." Unpublished DBA thesis. Seattle: University of Washington, 1965.

Feigenbaum, Edward A., and Julian Feldman, eds., *Computers and Thought*. New York: McGraw-Hill Book Company, Inc., 1963.

Feldman, E., F. A. Lehrer, and T. L. Ray, "Warehouse Location under Continuous Economies of Scale," *Management Science*, Vol. 12, No. 9 (May, 1966).

Gelernter, H. L. and N. Rochester, "Intelligent Behavior in Problem-Solving Machines," *IBM Journal of Research and Development*, Vol. 2, No. 4 (October, 1958).

Gere, William S., Jr., "Heuristics in Job Shop Scheduling," *Management Science*, Vol. 13, No. 3 (November, 1966).

Haines, George H., Jr., "The Rote Marketer," *Behavioral Science*, Vol. 6, No. 4 (October, 1961).

Hunt, Earl B., *Concept Learning: An Information Processing Problem*. New York: John Wiley & Sons, Inc., 1962, Chaps. 7 and 8.

Jones, Curtis H., "Parametric Production Planning," *Management Science*, Vol. 13, No. 11 (July, 1967).

Karg, Robert L. and Gerald L. Thompson, "A Heuristic Approach to Solving Travelling Salesman Problems," *Management Science*, Vol. 10, No. 2 (January, 1964).

Kilbridge, Maurice D. and Leon Wester, "A Heuristic Method of Assembly Line Balancing," *Journal of Industrial Engineering*, Vol. 12, No. 4 (July–August, 1961).

Kleinmuntz, Benjamin and Robert S. McLean, "Diagnostic Interviewing by Digital Computer," *Behavioral Science*, Vol. 13, No. 1 (January, 1968).

Kuehn, Alfred A. and J. Michael Hamburger, "A Heuristic Program for Locating Warehouses," *Management Science*, Vol. 9, No. 4 (July, 1963).

Lee, Robert C. and James M. Moore, "*CORELAP*—Computerized Relationship Layout Planning," *Journal of Industrial Engineering*, Vol. 18, No. 3 (March, 1967).

Levy, Ferdinand K., "An Application of Heuristic Problem Solving to Accounts Receivable Management," *Management Science*, Vol. 12, No. 6 (February, 1966).

Meinhart, Wayne A., "Artificial Intelligence, Computer Simulation of Human Cognitive and Social Processes, and Management Thought," *Academy of Management Journal*, Vol. 9, No. 4 (December, 1966).

Moodie, C. L. and H. H. Young, "A Heuristic Method of Assembly Line Balancing for Assumptions of Constant or Variable Work Element Times," *Journal of Industrial Engineering*, (January–February, 1965).

Newell, A., J. C. Shaw, and H. A. Simon, "A Variety of Intelligent Learning in a General Problem Solver," in *Self-Organizing Systems*, M. Yovits and S. Cameron, eds., New York: Pergamon Press, 1960.

Nugent, Christopher E., Thomas E. Vollmann, and John Ruml, "An Experimental Comparison of Techniques for the Assignment of Facilities to Locations," *Operations Research*, Vol. 16, No. 1 (January–February, 1968).

Samuel, A. L., "Some Studies in Machine Learning Using the Game of Checkers," *IBM Journal of Research and Development* (July, 1959).

Schussel, George, "Sales Forecasting with the Aid of a Human Behavior Simulator," *Management Science*, Vol. 13, No. 10 (June, 1967).

Simon, Herbert A., *The New Science of Management Decision*. New York: Harper & Row, 1960.

Simon, Herbert A. and A. Newell, *The Simulation of Human Thought*. RAND Publication, P-1734 (June, 1959).

——————————— "Heuristic Problem Solving: The Next Advance in Operations Research," *Operations Research*, Vol. 6, No. 1 (January–February, 1958).

——————————— "Simulation of Human Thinking," in *Management and the Computer of the Future*, Martin Greenberger, ed., New York: John Wiley & Sons, Inc., 1962.

Smith, Robert D. and Paul S. Greenlaw, "Simulation of a Psychological Decision Process in Personnel Selection," *Management Science*, Vol. 13, No. 8 (April, 1967).

Tonge, Fred M., "Assembly Line Balancing Using Probabilistic Heuristics," *Management Science*, Vol. 11, No. 7 (May, 1965).

———————————, *A Heuristic Program for Assembly Line Balancing*. Englewood Cliffs, N.J.: Prentice-Hall, Inc., 1961.

———————————, "Summary of a Heuristic Line Balancing Procedure," *Management Science*, Vol. 7, No. 1 (October, 1960).

———————————, "The Use of Heuristic Programming in Management Science," *Management Science*, Vol. 7, No. 3 (April, 1961).

Wester, Leon and Maurice D. Kilbridge, "Heuristic Line Balancing: A Case Study," *Journal of Industrial Engineering*, Vol. 13, No. 3 (May–June, 1962).

Wiest, Jerome D., "A Heuristic Model for Scheduling Large Projects with Limited Resources," *Management Science*, Vol. 13, No. 6 (February, 1967).

———————————, "Heuristic Programs for Decision Making," *Harvard Business Review*, September–October, 1966.

Wilson, Richard C., "A Packaging Problem," *Management Science*, Vol. 12, No. 4 (December, 1965).

Games and Gaming

6 The distinction between a game and a simulation is a subtle one. Both are dynamic numerical models, but they differ in purpose and mode of use. Simulation models are designed to generate a sequence of activities in a system and to record statistics regarding system operation. They are primarily tools for research into dynamic behavior of systems. Games are a form of simulation in which human beings make decisions at various stages; thus games are distinguished by the idea of play. Players feed into the model information about their decisions, and the game model simulates interactions between the simulated environment and decisions of participants. Results are fed back to the players, after which they make another set of decisions and the cycle is repeated.

Games, like simulation models, may be implemented by hand computations or may be programed for a computer. Although a computer is not essential to the gaming process, it performs necessary calculations rapidly and permits the use of more complex models than if calculations were done by hand by a game umpire. The computer also makes it possible to use structures that would involve an inordinate amount of computation for a manually scored game.

A game model may be used either to improve decision-making skills of the players or to improve performance of the system being simulated, or both. The term *operational gaming* will be used further to distinguish games used to study a process with the objective of finding and imparting optimal solutions.[1]

Development of Gaming Techniques

Current uses of games and operational gaming are extensions of the concepts of war games which have been utilized since the seventeenth and eighteenth centuries (even longer if the game of chess is considered). The

---

[1]C. J. Thomas and W. L. Deemer, Jr., "The Role of Operational Gaming in Operations Research," *Operations Research*, Vol. 5, No. 1 (February, 1957), p. 6.

modern war game, or Kriegspiel, was introduced into the Prussian army by von Reisswitz.[2] His game was played on maps with troops represented by blocks cut to the scale of the map. Situations were presented to the opposing officers, who issued orders that were evaluated by an umpire.

The classic three-room war game is a direct descendant of the von Reisswitz game. In this game participants are organized into two opposing teams and a control team. Thomas has described one version of the game as follows:

> The idealized version of the classic game may be pictured as the kind that is played largely for "research" purposes, at several military and research organizations which maintain gaming facilities, on a more or less continuing basis. Typically, there may be from ten to fifty players organized into three teams, a room for each team, maps, counters, slide rules or desk computers, clocks keeping "game time," and appropriate communication channels between rooms. The red team and the blue team represent opposing forces or nations or blocks of nations, with their players assuming pertinent military or political roles. Other nations, and the laws of nature generally, both deterministic and stochastic, are represented by the control team in accordance with a set of rules which it enforces. Play starts from the initial condition of a scenario, goes through a succession of red moves and blue countermoves, and finally is terminated at the discretion of the control team, usually after several days or weeks have elapsed. There may be one or more replays starting from the same basic situation. After the play has concluded, there may issue from it a succession of analyses, reports, and summaries.[3]

The actual exercises to be carried out and the structure of the game depend on the particular problem to be solved and the experts available for play. This classic war game, which had achieved the essentials of its modern form by World War I, has found increased use during this century in such applications as teaching military doctrine, testing war plans, and evaluating future military operations.

More recently the computer has been employed in war gaming with the machine doing much or all of the data reduction and analysis. Specialized games have also appeared, such as the inventory management game Monopologs developed at RAND in 1955 to simulate the United States Air Force logistics system.[4] This game, which has more in common with modern business management games than with earlier war games, was designed to simulate the operation of a supply depot and five Air Force bases. The players act as inventory managers and make monthly decisions on

---

[2]C. J. Thomas, "Military Gaming," in *Progress in Operations Research*, Vol. I, Russell L. Ackoff, ed. (New York: John Wiley & Sons, Inc., 1961), p. 426.

[3]*Ibid.*, p. 438.

[4]Jean R. Renshaw, *The Game Monopologs*, R. M.—1917–1 (Santa Monica, Calif.: The RAND Corporation, March 31, 1960).

procurement of new parts, repair of parts, and distribution of parts among bases.

Aside from military applications, undoubtedly the most extensive attempts to utilize games and gaming techniques have been in business and related areas. In the business field the use of games and gaming (we ignore the favorite old real estate business game of Monopoly) is about fifteen years old. It is generally agreed that the earliest business management game was the Top Management Decision Simulation, developed by the American Management Association in 1956.[5] This game is a computerized general management or total enterprise game, as opposed to functional and industry games, since all major functions of the enterprise are represented and decisions are those made at top management levels. The game is designed for team play in an interactive, competitive environment that is characteristic of other general management games. Participants are assigned to a team comprising the management of a hypothetical company producing a single product and competing with the other teams in a single market.

Each firm possesses information at each stage of the game about its own condition, and it has certain information about the industry and market in which it is selling. On the basis of this information players make decisions for the next time period. These are submitted to the computer, which has been programed to calculate results of the decisions. Financial statements reflecting results of the period's operations are delivered to the players, who then proceed with the next quarter's decisions, and the cycle is repeated until the desired number of periods have been completed. The A.M.A. game and the manual game designed by Andlinger had a considerable influence on the development of business games.[6]

One of the first uses of a management game on a university campus was the Top Management Decision Game developed by Schrieber at the University of Washington. This game, patterned after the A.M.A. game, was first used in the summer of 1957. At about the same time a number of universities and companies constructed management games, including the University of California at Los Angeles, Carnegie–Mellon University, International Business Machines, Remington Rand UNIVAC, General Electric, Westinghouse, and Pillsbury.[7] Besides general management games which initially received the most attention, a wide variety of games oriented

---

[5]Franc M. Ricciardi, et al., *Top Management Simulation: The AMA Approach*, Elizabeth Marting, ed. (New York: American Management Association Incorporated, 1957); and Richard Bellman, Charles E. Clark, Donald G. Malcom, Clifford J. Craft, and Franc M. Ricciardi, "On the Construction of a Multi-Stage, Multi-Person Business Game," *Operations Research*, Vol. 5, No. 7 (August, 1957).

[6]G. R. Andlinger, "Business Games—Play One!" *Harvard Business Review*, Vol. 36, No. 2 (March–April, 1958).

[7]A description of several of these games may be found in Joel M. Kibbee, Clifford J. Craft, and Bert Nanus, *Management Games* (New York: Reinhold Publishing Corporation, 1961).

to particular functional areas of business management have been developed. Marketing management, inventory control, scheduling, and finance are among the areas for which games are now available.[8] Although games have not received as much attention by economists as they have in the business field, at least one game has been designed to demonstrate economic principles related to market behavior.[9]

Following the introduction of business games, their number and use expanded rapidly, so that by 1961 it was estimated that there were over 100 games in existence and over 30,000 executives had played them. Greenlaw, Herron, and Rawdon catalogued 89 games;[10] Kibbee, Craft, and Nanus listed 85 games;[11] and a study by Dale and Klasson in 1962 disclosed that by then two-thirds of the major collegiate schools of business were using business games.[12]

Construction of a Management Game

To illustrate some basic concepts in construction of a game, we will describe a management game designed by one of the authors.[13] The game is typical of general management games, although lacking many of the refinements of management games currently in use. The game has purposely been kept simple in its design to permit investigation of a rather specialized application of the gaming idea which will be discussed later in the chapter. Because of its elementary nature, however, this game is well suited to illustrating the underlying structure of interactive games and some of the details of their construction.

The game environment is an oligopolistic industry composed of the participating players or teams who represent companies in the industry. A single product is made by the companies, and this product is sold in a single market. The companies (players) receive a balance sheet, profit and loss statement, statement of cash flow, and a summary of industry data each simulated period of play; a sample set of the reports given to each company is shown in Fig. 6.1. The period of operations covered by the reports

[8]References to several representative functional games are given in the bibliography at the end of the chapter.

[9]John Haldi and Harvey M. Wagner, *Simulated Economic Models* (Homewood, Ill.: Richard D. Irwin, Inc., 1963).

[10]Paul S. Greenlaw, Lowell W. Herron, and Richard H. Rawdon, *Business Simulation in Industrial and University Education* (Englewood Cliffs, N.J.: Prentice-Hall, Inc., 1962).

[11]Joel M. Kibbee, Clifford J. Craft, and Burt Nanus, *Management Games* (New York: Rinehold Publishing Corporation, 1961).

[12]Alfred G. Dale and Charles R. Klasson, *Business Gaming: A Survey of American Collegiate Schools of Business* (Austin: Bureau of Business Research, The University of Texas, 1964).

[13]Much of the actual computer programing for the game was done by Mr. Richard Burson.

is usually assumed to be three months, or one quarter of a year. For each simulated period the teams make decisions regarding price, marketing expenditures, production rate, plant and equipment purchases, and loan repayments. These decisions together with a value of the economic index for the period are given as input data to the computer program, which then calculates results of play for the next quarter. The program prepares a new set of reports, which are returned to the players, and the cycle continues until the end of the game.

The program that provides the environment for the game and calculates results of team decisions is composed of seven major sections. These sections perform the following functions in the order stated.[14]

1. Read in data regarding game environment, number of companies, characteristics of market, industry data for previous period, and previous period data for each company.
2. Read in economic index for current period and company decisions for each company for current period.
3. Edit company decisions for proper increments and check compatibility of production rate with plant capacity. (Decisions are rounded to even numbers of dollars and units and production rate decisions in excess of plant capacity are reduced to plant capacity.)
4. Compute size of total market and company sales in market.
5. Prepare data for company statements and revised industry data.
6. Print out results of play for period for each team. (See sample in Fig. 6.1.)
7. Punch out data to be used as input in step 1 above in next cycle and terminate computer run.

Input data are prepared for the program, and it is executed once for a simulated period of play. This is the usual structure of management game programs, although McKenney has designed a program that accepts input data representing a single set of decisions for a quarter but computes the status of the industry and each company 12 times (once each simulated week) before printing out results of play for the quarter.[15]

As suggested by the outline of the program above, much of the work done by the program is simply reading and writing of data and elementary arithmetic operations. Preparation of the company statements, for example, involves only basic arithmetic operations, but a substantial amount of calculation is required, since the program essentially maintains a small accounting system for each company.

From the standpoint of constructing an interactive game, the most

---

[14]For programing convenience the program is broken down into a main routine and certain subroutines. Since these programing details are not essential to understanding the structure and computations, we will not discuss them here.

[15]James L. McKenney, *Simulation Gaming for Management Development* (Boston, Mass.: Division of Research, Graduate School of Business Administration, Harvard University, 1967).

```
COMPANY   1    PERIOD   1

          ** PROFIT AND LOSS STATEMENT **                              ** STATEMENT OF CASH FLOW **

SALES - 52440. UNITS AT $ 4.95 PER UNIT -  $  259578.00        SALES                                    $  259578.00
LESS - COST OF GOODS SOLD      $  157320.00                    NEW BANK LOAN                                     0.00
       DEPRECIATION               17600.00                        TOTAL CASH PROVIDED                  $  259578.00
       MARKETING EXPENDITURES     45000.00                     LESS - MATERIAL AND LABOR               $  138000.00
       ADMINISTRATIVE EXPENSE     42000.00                            MARKETING EXPENDITURES              45000.00
       INTEREST PAID               1000.00                            ADMINISTRATIVE EXPENSE              42000.00
       TOTAL CURRENT EXPENSES               262920.00                 INTEREST PAID                        1000.00
                                                                      FEDERAL INCOME TAXES                    0.00
NET INCOME BEFORE FEDERAL INCOME TAXES      -3342.00                   ADDL. PLANT, EQUIPMENT                  0.00
FEDERAL INCOME TAXES                            0.00                   LOAN REPAYMENT                      20000.00
                                                                      TOTAL CASH OUTLAY                      246000.00
NET INCOME AFTER FEDERAL INCOME TAXES   $   -3342.00           NET CASH FLOW                            $   13578.00 *

***************************************************************************************************************

                                           ** BALANCE SHEET **

          ASSETS                                                     LIABILITIES

CURRENT ASSETS --                                    CURRENT LIABILITIES --
  CASH            $   88578.00                          LOANS OUTSTANDING  $   30000.00
  INVENTORY           25680.00                        LONG TERM LIABILITIES    50000.00
  TOTAL CURRENT ASSETS   $   114258.00                  TOTAL LIABILITIES              $   80000.00

FIXED ASSETS --                                                      NET WORTH
  PLANT AND EQUIPMENT $  880000.00                     CAPITAL STOCK        $  320000.00
  LESS - DEPRECIATION   197600.00                      RETAINED EARNINGS       396658.00
  TOTAL FIXED ASSETS        682400.00                    TOTAL NET WORTH              716658.00

TOTAL ASSETS               $   796658.00             TOTAL LIABILITIES AND NET WORTH  $  796658.00

***************************************************************************************************************

                         ** INDUSTRY DATA **

                                      PREVIOUS PERIOD    THIS PERIOD
ECONOMIC INDEX                             100.0            101.0
INDUSTRY WEIGHTED AVERAGE PRICE        $     5.00        $    5.39
INDUSTRY MARKETING EXPENDITURE         $  115000.00      $  524000.00
TOTAL MARKET (UNITS)                      400400.        404010.
COMPANY AVERAGE PROFIT AFTER TAXES     $   15000.00      $  -8242.06

      ** COMPANY DECISIONS **                            ** OTHER DATA **

PRICE PER UNIT            $    4.95                  SALES LOST (UNITS)        0.
MARKETING EXPENDITURES   $  45000.00
PRODUCTION RATE             46000.
ADDITIONAL PLANT, EQUIP. $      0.00
LOAN REPAYMENT           $  20000.00
```

FIGURE 6.1. Sample of Reports Given to Each Team in Business Game

184

interesting aspect of the program is computation of size of market and market shares in step 4 above. The market mechanism is designed to impart an appearance of realistic behavior but cannot be defended as representing any specific mechanism that has been shown to exist in reality. Unfortunately, the same shortcoming is present in most, if not all, games involving market interactions, since there is little quantitative knowledge of exactly how company decisions interact in an oligopolistic market.[16] The total base market B_t available to the industry in any period t is given by

$$B_t = T_{t-1}\left(\frac{I_t}{I_{t-1}}\right) \qquad\qquad (6.1)$$

where I is the economic index and T_{t-1} is total market from the previous period. To this base market are added the effects (positive or negative) of changes in average marketing expenditures by the industry and the weighted average price charged by the industry. The program reads a price effect table and marketing effect table in step 1 above. Price and marketing effect tables that have been used successfully in a simulated market for a single product with an average price of $5 are shown in Tables 6.1 and 6.2. Relation-

Table 6.1   SAMPLE PRICE EFFECT TABLE USED
IN BUSINESS GAME[a]

Last Period Industry Weighted Average Price[b]	Percentage Increase or Decrease in Market
$10.00 (and above)	−42.0
9.50	−40.5
9.00	−38.0
8.50	−34.5
8.00	−30.5
7.50	−26.0
7.00	−20.5
6.50	−15.0
6.00	− 9.0
5.50	− 4.5
5.00	0.0
4.50	+ 3.5
4.00	+ 6.5
3.50	+ 8.5
3.00	+11.0
2.50	+12.5
2.00	+14.5
1.00 (and below)	+17.5

[a]The table is for a product with an initial selling price of $5.00 at the start of the game.
[b]Note that the use of last period average price causes changes in the market due to price changes to lag one period behind actual price changes.

---

[16]The same shortcoming does not exist in certain other portions of the model, such as the accounting, cash flow, and inventory management aspects, which are accurate replicas of the real world.

Table 6.2 SAMPLE MARKETING EFFECT TABLE USED IN BUSINESS GAME

Ratio of Last Period Industry Marketing Expenditures to Expenditures Two Periods Previous[a]	Percentage Increase or Decrease in Market
2.40 (and above)	+10.0
2.20	+9.5
2.00	+9.0
1.80	+8.5
1.60	+7.0
1.40	+5.0
1.20	+3.0
1.00	0.0
0.80	−3.0
0.60	−6.5
0.40	−10.5
0.20 (and below)	−14.5

[a]Note that the use of last period expenditures to the previous period causes changes in the market due to changes in marketing expenditures to lag one period behind actual changes in expenditures.

ships shown in the tables were arrived at by trial and error by making an initial estimate as to what might give realistic market behavior and then adjusting the relationships somewhat as experience was gained with the game. These tables effectively define the responsiveness of size of market to industry pricing practices and industry marketing expenditures. Different table values can be used to obtain different behavior at the discretion of the game administrator. Price effect on the base market is found by calculating industry weighted average price for the preceding period of play and looking up the price effect in the table, or interpolating between values if necessary. Similarly, marketing effect is found by calculating the ratio of last period total marketing expenditures to expenditures for the period before that and looking up the marketing effect, again interpolating if necessary. Total market is obtained by

$$T_t = B_t \text{ (price effect + marketing effect)} \tag{6.2}$$

Both the price and marketing effect calculations cause the change in size of market to lag behind industry price and marketing expenditure movements.

The market share $s_{i,t}$ (expressed as a decimal) for each team i in period t is based on its share in the previous period and any changes due to pricing and marketing decisions. The change in market share $\Delta s_{i,t}$ of company i due to its marketing expenditure decision is given by

$$\Delta s_{i,t} = \alpha\left(\frac{m_i}{\bar{m}} - 1\right) \tag{6.3}$$

where m_i is the company's marketing expenditure in the current period and $\bar{m}$ is average industry expenditure. The constant α is read in as part of the data describing the characteristics of the market; it determines the general responsiveness of market share to marketing expenditures. Similarly, change in market share due to price $\delta s_{i,t}$ is calculated by

$$\delta s_{i,t} = \beta\left(1 - \frac{p_i}{\bar{p}}\right) \tag{6.4}$$

where p_i is the company's price in the current period, $\bar{p}$ is industry average price, and β is a constant similar to α which determines the responsiveness of market share to price. Market share for the current period t for company i, then, is found by

$$s_{i,t} = s_{i,t-1} + \Delta s_{i,t} + \delta s_{i,t} \tag{6.5}$$

Each company's share of the market in units is the product of T_t and $s_{i,t}$. However, because of lack of inventory and/or too low a production rate a company may not be able completely to fill demand placed on it. When this occurs, $s_{i,t}$ for that company is adjusted downward and the program distributes demand lost to the other companies in proportion to their relative market shares. If all companies in the industry cannot absorb demand that has been generated, any excess demand is lost to the market and the program adjusts T_t downward accordingly.

The market mechanism that we have described is the key interactive element in this game model. There is no justification for the market structure other than that it produces realistic behavior and the mechanisms have some semblance of plausibility. This structure also permits the game administrator to produce desired market volatility through his specification of α, β, and the price and marketing effect tables at the beginning of the game. There are, of course, countless other ways to construct a market mechanism, and the choice of relationships to be employed is largely a matter of judgment on the part of the game designer.

The game structure is deterministic in the sense that results of any set of decisions by the companies are completely determined by the environmental parameters, industry data, and company data which are input to the program when it calculates results of play for a period. Even with this deterministic structure the market mechanisms and interactions among decisions of the players are such that the game gives a considerable illusion of seemingly random and unexplained variation from play to play. True random elements could easily be inserted, if desired, by adding random terms to the right-hand side of one or more of Eqs. (6.1) through (6.5).

Structural Characteristics of Games

Games differ widely in terms of such differentiating characteristics as subject matter, method of calculation, inclusion of random elements, degree of interaction, and so forth. Some games are general management games because they include many of the major functions of an enterprise, and the decisions required are those that would typically be made at upper management levels. Others are functional games, since they focus on problems of particular functional areas of an organization. A number of games have been constructed around specific industries and products, and others deal with hypothetical products. Games vary in the inclusion of single or multiple products and single or multiple markets. Games may be designed for conflict and interaction among the players or for noninteraction. Some are completely deterministic, whereas others include stochastic elements. Most business games involve a sequence of individual decisions, but they may also be used for the development of decision rules to be followed over a period of time.

Method of scoring

Whether a game is manually scored or scored by a computer program is an important determinant of the structure of a game. Manually scored games are relatively cheap to develop, provide flexibility in administration, and make it possible to include qualitative factors or value judgments on the part of the umpire in the structure of the game. Manual scoring frees the user from dependence on the availability of a computer at the proper time and place, although this advantage is rapidly disappearing with availability of time-sharing computers that may be accessed remotely. Rather complex games can be scored manually if sufficient time is allowed, but computer programs are generally used for games in which computations are lengthy and rapid scoring is desired.

Computer game scoring programs are expensive to develop, but the cost of running them once they are written is likely to be less than hand scoring. Computers provide fast, accurate scoring, and complex models can be employed along with large volumes of output to the players. Rules for scoring must be predetermined when a computer is used, so in most cases it is impossible or impractical to use the judgment of umpires in scoring the play. This characteristic of computerized games is in sharp contrast to some war games, for instance, in which the play of opponents is subjectively evaluated by experts serving as umpires. A not inconsequential factor in the use of computers for scoring is the glamour associated with playing computer games; this has undoubtedly added to the prestige, excitement, and publicity surrounding gaming.

General management games

We have made reference previously to the scope of game models, that is, whether they encompass a total enterprise and are general management games or whether they stress a particular functional area such as marketing, production and manpower scheduling, inventory planning and control, or finance. Most general management games involve sequential decisions in a conflict situation, are computer scored, have few if any stochastic elements, and have many similarities to the original A.M.A. game. The games developed in the wake of the A.M.A. game differed mainly in types of decisions to be made, but more recently games of greatly increased scope and complexity have appeared.

The IBM Management Decision-Making Laboratory, one of the most widely known, provides for three companies operating competitively in four markets and permits players to use different strategies in each market.[17] A series of game models comprising the UCLA Executive Game have been constructed by Jackson and others at the University of California at Los Angeles,[18] and two versions, Game No. 2 and Game No. 3, have been widely distributed. Similar in many respects to the A.M.A. and IBM games, the UCLA Game No. 2 treats a single product in a single market, but it removes all restrictions imposed on the range of decisions and has an added feature of a depreciation rate which reduces production capacity unless new capacity is added. Game No. 3 is a multiproduct (up to three models differing in quality and price), multimarket game requiring a large-scale computer. Schrieber's Top Management Decision Game in its original version differed from the A.M.A. game primarily in that it provided for material purchases and used rate of return on investment as a criterion of success. In later versions it provided for increasing complexity as participants gained familiarity with the game mechanics. It will be described in more detail later in this section.

One of the early, and still one of the most complex, games is the Carnegie Tech Management Game.[19] It is modeled after a specific industry— packaged detergents—and provides for three companies marketing in

---

[17]*IBM Management Decision-Making Laboratory: Instructions for Participants* (White Plains, N.Y.: International Business Machines Corporation, 1963).

[18]James R. Jackson, "Learning from Experience in Business Decision Games," *California Management Review*, Vol. 1, No. 2 (Winter, 1959). Game No. 2 has been published as *The Executive Game*, by Richard C. Henshaw, Jr. and James R. Jackson (Homewood, Ill.: Richard D. Irwin, Inc., 1966).

[19]A complete description of the game, its development, and its use may be found in Kalman J. Cohen, William R. Dill, Alfred A. Kuehn, and Peter R. Winters, *The Carnegie Tech Management Game* (Homewood, Ill.: Richard D. Irwin, Inc., 1964). Detailed descriptions of the games models and available computer programs are contained in Kalman J. Cohen, William R. Dill, Alfred A. Kuehn, and Peter R. Winters, *Administrator's Manual for the Carnegie Tech Management Game* (Homewood, Ill.: Richard D. Irwin, Inc., 1964).

four regions. The game's complexity is demonstrated by the fact that players are permitted to make over three hundred decisions each period and that one to two thousand items of information are provided. Decision areas include production schedules, work force, inventory planning, plant investment, purchase of seven raw materials, pricing, product improvement and development, distributing and advertising each product in each region, market research, and a number of financial decisions. Its complexity is such that the teams of five to ten persons must organize themselves to assign functional responsibilities to each member.

Besides these university games, a number of companies have built and used general management games, often designed to simulate the firm's operations in its industry. Understandably, information on many of them is unavailable, either because they have not been successful or because they are treated confidentially if successful.[20]

Schrieber's Top Management Decision Game is illustrative of the complex nature of current management games. The game is designed to allow three to six teams of players, each representing a company, to manage the economic aspects of their respective companies and to compete with each other in a single consumer goods market. Each firm produces one product, which is identified only as a semiluxury item sold through retail outlets. The model provides a high degree of realism in types of cost, financial, and economic data provided to the players.

A typical simulation begins with each company in the same financial position. Plays of the game represent quarters of a year, and results are fed back to the companies in the form of quarterly operating reports representing a balance sheet, income statement, economic news letter, and market research report. At the end of each four periods annual summaries are prepared which include a work-in-process inventory, standard cost analysis, and a financial summary of the annual operations of the other competing firms.

The game is designed to progress through a series of phases, each enriching the game by adding complexity. This enrichment is intended to expand the decision variables and to add realism as participants gain experience with the behavior of the model. Fig. 6.2 is a balance sheet and Fig. 6.3 is an income statement for a typical firm in the third phase of the game (phase C). These reports provide the teams with fairly complete cost and financial data.

Phase A, which usually lasts through four periods, is completely deterministic. Each period eight decisions are made in this phase: selling price, marketing expenditures, research and development expenditures, production quantity, raw material purchases, plant expansion or contraction, and marketing research information expenditures. In addition each team

---

[20]Joel M. Kibbee, Clifford J. Craft, and Bert Nanus, *Management Games* (New York: Reinhold Publishing Corp., 1961), p. 176.

FORM 2B

ECHO COMPANY

BALANCE SHEET

AS OF END OF YEAR 7 QUARTER 3

ASSETS

CURRENT ASSETS

   QUICK ASSETS

      CASH $ 2181300.

      ACCOUNTS RECEIVABLE
        DUE FROM TRADE ACCOUNTS   2349694.
        DUE FROM PLANT DISPOSAL   0.
        DUE FROM TAX RECOVERY   0.
        OTHER ACCOUNTS RECEIVABLE   0.
        TOTAL QUICK ASSETS $ 4530694.

      INVENTORY

	UNITS	RATE		
RAW	710000.	2.248	1596188.	
WORK IN PROCESS	288000.	2.895	833760.	
FINISHED	55576.	3.389	188341.	
TOTAL INVENTORY				2618289.
TOTAL CURRENT ASSETS				7149283.

FIXED ASSETS
PLANT INVESTMENT (1900000. UNITS NEXT QUARTER)   9500000.

LESS DEPRECIATION RESERVE   3360000.
      NET PLANT INVESTMENT   6140000.
      TOTAL ASSETS   13289283.

LIABILITIES AND NET WORTH

LIABILITIES
  CURRENT LIABILITIES
    ACCOUNTS PAYABLE, PURCHASES   577278.

    ACCOUNTS PAYABLE, OPERATIONS   581200.

    NOTES PAYABLE, BANK   0.

    NOTES PAYABLE, TERM LOAN, CURRENT   100000.

    NOTES PAYABLE, OTHER   2750000.

    ACCRUED WAGES   133757.

    ACCRUED TAXES   112662.

       TOTAL CURRENT LIABILITIES   5154897.

   NOTES PAYABLE, TERM LOAN, FIXED   250000.

       TOTAL LIABILITIES   5404897.

NET WORTH
  CAPITAL STOCK   299000. SHARES AT   5.00 PAR   1495000.

  CAPITAL SURPLUS   1723487.

  PAID IN SURPLUS FROM TREASURY STOCK TRANSACTIONS   0.

  EARNED SURPLUS, END OF LAST QUARTER   4614273.

  NET PROFIT (OR LOSS) THIS QUARTER   51626.

  LESS DIVIDENDS   0.

  EARNED SURPLUS, END OF THIS QUARTER   4665899.
      TOTAL   7884386.
      LESS TREASURY STOCK   0. SHARES AT COST   0.
      TOTAL NET WORTH   7884386.
      TOTAL LIABILITIES AND NET WORTH   13289283.

FIGURE 6.2. Top Management Decision Game—Typical Balance Sheet

FORM 3B

ECHO COMPANY

PROFIT AND LOSS STATEMENT (PAGE 1)

AS OF END OF YEAR 7 QUARTER 3

SALES	1807457.	UNITS AT	3.900		$	7049082.
COST OF GOODS SOLD		UNITS	RATE			

RAW MATERIALS

OPENING INVENTORY		1760000.	2.222	$	3911029.	
PURCHASES		750000.	2.309		1731834.	
TOTAL AVAILABLE		2510000.	2.248		5642863.	
LESS CLOSING INVENTORY		710000.	2.248		1596188.	

WORK IN PROCESS

MATERIAL		1800000.	2.248		4046675.	

LABOR RATE PER HOUR 1.973
MAN HOURS PER UNIT   0.377

LABOR		1800000.	0.743		1337566.	
FACTORY OVERHEAD		1800000.	0.388		698000.	
TOTAL ADDED TO WIP		1800000.	3.379		6082240.	
OPENING INVENTORY		256000.	2.895		741120.	
TOTAL AVAILABLE		2056000.			6823360.	
LESS CLOSING INVENTORY		288000.	2.895		833760.	

FINISHED GOODS

MANUFACTURED		1768000.	3.388		5989600.	
OPENING INVENTORY		95033.	3.409		324010.	
TOTAL AVAILABLE		1863033.	3.389		6313610.	
LESS CLOSING INVENTORY		55576.	3.389		188341.	
COST OF GOODS SOLD		1807457.	3.389			6125270.

GROSS MARGIN   923813.

OTHER EXPENDITURES
MARKETING	(R.N. 150. PCT)	300000.	
RESEARCH AND DEVELOPMENT	(R.N. 82. PCT)	400000.	
MARKET RESEARCH INFORMATION		55000.	
TOTAL OTHER EXPENDITURES			755000.

RETURN ON OPERATIONS   166813.

INTEREST EXPENSE
TERM LOAN	30000.	
BANK LOAN	0.	
OTHER LOAN	39531.	
SUBTOTAL		69531.

OTHER NON-OPERATING CHARGES (OR INCOME)
PREMIUM ON ADVANCED TERM LOAN PAYMENT	0.	
FACTORING DISCOUNT	0.	
OTHER CHARGES (OR INCOME)	0.	
SUBTOTAL		0.

LESS TOTAL NON-OPERATING CHARGES (OR INCOME)   69531.
TAXABLE INCOME (OR LOSS)   99282.

INCOME TAXES (OR RECOVERY)
NORMAL TAX	21842.	
SURTAX	25813.	
TOTAL TAX		47655.
TAX ADJUSTMENT		0.
NET TAX		47655.

NET PROFIT (OR LOSS) AFTER TAXES   51626.

FIGURE 6.3. Top Management Decision Game—Typical Income Statement

submits forecasts of sales, profits, and cash position. Constraints are placed on expenditures of each firm to keep them from bankrupting themselves while learning the mechanics and basic behavior patterns of the model. Since no external financial transactions are permitted, an abbreviated balance sheet is prepared; the liabilities and net worth section contains only one consolidated figure instead of the complete set of data shown in Fig. 6.2.

In phase B the game is altered in three aspects: constraints on expenditures are removed, borrowing funds is permitted, and two random factors are introduced. The firms are free to manage their cash expenditures as they see fit, and funds may be obtained from short-term bank loans and from short-and long-term loans from private sources, including loans from other companies, as shown in Fig. 6.2. The two random factors apply to marketing and to research and development expenditures, as indicated in Fig. 6.3, and represent variations in the quality or effectiveness of those expenditures resulting from the element of risk. The number applying to each item is expressed as a percentage—100 per cent being average effectiveness.

In phase C the game is expanded to include changes in the equity structure of the firms and trading in capital stock. Four new decision variables are introduced: issue new capital stock, declare cash and stock dividends, buy and sell treasury stock, and buy and sell stock of other companies. The market price for stock at a given time is determined by a computed intrinsic stock price and adjusted by the influence of stock transactions.

Phase D introduces a major capital equipment replacement decision. The companies are presented with an impending loss of capacity because of equipment deterioration, and must decide whether to repair or replace the deteriorating equipment.

Market research information available to the teams is presented in the report in Fig. 6.4. Competitors' prices are made available at no cost, since this information could be expected to be readily obtained. Three other items of information must be purchased: industry sales, sales and market share of competitors, total industry expenditures for marketing, and total industry expenditures for research and development.

An important feature of this model is the inclusion of realistic economic data, illustrated in Fig. 6.5, as one determinant of the total industry market. Provision is made for the game administrator to input ten actual historical economic time series, thereby placing the game in a realistic economic environment. This also allows the administrator to assign the teams the task of analyzing the economy and developing economic forecasts. In order to forestall players from simply going to published sources and discovering their economic future, each series is disguised by a different scaling factor.

At the conclusion of the game, decision inputs and a large number of performance measures for each team for each period of play are plotted by

TOP MANAGEMENT DECISION GAME

FORM 6

ECHO COMPANY

MARKET RESEARCH INFORMATION BULLETIN
FOR YEAR 7 QUARTER 3

COMPANY		UNIT PRICES	SALES (UNITS)	PERCENTAGE SALES
ALPHA COMPANY	$	4.100	1980113.	16.6
BAKER COMPANY	$	3.800	3043910.	25.6
CHARLTON COMPANY	$	3.790	3994000.	33.6
DELTA COMPANY	$	3.900	1076092.	9.0
ECHO COMPANY	$	3.900	1807457.	15.2

TOTAL ACTUAL SALES   11901572.   100.000
SALES LOST TO INDUSTRY DUE TO OVERSOLD
CONDITION OF SOME COMPANIES   458797.

TOTAL POTENTIAL MARKET   12360370.

YOUR COMPANY LOST SALES OF   0.   UNITS DUE TO LACK OF AVAILABLE FINISHED INVENTOR

TOTAL INDUSTRY EXPENDITURES FOR MARKETING   1600000.

TOTAL INDUSTRY EXPENDITURES FOR
RESEARCH AND DEVELOPMENT   1501000.

FIGURE 6.4. Top Management Decision Game—Typical Market Research Information
Bulletin

TOP MANAGEMENT DECISION GAME

FORM 4

ECONOMETRIC NEWS LETTER

AS OF YEAR 7, AT THE BEGINNING OF QUARTER 4

UNIT RAW MATERIAL PRICES FOR THIS QUARTER---- $ 2.250

HOURLY DIRECT LABOR RATES FOR THIS QUARTER--- $ 2.007

GENERAL BUSINESS STATISTICS
=============================

SERIES	UNIT OF MEASURE	DATE	AMOUNT
GROSS NATIONAL PRODUCT	BILLION $	2 QUARTERS AGO	646.3
RETAIL SALES (ADJUSTED)	BILLION $	2 MONTHS AGO	21.3
FRB PRODUCTION INDEX (ADJUSTED)	INDEX NO.	2 MONTHS AGO	136.
BANK DEBITS, TOTAL	BILLION $	2 MONTHS AGO	312.3
CONSUMERS PRICE INDEX	INDEX NO.	3 MONTHS AGO	110.8
WHOLESALE PRICE INDEX	INDEX NO.	LAST MONTH	106.3
STANDARD AND POOR 500 STOCK INDEX	INDEX NO.	YESTERDAY	60.90
UNEMPLOYMENT	MILLIONS	2 MONTHS AGO	3.54
AVERAGE WEEKLY FACTORY EARNINGS	DOLLARS	2 MONTHS AGO	102.45
POPULATION	MILLIONS	2 MONTHS AGO	190.6

FIGURE 6.5. Top Management Decision Game—Typical Economic Data Report

the computer on large graphs. A separate graph is prepared for each variable, showing on the plot a comparison of the variable for all teams for the entire run of the game.

Figure 6.6 illustrates the basic structure of the game model, which is programed in FORTRAN. For each play data are input for team decisions, current economic data, status of the game from preceding plays, and parameters of the model functions. Total industry market is computed first and is a function of three factors: industry price, industry promotion, and economic conditions. The impact of price on the market is weighted by the price

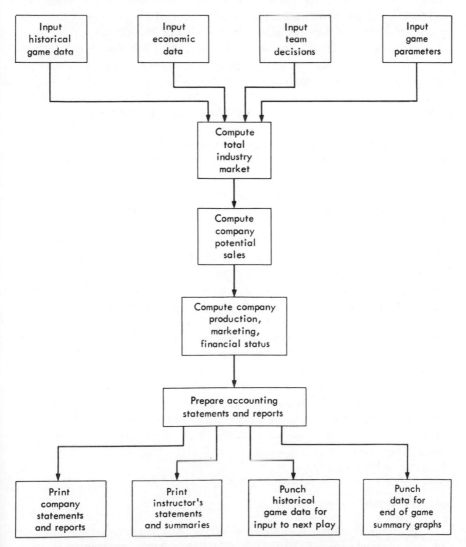

FIGURE 6.6. Structure of Top Management Decision Game Model

level in the economy, historical industry price level, and a price elasticity function. The impact of promotion is dependent upon current and past industry expenditures; expenditures have a carry-over effect from previous periods. Economic conditions are derived from the economic series input into the model.

Market share for each firm is a function of three factors: selling price, marketing expenditures, and research and development expenditures. Each of these factors is weighted by sensitivity parameters input for the game run. Both marketing expenditures and research and development expenditures have a carry-over effect from past periods. Research and development expenditures have two effects. They increase the attractiveness of the company's product to the market and lower its cost of production.

Results of internal operations of each firm are computed for the quarter. In the production sector output is constrained by availability of raw materials, and actual sales are restricted by availability of finished goods inventory. Costs of company operations and the firm's resultant raw material, work in process, and finished goods inventory quantities and values are then calculated. Following this, profits, taxes, and financial transactions for the company are determined. The process is repeated for each firm in the industry. Finally, accounting statements and reports for each company and a set of statements and summaries for the game administrator are prepared and printed, historical game data for input to the next play are punched on cards, and data for the end-of-game summary graphs and reports are punched.

The model is structured to allow the game administrator a wide latitude in developing a game to meet his requirements. The number of teams (from three to six), length of play, and phases to include are at his discretion. Model parameters that determine effects of decision variables, such as price elasticity and marketing expenditure impact, and parameters that determine basic functions, such as income tax rates, may be altered as part of the data input to the game. Initial price of the product, size of the companies, and financial condition of the companies are treated as data inputs and may be set at any desired level.

In use, this model with its progressive enrichment feature has proven to be quite flexible. Future plans are to increase its flexibility by a modular construction that will allow the addition and deletion of particular features at the discretion of the administrator, and to provide for reports in monetary units other than the dollar and languages other than English to facilitate its use in other countries.

Functional games

Functional games focus on middle management decisions and emphasize particular areas of the firm. They cover such areas as production scheduling, materials management, logistics systems, maintenance scheduling, manpower requirements, resource allocation, personnel assignments, sales management, retail operations, advertising and promotion, stock transactions, and research and development management. The objective in the play of functional games is usually to minimize cost by achieving efficient operations. With emphasis on cost control rather than competition in a market, there is no interaction in many functional games between player decisions. However, the players may compete to see who can achieve lowest cost or some other criterion of success. Many functional games do not require computer scoring, since they deal with a relatively small portion of the operations of an organization.

When there is no interaction between decisions of the players, functional games bear a strong resemblance to simulation models. In fact, simulation models are often used for gaming purposes. The simulation program in Appendix B, for example, has been used as a game in conjunction with the presentation of inventory theory. When it is used in this mode, data regarding parameters of an inventory system are presented to the players. The players make decisions regarding controllable variables, and the simulation program computes total cost for each player's decisions. There is no interaction among decisions, and the objective is to achieve minimum cost by employing certain principles learned from inventory theory. Aside from random variations that occur when stochastic elements are included in the simulated system, the player with the best understanding of principles of optimization in inventory systems will achieve lowest total cost.

The Westinghouse Plant Scheduling and Warehouse Distribution Simulation Exercise is another example of a noninteractive functional game.[21] It is designed to demonstrate the application of decision rules to a distribution system. Decisions made in the game involve placing orders on a factory for one item of a line of industrial goods and distributing completed items to three field warehouses. Typical of manually scored functional games in this area are Greene and Sisson's Materials Inventory Management Game and Production Scheduling Management Game.[22] In the materials game, participants are given an order cost, inventory carrying cost, and shortage penalty cost, and they attempt to minimize total inventory cost. It is designed to demonstrate elementary forecasting and economic order quantities.

Greenlaw, Herron, and Rawdon's, X-Otol is a manual game that simulates operation of a distribution system and demonstrates effects of feedback, time lags, and amplification in a manufacturer-wholesaler-retailer-customer distribution chain.[23] It is patterned after Forrester's industrial

[21]James C. Emery, "A Simulation Exercise for Plant Scheduling and Warehouse Distribution," in Kibbee, et al., *Management Games* (New York: Rinehold Publishing Corporation, 1961).

[22]Jay R. Greene and R. L. Sisson, *Dynamic Management Decision Games* (New York: John Wiley & Sons, Inc., 1959).

[23]Paul S. Greenlaw, Lowell W. Herron, and Richard H. Rawdon, *Business Simulation in Industrial and University Education* (Englewood Cliffs, N.J.: Prentice-Hall, Inc., 1962), Chap. 5.

dynamics model. In the X-Otol game a team comprises a distribution system with each member taking the role of one of the links in the chain: manufacturers, wholesalers, and retailers. The game administrator takes the role of consumers and provides fluctuating demand for the retailers. The object of play is to control inventory levels and prevent shortages. Three other manual games of feedback systems are presented in *Problems in Industrial Dynamics*: a production-distribution system, a factory hiring and lay-off system, and an apartment construction industry system.[24]

Illustrative of a computer-scored game is the IBM Production Manpower Decision Game. Players make monthly production and manpower scheduling decisions for a paint manufacturing company and compete with a computer program that makes calculations using the linear decision rule developed at Carnegie–Mellon University.[25]

Marketing games often focus on top-level marketing decisions, involve competition, and may be interactive. Some top-level marketing games are similar to general management games with the marketing decisions sector expanded and other sectors reduced in emphasis. Remington Rand has a Marketing Management Simulation, which involves decisions in pricing, advertising, sales personnel administration, inventory, and market research.[26] Another comprehensive marketing game is MARKSIM, which provides decisions in national and local advertising market research, inventory allocation among two distribution channels, price, product quality, production volume, and debt repayment.[27] The market in this game is divided into three segments based on price and quality of goods offered.

Functional games are available in other areas as well. FINANSIM is a computer game that emphasizes capital cost and budgeting, cash utilization and acquisition, and the asset structure of the firm.[28] Marketing decisions are excluded; demand and price are considered exogenous factors.

Typical of very specialized games is PERT-SIM, a computerized game developed in part by one of the authors.[29] This game allows players to place bids on a construction project and then to supervise construction of the project within a simulated environment. The particular project is building a road under uncertainty as to type of terrain, composition of material

[24]W. Edwin Jarmain, ed., *Problems in Industrial Dynamics* (Cambridge, Mass.: The Massachusetts Institute of Technology Press, 1963).

[25]Charles C. Holt, Franco Modigliani, John F. Muth, and Herbert A. Simon, *Planning Production, Inventories, and Workforce* (Englewood Cliffs, N.J.: Prentice-Hall, Inc., 1960).

[26]Joel M. Kibbee, Clifford J. Craft, and Bert Nanus, *Management Games* (New York: Reinhold Publishing Corp., 1961), Chap. 2.

[27]Paul S. Greenlaw and Fred W. Kniffin, *MARKSIM: A Marketing Decision Simulation* (Scranton, Pa.: International Textbook Company, 1964).

[28]Paul S. Greenlaw and M. William Frey, *FINANSIM: A Financial Management Simulation* (Scranton, Pa.: International Textbook Company, 1967). Another functional game is projected for this series: *PROSIM*, a production management game.

[29]Lloyd A. Swanson and Harold L. Pazer, *PERT-SIM* (to be published by International Textbook Company, Scranton, Pa., during 1968).

beneath the overburden, and structure of cost information. More precise information may be obtained by each player, but an additional cost is incurred. Although all players supervise an identical construction project, the information supplied is not (except in rare instances) the same. Information purchased merely narrows the range of possibilities and brings it closer to the actual value.

After analyzing whatever additional information the participant desires to purchase, he submits a bid that includes both a dollar amount and a project completion date. Players are informed that the client desires to utilize the road as soon as it is completed and that both dollar and time figures will be considered. (In essence, the client assigns a fixed cost per day for each day that he is unable to utilize the road.)

The objective is to maximize profit, but the participant must remember that he is bidding in a competitive environment. In the real world, the individual with lowest combination of time and cost, a similar quality level being assumed, is awarded the job. However, in the game each bid is converted into a probability of winning, which is a function of the rank of the bid and the dollar difference between bids. Subsequently, this probability is multiplied by total profit (or loss) at the conclusion of the game to give an expected profit. This enables all participants not only to prepare a bid but also to supervise the construction project.

Supervision of the projects consists of specifying starting times for activities and time compression of the activities, if any. This information is input data for the computer program, which selects randomly from a beta distribution the actual length of time and resulting cost for each activity. Time and cost data are then given to the student so that he may change his scheduling of activities or compress some activities further to lower total cost. This cycle is repeated several times until the project is completed.

Throughout the simulated construction of the project, the player has the opportunity to purchase additional information about all activities. After completion of the project, total cost of the project itself and cost of information purchased is computed for each participant, subtracted from the respective bid, and multiplied by the probability of obtaining the bid to compute total project profit (or loss) for each player.

Programed play[30]

In our discussion of game structures so far we have not distinguished explicitly between structures that require a sequence of decisions on the part of the players and those requiring only a single decision or set of decisions at the outset which is then used throughout the computer run by the game

---

[30]Some of the material in this section has appeared previously in: Robert C. Meier, "Decision Making Versus Strategy Determination: A Gaming and Heuristic Approach," *University of Washington Business Review*, Vol. 25, No. 4 (April–June, 1966).

program. We will call the latter type of play programed play, since the player essentially programs his decisions ahead of time, and no further inputs are made during the run of the game.

The programed play concept has commonly been used in noninteractive functional games. In an inventory game, for example, the players might decide on a lot size or order point, or perhaps on a mathematical formula for calculating the appropriate quantity, and the game program would determine the results of applying that decision for a specified number of periods. In effect, players program decisions or plays of the game ahead of time. If mathematical formulas or more complicated decision rules are employed, the decisions that result may exhibit an ability to adapt to changing conditions in the simulated environment during a run of the game in much the same way that a player might respond if he were making decisions himself.

The concept of programed play has not been applied to any great extent in interactive general management games. Almost universally, general management game structures provide for period-by-period decision making by the participants rather than the use of decision rules developed by them. However, programs have been designed to play competitive, interactive games such as checkers and chess[31] and to play the strategies of opposing sides in computerized war games,[32] and the same structure can be employed in management games.

The use of programed play in interactive, general-management-type games is an important extension of the gaming technique, since it shifts attention away from period-by-period decision making, emphasizing, instead, the determination of long-range strategy. Figure 6.7 illustrates the difference between play of a conventional management game and play of a game in which preprogramed strategies provide decisions for the teams each period. The elementary business game discussed previously in this chapter in the section dealing with construction of a game was specifically designed to operate using the idea of programed play as shown in Fig. 6.7(b), although it can be run as a conventional game, as shown in Fig. 6.7(a).[33] When the programed play mode is used, input to the game program by the players is in the form of decision-making subroutines. Each player or team of players works out a decision strategy for the five decisions—price, marketing expenditures, production rate, plant and equipment purchases, and loan repayments—that must be made each period of play. The strategy

---

    [31]See A. L. Samuel, "Some Studies in Machine Learning Using the Game of Checkers," *IBM Journal of Research and Development*, (July, 1959).

    [32]See, for example, E. S. Quade, *Analysis for Military Decisions* (Chicago: Rand McNally & Company, 1964), Sec. 4.7; and George W. Evans, II, Graham F. Wallace, and Georgia L. Sutherland, *Simulation Using Digital Computers* (Englewood Cliffs, N.J.: Prentice-Hall, Inc., 1967), Chap. 4.

    [33]The game program is discussed more fully in H. R. Burson, "An Application of Heuristic Programming in a Business Gaming Situation," unpublished MBA research report (Seattle: University of Washington, 1966).

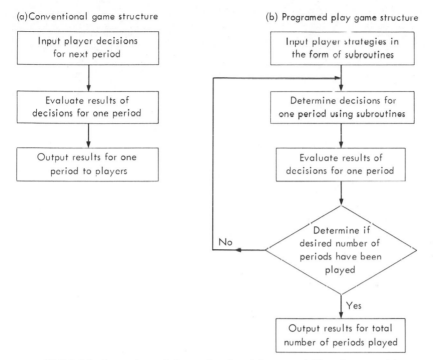

(a)Conventional game structure   (b) Programed play game structure

FIGURE 6.7. Comparison of Conventional and Programed Play Game Models

is converted into a computer program, a subroutine, and the subroutines play each other for as many periods as are desired without further intervention on the part of the players.[34] As the play proceeds automatically from period to period, profit and loss statements, statements of cash flow, balance sheets, summaries of industry data, and summaries of company decisions are prepared for each period so that events taking place and relative standings of the companies can be traced at the conclusion of the run. We have already shown a sample of output produced for the teams each period in Fig. 6.1.

While it is not difficult to play a game such as this reasonably well when one is making *ad hoc* decisions on a period-by-period basis, it is quite a different matter to select a strategy for each of the five variables which will be effective against the strategies of competitors, whatever these may be.[35] Since there are no mathematical techniques that would enable a team to

---

[34]A similar example of the examination of long-run strategies in a competitive market is found in; Philip Kotler, "Competitive Strategies for New Product Marketing Over the Life Cycle," *Management Science*, Vol. 12, No. 4 (December, 1965).

[35]One strategy that we have ruled out is that of industrial espionage. Since all data concerning the industry and companies are available in common storage in the computer memory, it would be possible to obtain perfect information about the other companies. Although it is doubtful that even this information would permit a company to select overwhelmingly successful strategies, we have established the ground rules that a company may use only its own company data and general industry data as shown in Fig. 6.1.

win the game[36] (or, for that matter, even to play the game), the subroutines that have been devised so far for playing the game fall under the broad classification of heuristic techniques, as discussed in Chap. 5. That is, player strategies as programed in the game-playing subroutines are heuristic in the sense that they involve selection of values for the decision variables from a very large number of possibilities in somewhat the same way that a human decision maker might make the selection.

To illustrate the character of strategies which might be employed, let us consider the decision strategy for price. Among several elementary strategies that might be imagined are

1. Hold price constant at some value.
2. Set price at the previous industry average.
3. Set price at some multiple or fraction of the previous industry average.
4. Select price at random from a specified distribution.
5. Increase the price if sales are above the last period industry average, and decrease it if sales are below.

These and many others are eligible candidates for strategies for just the one decision variable, price, and their effectiveness must be weighed in conjunction with the selection of strategies for the other four decision variables. Following is an example of a somewhat more sophisticated set of decision rules for setting price and marketing expenditures which was developed by one team in an experimental play of the game. In the decision rules, T is total market for the industry, S is sales of the company, P is company price, and M is company marketing expenditure. The subscripts t, $t-1$, and $t-2$ refer to the current period, last period, and two periods previously.

If $T_{t-1} > T_{t-2}$ and $S_{t-1} > S_{t-2}$, let $P_t = 1.00P_{t-1}$ and $M_t = 1.15M_{t-1}$

If $T_{t-1} > T_{t-2}$ and $S_{t-1} \leq S_{t-2}$, let $P_t = 0.98P_{t-1}$ and $M_t = 1.10M_{t-1}$

If $T_{t-1} \leq T_{t-2}$ and $S_{t-1} > S_{t-2}$, let $P_t = 1.00P^{t-1}$ and $M_t = 1.10M_{t-1}$

If $T_{t-1} \leq T_{t-2}$ and $S_{t-1} \leq S_{t-2}$, let $P_t = 0.96P_{t-1}$ and $M_t = 1.18M_{t-1}$

These rules are not meant to be indicative of what constitutes a "good" set of rules, but they are illustrative of how more complex rules can be constructed.

As yet, there is very little accumulated experience with the utilization of the concept of programed play in management games. We have found in experiments with this elementary game that teams are capable of constructing strategies that exhibit excellent competitive characteristics and produce

---

[36]"Winning" in the context of the game is itself an ambiguous concept, since the criteria for evaluating success are not as clear-cut as in games such as checkers and chess.

decision-making behavior that is similar to that of human participants in such a game. We regard this type of structure in management games as being very much in the experimental stage, but it is a structure that offers promise as a vehicle for looking into the nature of long-range strategic planning in a competitive management environment.

Selection of model structure

The game designer is faced with the problem of establishing the proper boundary for the system he is modeling. This boundary will determine the particular decisions to be included. Information feedback must be provided on which to base decisions, and there must be some resultant reward or penalty in order for each decision variable to involve a choice problem. As an example, in a marketing system model where the penalty for too small an inventory is lost sales, there should also be a penalty for too large an inventory. If a capital structure that will provide such a penalty is not included, then an inventory carrying charge may be needed.

Developers and users of business games face the same basic dilemma that has confronted developers of military games, and in fact of all types of simulation models: the conflict between realism and simplicity of computation and play. Since the model—in fact, any simulation or mathematical model—is an abstraction from some real process and hence only an approximation, the problem is to determine the degree of realism and resultant complication desirable in the model. It is fundamental that a game should appear to be realistic and behave in a realistic fashion, but realism adds complexity. As a game model becomes more complex, the game becomes more difficult to learn, to play, and to administer. A game model that is too complex does not permit identification of the impact of important policies and decisions and isolation of underlying structural relationships and causal factors. Determining the desired level of complexity is often a trial and error process. The game designer must choose carefully between oversimplification and overcomplication, but it is generally better to begin with simpler models and to increase complexity as the need develops than to begin with an unmanageable model. Several game designers have commented upon the depth of analysis obtainable with rather simple formulations.[37]

Simplicity in game design includes simplicity in the model structure, computation, decision making, and administration. The criteria for deciding on the degree of simplicity depend upon the uses for the game and the resources available. The rules must be easily learned for a game designed for use in a training situation requiring a short briefing session and rapid decisions, whereas those in a game permitting more learning time, such as the

---

[37]Richard Bellman, et al., "On the Construction of a Multi-Stage, Multi-Person Business Game," *Operations Research*, Vol. 5, No. 7 (August, 1957).

Carnegie Tech Management Game, may be rather elaborate. The decision-making sector of the game includes the rules of procedure, information feedback provided to the participants, and the arithmetic calculations required of them. Information feedback and arithmetic calculations involved can be simplified while decisions are still permitted that are difficult to make in the sense of choice criteria and strategy. The sequence of decisions in even a relatively simple multistage process can combine to result in a set of very complex interactions. Computational complexity increases rapidly with small increases in model complexity.

There is some evidence to suggest that simple game models may be as effective as more complex models. There may be a trade-off between factors —such as simplifying the arithmetic calculations of the participants and administrators by increasing the complexity of computation in a computer game. Thus, there are no rules to follow except for the suggestion to begin with the simplest feasible model and add complexity only as the need is carefully demonstrated.

An important distinction should be made between realism and verisimilitude, the appearance of reality. A simple hypothetical model may, if properly structured, appear quite realistic to the players. Most gaming relies heavily on illusion, whether it be the movement of wooden blocks (representing troops) across a map of a battle field, or the generation of an imaginary product's sales through expenditure of imaginary funds. The effect may be seen in this reaction to von Reisswitz's war game:

> In 1894, von Mueffling, then Chief of the German General Staff, consented to witness an exhibition of the game. He received the players somewhat coldly, but as the operation expanded on the map, the old general's face lighted up, and at last he broke out with enthusiasm, "It's not a game at all! It's a training for war; I shall recommend it most emphatically to the whole army."[38]

The effectiveness of the illusion has also been observed many times in business games.

Of course, verisimilitude can be achieved with a realistic model, and quite realistic models have been developed. The cost of these models is high, but if the purpose for which the game is to be used necessitates the added realism, it is worth the added cost. As an example, if in a marketing game the object is to demonstrate the general principles of the effects of interaction, price elasticity, managerial planning, and cash flows, model realism is of relatively minor importance, provided the model has the appearance of reality and behaves in a manner which the participants feel is realistic. The shape of the demand function represented in the model is not so important

---

[38]Farrand Sayre, *Map Maneuvers and Tactical Rides* (Springfield, Mass.: Springfield Printing and Binding Co., 1908). Cited in Clayton J. Thomas, "Military Gaming," in *Progress in Operation Research*, Russell L. Ackoff, ed. (New York: John Wiley & Sons, Inc., 1961), p. 426.

if it approximates the type of elasticity or inelasticity which does not seem unrealistic to the participants. However, if the objective is to demonstrate dynamic behavior of a particular product under various sets of conditions in a particular market, the model must have a high degree of realism. Price elasticity, seasonal variation, and advertising and promotional effects must necessarily be carefully represented. Realistic models have the added advantage that they may be used for operational gaming and for research purposes.

Three other factors affect the acceptability of a game model: its stability, elasticity, and protection from extreme policies.[39] Stability refers to its ability to resist wide fluctuations due to single moves by the players, for instance, one team capturing a whole market in one period by a drastic price reduction.[40] Elasticity refers to the sensitivity of the model to gross changes in strategy by the players. Achieving both may require careful trial and error, since striving for stability may be at the expense of elasticity, and vice versa. Attaining a balance between them is a function of having the proper time lags and damping factors in the model. Protection from extreme policies is achieved by checks and balances built into the model which prohibit unrealistic policies from being successful. Highly realistic models are potentially less subject to these defects, as they presumably reflect more closely actual behavior of the process being modeled.

Another consideration in designing a game structure is the criteria for measuring successful playing. In some functional games, such as a maintenance game, the object may be to find a minimum cost operating policy, which is acceptable if all the relevant costs have been included. In others, and especially in general management games, the criterion function for success may be more difficult to formulate. Certain measures are available, to be sure, such as total profits, return on investment, and market share, but these are static measures. To evaluate dynamic systems, measures of rates of change of these factors are also needed. The same type of measurement and evaluation problems exist here as in the real world; there is no unanimous agreement on how to weigh the criteria by which success of an organization may be measured.

All this is further complicated by a technical, but important aspect known as an "end effect." If the participants know that a game is to end after the twentieth play, they may be expected to employ an end-game strategy simply to maximize the criterion function. As an example, if in a general management game this function is stated in terms of total profit, the end-game strategy might be to discontinue all research and development expenditures and promotional expenditures for the last few plays, counting

---

[39]Richard Bellman, et al., "On the Construction of a Multi-Stage, Multi-Person Business Game," *Operations Research*, Vol. 5, No. 7 (August, 1957), pp. 484–485.

[40]Unless, of course, the model is designed to demonstrate a high degree of price elasticity.

on some residual effect to maintain short-run sales and thus increase short-term profits. In some instances this can be partially taken into account in the design of the game by careful formulation of the criterion function, such as determining at the game's end a market value for the entire firm as an on-going enterprise by some discounting process. In the original American Management Association game, participants were asked to formulate their own criteria. Others have tried to avoid the problem by not announcing the termination prior to the final decision.

Value of Gaming Techniques

Games have rather consistently been received with enthusiasm by participants, and players often become highly involved. Involvement and enthusiasm do contribute to their potential value, but in view of the cost of gaming in comparison with other teaching techniques, entertainment value alone is insufficient to justify their use. Shubik noted that if player involvement was the primary criterion, he would suggest "poker or the reading of the biographies of Messrs. Fiske, Gould, Drew and Vanderbilt as more than adequate alternatives for glorified monopoly."[41] That games have an important and accepted place in education and research is attested by their continued use and development by many highly respected institutions. However, an ill-structured and inappropriate game may be worse than not using any game.

The educational values claimed by proponents of gaming are impressive. High on the list are the interest aroused and emotional involvement on the part of participants. Perhaps more important is that a game provides a dynamic environment in which students can make decisions and obtain a direct feedback of the results. In this connection a game has been compared to a living case. Referring to the Carnegie Tech Management Game, Cyert noted:

> Essentially, the game is a living case. The student is put in a situation with a variety of problems to be identified and solved. More important, the student must be prepared to live with his decisions. In this respect, the game is unique. No other educational tool presents this opportunity and challenge.[42]

Many functional games are designed to facilitate teaching the value of particular analytic techniques. For instance, a scheduling game may be designed to explore the advantages of different dispatching rules. General management games usually have no such specific goal. The claim has been made that they are designed to teach people to make better decisions, but

---

[41]Martin Shubik, "Review of Dynamic Management Decision Games," *Management Science*, Vol. 5, No. 3 (April, 1960), p. 358.

[42]Kalman J. Cohen, et al., *The Carnegie Tech Management Game: An Experiment in Business Education* (Homewood, Ill.: Richard D. Irwin, Inc., 1964), p. 106.

in view of the highly simplified and unrealistic nature of most general management games it is questionable whether this is a reasonable goal. A more modest goal, that of teaching some of the dynamic functional and accounting interrelationships in a total enterprise, is undoubtedly attained. For example, the necessity of considering the effects of price, marketing expenditures, plant and equipment purchases, and production rate decisions on the cash position of a firm has considerable educational value.

Most general management games are of necessity so highly oversimplified in comparison with real business situations that they cannot fairly be said to teach business decision making. They do not often include any of the essential qualitative elements of decision making, but instead measure results almost entirely on quantitative factors. However, such games do have a potentially valuable contribution to the development of decision-making skills which is not dependent upon practice in a realistic environment. Kossack of IBM observed that gaming gave people experience in making decisions in an unreal world.

> Within this admittedly artificial environment, gaming gives participants an opportunity to compare their decision making assumptions with those of the game model, to discuss and evaluate both and compare them critically. In other words, the game serves as a sort of catalyst to critical self-analysis and introspection.[43]

Viewed thus, such games may be considered environments for self-instruction. The Carnegie Tech game is said to be designed to provide four types of experience: competitive, negotiating, organizational, and reflective.[44] A similar observation could be made for other games as well.

Another use for game models is as a basis for training in modeling. In this situation the game model is designated as the "real world" and the players attempt to determine the behavior characteristics of this world by playing the game. The primary object is not the play of the game, but to gain enough evidence to analyze the basic structure of this world, to build a simulation model of it, and to simulate its behavior. The advantage of modeling and simulating the game model is that the "world" can be dissected and examined, giving the modelers an opportunity to see how right or wrong they were.

There is considerable evidence that games, both of the general management and the specific function type, do have educational value. McKenney undertook to compare the effectiveness of a business game with a series of cases for two groups of students in production management courses identical except for the use of the game. On the basis of scores from written examinations, which were higher for those students who had participated in the game,

---

[43]*Simulation and Gaming: A Symposium*, Management Report No. 55. (New York: American Management Association, 1961), p. 49.

[44]Kalman J. Cohen, et al., *The Carnegie Tech Management Game: An Experiment in Business Education* (Homewood, Ill.: Richard D. Irwin, Inc., 1964), p. 251.

he concluded that the time taken for the game was worthwhile.[45] Dill and
Doppelt have reported on studies involving the Carnegie Tech Management
Game.[46] They reported that students improved in their ability to handle the
analytic tasks and to utilize information as the game progressed. Students
learned from their game experience, and placed a heavy emphasis on interpersonal learning, that is, learning derived from interpersonal relationships
with other members of their teams and with outside groups, as opposed to
learning solely from experiences with the game model. A study undertaken
at the University of Maryland examined the performance and interest of
students in a business policy course, comparing cases plus outside readings,
cases plus a relatively simple game, and cases plus a more complex game.[47]
Game participants scored significantly higher on the final examination and
did not suffer in their ability to analyze cases in comparison with nongame-
playing groups. Interest and motivation were increased by the game, but
participants did not develop more favorable attitudes toward the course.
An important conclusion was that there was no significant difference between
students playing the complex game and those playing the simple game.

Games may be used to determine optimal solutions or strategies for
play and to find optimal structures for systems. This has been called operational gaming by Thomas and Deemer who define it as "the serious use of
playing as a primary device to formulate a *game*, to solve a *game*, or to impart
something of the solution of a *game*."[48] Military gaming has long had this
purpose. In the functional business game involving a single person, optimal
play may be achieved through attempts by the player to maximize some
criterion in the game. In a multiperson, interactive game this is much more
difficult, because there may be no single acceptable measure of success and
methods of achieving success against the play of opponents are difficult to
devise.

Since control can be exercised over conditions surrounding the play,
a game can be used as a laboratory for behavioral research. The typical
business game involves small task-oriented groups in an environment which,
while artificial, is similar to a business environment. It is possible to observe
interactions in such small groups and observe effects of changes in group
size and composition. A related area is that of organizational research.
The game situation provides an opportunity to study the effects of organization structure on goal formation, intragroup conflict, identification of
members with the group, and evolution of leadership patterns. In addition,

[45]J. L. McKenney, "An Evaluation of a Business Game in an MBA Curriculum,"
Journal of Business, Vol. 35, No. 3 (July, 1962).
[46]William R. Dill and Neil Doppelt, "The Acquisition of Experience in a Complex
Management Game," *Management Science*, Vol. 10, No. 1 (October, 1963).
[47]Anthony P. Raia, "A Study of the Educational Value of Management Games,"
Journal of Business, Vol. 39, No. 3 (July, 1966).
[48]Clayton J. Thomas and Walter L. Deemer, Jr., "The Role of Operational Gaming in
Operations Research," *Operations Research*, Vol. 5, No. 1 (February, 1957), p. 6.

the game environment provides an opportunity to observe organizational processes: planning, translation of plans into action, and the use of procedures and controls. A realistic industry game permits research into organizational changes such as altering the grouping of functions and adding new functions to existing organizations.

Since interactive games typically involve an oligopoly market structure, they can be used to explore some aspects of the interaction of firms in an oligopoly situation. Games involving only a few competing firms in which the players are very much aware of the impact of their actions on competitors may provide some useful insights into the pattern of such interaction.[49] For research of this nature the programed play structure discussed earlier in the chapter would provide a method to compare effects of various strategies. Cohen, et al., have also suggested that games may be useful in exploring problems associated with the behavioral theory of the firm.[50] They suggest that a complex game situation could be used to study the impact of organization structure and institutional factors on the price and output policies of the firm. Additionally, companies might use game models of their own industry to predict competitors' reactions to company decisions and policy changes.

Summary

There is no clear distinction between games and gaming and simulation models as discussed in previous chapters. Games in which there is little or no interaction between the decisions of players and games which do not require inputs by the players after the initial decisions strongly resemble simulation models; indeed, many of the simulation models previously discussed may be used as noninteractive gaming models with little or no change in structure. Highly interactive, competitive game models, on the other hand, are quite different from the usual simulation models and are distinguished by the element of periodic decision making and play by the participants. The many different types of gaming and simulation models which are now in existence may be thought of as falling on a continuum with highly interactive, highly participative games at one end and noninteractive, nonparticipative simulation models at the other.

Although games are used both as educational devices and as tools for analysis and research, the greatest use of the gaming technique has been for educational purposes. Objectives of gaming for educational purposes vary from developing decision-making and organizational skills to imparting knowledge regarding specific techniques of analysis and optimi-

---

[49]For instance, see Austin C. Hoggatt, "An Experimental Business Game," *Behavioral Science*, Vol. 4, Number 3 (July, 1959).

[50]Kalman J. Cohen, et al., *The Carnegie Tech Management Game* (Homewood: Ill.: Richard D. Irwin, Inc., 1964), p. 277.

zation. Research uses of games have been mainly to investigate behavioral and organizational aspects of the play of the game, but games also have research uses in the development of dynamic theories of the firm and economic theories of oligopoly behavior. Programed play game structures offer an approach to the investigation of effective long-range strategies and automated decision making.

EXERCISES

6.1 Look through the text illustrations and exercises in previous chapters and determine the models that would be suitable to use as noninteractive games. Describe how they would be used.

6.2 A business game involves a market in which three companies compete. The initial base market is 1,000,000 units, price is $5.00 per unit, marketing expenditures for the industry are $750,000, and the economic index is initially 100. The following data describe the economic index and sequence of plays for 10 periods.

			Company 1		Company 2		Company 3
Period	Economic Index	Price	Mktg.[a] Expend.	Price	Mktg.[a] Expend.	Price	Mktg.[a] Expend.
1	101	$5.00	$250	$5.00	$260	$4.75	$250
2	102	5.25	250	5.00	265	4.75	260
3	107	5.25	260	5.00	275	4.50	265
4	110	5.00	265	4.75	280	4.50	280
5	114	4.75	265	4.75	280	4.50	285
6	113	4.75	265	4.25	280	4.50	285
7	115	4.75	275	4.25	285	4.25	300
8	116	4.75	285	4.25	300	4.25	305
9	118	4.75	300	4.50	300	4.25	310
10	119	4.75	300	4.75	300	4.25	320

[a]Marketing expenditures are shown in thousands of dollars.

a. Using Eqs. (6.1) and (6.2) and Tables 6.1 and 6.2, trace the behavior of total market for the 10 periods. (Read Table 6.1, using industry average price rather than weighted average price.)

b. Repeat part a. above but with Eq. (6.2) modified to

$$T_t = B_t \text{ (price effect + marketing effect)} + 25,000\ \mu_t$$

were μ_t is normally distributed with zero mean and unit variance.

6.3 Repeat Exercise 6.2a, including the calculation of company market shares by Eqs. (6.3) through (6.5) and using the following values of α and β.

a. $\alpha = 0.10$, $\beta = 0.25$

b. $\alpha = 0.25$, $\beta = 0.10$

c. $\alpha = 0.50$, $\beta - 0.50$.

Comment on your results.

6.4 Repeat Exercise 6.2a, calculating the company market shares by Eqs. (6.3) through (6.5) and using $\alpha = 0.10$ and $\beta = 0.25$. However, modify Eq. (6.3) by including a random factor to represent variation in the effectiveness of marketing expenditures. Select a distribution for this random factor which you feel would yield realistic behavior, and compare your results with the results in Exercise 6.3a.

6.5 Construct a simple business game, using the market structure outlined in Eqs. (6.1) through (6.5) and Tables 6.1 and 6.2. Assume that sufficient product is always available for sale so that inventory level, production rate, and production capacity are not relevant in the model. Each company is to have a certain fixed cost of operating each period and variable costs of a fixed amount for each unit sold. Develop a set of input data for your models and play the game for several periods to see whether the game yields reasonable behavior.

6.6 Restructure the model developed in Exercise 6.5 so that it has the programed play structure outlined in Fig. 6.7. Develop different decision strategies for price and marketing for several companies and run the game with these strategies making the decisions. Use the input data from Exercise 6.5 where possible.

6.7 Construct a flow chart for the computations required for the business game whose output is illustrated in Fig. 6.1.

BIBLIOGRAPHY

American Management Association, Inc., *Simulation and Gaming: A Symposium.* Report No. 55. New York: American Management Association, 1961.

Andlinger G. R., "Business Games—Play One!" *Harvard Business Review*, Vol. 36, No. 2 (March–April, 1958).

———— "What Can Business Games Do?" *Harvard Business Review*, Vol. 36, No. 4 (July–August, 1958).

Babb, E. M., M. A. Leslie, and M. E. Van Slyke, "The Potential of Business-Gaming Methods in Research," *The Journal of Business*, Vol. 39, No. 6 (October, 1966).

Bellman, Richard, Charles E. Clark, Donald G. Malcom, Clifford J. Craft, and Franc M. Ricciardi, "On the Construction of a Multi-stage, Multi-person Business Game," *Operations Research*, Vol. 5, No. 7 (August, 1957).

Burson, H. R., "An Application of Heuristic Programming in a Business Gaming Situation." Unpublished MBA research report. Seattle: University of Washington, 1966.

Cohen, Kalman J., William R. Dill, Alfred A. Kuehn, and Peter R. Winters, *The Carnegie Tech Management Game: An Experiment in Business Education.* Homewood, Ill.: Richard D. Irwin, Inc., 1964.

Cohen, Kalman J. and Eric Rhenman, "The Role of Management Games In Education and Research," *Management Science*, Vol. 7, No. 2 (January, 1961).

Dale, Alfred G. and Charles R. Klasson, *Business Gaming: A Survey of American Collegiate Schools of Business.* Austin, Tex.: Bureau of Business Research, The University of Texas, 1964.

Dill, William R. and Neil Doppelt, "The Acquisition of Experience in a Complex Management Game," *Management Science*, Vol. 10, No. 1 (October, 1963).

Dill, William R., James R. Jackson, and James W. Sweeney, eds., *Proceedings of the Conference on Business Games.* New Orleans, La.: Tulane University, 1961.

Dolbear, F. Trenery, Jr., Richard Attiyeh, and William C. Brainard, "A Simulation Policy Game for Teaching Macroeconomics," *American Economic Review*, Vol. 58, No. 2 (May, 1968).

Geisler, Murray A., "The Simulation of a Large Scale Military Activity," *Management Science*, Vol. 5, No. 4 (July, 1959).

Green, Paul E., Patrick J. Robinson, and Peter T. Fitzroy, *Experiments on the Value of Information in Simulated Marketing Environments.* Boston: Allyn & Bacon, Inc., 1967.

Greene, Jay R. and R. L. Sisson, *Dynamic Management Decision Games.* New York: John Wiley and Sons, Inc., 1959.

Greenlaw, Paul S., Lowell W. Herron and Richard H. Rawdon, *Business Simulation in Industrial and University Education.* Englewood Cliffs, N.J.: Prentice-Hall, Inc., 1962.

Greenlaw, Paul S. and M. William Frey, *FINANSIM: A Financial Management Simulation.* Scranton, Pa.: International Textbook Company, 1967.

Greenlaw, Paul S. and Fred W. Kniffin, *MARKSIM: A Marketing Decision Simulation.* Scranton, Pa.: International Textbook Company, 1964.

Haldi, John and Harvey M. Wagner, *Simulated Economic Models.* Homewood, Ill.: Richard D. Irwin, Inc., 1963.

Henshaw, Richard C., Jr., and James R. Jackson, *The Executive Game.* Homewood, Ill.: Richard D. Irwin, Inc., 1966.

Hoffmann, T. R., "Programmed Heuristics and the Concept of Par in Business Games," *Behavioral Science*, Vol. 10, No. 2 (April, 1965).

Kahn, H. and I. Mann, *War Gaming.* Santa Monica, Calif.: The RAND Corporation, P-1167, July 30, 1957.

Kibbee, Joel M., Clifford J. Craft, and Bert Nanus, *Management Games.* New York: Reinhold Publishing Corporation, 1961.

Kotler, Philip, "Competitive Strategies for New Product Marketing over the Life Cycle," *Management Science*, Vol. 12, No. 4 (December, 1965).

Malcolm, Donald G., J. R. Hibbs, J. W. Taul, and M. J. Vaccaro, "*GREMEX*—A Research and Development Management Simulation Exercise," *Management Technology*, Vol. 3, No. 2 (December, 1963).

McDonald, John and Franc Ricciardi, "The Business Game," *Fortune*, Vol. 57, No. 3 (March, 1958).

McKenney, James L., "An Evaluation of a Business Game in an MBA Curriculum," *Journal of Business*, Vol. 35, No. 3 (July, 1962).

————, *Simulation Gaming for Management Development*. Boston, Mass.: Graduate School of Business Administration, Harvard University, 1967.

Meier, Robert C., "Decision Making Versus Strategy Determination: A Gaming and Heuristic Approach," *University of Washington Business Review*, Vol. 25, No. 4 (April–June, 1966).

Mood, Alexander M., *War Gaming as a Technique of Analysis*, P-899. Santa Monica, Calif.: The RAND Corporation, September 3, 1954.

Raia, Anthony P., "A Study of the Educational Value of Management Games," *Journal of Business*, Vol. 39, No. 3 (July, 1966).

Renshaw, Jean R., *The Game Monopologs*, R. M.–1917–1. Santa Monica, Calif.: The RAND Corporation, March 31, 1960.

Ricciardi, Franc M., et al., *Top Management Simulation: the AMA Approach*, Elizabeth Marting, ed. New York: American Management Association, Inc., 1957.

Schrieber, Albert N., "Gaming—A New Way to Teach Business Decision Making," *University of Washington Business Review*, Vol. 17, No. 7 (April, 1958).

Smith, W. Nye, Elmer E. Estey, and Ellsworth F. Vines, *Integrated Simulation*. Cincinnatti: South-Western Publishing Company, 1968.

Symonds, Gifford H., "A Study of Consumer Behavior by Use of Competitive Business Games," *Management Science*, Vol. 14, No. 7 (March, 1968).

Thomas, Clayton J., "Military Gaming," *Progress in Operations Research*, Vol. I, Russell Ackoff, ed. New York: John Wiley & Sons, Inc., 1961.

Thomas, Clayton J. and Walter L. Deemer, "The Role of Operational Gaming in Operations Research," *Operations Research*, Vol. 5, No. 1 (February, 1957).

Thorelli, H. G. and R. L. Graves, *International Operations Simulation*. New York: The Free Press, 1964.

Computer Programs and
Languages for Simulation

7 In previous chapters occasional references were made to computer programs and languages used in simulation studies. This chapter will discuss major approaches that might be taken in implementing simulation studies on a digital computer. The discussion is not intended to take the place of manuals and other reference materials which describe these programs and languages in detail. Rather, we will outline various possibilities and their characteristics so that the prospective user can make an intelligent assessment of the technology that is available.

A large number of special purpose programs have been written to simulate specific problems or types of systems. When a suitable special purpose program is available, the use of such a program is the quickest and cheapest way to implement a simulation study on the computer. However, there are substantial problems that may be encountered in obtaining program descriptions, detailed documentation, and program decks or tapes. It is also frequently the case that existing programs do not have quite the capabilities that the user desires. In the fortunate instance when a suitable program in a form compatible with the user's computing equipment can be located, the user need supply only the problem data. For example, the inventory simulation program described in Appendix B permits the user to select certain backorder, lead time, and demand options and to set problem parameters through input data. This makes the program somewhat general in nature, but there are many inventory systems that cannot be simulated with it. In comparison with other approaches the use of an already existing program is by far the preferable way to carry out a simulation study—provided that the program does what is it is supposed to do and no unanticipated "bugs" turn up.

When previously written programs with proper characteristics are not available, a simulation model must be programed either in a general purpose language such as FORTRAN, COBOL, ALGOL, and PL/I or in one of the simulation languages. In general, the simulation languages reduce programing effort by providing routines to perform certain operations peculiar to simulation

214

which would otherwise have to be programed in detail. One such capability provided by simulation languages is a mechanism for moving the model ahead in time. Other capabilities are specific for each language and will be discussed later. Despite the apparent advantages of simulation languages over general purpose languages, a simulation language is not necessarily the best programing vehicle. One must consider availability of simulation languages for the computing equipment to be used, the cost of learning a new language, which may involve considerable investment of time by the programer, and whether the unique capabilities and structure of available languages are appropriate for the problem.

General Purpose Languages

Virtually any simulation model can be programed in a general purpose computer language. It is difficult to suggest the form that simulation programs written in general purpose languages might take, since much depends on the nature of the problem and the programer's taste and skill. In all cases, however, some technique is necessary for dealing with simulated time in the program.[1] Since digital computers carry out program instructions in sequential fashion, the simplest way to deal with time is to write the program with a philosophy that the sequence of instructions is executed once for each simulated time increment. The time increment can be assumed to represent as long or short a period of real world time as desired. The program updates the status of the system being simulated once for each time increment, changing the status of the parts of the system according to the events taking place in the system. In effect, the simulation program operates as if it were constructing a static picture of the system for one frame of a movie film. It then constructs another picture for the next frame by determining changes that take place in the intervening time period and so on through the total number of time increments. Just as a movie film, which is a series of static pictures, gives an illusion of dynamic movement, the computer program simulates dynamic behavior of a system over time. Unlike the movie film, which is always replayed to watch the action, we may not choose to print out the new status of the system after each time increment, printing out, instead, only periodic reports and summary statistics.[2]

---

[1]If the reader chooses to include model sampling as defined in Chap. 1 under the term "simulation," this statement is not strictly true. We will briefly discuss approaches to model sampling in a later section of this chapter.

[2]It is also feasible to make a moving picture if the state of the system can be displayed pictorially in a computer-prepared diagram. Period-by-period printed output from the program would be photographed one frame at a time on a movie film and then projected in the usual fashion to show the dynamic behavior of the system. Although this technique has never, to the author's knowledge, been used for business or economic problems, it has been used to show the results of simulations of wave actions and meteor impacts on space vehicles. See *IBM Computing Report*, Vol. 2, No. 2 (July, 1966), pp. 3-7, and Kenneth C. Knowlton, "Computer-Produced Movies," *Science*, Vol. 150, No. 26 (November, 1965).

Figure 7.1 illustrates the timing concept discussed in the previous paragraph. Using this philosophy, we make one cycle through the program for each time increment. Figure 7.2 is a simplified flow diagram for an inventory simulation program written with this timing structure. The program reads input data describing the problem parameters, cycles repetitively through the program for n periods, and finally prints a summary of the run. Each cycle represents advancement in time for one Δt as illustrated in Fig. 7.1, and a counter would be included in the program both to keep track of simulated time and to determine when the program should stop cycling and prepare summary statistics.

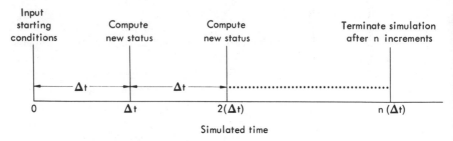

Δt = simulated time increment between updating of status (constant during simulation run)

FIGURE 7.1. Equal Time Increment Programing Concept

The sequence shown in Fig. 7.1 is not difficult to program, since the program essentially runs through the same set of computations once for each time increment. The method makes efficient use of computer time for models in which events that change the status of the system occur in most time increments. To illustrate, the program flow-charted in Fig. 7.2 would be reasonably efficient if the simulated time increment were chosen to be one day and if demand occurred on most days. At least part of the program would then perform useful work on most cycles. In another case, if a continuously changing system such as an economic system were being modeled, the program would be working usefully on every cycle. However, suppose that in the inventory example demand occurred on irregularly scattered days. Then many cycles would be made through the program without accomplishing anything, and considerable computer time might be wasted. Another possible disadvantage of the equal time increment approach is that accuracy may be lost when events that occur during the time increment Δt are assumed to occur either at the beginning or end of the increment.

When events that change the status of the system occur at irregular intervals, it may be more efficient and accurate to "look ahead" to the next most imminent event and advance directly to that point in simulated time. Using this philosophy, we find that the program moves ahead in unequal time increments as shown in Fig. 7.3. To use the unequal time increment concept, however, it is necessary to provide methods for maintaining a schedule of future events, selecting the most imminent event, and going directly to that

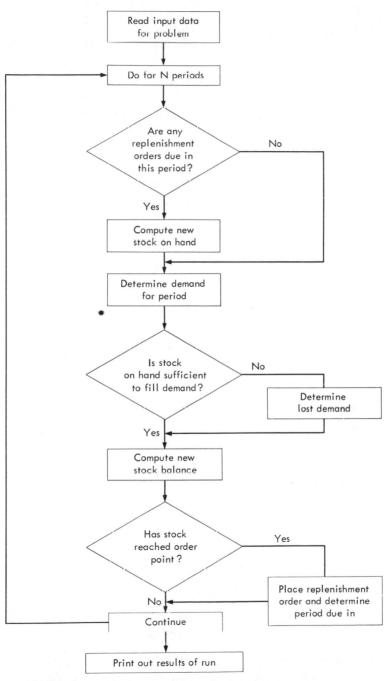

FIGURE 7.2. Flow Chart of Inventory Simulation Program Using Equal
Increment Concept

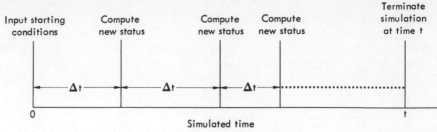

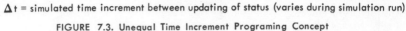

Δt = simulated time increment between updating of status (varies during simulation run)

FIGURE 7.3. Unequal Time Increment Programing Concept

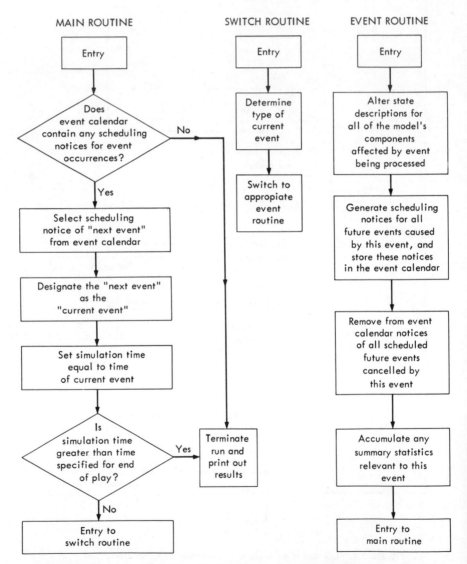

FIGURE 7.4. Flow Diagrams for Programing Unequal Time Increment Concept (adapted from George W. Evans, Graham F. Wallace, and Georgia L. Sutherland, *Simulation Using Digital Computers*, Englewood Cliffs, New Jersey: Prentice-Hall, Inc., 1967)

part of the program which can alter the status of the system properly. From a programing standpoint, this approach may be considerably more complex than the approach shown in Fig. 7.2. Flow diagrams showing in general how the unequal time increment concept can be programed are shown in Fig. 7.4, Since several of the specialized programing languages discussed in the next section automatically provide unequal time increment capability, the use of one of these languages may be preferable to programing this capability in a general language.

Simulation Languages[3]

In this section we will outline principal characteristics of the better known simulation languages. Space does not permit a complete discussion of the languages; rather, we will describe their general capabilities and philosphy. Although language developers often imply that their particular language is all-encompassing in application, our discussion will show that languages are sufficiently different so that proper selection may result in considerable time and cost savings in implementing a simulation model.

GPSS

The General Purpose Systems Simulator is a simulation program developed and maintained by IBM for its 7040/44, 7090/94, and 360 series of computers. Two earlier versions, GPSS I and GPSS II, were the forerunners of the current version GPSS III,[4] which we will discuss.

GPSS III is a two-part program. The first part is an assembly program that converts the user's description of the system to be simulated into suitable input for the second. The second part actually performs the desired simulation runs on the computer. In a normal successful run, the two parts operate in sequence without interruption.

The developers of GPSS III refer to it as a program rather than a language, since the user does not write computer programs in the usual sense. Normal procedure is to prepare a block diagram of the system to be simulated, the block types supplied by GPSS III being used. The block diagram is then described on punch cards, conventions established by the GPSS III manual being used. Unless certain special features are utilized, no previous knowledge of computer programing is necessary.

The orientation of GPSS III is one of transactions moving in time through a system composed essentially of facilities, storages, and queues.

---

[3]Although this section is entitled *Simulation Languages*, we will use the words *program* and *language* somewhat interchangeably in our discussion, since there is no clear distinction between the two. Generally we will use the terminology used by the developers of the various languages to describe their own simulation packages.

[4]A complete description of GPSS III and instructions for use are contained in: *General Purpose Systems Simulator III: Introduction*. IBM Application Program (White Plains, N.Y.: IBM Corporation, 1965), and *General Purpose Systems Simulator; User's Manual* (White Plains, N.Y.: IBM Corporation).

The program automatically compiles and prints out certain statistics regarding facility utilization, storage utilization, queue contents, and number of transactions flowing through the blocks in the system. In addition, other information can be collected and printed out in table form as desired by the user.

A great deal of flexibility in constructing a model is offered, since the program permits multiple transactions, facilities, stores, and queues. Powerful logical capabilities are provided through block types which perform such functions as matching similar transactions, gating transactions, and transferring transactions from one point in the system to another. By using these capabilities, systems of considerable complexity can be constructed out of the basic block types. Although the user is generally restricted to the GPSS III block types with their particular characteristics, the program also affords the opportunity to go outside the basic block types through the use of HELP routines. HELP routines are most likely to be employed only by the experienced user.

Simulated time moves forward in GPSS III in unequal time increments, following the concept in Fig. 7.3. Timing routines are provided by GPSS III and involve a current events chain and a future events chain. Transactions scheduled to move from their current position in the simulated system at some time in the future are placed on the future events chain. Transactions scheduled to move at current simulated time are in the current events chain, as are transactions with scheduled times *less than* current time which have been delayed because of some condition in the simulated system. The program scans the current events chain for transactions that can be moved and moves them, updating their status and statistics regarding operation of the system. When all transactions in the current events chain are either delayed by some condition in the system or have been moved to the future events chain because their next scheduled move is some time in the future, the "clock" is moved ahead to the next earliest scheduled time of the events on the future events chain. All transactions on the future events chain with this earliest scheduled time are moved to the current events chain, and the whole process is repeated.

Only integral time units are permitted in GPSS III. Simulated time may move ahead in unequal increments, but these increments are always integers. The program simply truncates the result whenever the next scheduled move time for a transaction is computed, thereby preventing any event from ocurring at a noninteger time. Some difficulties can arise if the user does not take this into account when specifying such things as time between entrance of transactions into the system and system service times.

An example will, perhaps, best explain the process of constructing a simulation model in GPSS III. In the section dealing with waiting lines in Chap. 2, we discussed a simple order taking system and how its operation could be investigated either analytically or by simulation. We will show how GPSS III can be used as the vehicle for performing the simulation.

The system consists of an order taker capable of serving one customer at a time at an average rate of 15 customers per hour. Service times are exponentially distributed. Customers arrive randomly at a rate of ten per hour, and the number of arrivals follows a Poisson distribution. The service time and interarrival time frequency functions are given in Eqs. (2.8) and (2.9), and the corresponding cumulative distributions are shown graphically in Figs. 2.6 and 2.7. The first step in using GPSS III is to represent the system, as in Fig. 7.5, by using blocks which are provided by GPSS III. The special block symbols follow suggestions made in the manuals but are not necessary except as an aid to visualizing the system.

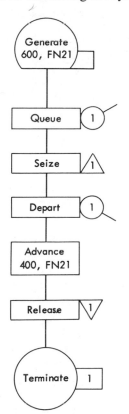

FIGURE 7.5. GPSS III Block Diagram of Order Taking System

The first block in Fig. 7.5 is a GENERATE block which creates transactions and enters them into the system. We have set the basic time increment to be $\frac{1}{100}$ of a minute, and 600 in the GENERATE block indicates that transactions (customers) are to be entered into the system on the average once every 600 simulated time units—or once every 6 minutes. The symbol FN 21 in the GENERATE block indicates that the mean interarrival time of 6 minutes is to be modified by a function arbitrarily called function 21. That is, the time between arrivals is to be a random quantity whose distribution is 600 times the distribution specified by function 21. We will show how function 21 is defined later in this section.

The QUEUE block indicates that transactions (customers) enter a waiting line called queue one as soon as they are generated. A QUEUE block immediately passes transactions through the block if the following block can be entered. Otherwise, a QUEUE block holds a transaction until the next block can be entered. In the model the next block is a SEIZE block, and the 1 in this block indicates that transactions entering this block seize, or occupy, facility one. The SEIZE block has the property that transactions can enter only if the specified facility is unoccupied. In our model, facility one is the order taker.

When a transaction is able to enter a SEIZE block, it immediately proceeds to the following block with no time delay. The following block is a DEPART block, which removes the transaction from the contents of queue one and updates the statistics for queue one accordingly. Together, the SEIZE block and QUEUE block allow the transaction (customer) to occupy the facility (order taker) and leave the queue whenever the facility is empty. Neither of these blocks by itself causes the transaction to be delayed for any amount of simulated time.

In Fig. 7.5, 400 in the ADVANCE block indicates that the average time that a transaction is to be delayed in the block is 400 units of simulated time— 4 minutes in our assumed time scale. The symbol FN 21 specifies that the function, arbitrarily designated function 21, is to be used as a modifier. Delay time in the block will, consequently, be a random quantity whose distribution is 400 times the distribution specified by function 21.

After a transaction has spent time in the ADVANCE block as determined by drawing randomly from the delay time distribution specified for the block, the transaction enters the RELEASE block. This releases facility one and makes it possible for transactions waiting in the queue (if any) or arriving at a later time to enter the facility. Finally, the transaction enters the TERMINATE block, where it is counted and destroyed to remove it from the computer memory. A simulation run is terminated by specifying on a START control card the number of terminations that are to take place before the simulation is to stop.

Figure 7.6 shows the model in Fig. 7.5 prepared for keypunching on a GPSS III coding form according to rules established by the GPSS III manual. Aside from the * SIMULATE card, which indicates that the model is to be run if no serious errors are found, the other cards with the asterisk in column one are simply comment cards for the user's convenience. The START card indicates that the simulation run is to continue until 10,000 transactions (customers, in this model) have terminated. The model also includes several cards which specify the form of FN 21, which is used to

LOCATION	OPERATION	A,B,C,D,E,F
*	SIMULATE	
*	TIME UNIT IS .01 MINUTE	
*	CUSTOMER ARRIVAL TIMES ARE EXPONENTIAL, 10 ARRIVALS PER HOUR
*	SERVICE TIMES ARE EXPONENTIAL, 15 SERVED PER HOUR
*	EXPONENTIAL DISTRIBUTION
21	FUNCTION	RN1,C24
0	.1	.104 .2 .222 .3 .355 .4 .509 .5 .69
.6	.915 .7	1.2 .75 1.38 .8 1.6 .84 1.83 .88 2.12
.9	.3 .92	2.52 .94 2.81 .96 2.99 .97 3.2 .98 3.5
.98	.9 .99	4.6 .995 5.3 .998 6.2 .999 7. .9998 8.
*	SYSTEM MODEL	
	GENERATE	600,FN21 GENERATE CUSTOMER ARRIVAL
	QUEUE	1 WAIT FOR SERVICE
	SEIZE	1 BEGIN SERVICE
	DEPART	1 LEAVE QUEUE
	ADVANCE	400,FN21 SERVICE CUSTOMER
	RELEASE	1 LEAVE ORDER TAKER
	TERMINATE	1 TERMINATE CUSTOMER
	START	10000
	END	

PROGRAM TITLE: ORDER TAKING SYSTEM

FIGURE 7.6. GPSS III Coding Form with Order Taking System Model

define the cumulative distributions of service time and interarrival time shown in Figs. 2.6 and 2.7.

GPSS III interprets a function, such as FUNCTION 21 in Fig. 7.6, as pairs of values of an independent and dependent variable. For instance, the sixth pair of values on the first of the four cards defining FUNCTION 21, 0.5 and 0.69, are interpreted to mean that a value of 0.5 of the independent variable corresponds to a value of 0.69 of the dependent variable. In effect, pairs of values on the four cards define a curve showing the relationship between the independent and dependent variables. The symbol C24 on the FUNCTION card specifies that there are 24 pairs of values and that the program is to interpret the relationship as a continuous one. We will not plot the relationship specified by FUNCTION 21; however, the function is a cumulative exponential of the sort shown in Figs. 2.6 and 2.7. The independent variable in FUNCTION 21 corresponds to the cumulative probability plotted on the vertical axis of either Fig. 2.6 or 2.7. The dependent variable corresponds to time, as shown on the horizontal axes of those figures.

The symbol RN1 is the identification of uniformly distributed random numbers between 0 and 1.00 which GPSS III provides automatically. The symbol RN1 on the FUNCTION card is interpreted as an instruction to use these uniformly distributed random numbers as the independent variable when selecting values of the dependent variable from the probability distribution. For instance, suppose that a transaction (customer) has just been generated (arrived). The program must then determine the time of arrival of the next customer. Since the GENERATE block specifies FN 21 as a modifier, a value of the independent variable RN1 specified in FUNCTION 21 is obtained automatically through a random number generation procedure. Suppose that this value happened to be 0.5. The corresponding value of the dependent variable is 0.69, and this would be used by the GENERATE block to determine the time before the next arrival simply by multiplying 0.69 by 600. In other words, the time between arrivals would be $600 \times 0.69 = 414$ time units. The procedure is precisely analogous to that shown in Fig. 2.6. The reader may verify this by determining from Fig. 2.6 the value of t_a which corresponds to a value of 0.5 for $F(t_a)$.

A simulation run of the model in Fig. 7.6 produced results comparable, but not identical, to results of the theoretical analysis of the system in Chap. 2. Statistics regarding facility utilization and queue contents, which are automatically compiled and printed out by GPSS III, showed that average utilization of the order taker was 0.6768 as compared to a theoretical value of 0.6667 obtained by Eq. (2.10), and the average queue contents were 1.46 as compared to a theoretical average queue length of 1.33 obtained by Eq. (2.12). Part of the reason for the upward bias is that the average service time during the run was 406.5, about 1.5 per cent higher than expected. This could be due either to chance variation or the possibility that the function described by the 24 points of FUNCTION 21 and the method of interpolation between these points only approximate the theoretical service time function described by Eq. (2.14).

Simulating the order-taker system with GPSS III confirmed results obtained previously by theoretical analysis. However, for more complicated systems theoretical analysis may not be possible, and simulation may be the only feasible method of analysis. For example, an analysis of the flow of steel through certain facilities in a batch process steel mill required about 150 GPSS III blocks to describe the basic system. The complex flow and logical operations embodied in this simulation model could not be analyzed by strictly mathematical or statistical means.

A new version of GPSS for the IBM 360 series of computers has essentially the same structure and philosophy as GPSS III.[5] However, some extensions have been made to add to the versatility and ease of use of the program. For example, entities such as facilities, queues, and storages which were formerly referenced only by number can now be referenced by names specified by the user. The model, accordingly, is easier to understand, and output statistics are more quickly associated with the parts of the model to which they refer. Boolean statements are provided in GPSS 360 to permit logical decisions to be made in a single block which formerly required a sequence of blocks. Another feature designed to reduce the number of blocks in a model is the provision for macro instructions which permit identical portions of a model to be coded only once and then used in several places in the model. Output format can also be modified easily in GPSS 360, and provision has been made for graphical as well as tabular output of statistics from a simulation run. These and other changes have added somewhat to the capabilities of GPSS 360 while maintaining the same basic structure as GPSS III.

DYNAMO

This language is an outgrowth of the development of the industrial dynamics concept at the Massachusetts Institute of Technology, discussed earlier in Chap. 3. DYNAMO was first completed at M.I.T. in 1959, and is available for the IBM 7090 and 7094 computers.[6] As discussed previously, industrial dynamics is based on the idea that managerial problems should be examined in terms of the total system and complex interactions that take place over time in the system. Emphasis is placed on information feedbacks and delays inherent in such systems and their impact on system behavior. The industrial dynamics approach is similar in many ways to engineering

---

[5]See *General Purpose Simulation System/360: Introductory User's Manual.* IBM Application Program (White Plains, N.Y.: IBM Corporation, 1967), and *General Purpose Simulation System/360: User's Manual* (White Plains, N.Y.: IBM Corporation, 1967).

[6]Complete documentation for the user is contained in: Alexander L. Pugh, III, DYNAMO *User's Manual*, 2nd ed. (Cambridge, Mass.: The Massachusetts Institute of Technology Press, 1963).

systems analysis in that the focus is on questions of stability of the system and response to external shocks or changes of parameters.

DYNAMO is a computer program which accepts as input a model in the form of a set of equations describing the system to be simulated. DYNAMO simulates the behavior of the system by evaluating the equations once for each simulated time increment. DYNAMO records the values of variables in the system through successive simulated time increments and prepares both tabulated and plotted time series of these values as may be desired.

Because of the basic philosophy underlying industrial dynamics and DYNAMO, the program has capabilities resembling those of analog computers. Probably the most significant difference is that, unlike an analog computer in which relationships and calculations are continuous and simultaneous, DYNAMO operates in a discrete and sequential fashion. In spite of this basic difference, however, the behavior of a model written in DYNAMO can be made very similar to the behavior of a model of the same system run on an analog computer.

Since DYNAMO uses a difference equation structure, the orientation is around aggregate rates of flow and levels rather than around transactions as in GPSS.[7] Levels are considered to exist at points in simulated time while rates exist over a time increment. In the DYNAMO philosophy, rates of flow over a time increment DT together with levels at the beginning of the increment determine levels at the end of the increment. Although DYNAMO may be viewed as a tool for solving difference equations independent of this rate and level concept, the terminology and equation formats of DYNAMO are such that the user is required to define at least parts of his model in these terms. In addition to rate variables and level variables, DYNAMO also provides for auxiliary variables defined by auxiliary equations which are used to reduce the complexity of rate equations. Constants are quantities which do not change in value during a run of the model, and their values are specified by input data at the beginning of a run. Equation forms available include algebraic manipulations and special operations such as common functions (exponential, natural logarithm, square root, sine, and cosine), switching functions, random numbers (uniform and normal), and input functions (pulse, step, and ramp). A functional relationship between an independent and dependent variable can be expressed in DYNAMO by a table of pairs of values of the variables. The user specifies pairs of values corresponding to points along the curve defining the relationship between the variables, and the table look-up function in DYNAMO finds the value of the dependent variable corresponding to any value of the independent variable. Values falling between the points are found by linear interpolation.

DYNAMO does not permit simultaneous equations and will reject a model containing them with a statement indicating the equations that are

---

[7] See pp. 84–85 for a further discussion of the rates and levels concept.

simultaneous. In this case, the user is expected to rework the model to remove simultaneity. This feature simplifies and speeds up DYNAMO, and little is lost through lack of simultaneity when the time increment between solution of the equations is sufficiently small.

The computation interval DT and total length of run are set at the beginning of the run, and all equations are evaluated once each DT, as shown in Fig. 7.7. In actuality, calculations never reach time L in Fig. 7.7, since the whole model is moved up an interval of time once the rates for the interval KL are calculated. That is, values at time K become values at J for a new set of calculations, and values for KL rates become JK rates for the next set of calculations. Since the model is evaluated once for each DT, the timing scheme is the same as that illustrated in Fig. 7.1.

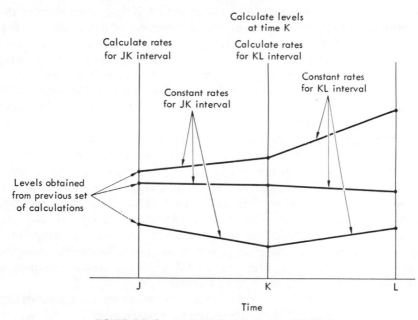

FIGURE 7.7. Sequence of Calculations in DYNAMO

The user of DYNAMO is required to construct his model in terms of certain equation forms listed in the DYNAMO manual, just as GPSS III users must use blocks specified in the GPSS III manual. Unlike GPSS III, which permits the user to go outside the standard block operations through the use of HELP routines, DYNAMO has no such facility for adding to existing equation forms. All equations are labeled according to the equation form numbers listed in the manual, and also the type of equation must be specified, e.g., rate, level, or auxiliary. In addition to equation labels, variables in the equations are given time subscripts according to conventions established by the DYNAMO manual.

A useful feature of DYNAMO is its provision for rerunning a model with different values for one or more constants without recompiling the basic model. If the user wishes to run a model several times, he can do so by following the basic model with additional cards specifying new values of constants. Equations can be altered between runs by embedding in the model switching functions regulated by values of constants. The program will rerun the model with new values and print or plot results as specified.

Figure 7.8 is a listing in DYNAMO format of the econometric model discussed earlier in Chap. 4. To the incomplete model shown in Fig. 4.1, we have added equation type and form designations, time subscripts (after the decimal points), and other details as required by the rules for keypunching DYNAMO models. Also in the complete model in Fig. 7.8 we have included DYNAMO direction cards and initial values for certain variables which are necessary to permit DYNAMO to perform the first cycle of evaluation of the equations. Two step-function equations have been added to the model in Fig. 4.1 which specify that wage payments to government and government purchases from business are to increase from their initial values to 55 and 110, respectively, in period four. It is the response of the model to these exogenous increases that is shown in Table 4.1. The cards starting with the word NOTE permit the user to insert titles or comments in the program, and they have no effect on the model.

We will not discuss all of the equations, since that would be too lengthy, but let us consider some examples of the basic equation types provided by DYNAMO which appear in the model. The first equation in Fig. 7.8 sums consumption CON, government expenditures GOV, and investment INV to arrive at a figure for gross national product GNP. Since gross national product does not appear elsewhere in the model, the only purpose in calculating it is to make it available when the results of a simulation run are printed out. Equations defining quantities of this nature are called supplementaries. The 8S label on the equation signifies that this is a supplementary equation punched according to equation form number eight.

The consumption sector of the model consists of two rate equations and two auxiliary equations. Referring to the time diagram in Fig. 7.7, we see that the rate of consumption CON for the time increment KL is the product of the average propensity to consume APCON and the disposable income rate DIN during the previous time increment JK. Thus consumption lags behind disposable income somewhat, depending on the length of simulated time interval DT which we select. A realistic extension of the model might be to lag consumption behind income in some other fashion, and DYNAMO has capabilities for inserting other types of delays.[8] The disposable income rate for period KL is computed by the second equation in the consumption sector. On the next cycle of computations this KL rate becomes the JK dis-

---

[8]See pp. 88–92 for a further discussion of delay functions.

```
*        DYNAMO
RUN
NOTE     HYPOTHETICAL ECONOMETRIC SIMULATION MODEL
SPEC     DT=0.05/LENGTH=10/PRTPER=.25/PLTPER=.25
PRINT    1)GNP/2)CON/3)GOV/4)INV/5)DIN/6)BUS
PLOT     GNP=Y,CON=C,GOV=G,INV=I
NOTE
NOTE        GROSS NATIONAL PRODUCT DEFINITION
NOTE
8S       GNP.K=CON.JK+GOV.JK+INV.JK                     GROSS NATIONAL PRODUCT
NOTE
NOTE        CONSUMPTION SECTOR
NOTE
12R      CON.KL=(APCON)(DIN.JK)                         CONSUMPTION
1OR      DIN.KL=WPB.K+WPG.K+TRN+DIV.K-PTX.K+0           DISPOSABLE INCOME
19A      PTX.K=(PTXRT)(WPB.K+WPG.K+DIV.K+0)             PERSONAL TAXES
7A       SAV.K=DIN.JK-CON.JK                            SAVINGS
NOTE
NOTE        GOVERNMENT SECTOR
NOTE
8R       GOV.KL=TRN+WPG.K+GPB.K                         GOVERNMENT EXPENDITURES
7R       TAX.KL=PTX.K+BTX.K                             TAX RECEIPTS
1L       DBT.K=DBT.J+(DT)(GOV.JK-TAX.JK)                ACCUMULATED DEBT
NOTE
NOTE        BUSINESS SECTOR
NOTE
7R       INV.KL=SAV.K+RET.K                             BUSINESS INVESTMENT
8R       BUS.KL=CON.JK+GPB.K+BPB.K                      TOTAL BUSINESS ACTIVITY
14A      BPB.K=INV.JK+(PRPCT)(BUS.JK)                   BUSINESS PURCH. FROM BUS.
12A      WPB.K=(WGPCT)(BUS.JK)                          WAGE PAYMENTS BY BUSINESS
19A      BPR.K=(BUS.JK)(1-PRPCT-WGPCT+0)                BUSINESS PROFITS
12A      BTX.K=(BTXRT)(BPR.K)                           BUSINESS TAXES
18A      DIV.K=(DIVRT)(BPR.K-BTX.K)                     DIVIDENDS
8A       RET.K=BPR.K-BTX.K-DIV.K                        RETAINED EARNINGS
NOTE
NOTE        CONSTANTS
NOTE
C        APCON=.95                                      AVG. PROPENSITY TO CONSUME
C        PTXRT=.25                                      PERSONAL TAX RATE
C        BTXRT=.50                                      BUSINESS TAX RATE
C        PRPCT=.72                                      BUSINESS PURCHASES PERCENT
C        WGPCT=.25                                      BUSINESS WAGES PERCENT
C        DIVRT=.50                                      DIVIDEND RATE
C        TRN=25                                         GOVERNMENT TRANSFER PAYMENTS
NOTE
NOTE        INITIAL VALUES
NOTE
6N       CON=435                                        CONSUMPTION
6N       DBT=250                                        ACCUMULATED DEBT
6N       BUS=2050                                       TOTAL BUSINESS ACTIVITY
6N       WPG=50                                         WAGE PAYMENTS BY GOVT
6N       GPB=100                                        GOVT PURCH. FROM BUS.
NOTE
NOTE        STEP FUNCTIONS
NOTE
45A      WPG.K=STEP(55,4)                               WAGE PAYMENTS BY GOVT
45A      GPB.K=STEP(110,4)                              GOVT PURCH. FROM BUS.
```

FIGURE 7.8. Hypothetical Econometric Model Written in DYNAMO

posable income rate in the consumption equation, and the same process is repeated in succeeding time increments. The third equation in the consumption sector is an auxiliary equation and is used to calculate a value for personal taxes PTX which appears in the rate equation for disposable income.

The third equation for accumulated national debt DBT in the government sector illustrates the use of a level equation. In DYNAMO rate equations define flows in the system and level equations define accumulations or levels of stocks in the system. Accumulated debt is the only level in the model.

Levels are calculated by taking the level at time J and adding to it the net inflow or outflow for the time increment from J to K to arrive at a new level at time K. Since rates are constant over the time interval, the net inflow or outflow is the product of DT and the sum of the constant rates of flow in and out. Net change in accumulated debt is the product of DT and the difference between the rate of government expenditures GOV and the rate of tax receipts TAX.

The last two equations in the model specify that wage payments by government WPG and government payments to business GPB are to be step functions. Initially these variables take on values given by the equations in the initial value section of the model. At the simulated time shown by the last number in the brackets, in both cases time period 4, the variables assume the values shown by the first number in the brackets and remain that way for the remainder of the run. DYNAMO has similar built-in capabilities to produce random values, pulses, delayed values, and several other types of functions as desired by the user.

There are several direction cards listed at the beginning of the model which give necessary instructions about the simulation run. The SPEC card specifies the length of DT, total length of simulated time for the run, length of time between printing of results, and interval between plotting of results. The length of run and DT, in effect, determine how many times DYNAMO will cycle through the equations during the computer run; 201 times with a length of 10 and DT of 0.05 as shown in Fig. 7.8. The PRINT card identifies variables that are to be printed, and the PLOT card identifies variables to be plotted, together with the single character symbol to be used in plotting. DYNAMO automatically prints and plots results of the simulation without further directions.

The sequencing of equations in our model in Fig. 7.8 is strictly for the convenience of the model builder, since DYNAMO determines its own sequence for solving the equations. If it cannot find a sequence, a diagnostic message is printed to the effect that certain quantities cannot be defined or that simultaneous equations exist in the model.

The econometric model that we have used as an illustration is relatively small in terms of DYNAMO's capabilities. Models of over 1000 equations can be handled by DYNAMO. Appendix C contains a complete listing of the DYNAMO model discussed in Chap. 3 and illustrates additional features of the language which are not utilized in the econometric model.

Another version, DYNAMO II, is under development by the Industrial Dynamics Research Group at the Massachusetts Institute of Technology. DYNAMO II retains the basic structure and philosophy of DYNAMO but removes several restrictions and adds new features. DYNAMO II is written in AED, an ALGOL-type language, and will be usable on a larger variety of computers than DYNAMO. In addition, DYNAMO II is formulated for use on time-sharing computer systems.

The change most apparent to the programer is removal of restrictions on equation types. Equations in DYNAMO are limited to the set listed in the manual and must be identified by the appropriate equation form number. In DYNAMO II equations may be formulated by the rules of algebra without limitation. It is necessary only to indicate whether an equation is a level L, rate R, auxiliary A, supplementary S, or initial value N. For example, Eq. (3.14) for first-order exponential smoothing might be written

$$\text{L} \quad \text{AVG.K} = \text{AVG.J} + (\text{DT/T}) * (\text{DATA.JK} - \text{AVG.J}) \qquad (7.1)$$

The error checking routine is revised for a more thorough check of subscripts. Where in DYNAMO any error causes the model to stop, in DYNAMO II the program will try to recover and run unless the error is classed as fatal, such as the existence of simultaneous equations.

Additional macro equations which represent two or more separate elementary equations are made available. DELAY3 can be used as a variable third-order delay in physical flows as explained in Chap. 3. SMOOTH can be used for a first-order exponential average of a physical rate of flow, and DLINF1 and DLINF3 are provided for first- and third-order exponential smoothing in information flows. The user may define other macro equations as part of his model.

In the place of the single SPEC card, equations may be used to define time, the length of run, print period, and plot period. The simulation can be started at any time, such as 1960. An equation for LENGTH, the length of time the simulation is to run, might be formulated to stop the model when some condition occurs. Equations can be provided for the print period and plot period to change the interval between printing and plotting.

In the time-sharing version a model may be input to the computer through a remote terminal and plotted or printed output may be received on the terminal. Certain restrictions are imposed by a time-sharing system, such as a requirement to number each equation and a limitation on the length of line of output to the typewriter carriage width. Other features and instructions for using DYNAMO II are explained in the *DYNAMO II User's Manual*, which is forthcoming.

SIMSCRIPT

This language was developed at the RAND Corporation and has its origins in work done at General Electric on the General Electric Manufacturing Simulator. It was originally designed at RAND for the IBM 709/7090 computers, and California Analysis Center, Inc., has since developed SIMSCRIPT compilers both for IBM equipment and that of other manufacturers such as Control Data, Philco, General Electric, RCA, and Univac. Unlike GPSS and DYNAMO, which require the user to have little or no previous knowledge of computer programing, SIMSCRIPT requires a knowledge of programing. Acquaintance with FORTRAN is particularly helpful, since the language is based on FORTRAN. The user of SIMSCRIPT prepares a simulation program, according to the conventions established by the SIMSCRIPT manual,[9] consisting of a description of the system to be simulated and programs to perform desired operations in the system. The SIMSCRIPT tape essentially treats the system description and operating programs as data and prepares from them the actual set of computer instructions for performing the simulation. In the process, SIMSCRIPT supplies a timing routine and certain other parts of the final simulation program, thereby relieving the user of a considerable amount of programing detail.

The original SIMSCRIPT system converted a part of the user's program into FORTRAN, which was then converted by the FORTRAN system into machine language instructions. Since this process requires two passes in the computer, another version has been developed which requires only one pass. We will discuss this version, SIMSCRIPT I.5, after explaining the basic concepts of SIMSCRIPT, which are the same for both versions.

In SIMSCRIPT, the system to be simulated is defined in terms of entities, attributes of the entities, attributes of the system, and sets. Entities may be permanent, in the sense that they exist throughout a simulation, or temporary, in which case they are created and destoyed in the course of the simulation. For instance, in a simulation of the operation of the tellers' windows at a bank, the number of windows might be constant during a simulation run, and they would be considered to be permanent entities. Customers, on the other hand, might be viewed as temporary entities that are created and destroyed to simulate the arrival and departure of customers during the simulation run. Sets are thought of as being "owned" either by the system or the entities in the system and entities can be filed in these sets. SIMSCRIPT provides the capability for searching these sets and removing entities from them. In a bank simulation, for example, customers (temporary entities) might be filed in sets belonging to the teller windows (permanent entities). Each teller window would "own" one set representing the queue in front of the teller window, and a customer would be filed in one of these sets to simulate his entry into the queue in front of the window.

Events that change the status of the system in SIMSCRIPT are of two types, exogenous and endogenous. The user writes event routines which specify the way in which the system is altered by the occurrence of the events. One exogenous or endogenous event routine is written for each type of event that can take place to change the status of the simulated system. An exogenous event is made to occur by specifying the type of exogenous event and simulated time at which it is to occur on a data card prior to the start of a simulation

[9]H. M. Markowtiz, B. Hausner, and H. W. Karr, *SIMSCRIPT: A Simulation Programming Language*. Memorandum RM-3310-PR (Santa Monica, Calif.: The RAND Corporation, November, 1962). This manual was later published commercially by Prentice-Hall, Inc., in 1963.

run. Endogenous events take place as a result of their being scheduled during the course of the simulation run. SIMSCRIPT provides a routine which automatically keeps track of the exogenous and endogenous events that are to occur in the future and causes them to occur in their proper sequence. SIMSCRIPT selects the next most imminent event, advances simulated time to that point, and calls the proper event routine which changes the status of the system. Since events need not be, and usually are not equally spaced in simulated time, time advances in unequal increments in the manner shown in Fig. 7.3.

The preceding discussion of the basic philosophy of SIMSCRIPT will, perhaps, be clarified with an example of a SIMSCRIPT simulation program. The example will also demonstrate some of the many capabilities of SIMSCRIPT which were not touched upon in the discussion.

In Chap. 2 we discussed the simulation of inventory systems, and Fig. 2.2 is a schematic diagram of a production-inventory-distribution simulator programed in SIMSCRIPT by the authors. Although the complete program is too lengthy to be used here for illustrative purposes, we will discuss a simplified version. In this version we have reduced the complexity by assuming that the system consists of branch warehouses which receive orders for products from customers and that these branches obtain their supplies from a single plant rather than multiple plants as shown in Fig. 2.2. We assume that all demand which cannot be filled immediately from branch inventory is lost and that the branches manage their inventories on an order point-order quantity basis with review of stocks and replenishment orders taking place only at periodic intervals. The plant produces all products in a single facility upon receipt of orders placed by the branches.

Figure 7.9 is a completed SIMSCRIPT Definition Form which describes the system to be simulated. In the "permanent system variables" section of the form we have defined two permanent entities, branches BRNCH and products PRDCT. When the program is run, these variables are given initial values to specify the number of branches and products during that particular run. Since we assume only one plant in the system, it does not need to be defined explicitly. The next four variables defined in this section are branch stock level BRSTK, order point BORDP, order quantity BORDQ, and stock on order from the factory BRORD. Each of these has two subscripts, since each variable must be defined for each branch and product combination. Shipping time SHTIM is a random variable and has one subscript, which refers to the branch to which a replenishment order is being shipped. When simulated shipments are made from the plant to a branch, SIMSCRIPT selects the transit time at random from the shipping time distribution for that branch. Production rate PRATE at the plant has one subscript, which refers to the product. Total demand TOTLD and lost demand LOSTD have two subscripts and are used to collect summary statistics for each branch and product combination. The review period REVPR is the number of simulated

SIMSCRIPT DEFINITION FORM

PROGRAMMER ______________________

PROBLEM ______________________

DATE ______________________

TEMPORARY SYSTEM VARIABLES

Temporary and Event Notice Entities

01	Temporary or Notice (T,N)	Name	Record Size: Master	Satellite 1*	Satellite 2*	3	4	5	6	7	8
+	T	BØRDR	8								
+	N	BØRFL	4								
+	N	BRREV	2								

*NOT AVAILABLE TO EVENT NOTICES

Attributes

Temporary or Notice (T,N)	Name	Record	Word	Packing	Signed	Mode (I,F)
T	BBRCH		1	/		I
T	BPRØD		2	/		I
T	BQUAN		3	/		I
T	BCØMP		4	/		F
T	BARRV		5	/		F
T	PSCED		6	/		I
T	SSCED		7	/		I
N	ØRDER		3	/		I

PERMANENT SYSTEM VARIABLES

Array Number	Name	Number of Subscripts or "E"	Packing	Signed	Mode (I,F)	Constant	Random: Unsubscripted or Subscripted (U,S)	Random: Step or Linear (S,L)
1	BRNCH	E	/					
2	PRDCT	E	/					
3	BRSTK	2	/	*	I			
4	BØRDP	2	/		I			
5	BØRDQ	2	/		I			
6	BRØRD	2	/		I			
7	SHTIM		/		F		S	S
8	PRATE	1	/		I	*		
9	TØTLD	2	/		I			
10	LØSTD	2	/		I			
11	REVPR	0	/		F			
12	FSCED	0	/		I			
13	LSCED	0	/		I			

SETS

Name	Number of Subscripts	LIFO	FIFO	Ranked	Attribute Used in Ranking	High or Low is Best (H,L)
SCED	O			*	BCØMP	L

FUNCTIONS

Name	Mode (I,F)

PREVIOUSLY COMPILED

Prefix to Set Name		LIFO	FIFO	Ranked	
P SET NAME	Predecessor in set			✓	Required attributes for member entities
S SET NAME	Successor in set	✓	✓	✓	Required attributes for member entities
F SET NAME	First in set	✓	✓	✓	Required attributes for owner entities
L SET NAME	Last in set		✓	✓	Required attributes for owner entities

FIGURE 7.9. SIMSCRIPT Definition Form with Production-Inventory-Distribution Model

time periods between reviews of branch inventories for possible replenishment orders. Finally, FSCED and LSCED are variables required by SIMSCRIPT to automatically maintain the list of orders placed by the branches with the plant.

Prior to a simulation run, a deck of initialization cards is prepared in a form specified by the SIMSCRIPT manual to give initial values to the permanent system variables. Although we will not illustrate the initialization cards themselves, Fig. 7.10 summarizes initializing data for a sample run of the model. This deck of cards, together with a systems specification card, which we will not discuss, is treated as a data deck by the simulation program

Number of branches – 2

Number of products – 3

Initial branch stocks

Product	1	2	3
Branch 1	400	175	600
Branch 2	750	480	1100

Order points

Product	1	2	3
Branch 1	100	125	150
Branch 2	500	250	1000

Order quantities

Product	1	2	3
Branch 1	500	500	1000
Branch 2	1000	500	2000

Shipping times

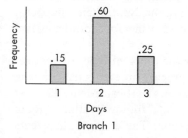
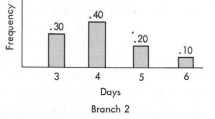

Production rates

Product 1 – 400 units per period

Product 2 – 200 units per period

Product 3 – 500 units per period

Interval between reviews – 5 periods

FIGURE 7.10. Initializing Data for Run of SIMSCRIPT Model

at the beginning of a run and establishes initial parameters for the system. A very convenient feature of SIMSCRIPT is that current values of permanent system variables are available to all routines during the simulation without the necessity of naming them in a COMMON statement or transferring them between routines in argument lists.

In the "temporary system variables" section of the definition form we have defined branch order BORDR as a temporary entity which may be created or destroyed in the course of the simulation. SIMSCRIPT permits any number of temporary entities of the same type (or other types, if they have been defined) to exist at one time during the course of the simulation. The attributes of each branch order are the originating branch BBRCH, product ordered BPROD, quantity ordered BQUAN, scheduled completion time BCOMP, and arrival time at the branch BARRV. PSCED and SSCED are also attributes, but they do not describe the order as do the other attributes. These are required by SIMSCRIPT so that it can automatically maintain the list of branch orders at the production facility.

The list of branch orders at the plant is defined in the "sets" portion of the definition form. The list is named SCED and has no subscripts, since there is only one such list in our system. Branch orders are placed in this set ranked according to completion date BCOMP.

Reviews of branch inventory levels for possible placement of replenishment orders and arrivals of completed replenishment orders at the branches are *endogenous* events that occur as a result of their being scheduled in the course of the simulation run. SIMSCRIPT requires that event notices be defined for each type of endogenous event, and BORFL and BRREV are the notices for order arrivals and branch reviews. These event notices are used by SIMSCRIPT in maintaining a schedule of future events and causing their occurrence at the proper point in simulated time. Also, as in the case of ORDER, an attribute of the event notice BORFL, the attributes of event notices may be used to carry over information to the event when it happens. The attribute ORDER of BORDR, for instance, identifies for the order arrival routine the specific order which is arriving.

In addition to defining event notices for the different types of endogenous events in the model, the user must also prepare an events list showing the names of all endogenous and exogenous events that can occur. This list is used by SIMSCRIPT to generate an appropriate timing routine. Figure 7.11 shows the events list for the simulated system. The endogenous events are branch review BRREV and order arrival BORFL as already mentioned, and there are three exogenous events called BEGSIM, DEMAND, and ENDSIM. In our model the exogenous events BEGSIM and ENDSIM each occur only once in the simulation, at the begining and end of the run, respectively, and their function will be clear when we discuss the routines. An exogenous event DEMAND takes place each time there is a customer demand for some quantity of a product from one of the branches. After defin-

```
EVENTS
   3 EXOGENOUS
        BEGSIM  (1)
        DEMAND  (2)
        ENDSIM  (3)
   2 ENDOGENOUS
        BRREV
        BORFL
END


SIMULATION
```

FIGURE 7.11. SIMSCRIPT Events List and Card for System Package

ing these exogenous and endogenous events in the events list, the user must prepare event routines, as shown in Fig. 7.12, for each event listed. Also shown in Fig. 7.11 is a single card with the word SIMULATION which instructs SIMSCRIPT to provide a system package. Except in a minor fashion, the user's pogram does not affect the system package, as it is substantially the same for all simulation programs written in SIMSCRIPT.

Besides the events list and event routines, a deck of cards is prepraed consisting of one card for each occurrence of an exogenous event. Each card, which we have not illustrated, is punched with the exogenous event number, the time at which the event is to occur, and—if desired by the user—additional data regarding the event. These exogenous event cards are treated as data at the time the program is executed and cause the occurrence of exogenous events at the proper times during the run. Endogenous events do not require such a deck, since their occurrence is governed by event notices that are generated internally during the course of the simulation run.

In Fig. 7.12 the first routine is the exogenous event routine BEGSIM. The only function of this routine is to create an event notice for a branch review and schedule the first review to occur at the current value of time plus the review period. When using this procedure to start the cycle of reviews, we specify time zero in the event card that causes BEGSIM, thereby causing the first review of branch stocks to occur a number of time periods in the future equal to the review period.

The second routine in Fig. 7.12 is the exogenous event routine DEMAND. Exogenous event cards which cause DEMANDs to occur contain the event number and time together with information regarding branch, product, and quantity demanded. The information is read from the card and transferred to variables named IBRAN, JPROD, and NQUAN. In SIMSCRIPT, these are local variables, since they do not appear on the definition form. Unlike system variables, which appear on the definition form, the values of local variables are not available from one routine to another unless transferred in an argument list. After reading the values of these variables, the routine updates the total demand accumulating variable TOTLD and subtracts demand from the proper branch stock BRSTK. If the resulting branch stock is greater than or equal to zero, the routine returns to the timing routine, and the next scheduled event is called. However,

```
      EXOGENOUS EVENT BEGSIM
      CREATE BRREV
      CAUSE BRREV AT TIME + REVPR
      RETURN
      END



      EXOGENOUS EVENT DEMAND
      SAVE EVENT CARD
      READ IBRAN,JPROD,NQUAN
      FORMAT (2I3,I6)
      LET TOTLD(IBRAN,JPROD) = TOTLD(IBRAN,JPROD) + NQUAN
      LET BRSTK(IBRAN,JPROD) = BRSTK(IBRAN,JPROD) - NQUAN
      IF (BRSTK(IBRAN,JPROD)) GE (0), GO TO 10
      LET LOSTD(IBRAN,JPROD) = LOSTD(IBRAN,JPROD) - BRSTK(IBRAN,JPROD)
      LET BRSTK(IBRAN,JPROD) = 0
   10 RETURN
      END



      EXOGENOUS EVENT ENDSIM
      CALL RESULT
      STOP
      END



      ENDOGENOUS EVENT BRREV
      DESTROY BRREV
      DO TO 10, FOR EACH BRNCH I, FOR EACH PROCT J
      IF (BRORD(I,J)) GR (0), GO TO 10
      IF (BRSTK(I,J)) GR (BORDP(I,J)), GO TO 10
      LET BRORD(I,J) = BORDQ(I,J)
      CREATE BORDR
      LET BBRCH(BORDR) = I
      LET BPROD(BORDR) = J
      LET BQUAN(BORDR) = BORDQ(I,J)
      CALL SCHED(BORDR)
   10 LOOP
      CALL STATUS
      CREATE BRREV
      CAUSE BRREV AT TIME + REVPR
      RETURN
      END



      SUBROUTINE SCHED(BORDR)
      LET QUAN = BQUAN(BORDR)
      LET RATE = PRATE(BPROD(BORDR))
      LET RUNTM = QUAN/RATE
      FIND START = MAX OF BCOMP(KORDR), FOR EACH KORDR OF SCED, WITH
     X(BCOMP(KORDR)) GR (TIME), IF NONE, GO TO 10
      LET BCOMP(BORDR) = START + RUNTM
      GO TO 20
   10 LET BCOMP(BORDR) = TIME + RUNTM
   20 LET BARRV(BORDR) = BCOMP(BORDR) + SHTIM(BBRCH(BORDR))
      CREATE BORFL
      STORE BORDR IN ORDER(BORFL)
      CAUSE BORFL AT BARRV(BORDR)
      FILE BORDR IN SCED
      RETURN
      END



      ENDOGENOUS EVENT BORFL
      STORE ORDER(BORFL) IN KORDR
      DESTROY BORFL
      REMOVE KORDR FROM SCED
      LET BRSTK(BBRCH(KORDR),BPROD(KORDR)) = BRSTK(BBRCH(KORDR),
     X BPROD(KORDR)) + BQUAN(KORDR)
      LET BRORD(BBRCH(KORDR),BPROD(KORDR)) = 0
      DESTROY BORDR CALLED KORDR
      RETURN
      END
```

FIGURE 7.12. Listing of Event Routines and Subroutines

if branch stock becomes negative, unfilled demand is assumed to be lost, the lost demand accumulating variable LOSTD is updated, and branch stock is set equal to zero before control is returned to the timing routine.

The last exogenous event routine ENDSIM in Fig. 7.12 calls a report routine named RESULT, which prints out a summary of statistics collected during the run, and the simulation is then terminated. We have not listed the program for the report routine, but a sample of output is shown in Fig. 7.13. The last table in Fig. 7.13 is output from the report routine RESULT for a run of the model for 60 periods.

An event notice called BRREV is created and placed on the schedule of events in the exogenous event BEGSIM. At the proper point the timing routine automatically calls the exogenous event routine BRREV. The first instruction in the exogenous event BRREV destroys the event notice to clear the memory locations occupied by the notice. The routine then checks

```
STATUS REPORT, PERIOD    55.00


ON HAND


PRODUCT              1            2            3

BRANCH   1          65          475           0
BRANCH   2         310          175         2000


ON ORDER


BRANCH       PRODUCT       QUANTITY       COMPLETION DATE       ARRIVAL DATE

   1            3            1000              54.50                57.50
   1            1             500              56.25                57.25
   2            1            1000              58.75                62.75
   2            2             500              61.25                65.25


RESULTS OF SIMULATION RUN, PERIOD    60.00


TOTAL DEMAND


PRODUCT              1            2            3

BRANCH   1        1565         1445         2780
BRANCH   2        3100         1515         5950


LOST DEMAND


PRODUCT              1            2            3

BRANCH   1          65          140          180
BRANCH   2         465          100          405
```

FIGURE 7.13. Sample Output from Run of SIMSCRIPT Model

inventory status for all branch and product combinations. If a replenishment order has previously been placed but not delivered, the quantity on order BRORD is greater than zero and no additional order is placed. Also, if branch stock BRSTK is greater than the order point BORDP, no order is placed. However, if the inventory level is below the order point, the quantity on order BRORD is set equal to the order quantity BORDQ and a branch order BORDR is created. Attributes of the branch order are set equal to the values of branch I, product J, and quantity BORDQ, after which a subroutine SCHED is called which actually schedules the order. After all branches and products have been reviewed a report routine named STATUS is called which prints out the status of branch stocks and orders as illustrated in Fig. 7.13. Finally, another branch review is scheduled to take place at the current value of time plus the review period.

The subroutine SCHED[10] actually places the branch replenishment order in the shedule file. It calculates production time RUNTM for the order and finds the earliest starting time START for production if there are other orders not yet completed in the production schedule file. Completion time of the order BCOMP is calculated and arrival time BARRV of the completed order at the branch. Arrival time is found by adding shipping time SHTIM to completion time BCOMP. Since shipping time to the branch was defined as a random variable in Fig. 7.9, a value is selected at random from the distribution of shipping times specified for the branch on the initialization cards. Finally, the routine creates an event notice called BORFL, gives to this notice the identification of the branch order that is due to arrive, schedules the arrival for the arrival time BARRV, and files the order in the production order file SCED.

The branch replenishment order remains in SCED until SIMSCRIPT causes the endogenous event BORFL to occur. When this event occurs, a local variable KORDR is given the identification of the order that is arriving, and the event notice is destroyed to avoid keeping unnecessary information in memory. The routine then removes the branch replenishment order from the production order file, updates branch stock BRSTK and quantity on order BRORD, and destroys the replenishment order.

The definition form in Fig. 7.9, the events list in Fig. 7.11, and the routines in Fig. 7.12 define the basic structure of the simulation program for SIMSCRIPT. Other inputs that must be provided when the simulation is run are initialization cards to give initial values to the permanent system variables shown in Fig. 7.9 and the exogenous events deck. Although all of these constitute a relatively large amount of material to be prepared, programming this model in a general language would require even more work. SIM-

---

[10]This scheduling routine could have been included in the endogenous event BRREV. We have made it a separate subroutine to illustrate the use of subroutines; also, the endogeneous event BRREV is much shorter and comprehensible without the scheduling routine.

SCRIPT automatically provides a timing routine, set operations, automatic location of variables in memory, transfer of system variables from one routine to another, and other details which the programer would otherwise have to provide.

Our general discussion of SIMSCRIPT and the illustrative model have covered many of SIMSCRIPT's capabilities. SIMSCRIPT also provides a report generator, automatic computation of statistics, and certain features which we do not have space to discuss here.

SIMSCRIPT I.5 is an improved version of SIMSCRIPT.[11] SIMSCRIPT I.5 compilers are written by the Consolidated Analysis Centers Inc., and are available for machines made by several different manufacturers. The basic structure of SIMSCRIPT I.5 is the same as that of SIMSCRIPT. Relatively minor changes have been made in the language to simplify and expand certain statements, and some changes have been made to eliminate possibilities for errors existing in the original version. A major improvement in SIMSCRIPT I.5 is elimination of translation of part of the program into FORTRAN so that programs are compiled directly on a single pass. The result is a much simpler system from the standpoint of the computer center running a SIMSCRIPT job.

Still another version, SIMSCRIPT II, is under development. This version, which has not been released at this writing, is best described in the words of one of the members of the development team.

> The basic design rule that has influenced SIMSCRIPT II is "make the language easy to use." Since use, in a practical sense, extends from problem analysis and coding to debugging and documentation, this rule has been foremost at all times. It has prompted the language to evolve into a free-form, English-like sentence structure that is easy to write and easy to read. This structure has made SIMSCRIPT II very much self-documenting. Statements can be written so that they convey, through their wording as well as their structure, the intent of the tasks they perform. This can be seen in some statements that might be part of a manufacturing simulation program:
>
> IF JOB IS IN PROCESS CAUSE
> EXIT IN 5 MINUTES OTHERWISE . . .
>
> Programs are written in free-form with blanks separating the statements and statement words. . . .
>
> The choice of statements and the selection of statement words has been guided by the principle "make every statement easy to remember, easy to write, self-descriptive and necessary." This last factor has been important in keeping the number of statements in the language down. A rule-of-thumb has been to reject the addition of a new statement if its actions can be accomplished by two or three existing statements. For example, there is no single statement to empty a set, as this can be done by the compound statement:

---

[11]Herbert W. Karr, Henry Kleine, and Harry M. Markowitz, SIMSCRIPT I.5 C.A.C.I.66-INT-2 (Santa Monica, Calif.: California Analysis Center, Inc., October 1, 1966).

UNTIL THE QUEUE IS EMPTY,
REMOVE THE FIRST ITEM FROM QUEUE.

Implementation guidelines have been few, but permissive. The compiler is written so that the language is extendable and implementable on many computers. SIMSCRIPT II is written in SIMSCRIPT II, so it is self-documenting to a SIMSCRIPT II programmer and has minimal dependence on machine language instructions. . . .

The language can be expanded by writing new commands in terms of existing commands (what is called "scripting") or by adding to the recognition and code generation sections of the compiler and then compiling the new compiler program. The result is a SIMSCRIPT II compiler that is augmented by the new commands. The language is open-ended in the sense that it can be expanded or modified at any time. . . .

The SIMSCRIPT definition form has been done away with and definitions are declared in sentence-like statements. . . .

Other features of SIMSCRIPT II that make it distinctively different from SIMSCRIPT are its format-free input and output statements, its debugging facilities, its improved event definition and scheduling statements and its data bank concept. The SIMSCRIPT initialization form has been done away with; initialization is accomplished by executable program statements that read ordinary data cards. . . .

SIMSCRIPT II is structured so that it can be taught to users with a great diversity of knowledge and background. To solve the teaching problem, the problem of merging the many ideas of SIMSCRIPT II into a coherent whole and to show that the language has a wide range of uses, SIMSCRIPT II is defined in a series of seven levels. Each level contains the preceding levels as a compatible subset and enough new commands and features to make it distinctly more useful than its preceding level. A programmer in a particular environment need read only those levels that contain the concepts and statements needed to solve his problems. A novice can be led gradually from the fundamentals of programming to the subtleties of the Level VII SIMSCRIPT II-in-SIMSCRIPT II language.[12]

OTHER LANGUAGES.

We have discussed GPSS, DYNAMO, and SIMSCRIPT because they are the best known and most frequently used simulation languages at this time. They each represent a different approach to the design of simulation packages, and the discussion should serve to alert the reader to the fact that simulation languages can have quite different underlying capabilities. Other languages besides these three have been developed. Some of the better known of these languages are briefly described below. Specific references to further documentation of the languages may be found in the bibliography at the end of the chapter together with citations of several articles in which languages are compared.

[12]Philip J. Kiviat, "Development of New Digital Simulation Languages," *The Journal of Industrial Engineering*, Vol. 17, No. 11 (November, 1966), pp. 605, 606, and 607.

CSL —Control and Simulation Language developed by Buxton and Laski of IBM United Kingdom, Ltd., and Esso Petroleum, respectively. Uses concepts of entities, set, and activities. Based on FORTRAN.

SIMPAC—Developed at Systems Development Corporation. Uses concepts of activities, transactions, queues, and resources. Requires knowledge of SCAT and is closer to machine language than most other simulation languages.

GASP —Developed at United States Steel. Consists of a collection of about 30 FORTRAN subroutines. Uses concepts of elements, attributes, queues, and events which cause activities.

OPS-3 —Developed at the Massachusetts Institute of Technology for on-line, time-sharing computer system. OPS is a general system of which simulation is a part. Uses concepts of activities placed on an agenda.

SIMULA—Developed at Norwegian Computing Center as an extension of ALGOL. Uses concepts of processes which become active, suspended, passive, or terminated due to occurrence of events.

Of the simulation languages we have discussed, DYNAMO is the only language that is oriented toward continuous systems. The others are structured toward the representation of systems in which events that change the state of the system take place at discrete times. The reason for this bias is fairly obvious if we consider the applications of simulation discussed in previous chapters. Most of the models involve discrete phenomena, and the use of languages oriented toward continuous change would involve in many cases a substantial degree of abstraction and aggregation and perhaps a loss of some essential detail. No generalizations can be made as to which orientation is better, since the nature of the problem and philosophy and objectives of the analyst are the controlling factors. However, simulation languages used in business and economic analysis are almost all discrete change languages, and none of the laguages have an easy and natural facility for handling both discrete and continuous models. In the next chapter we will show how a discrete change language can be used to model continuous phenomena.

Simulation languages and programs that are an outgrowth of work on problems in the physical sciences and engineering present quite a contrast. In these fields differential equation model structures and analog computers have long been principal tools of analysis,[13] and a number of digital simulation languages have been developed to permit analysis of continuous systems on digital computers.[14] However, these languages have seldom, if ever, been

[13]See the first part of Chap. 4 for a related discussion of differential equation model structures and the use of analog computers in economic model building.

[14]Two excellent summaries of simulation languages oriented toward continuous systems appear in: Daniel Teichroew and John Francis Lubin, "Computer Simulation—Discussion of the Technique and Comparison of Languages," *Communications of the A.C.M.* Vol. 9, No. 10 (October, 1966); and Robert Linebarger and Robert D. Brennan, "Digital Simulation for Control System Design," *Instruments and Control Systems*, October, 1965.

used in business or economic analysis, and references to them are virtually nonexistent in the business and economics literature.

CHOICE OF A LANGUAGE.

In most cases the analyst is not free to choose without restriction from the simulation languages. Limitations on time and funds usually reduce the possibilities to languages that can easily be obtained for available computing equipment.

When the analyst is in the fortunate position of having several alternatives, consideration must be given to the selection of an appropriate language. As our detailed discussion of the characteristics of GPSS, DYNAMO, and SIMSCRIPT has suggested, there are major differences between languages in spite of the fact that language developers tend to speak of their particular language as if it were *the* approach to simulation. Each language has an underlying structure or philosophy that may make it more efficient and convenient than other languages for certain types of problems. And, as yet, there has been no incorporation of all desirable features into a single package. Accordingly, the user must exercise care, when several languages are available, to choose the one most appropriate to the problem at hand.

To give an illustration, suppose that we wished to develop a model of a system in which transactions flowed through a number of facilities with possibilities for delay caused by congestion in the system and with various branching possibilities. For this problem, GPSS would be the first language to consider of the three that we discussed. GPSS provides automatic queue maintenance, easy collection of statistics relating to queues and waiting times, and ease of programing through the use of block diagrams. The same system could be modeled in SIMSCRIPT, but the user would have to provide some of the routines provided automatically be GPSS. Programing would require a higher level of skill and would be more difficult in SIMSCRIPT. Unless there were some particular reason why GPSS would not work, GPSS would be a logical choice over SIMSCRIPT. DYNAMO would probably not be suitable for the problem, since its basic philosophy is one of dealing in terms of aggregate flows. Modeling of individual transactions, if that were desired, would be difficult, if not impossible, with DYNAMO. The choice of a language, then, requires an understanding of language structures and making informed judgments regarding ease of programing and possibility of obtaining desired statistics.

Languages for Model Sampling, Heuristics, and Gaming

Throughout this text we have maintained a distinction between simulation, model sampling, heuristics, and gaming. Therefore, it is appropriate to discuss briefly languages that might be used in model sampling, heuristics, and gaming, since they are not necessarily the same languages used in simulation studies.

MODEL SAMPLING

Model sampling as we have defined it does not involve dynamic movement of a model through simulated time. Consequently, the availability of a timing routine, which is a feature of the simulation languages that we have discussed, does not represent a positive factor in the selection of a simulation language over a general programing language for model sampling applications. Choice of a language would be based on ease of programing, availability of random number generation routines, and ease of calculating statistics, and in this regard a simulation language would not necessarily have an advantage.

For instance, in the case of DYNAMO, the strong orientation of the language around a timing mechanism is a distinctly negative factor which probably makes DYNAMO unsuitable for model sampling problems. In SIMSCRIPT, the timing routine can be suppressed, and built-in routines for generating random variables with desired frequency distibutions and routines for calculating statistical quantities are useful features from the standpoint of model sampling applications. Although GPSS is rather strongly oriented around time, its structure is such that it is suitable for some model sampling applications. Also, GPSS has very excellent mechanisms for gathering statistics, and this could be an important positive factor in its use for model sampling.

Two examples of model sampling discussed previously in this text, the PERT analysis in Chap. 2 and the use of model sampling in evaluating parameter selection techniques discussed in Chap. 4, were programed in FORTRAN rather than one of the simulation languages. At the time the PERT problem was being investigated, consideration was given to the use of GPSS. However, it was decided after some experimentation that, although GPSS could be used, it was more convenient to use FORTRAN. GPSS has been used in at least one model sampling study reported in the literature. This application was the analysis of an investment decision tree, where the ability of GPSS to route and split transactions and tabulate statistics in the form of probability distributions made it an ideal tool for tracing possible results of investment decisions.[15]

HEURISTICS

Heuristic programing is often characterized by complex data structures. It may be difficult to handle this structural relationship in the data using the more common scientific or business programing languages, and none of the simulation languages are particularly suitable. Development of some forms of heuristic programing has been dependent upon the development of langu-

---

[15]Richard F. Hespos and Paul A. Strassmann, "Stochastic Decision Trees for the Analysis of Investment Decisions," *Management Science*, Vol. 11, Number 10 (August, 1965).

ages that provide the capability for the computer to manipulate complex data relationships. These languages include COMIT, LISP, SLIP, and IPL.[16] The last-named will be discussed, because several of the examples of heuristic methods in Chap. 5 were programed in IPL-V or a predecessor. It should be noted, however, that IPL-V and similar languages are certainly not used exclusively in the application of heuristic techniques. Many applications of heuristics, for example in layout planning and vendor selection in Chap. 5, make use of general languages such as FORTRAN.

The language IPL-V is designed to handle lists of data, either in numeric or symbolic form, and is one of the better known list-processing languages. The general characteristic of these languages is that symbolic or numeric data are stored and can be manipulated by utilizing the concept of a list. A list is a sequence of elements stored in the computer and interconnected by links that indicate where the next element in a list is stored.[17] By using the linking concept, elements in a list need not be stored in consecutive locations in a table, and complex interconnected data structures can be represented and manipulated.

In addition to the ability of IPL-V to manipulate symbols and lists of symbols, the language has other desirable characteristics. Recursiveness, or the ability of subroutines to call upon themselves, is accomplished by having the system store the environment of the current routine until the subroutine is completed. The routine can then proceed from where it paused (with changes which were outputs from the subroutine) by taking its own environment out of storage.

Memory allocation is expedited by the maintenance of a list of all available memory space.

> All words not otherwise in use form the cells of a list, each cell linking to the next. This list has a known name (it is H2 in IPL-V). Any process that needs space can get the address of an available cell from H2. This cell in turn gives the address of another available cell, and so on. A general responsibility is imposed on all processes of the system to put any cells they make available back on the available space list. Thus at all times the free cells are linked together and available to whatever process needs them. This technical device clears the way for the programmer to become almost completely free from problems of memory assignment and to apply at will various processes that modify the structure of memory.[18]

---

[16]An excellent comparison of the four languages is contained in: Daniel G. Bobrow and Bertram Raphael, "A Comparison of List-Processing Computer Languages," *Communications of the ACM*, Vol. 7, No. 4 (April, 1964). References to further documentation for these languages will be found in the bibliography at the end of this chapter.

[17]SIMSCRIPT utilizes a similar concept to maintain its sets, which are essentially lists of the members of the set. The links between the members of the SCED set in our SIMSCRIPT illustration are the PSCED and SSCED attributes of the branch orders, which are members of the set.

[18]Allen Newell, *Information Processing Language—V Manual* (Englewood Cliffs, N.J.: Prentice-Hall, Inc., 1961), p. 11.

Although the basic structure is the list, the list can itself be composed of lists, or it may have the last list cell linked to the first cell of the list (or some intermediate part of the list). The ability to have compound lists allows the creation of elaborate tree structures and even more complex nets in which the various branches are interrelated at more than just a single juncture. IPL-V permits finding the Nth cell on a list by writing a single high level instruction. Other instructions permit merging lists, creation or modification of lists that describe characteristics of a portion of the environment, erasing or copying lists, and performing basic arithmetic operations on numerical data terms. The following is an example of the use of IPL-V.

> Data lists are processed by means of *routines*. A routine has a name, say R1, and it has *inputs* and *outputs*. Suppose, for example, that R1 is a routine that will find the last symbol on a list. This means that R1 takes as input the name of a list (say L1, . . .) and provides as output the last symbol on the list (in this case, S4). Suppose, further, that we wanted to store the last symbol of L1 in a cell, W0. Then, on the coding sheet we would write:

Name	P	Q	SYMB	LINK	COMMENTS
1	0		L1		Input name of list, 'L1'
			R1		Find last symbol on list
2	0		W0		Output last symbol to W0

> Each line on this coding sheet is an *instruction*. The first instruction, 10L1, makes the symbol L1 the input to the process. The code P = 1 indicates that the symbol is an input, and the code Q = 0 indicates that the symbol we are designating is 'L1.' The second instruction is really 00R1, but we do not need to write the zeros in the PQ field. P = 0 indicates that the routine is to be executed, and again, Q = 0 shows that the name of the routine is 'R1.' Finally, the instruction 20W0 puts the output of R1—the symbol that R1 has found at the end of the list L1—into cell W0. The P = 2 indicates that the output symbol is to be put in a specified cell, and the Q = 0 shows that the name of the cell is 'W0.'[19]

This illustration suggests some of the power of list processing languages such as IPL-V to manipulate data structures in ways that would be difficult with conventional programing languages, For this reason, list processing languages have found considerable application in programing heuristic methods.

GAMING

As discussed in Chap. 6, most business games involve only one time period on each set of computations. That is, participants in the games make decisions based on the results of previous periods of play, these decisions are given to a computer program as input data, and the program computes and

---

[19]Allen Newell, *Information Processing Language—V Manual* (Englewood Cliffs, N.J.: Prentice-Hall, Inc., 1961), pp. 21–22.

prints out results of play for one period. The results in turn are given to the participants, and the cycle is repeated.

Computations of the results of play for each period may be quite complex if the game involves many variables with elaborate interrelationships. Simulation languages of the sort discussed earlier in the chapter, however, offer no particular programing advantages and, consequently, they are little used for writing game programs. Almost all programs used in business games are written in general programing languages such as FORTRAN, COBOL, and ALGOL.

A small number of business games involve the use of decision *rules* which move the game through a sequence of plays (or periods) on a single computer run. Figure 6.7 outlines the general structure of this type of game. Even though play is continuous, in cases where time always advances in equal increments it may still be easier to employ a simple loop structure using a general purpose language than to write a program in a special purpose language. The business game with the continuous play structure for instance, was written in FORTRAN with each loop through the program representing one period of play.

When simulation programs of the sort that might be used in analytical studies are used as gaming devices, then simulation languages are useful programing vehicles. As an example, the production-inventory-distribution simulator discussed in Chap. 2 could be used as a gaming device by allowing participants to select inventory replenishment rules or scheduling rules and then simulating the consequences of applying the rules suggested by each participant. For this type of gaming, simulation languages would be useful, but the situation is somewhat different from that encountered in the usual business game.

Summary

Simulation languages provide powerful capabilities that permit simulation models to be developed which would be too time consuming or costly to program with general purpose programing languages. This does not rule out the use of general purpose programing languages, since in many cases, and particularly when time moves ahead in equal increments in the simulation, they may be the cheapest and most efficient method of implementing a model on the computer. The simulation languages that have been developed vary widely in characteristics, so a good choice of a language may mean considerable savings over a poor one.

We have not attempted to compare the relative efficiencies of various languages, since it is only in rare instances that the results which can be obtained from different languages are directly comparable in terms of programing effort and computer running time. So much depends on the computing equipment that is available, the programing approach used, and the objectives of the study that meaningful direct comparisons are almost impossible to make. In selecting a language the analyst must understand the structure and capabilities of available languages, the nature of the model, and results desired, and then make an informed judgment as to the best method of implementing a model on the computer.

EXERCISES

7.1 Work Exercise 2.3, using GPSS.

7.2 Work Exercise 2.9, using GPSS.

7.3 Work Exercise 2.13, using GPSS.

7.4 Work Exercise 2.19, using GPSS.

7.5 Work Exercise 3.1, using DYNAMO. Let DT equal 0.1 week.

7.6 Work Exercise 3.3, using DYNAMO. Let DT equal 0.1 week.

7.7 Work Exercise 3.7, using DYNAMO. Let DT equal 0.1 week.

7.8 Work Exercise 4.2, using DYNAMO.

7.9 Work Exercise 4.6, using DYNAMO.

7.10 Work Exercise 2.5, using SIMSCRIPT.

7.11 Work Exercise 2.12, using SIMSCRIPT.

7.12 Work Exercise 2.15, using SIMSCRIPT.

BIBLIOGRAPHY

"A General Purpose Digital Simulator and Examples of Its Application," *IBM Systems Journal*, Vol. 3, No. 1 (1964).

An Introduction to COMIT Programming. Cambridge, Massachusetts: The Massachusetts Institute of Technology Press, 1962.

Berkeley, Edmund C., Daniel G. Bobrow, eds. *The Programming Language LISP: Its Operations and Applications*. Cambridge, Massachusetts: The Massachusetts Institute of Technology Press, 1966.

Blake, K., and G. Gordon, "Systems Simulation with Digital Computers," *IBM Systems Journal*, Vol. 3, No. 1 (1964).

Bobrow, Daniel G. and Bertram Raphael, "A Comparison of List Processing Languages," *Communications of the ACM*, Vol. 7, No. 4 (April, 1964).

Buxton, J. N. and J. G. Laski, "Control and Simulation Language," *The Computer Journal*, Vol. 5, No. 3 (1962).

Chu, Kong and Thomas H. Naylor, "Two Alternative Methods for Simulating Waiting Line Models," *Journal of Industrial Engineering*, Vol. 16, No. 6 (November–December, 1965).

COMIT Programmer's Reference Manual. Cambridge, Massachusetts: The Massachusetts Institute of Technology Press, 1962.

Control and Simulation Language, Introductory Manual (A Guide to C.S.L.), ESSO Petroleum Co., Ltd., Victoria Street, London S.W. 1, and IBM United Kingdom Ltd., 101 Wigmore Street, London W. 1, March, 1963.

Dimsdale, B. and H. M. Markowitz, "A Description of the SIMSCRIPT Language," *IBM Systems Journal*, Vol. 3, No. 1 (1964).

Dahl, Ole-Johan and Kristen Nygaard, *Basic Concepts of SIMULA, An ALGOL Based Simulation Language*. Oslo, Norway: Norwegian Computing Center.

————, *SIMULA: A Language for Programming and Description of Discrete Event Systems. Introduction and User's Manual*. Oslo, Norway: Norwegian Computing Center, May, 1965.

Efron, R. and G. Gordon, "A General Purpose Digital Simulation and Examples of Its Application: Part I—Description of the Simulator," *IBM Systems Journal*, Vol. 3, No. 1 (1964).

Evans, George W., Graham F. Wallace, and Georgia L. Sutherland, *Simulation Using Digital Computers*. Englewood Cliffs, New Jersey: Prentice-Hall, Inc., 1967, Chap. 7.

Forrester, Jay W., *Industrial Dynamics*. Cambridge, Massachusetts: The Massachusetts Institute of Technology Press, 1961.

GASP Manual. UNIVAC Data Processing Centers, UNIVAC Division of Sperry Rand Corporation, 1290 Avenue of the Americas, New York, March, 1965.

Gordon, G., "A General Purpose Systems Simulator," *IBM Systems Journal*, Vol. 1 (September, 1962).

General Purpose Simulation System/360: Introductory User's Manual. IBM Application Program. White Plains, New York: IBM Corporation, 1967.

General Purpose Simulation System/360: User's Manual. White Plains, New York: IBM Corporation, 1967.

General Purpose Systems Simulator III: Introduction. IBM Application Program. White Plains, New York: IBM Corporation, 1965.

General Purpose Systems Simulator III: User's Manual. White Plains, New York: IBM Corporation.

Green, Bert F., "Computer Languages for Symbol Manipulation," *IRE Transactions on Electronic Computers*, (December, 1961).

Greenberger, M., M. M. Jones, J. H. Morris, and D. N. Ness, *On-Line Computation and Simulation: The OPS-3 System*, Cambridge, Massachusetts: The Massachusetts Institute of Technology Press, 1965.

Hausner, B. and H. M. Markowitz, *Technical Appendix on the SIMSCRIPT Simulation Programming Language*. The RAND Corporation, RM-3813-Pr, August, 1963.

Herskovitch, H. and T. H. Schneider, "GPSS III—An Expanded General Purpose Simulator," *IBM Systems Journal*, Vol. 4, No. 3 (1965).

Hills, P. R., "SIMON: A Simulation Language in ALGOL," in *Digital Simulation in Operational Research*, S. H. Hollingdale, ed. New York: American Elsevier Publishing Company, Inc., 1967.

Kagdis, J. and M. R. Lackner, "A Management Control Systems Simulation Model," *Management Technology*, Vol. 3, No. 2 (December, 1963).

Kiviat, P. J., "Development of New Digital Simulation Languages," *The Journal of Industrial Engineering*, Vol. 17, No. 11 (November, 1966).

————, *GASP—A General Activity Simulation Program*. P-2864. Santa Monica, California: The RAND Corporation, 1964.

Karr, H. W., H. Kleine, and H. M. Markowitz, *SIMSCRIPT I.5*, C.A.C.I. 66—INT—2. Santa Monica, California: California Analysis Center, Inc., October 1, 1966.

Krasnow, Howard S. and Reino A. Merikallio, "The Past, Present and Future of General Simulation Languages," *Management Science*, Vol. 11, No. 2 (November, 1964).

Kribs, C. A., *Building a Model Using SIMPAC*. Technical Memorandum TM—602/300/00, System Development Corporation, November, 1962.

Lackner, Michael R., "A General Simulation Capability," *Data Processing*, November, 1962.

Laski, J. G., "On the Time Structure in (Monte Carlo) Simulations," *Operational Research Quarterly*, Vol. 16, No. 3 (September, 1965).

Lave, Roy E., Jr., "Timekeeping for Simulation," *The Journal of Industrial Engineering*, Vol. 28, No. 7 (July, 1967).

Ledley, R. S. and L. S. Rotolo, "A Heuristic Concept and an Automatic Computer Program Aid for Operational Simulation," *Naval Research Logistics Quarterly*, Vol. 9, Nos. 3 and 4 (September–December, 1962).

Linebarger, Robert and Robert D. Brennan, "Digital Simulation for Control System Design," *Instruments and Control Systems*, October, 1965.

Markowitz, H. M., "Simulating with SIMSCRIPT," *Management Science*, Vol. 12, No. 10 (June, 1966).

Markowitz, H. M., B. Hausner, and H. W. Karr, *SIMSCRIPT: A Simulation Programming Language*. RM-3310-PR, Santa Monica, California: The RAND Corporation, November, 1962 (Prentice-Hall, Inc., 1963).

McCarthy, John, et al., *LISP 1.5 Programmer's Manual*. Cambridge, Massachusetts: The Massachusetts Institute of Technology Press, 1962.

Newell, Allen, *Information Processing Language—V Manual*. Englewood Cliffs, New Jersey: Prentice-Hall,Inc., 1961.

Newell, Allen and Hugh S. Kelley, *Information Processing Language—V* 2nd ed. Englewood Cliffs,New Jersey: Prentice-Hall, Inc., 1964.

Pugh, Alexander L., *DYNAMO User's Manual*, 2nd ed. Cambridge, Massachusetts: The Massachusetts Institute of Technology Press, 1963.

————, *DYNAMO II*. Memorandum D-1000–1. Cambridge, Massachusetts: Alfred P. Sloan School of Management, Massachusetts Institute of Technology, September 27, 1967.

————, "Time Sharing DYNAMO User's Manual," Memorandum D-805–2. Cambridge, Massachusetts: Alfred P. Sloan School of Management, Massachusetts Institute of Technology, June 6, 1967.

SIMPAC User's Manual, Technical Memorandum TM-602/000/00, System Development Corporation, April, 1962.

Teichroew, Daniel and John Francis Lubin, "Computer Simulation—Discussion of the Technique and Comparison of the Languages," *Communications of the ACM*, Vol. 9, No. 10 (October, 1966).

Tocher, K. D., "Review of Simulation Languages," *Operational Research Quarterly*, Vol. 16, No. 2 (June, 1965).

Weissman, Clark, *LISP 1.5 Primer*. Belmont, California: Dickenson Publishing Company, Inc., 1967.

Weizenbaum, J., "Symmetric List Processor," *Communications of the ACM*, Vol. 7, No. 4 (April, 1964).

Concepts in Model Construction

8 In this and the following chapter we deal with concepts that may be useful in constructing and running a simulation model. Although some authors have spoken of an emerging theory of simulation, model structures are so diverse as to make it unrealistic to speak in terms of a unified theory of simulation. Rather, many concepts and techniques have been developed, some of which may be useful in conducting a specific simulation study.

Probably the closest resemblance to a well-organized body of theory may be found in the areas of random variable generation and use of variance reduction techniques. Sufficient work has been done in developing these techniques so that the use of the word theory is probably warranted. However, neither is a necessary part of a useful simulation model; in fact, variance reduction techniques that have been most fully developed in theory are, for reasons discussed later in this chapter, little used in current business and economics simulation models.

Our treatment of the technical aspects of simulation is divided into two parts: Chap. 8, dealing with concepts applicable to the construction of a model, and Chap. 9, which deals with concepts most closely related to model operation and interpretation. This division is rather arbitrary, and the two chapters, together with the preceding one dealing with simulation languages, might well be regarded as a single unit setting forth the principal technical tools available at the present time which may be found useful in constructing and operating simulation models.

Random Number Generation

Following terminology that is fairly consistently used in the literature, we will refer to a random variable uniformly distributed over the interval 0 to 1 simply as a random number. A graph of the distribution is shown in Fig. 8.1, and the frequency function is

$$f(x) - \frac{1}{1 - 0} = 1, \qquad 0 \leq x \leq 1 \tag{8.1}$$

where x is a random number. By moving the decimal point appropriately, random numbers may be converted to numbers uniformly distributed over the interval 0 to 0.1, or 0 to 100, or 0 to 10,000 and so forth. When simulation models contain stochastic elements, the ability to generate random numbers is fundamental to operation of the model. Random numbers may be used directly or to generate sequences of numbers with other distributions through methods described in the next section of this chapter.

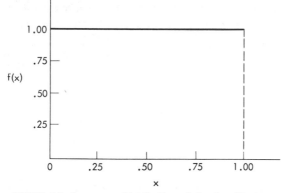

FIGURE 8.1. Frequency Distribution of Random Numbers

For simulations performed by manual methods, elementary physical processes such as drawing prenumbered slips of paper out of a container can be devised to generate sequences of random numbers, and such methods may be useful for short demonstrations. For most work, however, more efficient and reliable sources of random numbers are required. One possibility is to use one of the tables of random numbers which have been available for many years. The earliest was prepared by Tippett[1] in 1927, and several have appeared since then; the RAND Corporation[2] table is one of the largest and best known. Specially designed machines to produce random numbers are another source of numbers of sufficient volume and reliability, and one such machine was used to produce the RAND table. But neither tables nor special machines are very satisfactory sources of random numbers for digital computers. Tables are awkward because they must either be stored in memory (where they use up capacity needed for other purposes) or externally on tape or cards and read when random numbers are required, and special machines for random number generation are not easily attached to digital computers.

---

[1]L. H. C. Tippett, "Random Sampling Numbers," *Tracts for Computers*, No. XV (Cambridge, England: Cambridge University Press, 1927).

[2]RAND Corporation, *A Million Random Digits with 100,000 Normal Deviates* (New York: The Free Press, 1955).

Consequently, considerable effort has been expended in devising efficient numerical processes for generating pseudo-random numbers within the computer itself.

One of the earliest numerical processes which was suggested is the mid-square method described by Metropolis as follows:

> One scheme, proposed by von Neumann, is the so-called "middle square." Beginning with some n (usually even) digit number x_0, one obtains the first iterate x_1 by forming x_0^2, and extracting the middle n digits from it. x_2 is obtained by squaring x_1, etc. The iterative scheme is simple and requires the storage in the computer of a single number. The sequence of iterates is the set of random numbers.[3]

Table 8.1 is a sequence of 30 four-digit random numbers generated by the mid-square method starting with an initial number of 3456. Using Metropolis' terminology, we obtain the sequence in Table 8.1 as follows:

$$x_0 = 3456$$

and

$$x_0^2 = 11943936$$

therefore,

$$x_1 = 9439$$

Table 8.1   FOUR DIGIT RANDOM NUMBERS PRODUCED
BY MID-SQUARE METHOD

9439	4501	0756
0947	2590	5715
8968	7081	6612
4250	1405	7185
0625	9740	6242
3906	8676	9625
2568	2729	6406
5946	4474	0368
3549	0166	1354
5954	0275	8333

Successive numbers in the table are generated by the same procedure. The method is simple and easily programed, and is more attractive as a source of random numbers in a digital simulation program than either a table or an external generating device.

Whether a random number generation technique such as the mid-square method is a good one or not depends on factors other than just the ease of producing the sequence of numbers. One criterion which might be applied is whether a sequence is reproducible, since in some models we might be interested in rerunning the model with the same sequence of random

---

[3]N. Metropolis, "Phase Shifts—Middle Squares—Wave Equation," in *Symposium on Monte Carlo Methods*, Herbert A. Meyer, ed. (New York: John Wiley & Sons, Inc., 1956).

numbers but with some parameter or structural relationship altered. The mid-square method meets this criterion, since a sequence is completely determined by the initial number.

Another criterion for judging a random number generation technique is whether the numbers are, in fact, random. Several tests for randomness have been suggested, but there is no agreement on the tests that a sequence of random numbers should be able to pass. To illustrate some possibilities, we will apply two simple tests to the sequence of numbers in Table 8.1.

If the numbers in Table 8.1 are random, each digit would be expected to appear with equal frequency. Since there are 120 total digits in the table, each digit should appear 12 times. We can make a comparison of observed frequencies of the digits in the table with theoretical frequencies, using the χ^2 statistic.[4] Table 8.2 summarizes the calculation of χ^2, using the observed frequencies of digits in Table 8.1. If observed frequencies differ significantly from theoretical frequencies so that the digits cannot be considered random, the computed value of χ^2 will be larger than the critical value given in a table of χ^2. In this case, there are nine degrees of freedom, and the critical value for a level of significance of 0.05 is 16.916. Consequently, we conclude that the test does not reveal any nonrandomness at this level of significance. More complicated χ^2 tests have been suggested which we will not discuss here.[5]

Table 8.2 APPLICATION OF χ^2 TEST FOR RANDOMNESS TO DIGITS
IN TABLE 8.1

Digit	Frequency (o_i)	Expected (e_i)	$(o_i - e_i)$	$(o_i - e_i)^2$	$(o_i - e_i)^2/e_i$
0	14	12	2	4	0.333
1	8	12	−4	16	1.333
2	11	12	−1	1	0.083
3	8	12	−4	16	1.333
4	15	12	3	9	0.750
5	17	12	5	25	2.083
6	17	12	5	25	2.083
7	10	12	−2	4	0.333
8	8	12	−4	16	1.333
9	12	12	0	0	0.000

$$\chi^2 = \sum_{i=0}^{9} \frac{(o_i - e_i)^2}{e_i} = 9.664$$

There are several tests of randomness which analyze runs in the sequence.[6] One of these is the analysis of the number of runs up and down.

[4]See Chap. 9, particularly Sec. 9.2 of Paul G. Hoel, *Introduction to Mathematical Statistics*, 2nd ed. (New York: John Wiley & Sons, Inc., 1954). Appendix Table III of Hoel is a table of the χ^2 distribution which will be used in testing the computed χ^2 value.

[5]See J. M. Hammersley and D. C. Handscomb, *Monte Carlo Methods* (New York: John Wiley & Sons, Inc., 1964), pp. 30-31.

[6]A complete discussion of tests of runs is contained in: Acheson J. Duncan, *Quality Control and Industrial Statistics*, 3rd ed. (Homewood, Ill.: Richard D. Irwin, Inc., 1965), Chap. VI, Sec. 7.

From Table 8.1 we can determine that there are 14 downward *changes* in the values of the numbers in the sequence and 15 *changes* upwards. There are also 10 *runs* downward and 10 *runs* upward. Using tables supplied by Duncan,[7] we conclude that the number of runs is not inconsistent with a hypothesis of randomness.

The sequence in Table 8.1 meets these two simple tests of randomness, and there are others, such as the series, gap, and poker tests, which could be applied.[8] One reason for not proceeding further with tests of randomness on the sequence in Table 8.1 is that the mid-square method fails to meet another criterion for judging random number generation procedures in that sequences produced by this method may degenerate. For instance, if the sequence started in Table 8.1 is continued as in Table 8.3, we note that it quickly enters a short loop of four numbers. In general, we would like a generator to produce long sequences of random numbers before the sequence repeats, and the mid-square method may fail to meet this criteria.[9]

Table 8.3   CONTINUATION OF SEQUENCE OF RANDOM NUMBERS FROM TABLE 8.1 TO POINT OF LOOPING

4388	1030	6100	4100
2545	0609	2100	8100
4770	3708	4100	6100
7529	7492	8100	2100
6858	1300	6100	4100
0321	6900	2100	8100

A number of other random number generation procedures have been developed with characteristics superior to the mid-square method. At the present time congruential methods are, perhaps, the most widely used.[10] In the multiplicative congruential method the ith random number x_i in the sequence is found by

[7]Acheson J. Duncan, *Quality Control and Industrial Statistics*, 3rd ed. (Homewood, Ill.: Richard D. Irwin, Inc., 1965), Appendix II, Tables N1 and N2.

[8]The interested reader may find a discussion of further tests of randomness and additional references in: Daniel Teichroew, "A History of Distribution Sampling Prior to the Era of the Computer and Its Relevance to Simulation," *American Statistical Association Journal*, Vol. 60, No. 309 (March, 1965), pp. 36-37.

[9]It should be noted, however, that the mid-square method can produce some very long sequences of random numbers with properly chosen starting points and values of n. For an analysis of some characteristics of the method, see: N. Metropolis, "Phase Shifts—Middle Squares—Wave Equation," *Symposium on Monte Carlo Methods*, Herbert A. Meyer, ed. (New York: John Wiley & Sons, Inc., 1956), pp. 30-34.

[10]For an early discussion of congruential methods see: D. H. Lehmer, "Mathematical Methods in Large Scale Computing Units," in *Proceedings of a Second Symposium on Large Scale Digital Calculating Machinery*. The Annals of the Computation Laboratory of Harvard University, Vol. XXVI (Cambridge, Massachusetts: Harvard University Press, 1951). A variation on the multiplicative method, the additive method, is discussed in: Olga Taussky and John Todd, "Generation and Testing of Pseudo-Random Numbers," in *Symposium on Monte Carlo Methods*, Herbert A. Meyer, ed. (New York: John Wiley & Sons, Inc., 1956), pp. 21-25.

$$x_i - \frac{n_i}{m} \qquad\qquad (8.2)$$

where

$$n_i = cn_{i-1}(\text{modulo } m)$$

and c and m are constants. The symbol (modulo m) means that the quantity cn_{i-1} is to be divided by m, and the result n_i is the remainder. An initial value n_0 is chosen as a starting point together with values for c and m, and the sequence of n_i's and x_i's is generated by using the relationships indicated above. When using this method on a digital computer in which information is represented in binary form, we choose m as an integral power of 2 so that the remainder is obtained efficiently by discarding or shifting off binary bits from the product cn_{i-1}. We select specific values of c, m, and the starting point n_0, taking into consideration the characteristics of the computer to be used and analysis based on number theory.[11]

Congruential methods are efficient in terms of computer time, and sequences produced by them are reproducible. They generate numbers which have passed many tests of randomness, and the sequences can be made quite long before the sequence repeats itself. These are sufficient reasons for favoring them over the mid-square method discussed previously.

We have outlined major concepts that have evolved in generating and testing random numbers, but in most cases the prospective user need not provide the mechanisms for generating them himself. Many computing installations provide library subroutines for generating random numbers, and simulation languages such as GPSS, DYNAMO, and SIMSCRIPT have built-in random number generation capabilities so that the user need only call for random numbers as required. Although these built-in capabilities have shifted attention of the simulation model builder away from random number generation, which is desirable, the user should have some basic knowledge of random number generation procedures and be alert to possible problems that may arise in their use.

Generation of Random Variates with Other Distributions

Although random numbers as defined in the proceding section may occasionally be utilized directly in a simulation model, it is more likely that random variates with other distributions must be generated. In almost all cases, random numbers are used to generate these random variates, techniques of the kind described in this section being used. Normally distributed random

---

[11]An extensive discussion of the proper choice of constants and starting point appears in: Guy H. Orcutt, Martin Greenberger, John V. Korbel, and Alice M. Rivlin, *Microanalysis of Socioeconomic Systems: A Simulation Study* (New York: Harper and Row, Inc., 1961), Chap. 16, Appendix: "Random Number Generation".

variates, however, may be obtained directly from published tables.[12] Because the use of such tables is not very practical in computer models even in this case computerized methods of generating normal random variates are needed.

The most direct way to obtain random variates with a desired distribution is to use the inverse of the mathematical expression for the cumulative distribution function. To illustrate the procedure in general terms, let us define y as a random variable with frequency function $f(y)$ and cumulative distribution function $F(y)$; then, if we let

$$x = F(y) \tag{8.3}$$

we note that x is a random number, varying from 0 to 1 depending on the value of the random variable y. If we denote the inverse function by F^{-1}, the relationship between x and y can be rewritten as

$$y = F^{-1}(x) \tag{8.4}$$

The importance of Eq. (8.4) is that it can be used to generate values of the random variable y whenever the inverse function F^{-1} is known for a distribution. This is done simply by generating random numbers and using them in the inverse function to find corresponding values of y. Direct application of the inverse function concept depends on whether the inverse function can be obtained in mathematical terms. We will demonstrate the application of the inverse function to generating random variates from two common distributions.

Earlier it was noted that random numbers can be used directly to provide random variates uniformly distributed over intervals such as 0 to 1, or 0 to 100, or 0 to 10,000 by moving the decimal point. The inverse function concept can be used to obtain random variates uniformly distributed over other intervals. For a random variable uniformly distributed over the interval a to b, the frequency function is

$$f(y) = \begin{cases} \dfrac{1}{b-a}, & a \le x \le b \\[2mm] 0, & x < a \quad \text{or} \quad x > b \end{cases} \tag{8.5}$$

The cumulative distribution function is found by integration.

$$F(y) = \int \frac{1}{b-a} dy$$

$$= \frac{y}{b-a} + C \tag{8.6}$$

---

[12]See, for instance: H. Wold, "Random Normal Deviates," *Tracts for Computers*, No. XXV (Cambridge, England: Cambridge University Press, 1948); and RAND Corporation, *A Million Random Digits with 100,000 Normal Deviates* (Glencoe, Ill.: The Free Press, 1955).

To find the value of the constant of integration C, we note that when $y = a$, $F(y) = 0$. Substituting these values into Eq. (8.6), we find

$$\frac{a}{b-a} + C = 0 \tag{8.7}$$

and

$$C = \frac{-a}{b-a} \tag{8.8}$$

Substituting in Eq. (8.6), we have

$$F(y) = \frac{y}{b-a} - \frac{a}{b-a}$$

$$= \frac{y-a}{b-a} \tag{8.9}$$

In accordance with the discussion of Eq. (8.3), we substitute x for $F(y)$ to give

$$x = \frac{y-a}{b-a} \tag{8.10}$$

and solving for y, we obtain the inverse function

$$y = a + x(b - a) \tag{8.11}$$

The procedure for generating random variates uniformly distributed over the interval a to b is to generate random numbers and substitute them for x in Eq. (8.11) to find corresponding values of y.

Another common distribution to which the inverse function method can be applied is the exponential distribution. The utilization of this distribution in connection with waiting line problems was discussed in Chap. 2. Illustrations of the cumulative distribution function are given in Figs. 2.6 and 2.7. To make the terminology consistent with our usage in this section, we rewrite the frequency function given in Eq. (2.9) as follows:

$$f(y) = \lambda e^{-\lambda y}, \qquad y \geq 0 \tag{8.12}$$

The interpretation of the parameter λ in the context of waiting line problems was discussed in Chap. 2. The cumulative distribution function is found by integration.

$$F(y) = \int \lambda e^{-\lambda y}\, dy$$

$$= -e^{-\lambda y} + C \tag{8.13}$$

Making use of the fact that at $y = 0$, $F(y) = 0$, we substitute to find the value of C.

$$0 = -e^{-0} + C \tag{8.14}$$

and

$$C = e^{-0} = 1 \tag{8.15}$$

Therefore, the cumulative distribution function is

$$F(y) = 1 - e^{-\lambda y} \tag{8.16}$$

which is the same function as was given previously without derivation in Eq. (2.13).

In accordance with the discussion of Eq. (8.3), we substitute x for $F(y)$ to give

$$x = 1 - e^{-\lambda y} \tag{8.17}$$

or

$$e^{-\lambda y} = 1 - x \tag{8.18}$$

By the definition of a natural logarithm, Eq. (8.18) can be rewritten

$$-\lambda y = \ln (1 - x) \tag{8.19}$$

and the inverse function is

$$y = -\frac{1}{\lambda} \ln (1 - x) \tag{8.20}$$

To find exponentially distributed random variates, we generate random numbers, substitute them for x in Eq. (8.20), and obtain corresponding values of y. Since x is uniformly distributed from 0 to 1, the quantity $(1 - x)$ in Eq. (8.20) has the same distribution. Therefore, Eq. (8.20) can be simplified slightly by using x instead of $(1 - x)$.

$$y = -\frac{1}{\lambda} \ln (x) \tag{8.21}$$

The demonstration that both Eqs. (8.20) and (8.21) produce exponentially distributed random variates will be left to the reader as an exercise (see Exercise 8.6).

Explicit mathematical expressions for the inverse functions were obtained in the preceding illustrations. However, the same concept can be used when the inverse function is expressed only as a table or graph. We have already illustrated the use of the concept without explanation in Figs. 1.6 and 2.6. In each case the usual interpretation of the dependent and independent variables was merely reversed. That is, normally we would use a value of the independent variable on the horizontal axis to determine the value of the cumulative frequency which is the dependent variable on the vertical axis. Instead, the value of a random number was plotted on the vertical axis and used to determine the value of the variable on the horizontal axis.

With computer hardware and software that are commonly available, graphs cannot be used directly as input. Consequently, the usual practice when mathematical functions are not used is to describe distribution functions by tables of values of the random variable y and corresponding values of $f(y)$ or $F(y)$. These tables are stored in memory so that when random variates are required during a simulation, a random number is generated and the corresponding value of the random variable is obtained from the table.[13] When the table represents a continuous distribution, an interpolation procedure is used to obtain intermediate values of y not defined explicitly by the table.

Some simulation languages such as GPSS, DYNAMO, and SIMSCRIPT allow input of either continuous or discrete probability distributions in table form and automatically provide random variates from these tables. The reader may recall that the model used to illustrate the use of GPSS III in Chap. 7 included as input a table of an exponential distribution used to determine interarrival and service times,[14] and the SIMSCRIPT model included a probability distribution of shipping times.

Two other general methods for generating random variables are the rejection method and the composition method.[15] We will discuss the rejection method, since the principle on which it operates is basic and has found important application in evaluating definite integrals.

Suppose that it is desired to obtain random variates distributed according to the arbitrary frequency function $f(y)$ shown in Fig. 8.2. Note that when a frequency function is continuous, as this one is, the maximum value of $f(y)$ may be greater than 1, since, for a continuous distribution, the *area* under the curve determines relative frequency rather than the height of the curve.

---

[13]A manual method for obtaining random variates from a table has already been illustrated in Tables 1.1 and 1.4. A simple computer procedure is used in several places in the program in Appendix B; see statements 44 through 46, for instance.

[14]A minor idiosyncracy of GPSS III is that all times are truncated to integral values. Therefore, when random variates are generated to simulate such things as random times between arrivals and random service times, a bias may be injected into the distributions obtained in the simulation run. If this is severe enough, the user may have to compensate by adjusting the table of probabilities or scaling all parameters of the model in terms of a smaller time unit.

[15]An early discussion of these methods is contained in: James W. Butler, "Machine Sampling from Given Probability Distributions," in *Symposium on Monte Carlo Methods*, Herbert A. Meyer, ed. (New York: John Wiley and Sons, Inc., 1956), pp. 256–263.

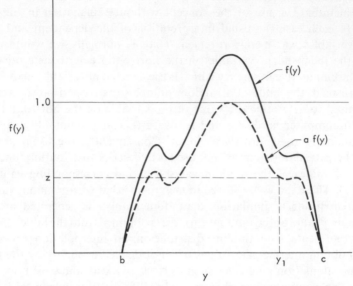

FIGURE 8.2. Rejection Method for Generating Random Variables

For reasons that will be clear as our discussion proceeds, $f(y)$ must be scaled so that the maximum is equal to or less than 1. In general, we may think of $f(y)$ as always being scaled by a constant a, where $0 < a \leq 1$. The resulting function $af(y)$ is also shown in Fig. 8.2. A random number x_1 is now generated and y_1 is found by using the relationship

$$y_1 = b + x_1(c - b) \qquad (8.22)$$

where b and c are the lower and upper limits, as shown in Fig. 8.2, on the values assumed by the random variable y. We now substitute y_1 into the scaled frequency function to find z; that is,

$$z = af(y_1) \qquad (8.23)$$

Of necessity the value of z will fall between 0 and 1. A second random number x_2 is now generated and compared with z. If $x_2 \leq z$, y_1 is accepted as a random variate from the distribution $f(y)$; if $x_2 > z$, y_1 is rejected and the process is repeated, two new random numbers being used. The frequency of acceptance of the y's depends on the vertical distance from the y axis to $af(y)$. It is easily seen that the rejection procedure produces a sequence of accepted y's with the same frequency distribution as specified by $af(y)$. In a *relative* frequency sense, $af(y)$ has the same distribution as $f(y)$, so that the sequence of accepted y's has the frequency distribution which is desired.

The principle used in the rejection method may also be used in the

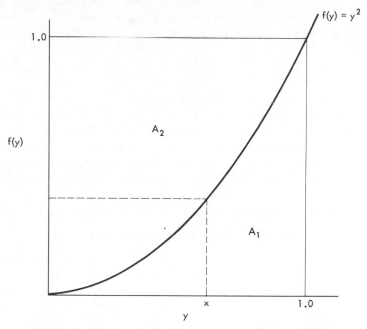

FIGURE 8.3. Rejection Method for Evaluating a Definite Integral

evaluation of definite integrals.[16] Although the procedure would be employed for complex, multidimensional integrals, a two-dimensional example is informative. The integral to be evaluated is $\int_0^1 y^2 dy$. The function $f(y) = y^2$ is shown graphically in Fig. 8.3, and the value of the definite integral $\int_0^1 y^2\, dy$ is the area A_1, under the curve between the limits. Because of the simplicity of the function the area is easily found mathematically.

$$A_1 = \int_0^1 y^2\, dy$$

$$= \frac{y^3}{3}\Big]_0^1 = \frac{1}{3} \tag{8.24}$$

To evaluate the integral by the Monte Carlo method, we generate a random number x_1 and let $y_1 = x_1$. We then compute $z = f(y_1)$. A second random number x_2 is generated, and we compare x_2 with z, recording

---

[16]The rejection method, however, is not the most efficient method that can be found. Several of the techniques for increasing efficiency discussed in the next section of this chapter are applicable to the problem, and one of these, called "crude Monte Carlo," is applied to the evaluation of this integral in the next section. A complete discussion of more efficient ways to evaluate integrals may be found in: J. M. Hammersley and D. C. Handscomb, *Monte Carlo Methods* (New York: John Wiley & Sons, Inc., 1964), Chap. 5.

whether $x_2 > z$ or whether $x_2 \leq z$. After n trials, x_2 will have been equal to or less than z some number of times u. Then an estimate $\hat{A}_1$ of the area under the curve is

$$\hat{A}_1 = \left(\frac{u}{n}\right)(A_1 + A_2) \qquad (8.25)$$

Since $A_1 + A_2 = 1$ in this problem, the estimate of the area is simply u/n. Table 8.4 shows the results of 50 trials using the third and fourth columns of the table of random numbers in Appendix A.1 as sources of x_1 and x_2, respectively. (For simplicity only the first two digits of each column have been used, and z has been rounded to three decimal places.) Our estimate of the area A_1 from Table 8.4 is 0.28 as compared with the true value of 0.33.

Table 8.4   EVALUATION OF $\int_0^1 y^2 dy$ BY MONTE CARLO METHOD USING REJECTION PRINCIPLE

x_1	z	x_2	$x_2 \leq z$	x_1	z	x_2	$x_2 \leq z$
0.71	0.504	0.72		0.11	0.012	0.01	*
0.31	0.096	0.81		0.32	0.102	0.41	
0.35	0.122	0.48		0.75	0.562	0.48	*
0.53	0.281	0.65		0.04	0.002	0.05	
0.31	0.096	0.47		0.44	0.194	0.50	
0.28	0.078	0.41		0.22	0.048	0.95	
0.18	0.032	0.66		0.35	0.122	0.01	*
0.15	0.022	0.58		0.40	0.160	0.51	
0.73	0.533	0.23	*	0.27	0.073	0.19	
0.75	0.562	0.85		0.01	0.000	0.40	
0.72	0.518	0.76		0.04	0.001	0.50	
0.77	0.593	0.40	*	0.42	0.176	0.41	
0.48	0.230	0.20	*	0.31	0.096	0.80	
0.05	0.002	0.16		0.79	0.624	0.37	*
0.68	0.462	0.91		0.12	0.014	0.54	
0.46	0.212	0.37		0.03	0.001	0.47	
0.84	0.706	0.29	*	0.78	0.608	0.01	*
0.48	0.230	0.73		0.70	0.490	0.43	*
0.13	0.017	0.96		0.12	0.014	0.26	
0.60	0.360	0.83		0.89	0.792	0.36	*
0.87	0.757	0.35	*	0.48	0.230	0.40	
0.53	0.281	0.73		0.86	0.740	0.57	*
0.90	0.810	0.89		0.90	0.810	0.66	*
0.26	0.068	0.74		0.38	0.144	0.22	
0.16	0.026	0.40		0.12	0.014	0.37	

Total trials, $n = 50$.
Number of times $x_2 \leq z = u = 14$.
Estimate of area, $\hat{A}_1 = u/n = 0.28$.

Because the normal distribution is often a reasonable approximation to frequency distributions found in the real world, it is important to be able to generate normally distributed random variates. For a normally distributed random variable y with mean a and standard deviation b, the frequency function is

$$f(y) = \frac{1}{b\sqrt{2\pi}} \exp\left[-\frac{1}{2}\left(\frac{y-a}{b}\right)^2\right] \qquad (8.26)$$

Unfortunately, the cumulative distribution function cannot be found explicitly. Therefore, the inverse function method cannot be employed to generate random normal variates unless we are willing to use a table rather than a mathematical expression to represent the cumulative distribution. The rejection method, which we have just discussed, can be used to generate normal random variates, provided the tails of the distribution are truncated. We will leave the application of the rejection method to the normal distribution to the reader as an exercise (see Exercise 8.7). Still other methods have been suggested for generating normal random variates.[17] One of the these makes use of the central limit theorem, which states that the distribution of the mean of samples from any distribution approaches a normal distribution as the size of sample is increased. The mean of the distribution of sample means is equal to the mean of the distribution from which the samples are drawn, and the standard deviation of the distribution of sample means is $\sigma/\sqrt{n}$, where n is the sample size and σ is the standard deviation of the distribution from which the samples are drawn.

These concepts can be utilized to generate normal random variates from samples of uniformly distributed random numbers. We note first that random numbers uniformly distributed between 0 and 1 have a mean μ of $\frac{1}{2}$. The variance σ^2 of random numbers uniformly distributed between 0 and 1 is found by applying the mathematical expression for the variance of any random variable y with frequency function $f(y)$ and mean μ.

$$\sigma^2 = \int_a^b (y - \mu)^2 f(y) dy \qquad (8.27)$$

In Eq. (8.27) we substitute 0 and 1 for a and b, $\frac{1}{2}$ for μ, and 1 for $f(y)$ [see Eq. (8.5)]. The variance of random numbers uniformly distributed between 0 and 1, accordingly, is

$$\sigma^2 = \int_0^1 \left(y - \frac{1}{2}\right)^2 dy$$

$$= \frac{y^3}{3} - \frac{y^2}{2} + \frac{y}{4}\Big]_0^1 = \frac{1}{12} \qquad (8.28)$$

and

$$\sigma = \frac{1}{\sqrt{12}} \qquad (8.29)$$

---

[17]An excellent summary of various methods of generating normal random variates is given in: K. D. Tocher, *The Art of Simulation* (London: The English Universities Press Ltd., 1963), pp. 31–34.

From the central limit theorem, the distribution of the mean $\bar{x}$ of samples of size n drawn from random numbers uniformly distributed between 0 and 1 is approximately normal with mean $\mu_{\bar{x}}$ equal to $\frac{1}{2}$ and standard deviation $\sigma_{\bar{x}}$ equal to $\sigma/\sqrt{n}$ or $1/\sqrt{12n}$. Samples of size n are obtained by generating n random numbers by one of the techniques discussed earlier in the chapter and their mean $\bar{x}$ is found by

$$\bar{x} = \sum_{i=1}^{n} \frac{x_i}{n} \qquad (8.30)$$

where the x_i are random numbers. The $\bar{x}$'s generated in this fashion, then, are approximately normally distributed with mean $\frac{1}{2}$ and standard deviation $1/\sqrt{12n}$. Rather than working with the mean of n random numbers, it is more convenient to work with the sum of the n random numbers. The sum is also normally distributed with

$$\mu_{\sum x_i} = n(\tfrac{1}{2}) \qquad (8.31)$$

and

$$\sigma_{\sum x_i} = \sqrt{n/12} \qquad (8.32)$$

To generate random variates with the standard normal distribution having zero mean and unit variance, it is convenient to choose n as 12, since from Eq. (8.32) the standard deviation of the sum of 12 random numbers is 1. This is also probably a sufficiently large n so that the distribution of the sum is approximately a normal distribution. To obtain a zero mean when n is 12, 6 is subtracted from the sum of the random numbers. With $n = 12$, then, the procedure for generating a standard normal random variate r is given by

$$r = \sum_{i=1}^{12} x_i - 6 \qquad (8.33)$$

where the x_i's are random numbers generated by one of the methods discussed previously. Normal variates R with a different mean m and standard deviation d may be obtained by

$$R = m + dr \qquad (8.34)$$

If n is selected as some value other than 12, Eqs. (8.33) and (8.34) would have to be adjusted accordingly.

Techniques for generating random variates from certain distributions other than those covered in this section have also been developed. References may be found in the bibliography at the end of the chapter. The reader may also wish to refer at this point to the short discussion of the generation of autocorrelated variables in Chap. 4, p. 140.

Techniques to Improve Model Efficiency

It was recognized at an early date that the use of Monte Carlo approaches to solving problems in the physical sciences often consumed large amounts of digital computer time. Attention quickly focused, as a result, on methods, commonly called variance reduction techniques, which could improve the efficiency of the computations. In fact, this emphasis became so strong that some writers considered the use of variance reduction techniques to be an integral part of a Monte Carlo study. Kahn, for instance, in an early paper on variance reduction techniques, describes the Monte Carlo approach in the following way:

> When doing a Monte Carlo problem one focuses attention on three main topics. They are:
> 1. Choosing or analogizing the probability process.
> 2. Generating sample values of the random variables on a given computing machine.
> 3. Designing and using variance reducing techniques.[18]

Variance reduction techniques, in general, are directed toward altering the probability structure of the model so that efficiencies in computation are obtained. According to Hammersley,

> A general Monte Carlo tenet is: *never sample from a distribution merely because it arises in the physical context of a problem, for we may be able to use a better distribution in the computations and still get the right answer.*[19]

Since our definition of simulation includes deterministic as well as stochastic models, techniques of variance reduction as originally conceived are not strictly relevant to all simulation models. And, for reasons discussed later, variance reduction may not be practical when one is designing models of the types used in business and economic analysis. However, the possibility of applying variance reduction concepts and other devices for increasing efficiency in both deterministic and stochastic models should not be ignored when one is constructing a simulation model. On occasion, significant economies of computing time may be obtained. In the remainder of this section, we will discuss some of the ideas that have been suggested for increasing computational efficiency in simulation models.

---

[18]Herman Kahn, "Use of Different Monte Carlo Sampling Techniques," in *Symposium on Monte Carlo Methods*, Herbert A. Meyer, ed. (New York: John Wiley & Sons, Inc., 1956), p. 146.

[19]J. M. Hammersley and D. C. Handscomb, *Monte Carlo Methods* (New York: John Wiley & Sons, Inc., 1964), p. 42.

Restructuring model

Orcutt gives the following illustration of how a model might be restructured to reduce the number of times that a certain type of calculation must be done without in any way changing the output from the model.

> Imagine a cohort of white females. Since they have all been born at the same time and will have identical ages on all subsequent dates, it is clear that our demise routine will at the start of any period calculate the same probability of death during the period for each surviving member of the cohort. We now use one random number for each woman to determine if she survives the period. At the start of the next period we repeat the above process with age and t both increased by one period. We again use one random number per woman.
>
> Instead of the above procedure for determining death, we could calculate the conditional probabilities of death as above but use them to build up a probability of survival to time t. Thus, if X_t = probability a unit will survive to time t, and if Y_t = the conditional probability that a unit surviving to time $t - 1$ will survive to time t, then $X_t = Y_1 \cdot Y_2 \ldots Y_t$, where Y_1 is the probability that a unit present at time 0 will survive to time 1. Clearly, one single random drawing from the uniform distribution ranging from 0 to 1 will be sufficient to determine the period in which a given individual must die. That random number can be drawn initially, and then successive values of X_1, X_2, X_3, etc., computed. As each one is computed it can be compared with the random drawing for the individual. When X_t exceeds the individual's random drawing, that individual dies. Thus the expected fraction of survivors in a cohort, by the time X_t is reduced to 0.90, will be 0.90.[20]

Crude Monte Carlo

In the preceding section of this chapter the rejection principle was applied to evaluating the definite integral in Eq. (8.24). A sample calculation using 50 trials is shown in Table 8.4. Although the rejection method is easily understood and computationally simple, improved efficiency can be obtained by using a different technique which Hammersley calls "crude Monte Carlo."[21]

Before explaining the crude Monte Carlo technique, let us return to the rejection principle for a moment. From our preceding discussion, it is apparent that application of the rejection principle to evaluating the integral in Eq. (8.24) involves selecting a point at random within the unit square in Fig. 8.3 and determining whether the point falls above or below the curve

---

[20]From pp. 400–401, *Microanalysis of Socioeconomic Systems: A Simulation Study* by Guy H. Orcutt, et al. Copyright © 1961 by Harper and Row, Publishers, Incorporated. Used by permission of the publishers. Before continuing further the reader may wish to review the section on socioeconomic systems in Chap. 4, which describes the model to which Orcutt refers in this discussion of model restructuring.

[21]J. M. Hammersley and D. C. Handscomb, *Monte Carlo Methods* (New York: John Wiley & Sons, Inc., 1964), pp. 51–55.

$f(y) - y^2$. The procedure may be viewed as making a selection at random from a binomial population, where the proportion p is given by

$$p = \frac{A_1}{A_1 + A_2} = A_1 \qquad (8.35)$$

If an estimate $\hat{A}_1$ of the area under the curve has been made by the rejection method, the standard error of the sample proportion $\hat{A}_1$ is[22]

$$\sigma_{\hat{A}_1} = \sqrt{\hat{A}_1(1 - \hat{A}_1)/(n - 1)} \qquad (8.36)$$

Now let us consider the crude Monte Carlo method and compare its standard error with that of the rejection method (called the hit-or-miss method by Hammersley). In the crude Monte Carlo method an estimate $\hat{A}_1$ is made by

$$\hat{A}_1 = \frac{1}{n} \sum_{i=1}^{n} f(x_i) \qquad (8.37)$$

where the x_i are random numbers and n is the number of trials. That is, random numbers are substituted for y in the function $f(y) = y^2$, and the mean of the $f(x_i)$ is found. (If the limits of integration were other than 0 to 1, the x_i would have to be scaled suitably before making the substitution.) Referring to Fig. 8.3, we see that crude Monte Carlo in effect estimates the mean distance between the y axis and $f(y)$, and since the width of the area is 1, the estimate of A_1 is simply the estimated mean distance between the y axis and $f(y)$.

If an estimate $\hat{A}_1$ is made using Eq. (8.37), the standard error of $\hat{A}_1$ is given by

$$\sigma_{\hat{A}_1} = \sqrt{\frac{\sum_{i=1}^{n}[f(x_i)]^2 - n(\hat{A}_1)^2}{n(n - 1)}} \qquad (8.38)$$

In Table 8.5 an estimate of A_1 is obtained by using Eq. (8.37) and $n = 50$. The third column of the random number table in Appendix A.1 was used as a source of random numbers; for simplicity only the first two digits were used. The estimate of A_1 from Table 8.5 is 0.27 (rounded to two places) which, by chance, is not quite as good an estimate of the true value as was obtained by using the rejection method in Table 8.4. However, let us compare

---

[22]For a discussion of the standard error of a proportion and standard error of the mean, which will be utilized in comparing the rejection method and crude Monte Carlo, see: Edward C. Bryant, *Statistical Analysis*, 2nd ed. (New York: McGraw-Hill Book Company, Inc., 1966), pp. 58, 66, and 112.

Table 8.5 EVALUATION OF $\int_0^1 y^2\,dy$ BY "CRUDE" MONTE CARLO METHOD

x	$f(x)$	$[f(x)]^2$
.71	.5041	.2541
.31	.0961	.0092
.35	.1225	.0150
.53	.2809	.0789
.31	.0961	.0092
.28	.0784	.0061
.18	.0324	.0010
.15	.0225	.0005
.73	.5329	.2839
.75	.5625	.3164
.72	.5184	.2687
.77	.5929	.3515
.48	.2304	.0530
.05	.0025	.0000
.68	.4624	.2318
.46	.2116	.0447
.84	.7056	.4978
.48	.2304	.0530
.13	.0169	.0002
.60	.3600	.1296
.87	.7569	.5728
.53	.2809	.0789
.90	.8100	.6561
.26	.0676	.0045
.16	.0256	.0006
.11	.0121	.0001
.32	.1024	.0104
.75	.5625	.3164
.04	.0016	.0000
.44	.1936	.0374
.22	.0484	.0023
.35	.1225	.0150
.40	.1600	.0256
.27	.0729	.0053
.01	.0001	.0000
.04	.0016	.0000
.42	.1764	.0311
.31	.0961	.0092
.79	.6241	.3895
.12	.0144	.0002
.03	.0009	.0000
.78	.6084	.3701
.70	.4900	.2401
.12	.0144	.0002
.89	.7921	.6274
.48	.2304	.0530
.86	.7396	.5470
.90	.8100	.6561
.38	.1444	.0208
.12	.0144	.0002
	$\Sigma f(x) = \overline{13.6338}$	$\Sigma [f(x)]^2 = \overline{7.2749}$

Estimate of area $\hat{A}_1 = \dfrac{1}{n}\,\Sigma f(x) = 13.6338/50 = 0.2727$

the standard errors of these estimates. From Eq. (8.36), the standard error of $\hat{A}_1$ obtained by the rejection method in Table 8.4 is

$$\sigma_{\hat{A}_1} = \sqrt{(0.28)(0.72)/(50 - 1)}$$
$$= 0.064 \qquad (8.39)$$

From Eq. (8.38) the standard error of $\hat{A}_1$ obtained by crude Monte Carlo in Table 8.5 is

$$\sigma_{\hat{A}_1} = \sqrt{\frac{7.2749 - 50(0.2727)^2}{50(50 - 1)}}$$
$$= 0.038 \qquad (8.40)$$

In this particular case, then, crude Monte Carlo produced a smaller standard error than did the rejection method using the same n.

Although the point estimate of A_1 by crude Monte Carlo happens, by chance, to be poorer than the estimate by the rejection method, let us establish the confidence interval for each of the estimates. If we use three standard deviations for the confidence interval, then the interval for the rejection method is $0.28 \pm 3(0.064)$ or from 0.09 to 0.47. For crude Monte Carlo, the confidence interval is $0.27 \pm 3(0.038)$ or from 0.16 to 0.38. The confidence interval for crude Monte Carlo is much smaller than and lies wholly within the interval for the rejection method.

Importance sampling

This method involves distorting a probability distribution to which the Monte Carlo method is applied in order that more events of interest to the investigator are obtained than would otherwise be the case. A weighting factor is then applied to the distorted results to remove the bias which has been introduced.

Kahn gives a simple illustration of how the probabilities can be distorted when one is attempting to determine empirically by the Monte Carlo method the frequency p with which 3 is obtained when two dice[23] are thrown. An estimate $\hat{p}$ is made by counting the number of successes μ in n trials and calculating:

$$\hat{p} = \frac{\mu}{n} \qquad (8.41)$$

Since we consider only two outcomes on a trial (i.e., a 3 may or may not occur) and the probability of success is the same for all trials, the problem is

---

[23]Herman Kahn, "Use of Different Monte Carlo Sampling Techniques," in *Symposium on Monte Carlo Methods*, Herbert A. Meyer, ed. (New York: John Wiley & Sons, Inc., 1956), p. 149.

one of sampling from a binomial distribution with an unkown value of p. If p is known, the standard deviation of the proportion of successes in n trials σ_p is

$$\sigma_p = \sqrt{\frac{p(1-p)}{n}} \qquad (8.42)$$

The value of σ_p may be converted to a percentage of p by dividing by p and multiplying by 100.

$$\frac{100\sigma_p}{p} = 100\sqrt{\frac{1-p}{np}} \qquad (8.43)$$

Kahn suggests that the concept of importance sampling can be applied to this problem by biasing the dice so that a 1 or a 2 would come up twice as frequently as would be normal. The probability of getting a 3 would then be $\frac{2}{9}$ instead of $\frac{1}{18}$, and the percentage of error is reduced to less than one half of its previous value. Because of the bias in the procedure, Eq. (8.41) cannot be used to estimate p, and an estimate, instead, is made by

$$\hat{p} = \frac{1}{4}\frac{u}{n} \qquad (8.44)$$

where the factor $\frac{1}{4}$ is used to remove the bias. The principle involved is to bias the sample to produce more results of interest to the investigator and then to use an appropriate weighting factor to remove bias from the final results.

Antithetic variates

An antithetic random variable is one which has the same expected value as another random variable, but which is negatively correlated with it.[24] In operational terms, y and y' must have the same mean μ, but when a high value of y is drawn at random a low value of y' should be generated, and vice versa. When y and y' are random variables with these properties, an estimate $\hat{\mu}$ of the mean after n random selections from each of the distributions is given by

$$\hat{\mu} = \frac{1}{n}\sum_{i=1}^{n}\left(\frac{y_i}{2} + \frac{y_i'}{2}\right) \qquad (8.45)$$

The process may be viewed as generating n pairs of values of y and y' or generating n values of y followed by n values of y' negatively correlated with the y's. A useful way to think of the procedure is that a new random

---

[24]A more complete discussion may be found in: J. M. Hammersley and D. C. Handscomb, *Monte Carlo Methods* (New York: John Wiley & Sons, Inc., 1964), pp. 60–66.

variable z is being generated, where $z = y/2 + y'/2$. The variance of z is given by

$$\sigma_z^2 = E(z^2) - [E(z)]^2 \tag{8.46}$$

where E is interpreted "expected value of."[25] Substituting $(y/2 + y'/2)$ for z, we have

$$\sigma_z^2 = E\left(\frac{y}{2} + \frac{y'}{2}\right)^2 - \left[E\left(\frac{y}{2} + \frac{y'}{2}\right)\right]^2$$

$$= \frac{1}{4}E(y^2) + \frac{1}{2}E(yy') + \frac{1}{4}E(y'^2) - \frac{1}{4}[E(y)]^2$$

$$- \frac{1}{2}E(y)E(y') - \frac{1}{4}[E(y')]^2$$

$$= \frac{1}{4}\{E(y^2) - [E(y)]^2\} + \frac{1}{4}\{E(y'^2) - [E(y')]^2\}$$

$$+ \frac{1}{2}[E(yy') - E(y)E(y')]$$

$$= \frac{1}{4}\sigma_y^2 + \frac{1}{4}\sigma_{y'}^2 + \frac{1}{2}\operatorname{cov}(y, y') \tag{8.47}$$

Since the cov (y, y') is negative if y and y' are negatively correlated, this factor will tend to reduce the variance of z as calculated by Eq. (8.47). Also, we see from Eq. (8.47) that by appropriately choosing an antithetic variable, the variance of z can be made smaller than the variance of either the original random variable y or the antithetic variable y'. Since the random variable z has the same mean μ as y and y' but can be made to have a smaller variance, it can be more efficient to generate values of z [that is, use Eq. (8.45)] to estimate μ than it is to generate values of y alone to estimate μ.

Although antithetic variables can be generated in different ways, one of the easiest is to use the following procedure:

1. Generate a random number x_i and use it to select a value of y_i from its distribution.

2. Find $(1 - x_i)$ and use it to select y_i' from the same distribution. It is clear that y' will have the same mean and variance as y and will also be negatively correlated with it, which are the desired properties for an antithetic variable. The application of the technique to an actual problem is left to the reader as an exercise (see Exercise 8.13).

Page gives an illustration of the use of the antithetic variable technique to estimate waiting time in a single server queue similar to that discussed in

---

[25]For a further discussion of expected values, variance, and covariance, see: Richard C. Clelland, John S. deCani, Francis E. Brown, J. Parker Bursk, and Donald S. Murray, *Basic Statistics with Business Applications* (New York: John Wiley & Sons, Inc., 1966), Secs. 6.2, 6.4, 6.5, and 11.6.

the waiting line section of Chap. 2 and used as an illustrative problem in the discussion of GPSS III in Chap. 7.[26]

On the basis of several trial runs with two different antithetic variates, Page concludes that the method may reduce by one-half the number of observations necessary to obtain a certain accuracy.

Other techniques

The preceding discussion of several variance reduction techniques by no means exhausts the methods which have been suggested. Other techniques discussed in the literature are

1. Stratified sampling
2. Systematic sampling
3. Correlated sampling
4. Regression methods
5. Use of expected values
6. Russian roulette and splitting
7. Control variates
8. Orthonormal functions

Kahn and Hammersley offer two rather complete discussions of variance reduction techniques.[27]

Usefulness of variance reduction techniques in simulation studies

Simulation has often been criticized as a "brute force" approach to problem solving, relying more on computing power than analysis to obtain answers. There is no question that careful investigation of possible ways to increase efficiency of operation of simulation models may result in substantial economies of computing time and eliminate some of the "brute force" aspects. However, it is questionable whether variance reduction techniques of the sort that have found favor in Monte Carlo studies in the physical sciences are directly applicable to most business and economics simulation models.

The principal arguments against their use are

1. With the high speed of modern digital computers, additional costs of analysis and programing may not be worth the savings in computing time and cost.
2. Variance reduction techniques designed for the types of problems found in the physical sciences may be inapplicable to models found in business and economics.

---

[26]E. S. Page, "On Monte Carlo Methods in Congestion Problems: II. Simulation of Queuing Systems," *Operations Research*, Vol. 13, No. 2 (March–April, 1965).

[27]Herman Kahn, "Use of Different Monte Carlo Sampling Techniques," in *Symposium on Monte Carlo Methods*, Herbert A. Meyer, ed. (New York: John Wiley & Sons, Inc., 1956). J. M. Hammersley and D. C. Handscomb, *Monte Carlo Methods* (New York: John Wiley & Sons, Inc., 1964), Chap. 5.

3. In contrast to physical science problems, many business and economics problems involve such detailed and complex systems that attempts to use variance reduction techniques would impose unreasonable additional burdens on the model builder.

4. Application of many of the techniques produces distortion in both the input and output from the simulation, thereby requiring further interpretation by the analyst. This negates one of the attractive features of simulation, that of easy communication regarding model structure and results between the analyst and the decision maker.

5. Simulation languages and the methods used in them to generate random numbers and to sample from probability distributions do not lend themselves to application of some of the variance reduction techniques.

In spite of these objections, variance reduction techniques and other methods for increasing efficiency are well worth keeping in mind. On occasion some of the more formal methods may be applicable, and on many other occasions, intelligent appraisal of the model structure will lead to common sense ways to improve efficiency. As Kahn has put it, ". . . the greatest gains in variance reduction are often made by exploiting specific details of the problem, rather than by routine application of general principles."[28]

Exogenous Inputs and Use of Tracking Devices

A frequent characteristic of simulation models is the inclusion of capability for introducing exogenous inputs to the model at various points in simulated time. Such inputs may occur regularly or as infrequently as only once in a run of the model. In previous chapters we have illustrated models both with and without exogenous inputs. Many models, of course, are self-contained in that once initial conditions and initial parameters for a run are established, there are no further inputs to affect the behavior of the model as simulated time elapses. But for many problems model structures are required which make it possible to inject exogenous data as the simulation proceeds.

One use of a time series input of data is illustrated by the production-inventory-distribution model used to explain SIMSCRIPT in Chap. 7. In this model, demand is an exogenous input to the model. Quantity, product, and location are read from data cards at the proper point in time and constitute exogenous input to the model at that point in time. An alternative structure in such a model would be to generate demand from probability distributions given to the model at the beginning of a run, thereby making the model self-contained during a run. However, if many demand distributions were required, or if demand characteristics were too complex to be summarized in a simple probability distribution, or if it were desired to use a specific

---

[28]Herman Kahn, "Use of Different Monte Carlo Sampling Techniques," in *Symposium on Monte Carlo Methods*, Herbert A. Meyer, ed. (New York: John Wiley & Sons, Inc., 1956), p. 146.

demand history, demand must be treated as an exogenous input rather than a quantity generated within the model. Simulation models are often constructed to accept input of exogenous time series data in this fashion, and in such cases the user must supply the data from historical records or from a generating process external to the model.

Another use of exogenous input of time series data is to keep the model "on the track." This device has been used in economic models to prevent errors from accumulating and producing grossly distorted results. When such a procedure is used, the predictive value for future time periods is questionable, since data to correct errors are not likely to be available. However, such a model may still be useful in short-range forecasting and also to examine the mechanisms underlying phenomena being simulated.

One of Cohen's models of the shoe, leather, hide, sequence that was discussed in Chap. 4 operates as a one-period-change model. In this scheme the model is used to predict the value of certain endogenous variables for just one period in the future. As simulated time advances by one period, predicted values of these endogenous variables are replaced by actual values known from historical data. The model then uses this new base of corrected information to predict for the following period. In this way cumulative errors are avoided and the model is constantly brought back into agreement with known data during the simulation run.

A similar scheme was used in a test for the period 1953–1965 of an econometric model developed at the Office of Business Economics.[29] In this case the econometric model was used to forecast (essentially simulate) the behavior of the economy for four quarters in the future. At the end of the four quarters, predicted values generated by the model were replaced by actual known values to be used as a starting point for the next four quarters.

Econometric models probably lend themselves better to using exogenous inputs to guide the model than do other types of simulation models, since time series of actual economic data are often available. Other devices, however, can be used to prevent a model from straying by chance too far from expected values. Orcutt in his socioeconomic model[30] incorporates correction factors to prevent mean values obtained in a simulation run from varying too far from expected mean values. This is accomplished by keeping track of the accumulated discrepancy between simulated and actual values. The discrepancy is then used as a multiplicative factor in the simulation model to alter the output to bring the discrepancy back to zero.[31]

Exogenous inputs may also be in the form of single inputs to the model

[29]Maurice Liebenberg, Albert A. Hirsch, and Joel Popkin, "A Quarterly Econometric Model of the United States: A Progress Report," *Survey of Current Business*, Vol. 46, No. 5 (May, 1966), pp. 20–23.

[30]See Chap. 4 for a discussion of the model.

[31]Guy H. Orcutt, Martin Greenberger, John Korbel, and Alice M. Rivlin, *Microanalysis of Socioeconomic Systems: A Simulation Study*. (New York: Harper and Row, 1961), p. 297.

rather than a time series. Such an input may be used to produce a policy, parameter, or structural change in the model at a certain point in simulated time so that the effect of the change can be observed. The econometric model discussed in Chap. 4 is a good example of the use of an exogenous input to study the direct and indirect effects of an increase in government expenditures. In this case, the increase may be viewed as a policy or parameter change. Table 4.1 shows how the model responded to the exogenous input in simulated time period 4. The same concept can be used to see how a model responds, for instance, to the addition of another station in a service facility model, or an increase in mean demand in an inventory simulation model. Figure 3.11, for example, shows the response of a distribution system to a step increase in customer demand.

Simulation of Continuous Processes

In Chap. 7, we noted that most computer languages oriented toward business and economic simulation models are based on a philosophy of modeling the occurrence of discrete events. Other languages suitable for simulating continuous systems are available, but, with the exception of DYNAMO, these are oriented toward scientific and engineering problems.[32] DYNAMO has a continuous system orientation and may be useful for modeling systems in which continuous flows are essential features of the analysis. However, DYNAMO has a structure that may not be suitable or convenient for all such problems, and DYNAMO may not always be available for the computer system at hand.

The basic DYNAMO concept for advancing the model in time as shown in Fig.7.7 results in an equal time increment model as shown in Fig. 7.1. The flow chart in Fig. 7.2 shows how a general programing language such as FORTRAN can be used to achieve the same result, and the same concept can be used to construct an approximation to a continuous system. Instead of modeling effects of the occurrence of discrete events on each pass through the loop, the program would be designed to calculate the new status of the system as a result of the rates of flow over the last simulated time increment and to compute new rates, which are assumed constant over the next time increment. By utilizing a sufficiently small time increment, continuous systems with nonlinear characteristics can be accurately modeled.

When using a linear approximation to model systems with nonlinear characteristics, it is important to recognize the influence of the choice of time increment on the results. To illustrate this point, we have rerun the econometric model written in DYNAMO, which was discussed in Chap. 4, with a time increment of 0.25 rather than 0.05, as was used originally. For brevity, we have not included complete output from the model, but Table 8.6

---

[32]See footnote 14, Chap. 7.

compares results obtained for one important endogenous variable in the model, GNP. As might be expected, the response of the model with DT = 0.25 was slower than with DT = 0.05, although by period 20 (which is not shown in Table 8.6) GNP in the run with DT = 0.25 achieved almost the same equilibrium value that was achieved in period 10 with DT = 0.05.

Table 8.6   COMPARISON OF RESULTS OBTAINED WITH DIFFERENT VALUES OF DT IN DYNAMO ECONOMETRIC MODEL

	GNP	
Time	DT = 0.05[a]	DT = 0.25
1.00	648.41	648.86
2.00	648.27	648.63
3.00	648.24	648.53
4.00	648.23	648.46
5.00	691.97	672.02
6.00	699.22	680.01
7.00	701.08	685.06
8.00	701.57	688.99
9.00	701.69	692.03
10.00	701.72	694.33

[a]See Table 4.1 for a complete tabulation of GNP and other variables for the run of the model with $DT = 0.05$.

SIMSCRIPT and several other simulation languages advance simulated time by selecting the next most imminent event from a list of previously scheduled events. After the event has been selected, the status of the system is updated and the following event is selected from the schedule. With this language structure, calculation of new rates of flow after each simulated time increment is accomplishd by a different mechanism than when a general purpose language such as FORTRAN is used. With this type of language, an initial review of the system can be scheduled to occur at the starting time plus one time increment. When the review takes place, in addition to calculating the new status of the system and new rates of flow, the review routine can be used to schedule another review at the current value of simulated time plus one time increment. This causes a second review to occur, and the process continues until termination of the simulation run. Because of the capability of a language like SIMSCRIPT for injecting into the model exogenous events, it is a simple matter to interrupt the sequence of reviews at any point in simulated time and inject policy, parameter, or structural changes.

Now let us suppose that we are simulating a system of storage tanks, connecting pipes, and processing machines with continuous flows between them with the intent of examining different scheduling rules. For purposes of illustration, we ignore the scheduling rules and look at the modeling process, initially just one storage tank in the system. If the equal time increment concept using a language like SIMSCRIPT were used, analysis of results of a simulation run might reveal that the simulated level of liquid in this tank

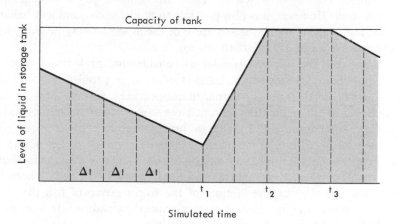

FIGURE 8.4. Hypothetical Tank Level During Simulation Run

during the run varies as shown in Fig. 8.4. The capacity of the tank is also shown in the figure.

Considering only the one storage tank, we see that an equal time increment approach to simulating this continuous sytem is not efficient, since we could have skipped some of the reveiws when rates of flow were constant. Looking at just the one tank, we see that the only conditions that will necessitate a review are

1. A change in the inflow rate.
2. A change in the outflow rate.
3. Filling of the tank to capacity.
4. Emptying of the tank.

Therefore, a more efficient method of simulating the operation of the tank is to look ahead and see which of the four conditions above is most imminent and move directly to it. In other words, referring to Fig. 8.4., we would move directly in simulated time to t_1 to t_2 to t_3, and so forth. This gives an unequal time increment model, which is efficient and also has the advantage that t_1, t_2, t_3, and other system-changing events can fall anywhere in simulated time, not just on even multiples of a time increment Δt. The practical usefulness of this approach when rates are constant between changes of state in the system depends on how difficult it is to determine the event that next changes the state of the system and whether the system remains in a steady state long enough so that a significant number of unnecessary reviews are avoided.

Our discussion of simulating continuous systems so far has dealt with approaches that rely on an assumption of constant rates of flow or rates of change over the interval between points in simulated time when the status of the system is updated and new rates established. By choosing suitably small time increments, models constructed in this way can be made closely to approximate systems in which the rates are continuously changing rather than constant. However, it is also possible to model such nonlinear behavior exactly, and, depending on the structure of the model, it may be worthwhile to expend the necessary effort to do so.

To give a specific example, let us consider the problem of modeling a fish population, which might be part of a larger problem of simulating the effects of different fishery management practices. One could keep track of each fish in the population in much the same way that Orcutt modeled a human population.[33] But, from a practical standpoint a more likely approach in this case is to model the aggregate population. Let us suppose that these are migrant fish having a two-year life cycle in which the fish hatch, go out to sea, where they mature, and finally return to rivers, where they spawn and die. During the lifetime of the fish a group of fish that hatch together—called a class—have a certain natural mortality rate and growth rate, both of which are changing through time.

In modeling such a population, one might be interested principally in the effects of fishing on a class during the later part of the life cycle. That is, months 18 to 21 might be the interesting part of the life cycle, whereas months 0 to 18 are relatively of less importance. The problem of simulating successive life cycles is one of simulating a system that is in a large part continuous and nonlinear. It could be accomplished by assuming constant rates for a small increment of time, computing new class size and weight, computing new constant rates for the next time increment, and so forth. However, when no events other than the continuous growth and mortality are taking place, it may be more efficient to move the model ahead in simulated time to the next "interesting" event and to compute mathematically the class size and weight at that point in time. This can be done if the rates of change are functions that can be integrated mathematically.

For example, when the natural mortality rate is the only influence, the rate of change of class size N with respect to time t since birth of the class might be

$$\frac{dN}{dt} = -0.21N + 0.01tN \qquad (8.48)$$

where the parameters in the equation are those appropriate for a particular type of fish and environment. Rewriting Eq. (8.48), we have

$$\frac{dN}{N} = (-0.21 + 0.01t)\, dt \qquad (8.49)$$

---

[33]Orcutt's model was discussed in Chap. 4.

Finding the integral of both sides

$$\int \frac{dN}{N} = \int (-0.21 + 0.01t)\, dt \tag{8.50}$$

we have

$$\ln N = -0.21t + \frac{0.01t^2}{2} + C \tag{8.51}$$

If we let N_0 be the initial class size at $t = 0$, it follows from Eq. (8.51) that

$$C = \ln N_0 \tag{8.52}$$

Substituting the value of C in Eq. (8.51) and solving for N, we find that the class size N_t at time t is

$$N_t = \exp\left(-0.21t + 0.01t^2/2 + \ln N_0\right) \tag{8.53}$$

Equation (8.53) can be used to find directly the class size at any time t after the birth of the class when the initial class size is known and there are no intervening events that affect class size or mortality rate.

In a typical case, the natural mortality rate might continue from the birth of a class until $t = 18$, when fishing begins. To simulate the decline in class size over the period, one could choose a Δt and approximate the exponential decline as in Fig. 8.5a, or one might use Eq. (8.53) to move directly to the value of N at $t = 18$ as in Fig. 8.5b. In other words, the simulation model can be constructed so that when only natural mortality is affecting a class of fish, the model moves ahead in simulated time to the first event affecting the class size and calculates the class size by Eq. (8.53). This, in effect, yields an unequal time increment model, which is more efficient and accurate than an equal increment linear approximation model. The usefulness of the technique in any particular instance depends on whether rates of change such as the one in Eq. (8.48) result in integrable expressions and whether the additional programing effort is more than balanced by increased accuracy or savings in computational time.

In concluding the discussion, it should be noted that care must be exercised in dealing with rates that are changing through time. Equation (8.53), for instance, is a proper expression for N_t based on the initial class size N_0. It cannot be used, however, to calculate N_t based on the size of class at another point in simulated time. In other words, if we know, for instance, the class size at $t = 10$, we cannot substitute that class size for N_0 in Eq. (8.53) to find the class size at $t = 15$. Instead, another expression similar to Eq. (8.53) must be derived which expresses class size in t in terms of class size at any other previous time.

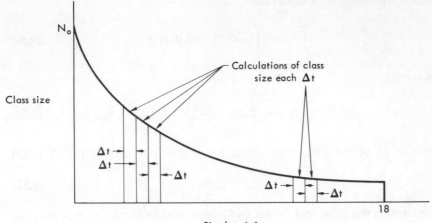

(a) Linear approximation to class size at end of period

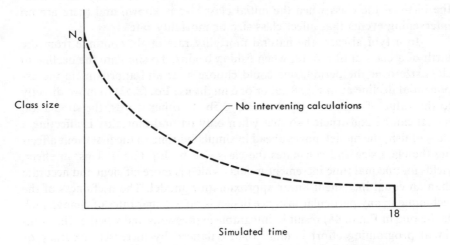

(b) Exact determination of class size at end of period

FIGURE 8.5. Alternative Approaches to Simulating Population Changes

Nonrecursive Model Structures

All of the model structures that we have discussed so far have been recursive; i.e., calculations in the model can be carried out in a sequential fashion, and there are no simultaneous equations to be solved. In most simulation problems, recursive structures are a normal result of the way in which the model builder is likely to look at a system. Since simulation represents the behavior of a system over time, the natural tendency is to think in terms of something happening in a system, which causes something else to happen, and so forth. Normally, the model builder traces a process through time, modeling the sequence of events, and simultaneous equation structures are not likely to arise.

On occasion, however, the structure of a problem or the conventional methods of analysis in an area are such that sequential modeling is not practical. One of the best examples is in the area of econometric model building. Almost all econometric models make use of simultaneous equations, and the methods that have been developed for parameter estimation are based on the assumption of simultaneous equation model structures.[34] Consequently, when present econometric models are used as a basis for simulating economic behavior, it may not be possible to avoid simultaneous equations.

To see how these may be incorporated into a simulation model, let us refer back to the model comprised of Eqs. (4.1) through (4.6). In Chap. 4, we used this model to explain the philosophy of econometric models, but we did not show how to use it as a simulator. When using this model as a simulator, we must calculate the values of the endogenous variables at time t, move simulated time ahead by one increment, recalculate the endogenous variables, and so forth. In fully recursive models, calculation of new values of the endogenous variables is accomplished by a sequential process, but this cannot be done in the model in Eqs. (41) through (4.6). At any point in time, the parameters of the model (the α's, β's, and γ's), C_{t-1} and K_{t-1}, and the exogenous variable G_t are known, but the values of the remaining endogenous variables must be found by simultaneous solution of Eqs. (4.1) through (4.6).[35]

To see clearly the structure of this econometric model, let us rewrite Eqs. (4.1) through (4.6), using matrix and vector notation in the general form $\mathbf{Ax} = \mathbf{c}$, where $\mathbf{A}$ is the matrix of coefficients of the endogenous variables, $\mathbf{x}$ is a column vector of endogenous variables, and $\mathbf{c}$ is a column vector of constants.[36] Equation (8.54) shows the model rewritten in this form.

$$
\begin{bmatrix}
1 & 0 & 0 & -\alpha_1 & 0 & 0 \\
0 & 1 & 0 & 0 & -\beta_1 & 0 \\
0 & 0 & 1 & -\gamma_1 & 0 & 0 \\
-1 & -1 & 0 & 1 & 0 & 0 \\
0 & 0 & 1 & -1 & 1 & 0 \\
0 & -1 & 0 & 0 & 0 & 1
\end{bmatrix}
\begin{bmatrix}
C_t \\
I_t \\
W_t \\
Y_t \\
P_t \\
K_t
\end{bmatrix}
=
\begin{bmatrix}
(\alpha_0 + \alpha_2 C_{t-1}) \\
(\beta_0 + \beta_2 K_{t-1}) \\
(\gamma_0 + \gamma_2 t) \\
G_t \\
0 \\
K_{t-1}
\end{bmatrix}
\tag{8.54}
$$

---

[34]See the previous discussion of econometric models in Chap. 4.

[35]Actually, only Eqs. (4.1) through (4.5) need to be solved simultaneously, since K_t can be found independently after I_t is obtained. However, with this small model the inclusion of the extra equation is immaterial in terms of computing time.

[36]An elementary discussion of the use of matrix and vector notation in describing a system of equations and the role of the inverse in the solution may be found in: Robert C. Meier and Stephen H. Archer, *An Introduction to Mathematics for Business Analysis* (New York: McGraw-Hill Book Company, Inc., 1960), Sec. 19.

From Eq. (8.54) we see that if the model is used as a simulator, the matrix of coefficients does not change during a simulation run as long as we do not input any changes exogenously to these parameters. The column vector on the right-hand side does change, depending on the value of t, the values of the endogenous variables C and K in the previous period, and the value of the exogenous variable G for the current period.

From a computational standpoint, the behavior of the model over time as a result of a certain set of starting conditions or the effects of changes in the level of G can be simulated quite easily when there are no changes to the parameters in the matrix. We invert the matrix of coefficients once at the beginning of the simulation and use the inverse to determine values of the endogenous variables each time period, using the relationship

$$\mathbf{x} = \mathbf{A}^{-1}\mathbf{c} \qquad\qquad (8.55)$$

where $\mathbf{x}$ is the column vector of endogenous variables, $\mathbf{A}^{-1}$ is the inverse of the coefficient matrix in Eq. (8.54), and $\mathbf{c}$ is the column vector shown on the right-hand side of Eq. (8.54). An abbreviated flow chart of a computer program for running the model as a simulator in this fashion is shown in Fig. 8.6.

To illustrate the use of the model as a simulator, we have assumed the following parameter values.[37]

$$\alpha_0 = 185$$

$$\alpha_1 = 0.25$$

$$\alpha_2 = 0.20$$

$$\beta_0 = 70$$

$$\beta_1 = 0.10$$

$$\beta_2 = 0.01$$

$$\gamma_0 = 250$$

$$\gamma_1 = 0.40$$

$$\gamma_2 = 1.5$$

In addition, the following initial values of consumption and capital stock at time 0 have been assumed.

$$C_0 = 460$$

---

[37]Note that these values are only for purposes of illustration and are not based on any attempts to collect real data for the model.

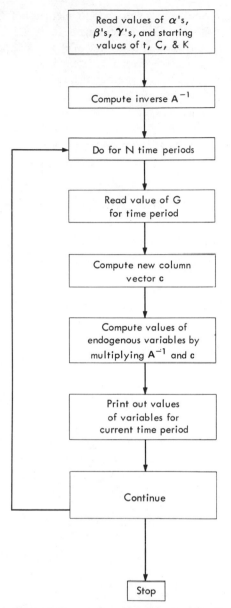

FIGURE 8.6. Flow Chart of Computations Using Econometric Model as Simulator

$$K_0 = 1000$$

The time increment between successive solutions of the model is assumed to be one quarter, which necessitates a slight change in Eq. (4.6). In this equation the coefficient of I must be changed from 1 to 0.25 to adjust for the fact that it is easiest to state the endogenous variables including I in terms of yearly rates. Therefore, the increase or decrease in K from quarter to quarter is

0.25 times the yearly rate of *I*. [The second element of the sixth row of the matrix in Eq. (8.54) must also be changed to 0.25.] Figure 8.7 shows first the inverse matrix and then the results of a run of the model for five years, using an assumed rate of government expenditures of 175 until year 2 and increasing this rate to 195 for the balance of the run.

When one is using an econometric model as a simulator in this fashion, it is a relatively simple matter to alter parameters or the value of exogenous

Inverse of matrix of coefficients [a]

1.362319	0.362319	-0.036232	0.362319	0.036232	0.000000
0.086957	1.086957	-0.108696	0.086957	0.108696	0.000000
0.579710	0.579710	0.942029	0.579710	0.057971	0.000000
1.449275	1.449275	-0.144928	1.449275	0.144928	0.000000
0.869565	0.869565	-1.086957	0.869565	1.086957	0.000000
0.021739	0.271739	-0.027174	0.021739	0.027174	1.000000

Time	C_t	I_t	W_t	Y_t	P_t	K_t	G_t
0.250	460.682	99.046	544.266	734.728	190.462	1024.762	175.000
0.500	460.944	99.286	544.842	735.230	190.388	1049.583	175.000
0.750	461.092	99.520	545.370	735.612	190.242	1074.463	175.000
1.000	461.209	99.752	545.884	735.961	190.076	1099.401	175.000
1.250	461.317	99.985	546.396	736.302	189.906	1124.397	175.000
1.500	461.424	100.217	546.906	736.641	189.735	1149.452	175.000
1.750	461.530	100.451	547.417	736.981	189.563	1174.564	175.000
2.000	461.636	100.685	547.928	737.321	189.393	1199.736	175.000
2.250	468.989	102.659	560.034	766.648	206.614	1225.400	195.000
2.500	471.072	103.025	561.389	769.097	207.708	1251.156	195.000
2.750	471.719	103.300	562.133	770.020	207.887	1276.982	195.000
3.000	471.976	103.551	562.711	770.527	207.816	1302.869	195.000
3.250	472.126	103.797	563.244	770.922	207.678	1328.819	195.000
3.500	472.247	104.040	563.765	771.287	207.522	1354.829	195.000
3.750	472.361	104.284	564.283	771.645	207.362	1380.900	195.000
4.000	472.473	104.529	564.801	772.002	207.201	1407.032	195.000
4.250	472.584	104.774	565.318	772.358	207.040	1433.226	195.000
4.500	472.696	105.020	565.836	772.716	206.880	1459.481	195.000
4.750	472.808	105.267	566.355	773.075	206.720	1485.797	195.000
5.000	472.920	105.514	566.874	773.434	206.560	1512.176	195.000

[a] The matrix at coefficients is shown in Eq. (8.54).

FIGURE 8.7. Results of Simulation Run of Econometric Model

inputs on different runs or during a run to see the effects of such changes. Or the structure of the model could be altered to observe differences that result. We could also add disturbance terms, which are often a part of econometric models, to see how the model reacts with such random elements present.[38]

From a computational standpoint, the model that we have used for an illustration is relatively easy to program, since all equations are linear and none of the elements of the matrix of coefficients of the endogenous variables change during the simulation run. If nonlinearities are present, different solution methods more complicated than matrix inversion are necessary; or if the coefficient matrix changes in a linear model, a new inverse must be found whenever the matrix changes. As mentioned in Chap. 4 in the discussion of econometric models, program SIMULATE, which was developed in connection with the Brookings-SRCC econometric model, is a general program for operating econometric models as simulators. The program has capabilities for handling large models with more complex simultaneous equation structures than we have illustrated in this section.[39]

Man-machine Model Structures

Simulation models which include man as an integral part of the simulation procedure are usually referred to as game or gaming models. Game structures as described in Chap. 6 in most cases incorporate man as a decision maker between plays of the game and have tended to deal principally with aggregate aspects of system behavior and interaction. Operational gaming, however, can be used to explore the specific procedures and decision rules used in a system. Some characteristics of man-machine models used for this purpose may be illustrated by examining an important application of the operational gaming concept.

Significant efforts to incorporate man into simulation models that deal with the details of operating systems have been made at the RAND Corporation's Logistics Systems Laboratory.[40] In this laboratory, a number of man-machine simulations have been run in which both the computer and human participants are an integral part of the simulation. Structures of this sort have rarely been used elsewhere, possibly because of the relatively high cost and slow speed with which results can be obtained. However, highly realistic models can be developed, and the man-machine technique offers opportunities

---

[38]See Chap. 4, pp. 138–139, for a discussion of disturbance terms in connection with this model.

[39]Charles C. Holt, Robert Shirey, Donald V. Stewart, Joseph L. Midler, and Arthur H. Strand, *Program SIMULATE, a User's and Programmer's Manual.* University of Wisconsin, Social Science Research Institute, May, 1964 (mimeographed).

[40]For an excellent discussion of the laboratory and work that has been done there, see: M. A. Geisler, W. W. Haythorn, and W. A. Steger, "Simulation and the Logistics System Laboratory," *Naval Research Logistics Quarterly*, Vol. 10, No. 1 (March, 1963).

for evolving procedures, working out operational decision rules, and training personnel in a way that is not possible with completely computerized
models.

As an illustration of the man-machine technique, let us consider LP-
III, one of the laboratory problems run at the RAND Corporation.[41] LP-III
was designed to examine the performance of logistics systems designed to
support the needs of a base director of weapons systems who is responsible
for keeping aircraft or missiles operational. Spare parts are carried at the base
and reordered when necessary from a weapons system storage site. The weapons system storage site obtains parts from a depot storage site, which, in
turn, receives parts from the manufacturer or repair facility. In the system,
a weapons system manager operates the weapons storage site, while an
inventory manager is in charge of the depot storage site.

The purpose of the laboratory problem was to investigate two alternative management structures: one in which material management is assigned
primarily to the weapons system manager, and the other in which material
management is delegated to the inventory manager. Elements of the system
included in the simulation were weapons system managers, inventory
managers, repair activities, factories, transportation, and connecting information systems. The simulated system to be operated by the alternative
management structures consisted of two inventory classes and two weapons
systems in 18 bases. Each simulation run lasted for eight simulated months
with 15 runs being made in total. The role of the computer in the model was
to:

1. Generate the environment (such as parts failures and transportation
   delays).
2. Simulate logistics activity (such as issues, repair, and manufacturing
   activity).
3. Provide operational and management reports to participants for each
   week of operation.
4. Record data regarding the simulation for analysis and interpretation.
5. Analyze system performance.

Essentially the computer takes care of generating requirements, accomplishes
routine data processing, and presents information once every simulated week
to be acted upon by the participants.

The simulation model assumed an organization consisting of two
weapons system managers and two inventory managers for each management
structure. Human participants in these roles act upon information presented
by the computer and received in communications from other participants.
During the simulation run, actions by the participants and comnunications
are allowed only insofar as they are consistent with the logistics system and

---

[41]For a full discussion of LP-III, see: Jack D. Little and Wayne V. Skelton, *An
Example of Man-Machine Simulation in Logistics Research*, P-2050 (Santa Monica, Calif.:
The RAND Corporation, August 2, 1960).

management structure being simulated. Management decisions made by the participants involve such things as changing repair schedules and priorities, requesting overtime for repairs, and shipping parts from base to base.

For this particular laboratory problem, participants received output from the computer representing results from a week of simulated operation and in two or three hours made decisions for operating the system for the following week. These decisions were then put in proper form for input to the computer, which prepared results of the next week's operations. In addition to this weekly decision cycle, the participants performed certain other long-range planning activities. While the time scale in this laboratory problem was considerably compressed over the time scale of actual operations, running time using the man-machine approach was considerably longer than that of an equivalent completely computerized model.

Man-machine structures of the type that has just been described have significant advantages over all-computer simulation models in their ability to model the real world, including the influence of human factors, with a minimum of distortion. Additional benefits in terms of personnel training and development of procedural details are also gained by the man-machine approach. These benefits are partially offset by additional costs and time incurred by the man-machine structure. However, in cases where potential savings are great and where it is difficult to develop adequate all-computer models, a man-machine structure may be worth the extra effort.

Summary

Concepts discussed in this chapter are most likely to be useful in the earlier stages of construction of a simulation model. They do not provide any detailed guide as to how to construct a simulation model, but instead constitute a body of ideas which may be profitably drawn upon by the model builder. The final form of a simulation model and philosophy used in its construction are highly dependent upon the nature of the problem, results desired, and programing systems and computing machinery which may be available. Consequently, there can be no closely defined procedure to follow in developing a model. The construction of efficient simulation models is largely a function of the breadth of knowledge of relevant techniques and ingenuity of the model builder.

EXERCISES

8.1 Select one of the columns of five-digit numbers in the random number table in Appendix A.1. Use a simple χ^2 test to compare actual frequencies of digits in the column with theoretical frequencies that would be expected if the digits appeared at random. (Note that blanks in the table are zeroes.)

8.2   Generate a sequence of 50 four-digit random numbers, using the mid-square method. Use a simple χ^2 test to compare actual frequencies of digits with frequencies that would be expected if the digits appeared at random.

8.3   Generate a sequence of 50 four-digit random numbers, using the congruential method in Eq. (8.2). Use a simple χ^2 test to compare actual frequencies of digits with frequencies that would be expected if the digits appeared at random.

8.4   Generate a sequence of 50 random variates uniformly distributed over the interval 25 to 30 by the inverse function method.

8.5   Use a table of the cumulative unit normal distribution to generate a sequence of 50 normally distributed random variates.

8.6   Generate 50 exponentially distributed random variates by the inverse function method.
    a. Use Eq. (8.20) with $\lambda = 10$.
    b. Use Eq. (8.21) with $\lambda = 10$.
    c. In parts a. and b. above, plot the cumulative distributions and compare them with Fig. 2.6. (Figure 2.6 is the theoretical cumulative distribution for an exponentially distributed variable with $\lambda = 10$.)

8.7   Generate a sequence of 50 random normal variates with zero mean and unit variance by the rejection method.

8.8   Find the value of $\int_0^2 y^3 \, dy$.
    a. By evaluating the integral mathematically.
    b. By the rejection method with $n = 50$.
    c. By crude Monte Carlo with $n = 50$.
    d. Determine 95 per cent confidence limits for the estimates obtained in parts b. and c. above and compare the results in a., b., and c.

8.9   Estimate the total area under the unit normal curve by
    a. Rejection method.
    b. Crude Monte Carlo.

8.10   Add disturbance terms μ_{1t}, μ_{2t}, and μ_{3t} to the first three elements of the vector on the right-hand side of Eq. (8.54). The disturbance terms are normally distributed with zero mean and the following standard deviations: $\sigma_1 = 15$, $\sigma_2 = 5$, $\sigma_3 = 10$. Using the same parameter values and initial values as shown on pp. 284–85, run the model for 5 years and compare your results with those obtained without the disturbance terms as shown in Fig. 8.7.

8.11   Suits gives the following econometric model as an illustration (*American Economic Review*, March, 1962, p. 106).

$$C_t = 20 + 0.7(Y_t - T_t)$$

$$I_t = 2 + 0.1 Y_{t-1}$$

$$T_t = 0.2\,Y_t$$

$$Y_t = C_t + I_t + C_t$$

where

$$C = \text{consumption}$$

$$I = \text{investment}$$

$$T = \text{taxes}$$

$$G = \text{government spending}$$

$$Y = \text{income}$$

Use this model to simulate the operation of the economy for 25 periods, starting with initial values of $Y = 150$ and $G = 30$, and with G increasing to 40 in period 10.

8.12 Devise a method to increase the efficiency of sampling to locate the 95 per cent point on the distribution of demand during lead time in Exercise 1.4. (Hint: Note that the random selection of lead times and demands that are "too small" produces results that are relevant only to the lower tail of the demand during lead time distribution, whereas the upper tail is the portion of interest.)

8.13 In Table 8.5, take the first 25 samples from the table and combine them with 25 samples obtained by using the antithetic concept. Compute the estimated area from the combined sample of 50. Compare the estimate obtained using the antithetic concepts with results obtained without using the antithetic concept as shown in Table 8.5.

8.14 Use the same sequence of random numbers to generate 25 exponentially distributed random variates from Eq. (8.20) and 25 from Eq. (8.21) with $\lambda = 10$. Combine these into a single sample of 50 and compare the mean of this sample with the means of the samples in Exercises 8.6a and 8.6b. Explain your results. (Note that the theoretical mean is 0.1.)

BIBLIOGRAPHY

Brenner, Michael E., "Selective Sampling—A Technique for Reducing Sample Size in Simulation of Decision-Making Problems," *Journal of Industrial Engineering*, Vol. 13, No. 6 (November–December, 1963).

Brown, Robert G., *Statistical Forecasting for Inventory Control*. New York: McGraw-Hill Book Company, Inc., 1959, Appendix A.

Butler, James W., "Machine Sampling from Given Probability Distributions," in *Symposium on Monte Carlo Methods*. Herbert A. Meyer, ed. New York: John Wiley & Sons, Inc., 1956.

Clark, Charles E., "The Utility of Statistics of Random Numbers," *Operations Research*, Vol. 8, No. 2 (March–April, 1960).

————, "Importance Sampling in Monte Carlo Analyses," *Operations Research*, Vol. 9, No. 5 (September–October, 1961).

————, *Random Numbers in Uniform and Normal Distribution with Indices for Subsets*. Chicago: Science Research Associates, Inc., and Chandler Publishing Company, 1966.

Conway, R. W., B. M. Johnson, and W. L. Maxwell, "Some Problems of Digital Systems Simulation," *Management Science*, Vol. 6, No. 1 (October, 1959).

Ehrenfeld, S., and S. Ben-Tuvia, "The Efficiency of Statistical Simulation Procedures," *Technometrics*, May, 1962.

Forsythe, George E., "Generation and Testing of Random Digits at the National Bureau of Standards, Los Angeles," in *Monte Carlo Method*. U. S. Department of Commerce, National Bureau of Standards, Applied Mathematics Series, No. 12, June 11, 1951.

Galliher, Herbert P., "Monte Carlo Simulation Studies," in *Report of the System Simulation Symposium*. Sponsored by the American Institute of Industrial Engineers, The Institute of Management Sciences, and Operations Research Society of America, New York, May, 1957.

Geisler, Murray A., *Development of Man-Machine Simulation Techniques*, P-1945. Santa Monica, California: The RAND Corporation, March 17, 1960.

Geisler, Murray A., W. W. Haythorn, and W. A. Steger, "Simulation and the Logistics System Laboratory," *Naval Research Logistics Quarterly*, Vol. 10, No. 1 (March, 1963).

Hammer, Preston C., "The Mid-Square Method of Generating Random Digits," in *Monte Carlo Method*. U. S. Department of Commerce, National Bureau of Standards, Applied Mathematics Series, No. 12, June 11, 1951.

Hammersley, J. M., and D. C. Handscomb, *Monte Carlo Methods*. New York: John Wiley & Sons, Inc., 1964, Chaps. 3 and 5.

Harling, John, "Simulation Techniques in Operations Research—A Review," *Operations Research*, Vol. 6, No. 3 (May–June, 1958).

Holt, Charles C., "Validation and Application of Macroeconomic Models Using Computer Simulation," in *The Brookings Quarterly Econometric Model of the United States*. James S. Duesenberry, Gary Fromm, Lawrence R. Klein, and Edwin Kuh, eds. Chicago: Rand McNally and Company, 1965.

Holt, Charles C., Robert Shirey, Donald V. Stewart, Joseph V. Midler, and Arthur H. Strand, *Program SIMULATE, A User's and Programmer's Manual*. Madison, Wisconsin: University of Wisconsin, Social Science Research Institute, May, 1964 (mimeographed).

Hull, T. E. and A. R. Dobell, "Random Number Generators," *SIAM Review*, Vol. 4, No. 3 (July, 1962).

International Business Machines Corporation, *Random Number Generation and Testing*. Form C20–8011, New York, 1959.

Itzelberger, G., "Some Experiences with the Poker Test for Investigating Pseudo-Random Numbers," in *Digital Simulation in Operational Research*, S. H. Hollingdale, ed. New York: American Elsevier Publishing Company, Inc., 1967.

Kahn, Herman, "Use of Different Monte Carlo Sampling Techniques," in *Symposium on Monte Carlo Methods*. Herbert A. Meyer, ed. New York: John Wiley & Sons, Inc., 1956.

Kahn H. and A. W. Marshall, "Methods of Reducing Sample Size in Monte Carlo Computations," *Operations Research*, Vol. 1, No. 5 (November, 1953).

Kendall, M. G. and B. Babington-Smith, "Tables of Random Sampling Numbers," *Tracts for Computers*, No. XXIV. Cambridge, England: Cambridge University Press, 1939.

Lehmer, D. H., "Mathematical Methods in Large-Scale Computing Units," in *Proceedings of the Second Symposium on Large-Scale Digital Calculating Machinery*. The Annals of the Computation Laboratory of Harvard University, Vol. XXVI. Cambridge, Massachusetts: Harvard University Press, 1951.

Little, Jack D. and Wayne V. Skelton, *An Example of Man-Machine Simulation in Logistics Research*, P-2050. Santa Monica, California: The RAND Corporation, August 2, 1960.

Labiner, Kenneth H., *Experience in the Use of a Simulation Laboratory in the Design of a Management Information System*, P-2115. Santa Monica, California: The RAND Corporation, October 3, 1960.

Metropolis, N., "Phase Shifts-Middle Square-Wave Equation," in *Symposium on Monte Carlo Methods*, Herbert A. Meyer, ed. New York: John Wiley & Sons, Inc., 1956.

Naylor, Thomas H., Joseph L. Balintfy, Donald S. Burdick, and Kong Chu, *Computer Simulation Techniques*. New York: John Wiley & Sons, Inc., 1966, Chaps. 3 and 4.

Orcutt, Guy H., "Simulation of Economic Systems" (Section III), *The American Economic Review*, Vol. 50, No. 5 (December, 1960).

Orcutt, Guy H., Martin Greenberger, John Korbel, and Alice M. Rivlin, *Micro-Analysis of Socioeconomic Systems: A Simulation Study*. New York: Harper & Row, Inc., 1961, Chap. 16, Appendix: Random Number Generation.

Page, E. S., "On Monte Carlo Methods in Congestion Problems: II. Simulation of Queuing Systems," *Operations Research*, Vol. 13, No. 2 (March–April, 1965).

————, "The Generation of Pseudo-Random Numbers," in *Digital Simulation in Operational Research*, S. H. Hollingdale, ed. New York: American Elsevier Publishing Company, Inc., 1967.

RAND Corporation, *A Million Random Digits with 100,000 Normal Variates*. Glencoe, Illinois: The Free Press, 1955.

Tocher, K. D., *The Art of Simulation*. London: The English Universities Press, Ltd., 1963, Chaps. 2–6 and 9.

Teichroew, Daniel, "A History of Distribution Sampling Prior to the Era of the Computer and Its Relevance to Simulation," *American Statistical Association Journal*, Vol. 60, No. 309 (March, 1965).

Tippett, L. H. C., "Random Sampling Numbers," *Tracts for Computers*, No. XV. Cambridge, England: Cambridge University Press, 1927.

Taussky, Olga and John Todd, "Generation of Pseudo Random Numbers," in *Symposium on Monte Carlo Methods*, Herbert A. Meyer, ed. New York: John Wiley & Sons, Inc., 1956.

von Neumann, John, "Various Techniques Used in Connection with Random Digits," in *Monte Carlo Method*. U. S. Department of Commerce, National Bureau of Standards, Applied Mathematics Series, No. 12, June 11, 1951.

Wold, H., "Random Normal Deviates," *Tracts for Computers*, No. XXV. Cambridge, England: Cambridge University Press, 1948.

Operation of a
Simulation Model

9 In the previous chapter we discussed concepts relevant to the design and construction of simulation models. We will now discuss concepts which are most likely to be useful in the operating phases of a study after the model has been constructed. It is not good practice, of course, to construct a model without considering how it is to be employed; consequently, the ideas discussed in this chapter must be considered at the time the model is under development, although they may not be utilized until the actual simulation runs are made. The operation of a model can be made a good deal less cumbersome by planning in the early stages of model construction for the type of runs that will be made and the form of data to be extracted from the model.

Validation of Model

Exercising care in the early stages of formulation and construction of a simulation model is as important as any more specific procedures that can be suggested for validating a model. However, once the model is completed, validating it may be viewed as a two-step process. The first step is to determine whether the model is internally correct in a logical and programing sense. And the second is to determine whether it represents the phenomena it is supposed to represent.

The first step can be accomplished by a systematic series of runs designed to uncover defects in the model. The sort of test runs that can be made are dependent on specific characteristics of the model, but the following are some possibilities.

1. Run the model for a short time period or a small number of transactions so that results can be compared with hand calculations.
2. Run separate segments of complicated models alone so that results can be verified.

3. Eliminate random elements from stochastic models and run them as deterministic models.

4. Replace complex probability distributions with elementary ones so that results are more easily verified.

5. Construct simple test situations that test as many combinations of circumstances in the model as is feasible.

Many models are so complex that programing and logical errors cannot be detected by examination of output from a full-scale run of the model. In these cases it is essential that test runs along the lines of those suggested above be made to verify the correctness of the program.

Verification that a simulation model represents the real-world phenomena it is supposed to represent is the second step in the validation process. Where the model is designed to be descriptive of an existing system, output from the model can be compared with known data from the real world. Cohen and Cyert have suggested the following tests, where output from a model is in the form of time series data.[1]

1. Distribution-free statistical tests to see whether actual time series and generated time series have the same timing and amplitude.

2. Regression of generated time series on actual time series to see whether the regression equation has slope and intercept not significantly different from 1 and 0.

3. Factor analysis on two time series to see whether factor loadings are significantly different.

In cases where the results from a model are in the form of mean values, proportions, or probability distributions, these results can be compared with known values from the real world by standard statistical techniques. For instance, a test might be made of the significance of the difference between a mean value, such as the average number of transactions moving past some point in a system, obtained from the simulation model and the known mean value from the real world.[2] Or the χ^2 statistic might be used to compare a probability distribution generated by the simulation model with the known distribution from the system being simulated.[3] Unfortunately, because of the number of possibilities, it is not feasible to test all statistics that might be obtained from validation runs of the simulation model against comparable statistics from the real world. Accordingly, the model builder must usually select certain key statistics and distributions to test and rely on these to form some judgment as to the over-all validity of the model.

When a model is intended to simulate a new or proposed system for which no actual data are available, there is no good way to verify that the

---

[1]Kalman J. Cohen and Richard M. Cyert, "Computer Models in Dynamic Economics," *The Quarterly Journal of Economics*, Vol. 75, No. 1 (February, 1961), pp. 120–121.

[2]An illustration of such a test of significance of the difference between means is given later in this chapter in the section dealing with experimentation.

[3]Table 8.2 illustrates the use of the χ^2 statistic to compare two probability distributions.

model, in fact, represents the system. Under these circumstances, there is little alternative but to test the model thoroughly for logical or programing errors and to be alert for any discrepancies or unusual characteristics in the results obtained from the model.

Initial Conditions and Elimination of Transients

A simulation run represents the operation of a system from a given starting point for a period of time. Starting conditions, therefore, are relevant to results obtained from the model. To a certain extent, the problem of initial conditions can be viewed as a problem of sample size in that a long enough run, which is equivalent in simulation studies to taking a large sample, can usually obliterate the effects of starting conditions. However, initial conditions can also be dealt with independently of the question of sample size, and we will defer a complete discussion of that subject to a later section of this chapter.

On occasion a model may not present any problems in establishing initial conditions. For example, the simulation of a process that begins operation empty or virtually empty, such as a toll collection facility before the onset of a rush period, would not present any serious initializing problems. Starting such a model without any customers or queues would be highly realistic, and one might also expect that any slight distortions caused by this procedure would wash out quickly after relatively few arrivals. If the same toll collecting process were to be simulated and the analyst were interested in generating statistics associated with arrival and service rates representative of highly congested conditions at the peak of the rush hour, it could be quite misleading to start gathering statistics with empty queues. Under congested conditions, queues might be very long so that initial conditions closer to this state would be desirable.

One way to obtain the congested state is to start the model empty, let the contents of the system build up to the anticipated congested state, and then begin tabulating behavior of the system. Some experimentation may, of course, be necessary to determine how long to let the model run before beginning to gather statistics. The GPSS simulation language, for example, incorporates a control card specifically intended to permit this method of initialization. The RESET card allows a model to be run for any specified number of transactions after which all statistics are reset to zero without altering the contents of the system. The same scheme can be programed into models in other languages.

Another approach that achieves the same objective is to load the model initially with a representative sample of the traffic flowing through the system so that there is little or no startup effect. The difficulty with this method is that it may not be easy to determine *a priori* what the loaded model should look like. To illustrate how this type of loading can be accomplished, however, let us consider the simulation of the calibration system discussed in Chap. 2.[4] Figure 2.8 shows the circular nature of the system. In modeling a circular process such as this, initial loading of the model may be particularly important, since any transient conditions resulting from startup of the model could travel around the system more than once.

To avoid any such problems, the model was loaded with transactions (representing the known number of instruments in the system) so that they were distributed through the system in approximately the same way that they would be under normal operating conditions. For each type of instrument, an estimate was made from empirical data of the relative time spent in use, on the shelf, or in the calibration laboratory. For example, instruments of a certain type might on the average spend 15 days on the shelf, 75 days in use, and 10 days in the calibration laboratory. Transactions representing this instrument type were loaded at random into one of the three areas by drawing a random number and using it to make the assignment. A random number from 0.00 to 0.14 would assign the transaction to the shelf, 0.15 to 0.89 to use, and 0.90 to 0.99 to the calibration laboratory.

Once assigned to an area, each transaction also required an assignment of time left in the process. Where process times were constant, time left was determined by drawing a random number and multiplying the process time by this number. Where process times were themselves random variables, the total process time for the transaction was first selected at random from the probability distribution of processing times, then the *remaining* process time was found by multiplying by a random number. When these methods were used initially to distribute transactions through the processes in the system and to determine time left in the processes, it was found that little transient behavior occurred at startup of the model. The techniques used in loading this circular model would be applicable, perhaps with some modification, to any model that represents the progress of transactions or entities through a system.

Somewhat different problems are encountered in initializing simulation models that deal with aggregate behavior. The econometric models discussed in Chaps. 4 and 8 and industrial dynamics models discussed in Chap. 3 are examples of this type of model. In these models, initial values of the variables in the model determine whether any unusual transient behavior occurs at the beginning of a simulation run. Table 4.1 and Fig. 8.7 show the results of demonstration runs of two econometric models. Prior to these demonstration runs, test runs of both models were conducted to determine the effects of various initial values on the behavior of the models. Since the demonstration runs were designed to show how econometric models could simulate the effects of an exogenous increase in government expenditures,

---

[4]The reader may wish to reread pp. 48–51.

it was desired to have starting conditions close to equilibrium. Otherwise, initial movement of the models toward equilibrium might have been confused with response of the models to the exogenous increase.

In the case of the econometric model programed in DYNAMO,[5] test runs revealed that with initial values of 435 for consumption, 2050 for business activity, 250 for accumulated debt, and 175 for government expenditures, the model stabilized by period 3.5; the exogenous increase in government expenditures consequently was made to take place at period 4 after all transient behavior caused by starting conditions had subsided. Changes taking place in the model after period 4 as shown in Table 4.1 are exclusively the result of the exogenous increase.

The model defined by Eq. (8.54) presents somewhat different initializing problems when it is operated as a simulator. Although it is a deterministic model, it does not necessarily reach equilibrium in the sense that the endogenous variables reach certain constant values and stay at those values for as long as there are no exogenous inputs. Instead, with the structure shown in Eq. (8.54) and with parameter values and initial values used for the simulation run shown in Fig. 8.7, all of the endogenous variables (with the exception of P_t, which is essentially a residual) show continual upward movement. Under these circumstances, equilibrium conditions may be viewed as consisting of a stable growth pattern, and initial conditions are selected which lead rapidly to the long-run growth rate without undue fluctuation at the beginning of the run. For the demonstration run shown in Fig. 8.7, initial values were selected so that changes in the values of the endogenous variables after the exogenous increase in government expenditures in period 2.25 can be attributed almost entirely to the natural growth pattern and influence of the exogenous increase rather than to any transient behavior caused by starting conditions.

As a final comment on initialization problems, it should be noted that the question of starting conditions for simulation runs designed to compare alternate methods of operation or to ascertain the effects of parameter changes is not easily resolved. Conway suggests that the analyst has three choices and evaluates them as follows:

1. Test each system starting "empty and idle."
2. Test each system using a common set of starting conditions that is essentially a compromise between the two different sets of reasonable starting conditions.
3. Test each system with its own "reasonable" starting conditions.

The second strategy is clearly more efficient than the first; the choice between the second and third is less obvious. While presumably less time would be lost in achieving near-equilibrium conditions by using the third strategy, one must also consider the possibility that

---

[5]For a complete discussion of the model, see pp. 121–25.

the use of different starting conditions is biasing the results. In general, one should compare alternatives under as close to identical conditions as possible. In deference to this canon I would avoid using the third strategy.

I would be reluctant to report an investigation in the following manner:

1. I wished to compare two systems; A and B.
2. I anticipated that System A would yield a greater mean value of attribute M than would System B.
3. I performed an experiment in which the initial value of attribute M for System A was set greater than that for System B.
4. The experimental results demonstrate that the mean value of attribute M for System A is significantly greater than that for System B.

Constructing a "good compromise" set of starting conditions to materially shorten the necessary stabilization period is not a trivial task, even when possessing considerable knowledge of the nature of the equilibrium conditions for each alternative. But at least there is the consolation that it is almost impossible to do worse than "empty and idle" conditions so that any effort will allow some reduction in computing time.[6]

Although Conway's argument for the existence of bias when one is using the third method has some validity, the experience of the authors suggests that the case against the use of the third method may be overstated.

Sampling From Simulation Models

After a model is constructed, simulation runs provide observations of the phenomena represented by the model. From the observations, estimates can then be made of the operating characteristics of the model. These estimates in many cases are subject to error in that it is impossible to make a sufficient length or number of simulation runs to guarantee complete accuracy. We have, then, two ways in which results from a simulation model can be in error in describing the real world: the model itself may not be a completely accurate description of the real world, and estimates made from observation of the model may not be completely accurate in describing the model. In this section we concern ourselves only with making estimates based on observation of the model and establishing the degree of confidence in them.

Making estimates based on data from a simulation model may be viewed essentially as a sampling problem. But the sampling problem is not the same for all simulation models. The structure of a model and the information desired influence the types of samples that can be obtained and statistical difficulties encountered in interpreting them. Since it is impossible

---

[6]R. W. Conway, "Some Tactical Problems in Digital Simulation," *Management Science*, Vol. 10, No. 1 (October, 1963), p. 51.

to discuss all possible model structures, we will discuss several basic concepts regarding sampling in simulation studies which may serve as a starting point for establishing a sampling procedure appropriate to a particular model.

Length of Δt in equal time increment models

In a sense, a decrease in the length of Δt in models with an equal time increment structure can be viewed as an increase in sample size, since more observations are possible of the model's behavior in a given length of simulated time.[7] However, we would prefer to view changes in Δt as affecting the validity of the model rather than being a matter of sample size. In most cases, changes in the time increment affect how well the model represents the real world,[8] and this, in turn, determines the accuracy of the information which a model *can* yield. The selection of Δt, then, is largely a matter related to designing and validating the structure of a model rather than one related to extracting information from it, once the model has been developed. In the remainder of the discussion of sampling, we will assume that Δt in equal time increment models has been established and is not an issue in taking samples from these models.

Methods of sampling

Because of the time dimension in simulation models and the varying structures of simulation models, the concept of taking a sample can be given a number of different interpretations. The following are several possibilities:

1. If the length of run (in terms of simulated time) is fixed, then taking a sample of size n may be viewed as consisting of n separate runs of the model.

2. If only a single run is considered, the sample size can be interpreted as the length of run. That is, a run of a model for 2000 simulated time periods is twice as large a sample as a run for 1000 time periods.

3. Closely related to (2) is the concept of determining sample size by the amount of traffic that has flowed through the system. That is, a model is allowed to run until a certain number of transactions have flowed through the system; a sample of twice that size allows double the number of transactions to flow through the system.

4. Still another possibility is to take observations intermittently during a run and to determine sample size by how many times the sampling procedure is repeated during a run.[9]

---

[7]See Chap. 7, pp. 215–16, for a complete discussion of equal time increment models.

[8]Table 8.6 illustrates the effect of different choices of Δt on the behavior of a model.

[9]Conway suggests, and we agree, that this is not an efficient way to sample. See: R. W. Conway, "Some Tactical Problems in Digital Simulation," *Management Science*, Vol. 10, No. 1 (October, 1963), pp. 54–55.

The question of appropriate sample size and accuracy of results in a simulation study, then, is related to the method of sampling, type of model, and what is being sampled. We will consider next several types of models and the sampling procedures appropriate to them.

Deterministic models

Because of the absence of random elements, deterministic models would appear, at first glance, to offer few, if any, sampling problems. For deterministic models of processes of finite duration, this is likely to be true. With this type of model, one can simulate and record the behavior of the process for its entire duration, thereby yielding complete information on a single run which is not subject to sampling error.

Deterministic models of processes of infinite duration (or those of finite length that are too lengthy to be simulated to termination) present sampling problems in the sense of determining an adequate length of run. If the initialization problems that were discussed previously are ignored, the run must be sufficiently long so that a reasonable sample is obtained of all important phenomena that may occur in the model.

To illustrate this point, let us examine again the output from the inventory simulation model discussed in Chap. 1. It was noted in Chap. 1 that the 50-period simulation run shown in Fig. 1.4 yielded results somewhat different from theoretical results obtained by Eq. (1.6). The principal reason for the discrepancy is the excessive (from a long-run average standpoint) number of orders placed in the 50-period run. In terms of total cost, only $250 \times \frac{10}{316} \times 5 = 1.58$ orders should be allocated to 50 periods of operation. Actually, two orders occurred during the simulation run and contributed to total cost for the run.

The only way to get an accurate result is to run such a model sufficiently long so that there is an adequate sample of significant events which occur relatively infrequently. In the inventory model, the run must include enough replenishment orders to give an accurate picture of average total cost. Table 9.1 shows summarized results in terms of total cost for simulation runs of different lengths. From Table 9.1 it may be seen that runs longer than 250 periods yield essentially similar results so that for this particular deterministic inventory model and set of parameters a run of 250 periods is adequate. It is interesting to note that the total cost per year obtained from the simulation model does not appear to be converging on the theoretical value as length of run increases. The principal reason, aside from the effect of initial conditions, is a slight discrepancy, which almost always exists in simulation models, between the operation of the system assumed by the theoretical calculations and the actual operation of the simulation model. In this case, the theoretical calculations assume zero inventory at the time a replenishment order is received, whereas in the simulation runs this is not strictly the case.

Table 9.1   RESULTS OF SIMULATION RUNS OF DETERMINISTIC MODEL
FOR DIFFERENT NUMBERS OF PERIODS

| Number of simulated time periods | Simulation results | | Theoretical cost/year[b] |
	Total cost	Cost/year[a]	
50	$ 72[c]	$ 361	$ 316
100	122	304	316
150	196	327	316
200	264	330	316
250	320	320	316
500	639	320	316
750	958	319	316
1000	1277	319	316

[a]Computed by adjusting results to 250-period year.
[b]See Eq. (1.6). Fixed costs of $12,500/year not included.
[c]See Fig. 1.4 for complete tabulation of results of 50-period run.

Stochastic models

Sampling problems are more complex when one is dealing with stochastic simulation models than when one is dealing with deterministic models. The underlying random processes produce random variations in

1. The state of the system through time.
2. Statistics associated with transactions (if there are any) flowing through the system.
3. Aggregate measures of system operation.

The analyst may be interested in information relating to all three of these aspects of behavior of the simulated process. From a strategic standpoint, it is desirable to plan a simulation run or runs to ensure the reliability of aggregate statistics of operation after which reliability of statistics relating to the state of the system through time or relating to individual units of traffic can be ascertained. Our discussion will follow this order of presentation.

In working with stochastic models of finite duration, a run of a model until termination may be treated as one observation with regard to aggregate statistics of operation of the system; that is, a run would yield one observation for such quantities as total system throughput, maximum contents of system, maximum time taken for a unit of traffic to flow through the system, etc. Because of random elements, aggregate results will vary from run to run when different random number sequences are used. A sample of size n is obtained by making n runs of a model starting from the same initial conditions but using a different random number sequence in each. From this sample, estimates can be made of aggregate system parameters such as those mentioned above, and confidence limits may be established for these estimates.

For example, an estimate of a quantity such as the total amount of traffic that a system can handle might be made by making n runs of the model to obtain n observations of total traffic handled; let us designate them $y_1, y_2, \ldots, y_n$. Then the mean system capability μ would be estimated by $\bar{y}$, where

$$\bar{y} = \sum_{i=1}^{n} \frac{y_i}{n} \tag{9.1}$$

We find $\sigma_{\bar{y}}$ by

$$\sigma_{\bar{y}} = \sqrt{\frac{s_y^2}{n-1}} \tag{9.2}$$

where s_y^2 is the sample variance. In the case of large samples, a 95 per cent confidence interval, for instance, would be $\bar{y} \pm 1.96\ \sigma_{\bar{y}}$. For small sample sizes, say under 30, where it can be assumed that we are sampling from a normal population, the t distribution would be used instead of the confidence interval above.

When we are dealing with a characteristic such as system reliability where the system would either fail or not fail on the simulation run, results are in the form of percentages or fractions rather than mean values. Reliability r, for instance, might be estimated by p where

$$p = \frac{n_0}{n} \tag{9.3}$$

and n_0 is the number of simulation runs without failure. By computing

$$\sigma_p = \sqrt{\frac{p(1-p)}{n}} \tag{9.4}$$

the 95 per cent confidence interval, for example, would be established as $p \pm 1.96\sigma_p$. Again, the method of calculation assumes a large sample and must be modified for small samples. Estimates can also be made of the number of runs n necessary to achieve any desired accuracy for either mean values or percentages.[10]

Model sampling studies present approximately the same sampling situation as do simulation models of finite duration in that one run of the model results in one observation and n runs give rise to a sample of size n. An illustration of the effect of sample size on results obtained in a model sampling study has already been given in Table 2.5.

Obtaining aggregate measures of system operation from stochastic

---

[10]A more complete discussion of estimation, confidence intervals, and determination of sample size is found in: Richard C. Clelland, John S. deCani, Francis E. Brown, J. Parker Bursk, and Donald S. Murray, *Basic Statistics With Business Applications* (New York: John Wiley & Sons, Inc., 1966), Secs. 9.4–9.8.

simulation models of infinite duration can be approached in two ways. The model can be run for a period of time, stopped, and rerun with a different random number sequence but starting from the same initial conditions. A series of *n* runs of this sort yields a sample of size *n* which can be viewed statistically in the same way as a sample of *n* runs from a finite model. Alternatively, the model can be run continuously for a sufficient length of time to obtain an adequate sample. In this case sample size is governed by length of run rather than the number of runs.

The starting and stopping approach yields *n* independent observations that are straightforward to interpret statistically. But a penalty is paid in restarting the model *n* times, and it is necessary to estimate the length of run necessary to allow starting transients to disappear and a reasonable sample of system behavior to occur. In the continuous run approach, periodic observations must be made, since a single observation at the end of a run would not provide any information on variability from which to establish confidence limits. Sample size in the continuous run approach, then, is determined by the length of run and interval between the intermediate observations taken during the run. These intermediate observations must be spaced sufficiently so that they are independent in a statistical sense, or, if they are not, some changes must be made in the statistical treatment to take into account the correlation between observations.

In effect, determining the variability of an aggregate measure of system performance when one is using the continuous run sampling procedure presents many of the same problems as obtaining statistics related to the state of the system at successive points in time or statistics related to the transactions flowing through the system. If *n* observations of the state of the system or of units of traffic are made on a run (or runs, in the case of finite models) these may be treated as a sample of size *n* and estimates may be made of mean values or proportions together with confidence limits on these estimates. However, observations from simulation models at adjacent or nearly adjacent points in time are often correlated, so care must be exercised in computing confidence intervals. Conway gives a good illustration of the problem in connection with the collection and analysis of statistics relating to temporary entities in a system.[11]

> With attributes of temporary entities there is no question of the method of measurement—each entity contributes a single value. In fact, the problem is deceptively simple. The sample size is obviously the number of entities, and the variance of the individual values may be readily calculated as a basic measure of variability. Again the difficulty lies in the autocorrelation of the observations and arises when one would use the sample variance to estimate the variance of the sample mean. To equate the variance of the mean with the sample variance divided by the number of observations contributing to the

---

[11]Temporary entities in the sense that Conway uses the term are discussed in connection with the description of SIMSCRIPT, Chap. 7.

mean, requires that the observations be mutually independent and that is rarely the case. Temporary entities existing at the same time are subject to the same system conditions so that the values of the attributes tend to be positively and strongly correlated. The neglect of this correlation results in a substantial understatement of the variance of the mean.

For example, in a recent simulation investigation of a simplified manufacturing job shop the time in the shop was measured for each of 9600 jobs. Omitting the data for the first 300 jobs, as recommended earlier, a sample of 9300 may be used. The mean time in the shop for this sample is 73.505 and the sample variance is 5602.136. By assuming that these are independent observations, one could estimate that the variance of a mean of 9300 observations would be only 0.6024, and one might report a mean of 73.505 with a standard deviation of 0.776.

Assuming independence, the investigator would similarly estimate that the variance of the mean of 100 observations would be 56.02136. Now he can readily obtain 93 such means from these same data and estimate the variance of means of 100 observations from this sample of 93. That estimate turns out to be 469.98, more than 8 times the estimate based on the individual job variance. (1 per cent of the area of an F-distribution with 92 df [degrees of freedom] in the numerator and 9299 df in the denominator lies above 1.6.) The width of a confidence interval for a mean for 100 jobs, based on the variance of the individual job values, would be understated by a factor of almost three. . . . The procedure that I have found most satisfactory for measuring attributes of temporary entities is to number the entities in their order of creation and to divide the sequence into blocks of equal numbers with consecutively numbered entities. For purposes of estimating the precision of results the block means should be considered as the basic observations.[12]

Automatic termination procedures

From a procedural standpoint, our discussion of sampling has been based on an implicit assumption that the analyst determines the number of runs and/or length of run prior to making the computer runs. At the conclusion of the run or runs, results must be analyzed and the model restarted or additional runs made if desired accuracy has not been attained. A natural addition to a computer simulation program would be the incorporation in the program of rules for terminating the run when sufficiently accurate or stable results have been achieved. Tocher discusses "stopping rules,"[13] but there is no evidence in the literature of any extensive use of automatic termination procedures. It is obvious, however, from Table 9.1, that it would be relatively easy to program decision rules into the simulation model that

---

[12]R. W. Conway, "Some Tactical Problems in Digital Simulation," *Management Science*, Vol. 10, No. 1 (October, 1963), pp. 58 and 60.
[13]K. D. Tocher, *The Art of Simulation* (London: The English Universities Press, Ltd., 1963), p. 114.

would terminate a run when a critical statistic, such as total cost per year in this model, ceased to fluctuate beyond certain limits. Similarly, in stochastic models it would be possible to program into the model decision rules that would terminate a run or stop the replication procedure when a certain standard error is attained.

Illustration of joint analysis of sample size, initial period, and random number seed

An example of combined analysis of three factors in a simulation model —sample size, initial period, and random number seed—is reported by Fetter and Thompson.[14] To determine the effects of these three factors on a model of a hospital maternity suite, results from experimental runs of the model were analyzed by using analysis of variance and a Latin square experimental design.[15] Three levels of the three factors were systematically combined in nine experimental runs to permit evaluation of effects of each of the factors on behavior in the model. The experimental design is shown in Fig. 9.1. Entries in the body of the table are the number of periods used to initialize the model after startup before beginning collection of statistics. Results of the experimental runs revealed that the random number seed was the only significant source of variation, and this was taken into account when the model was actually used. This case illustrates a practical approach to examining model performance and sensitivity prior to using the model.

Random number seed	Sample size		
	1000	2000	3000
1	20[a]	40	30
57319	30	20	40
283	40	30	20

[a]Entries in body of table are initialization period.

FIGURE 9.1. Experimental Design to Investigate Effects of Three Factors on Simulation Model

---

[14]R. B. Fetter and J. D. Thompson, "The Simulation of Hospital Systems," *Operations Research*, Vol. 13, No. 5 (September–October, 1965).

[15]For a basic discussion of experimental design, see: Edward C. Bryant, *Statistical Analysis*, 2nd ed. (New York: McGraw-Hill Book Company, Inc., 1966), Chap. 8.

Experimentation with Simulation Models

Most simulation models are constructed to permit experimentation on the model rather than on the real world process. A model is used to reduce the time or cost involved or to permit experimentation that would not be possible in the real world. Experimentation may be undertaken with the intent of evaluating alternate structures, determining effects of parameter changes on behavior, or testing different decision rules in the model. Experiments take the form of making changes between or during runs of the model so that comparisons can be made between statistics describing behavior of the model.

Our discussion for the remainder of this section will center around statistical aspects of experimentation with simulation models. But it should be pointed out that it is possible to experiment with simulation models and draw conclusions without using any formal statistical analysis. Since simulation models are capable of providing complete histories of behavior during a run, the results can often be observed and evaluated on a judgmental basis without using formal statistical tests. For instance, industrial dynamics models such as those discussed in Chap. 3 are typically evaluated in terms of stability and long-term trend under varying conditions. Relative stability and trends in most cases are determined simply by observing plotted output from experimental runs. Statistical methods are not usually required to evaluate the results of the experiments.

When models are evaluated on a statistical basis, differences in statistics that are obtained when experimental changes are made may be attributed to:

1. Effects of starting conditions.
2. Random fluctuations in behavior caused by random processes in the model.
3. Effects of experimental changes that are made in the model.

Since the experimenter is primarily interested in (3), it is desirable to plan experiments to control the effects of (1) and (2).

We have already discussed the problem of starting conditions in an earlier section of this chapter and will not repeat the discussion here. However, let us note a particular problem of starting conditions which arises when experimental changes are made in a model. It is tempting to say that the best way to compare one version of a model with another version, which incorporates some change in parameter, structure, or decision rule, is to start simulation runs of both versions at the same point.[16] In many cases this is reasonable advice and eliminates any distorting effects caused by differences in starting conditions. In some models, this may turn out to be a poor procedure in that a common starting point may create unusual con-

---

[16]See Conway's remarks which were quoted previously, pp. 298–99.

ditions for one, or the other, or even both of the versions being compared. One can imagine, for instance, a situation in which initial behavior of an inventory model being run for comparative purposes with different ordering systems or parameters might be quite distorted in early periods if a common starting point for inventory level were used. In this case, different starting conditions would lead more quickly to normal operating conditions for the different systems, and there is less likelihood of producing biased results.

In deterministic models, the effects of changes in the model are not obscured by random fluctuations in behavior of the model. In stochastic models, observation of the effects of experimental changes is made more difficult by the random processes in the model. Variations in results occur without any changes in the model, and variations caused by experimental changes must be distinguished from these random variations. One possible way to reduce some of the random variation when experimental runs of different versions of a model are made is to use identical sequences of random variates in the experimental runs. For example, in a model of service facilities, the same random sequence of customer arrivals might be used in test runs of the model with different arrangements or number of facilities. This procedure eliminates some of the random variation caused by the stochastic nature of the underlying systems and which is not caused by differences in systems being compared. It should be noted that results of such a scheme may be valid only in a relative sense, since any bias in the sequence used is incorporated into results of the experimental runs.

As a practical matter, the use of identical random sequences may not be feasible for all factors. In a service facility simulation, for example, it would be difficult or impossible to arrange to use identical sequences of service times when one is experimenting with the number or characteristics of servers. An additional practical difficulty arises when random variates are generated during a simulation run rather than read in as a sequence of exogenous inputs. Random number sequences used to generate the random variates can easily be duplicated. But different versions of a model will, in many cases, use the random number sequence for different purposes. Therefore, unless a separate random number generator is provided for each random variable, the sequences will not be identical.

In the preceding section of this chapter we discussed the use of output from stochastic simulation models to estimate parameters of the model and placed confidence limits on these estimates. Samples obtained from experimental runs of different versions of a model can be used to test hypotheses concerning the similarity of results obtained from different versions of the model and to estimate the amount of difference.

As an illustration, suppose that we experiment with a simulation model using two sets of decision rules and we wish to compare results obtained in terms of one output of the model, total cost.[17] As discussed in the previous section on sampling, we can arrange experimental runs to obtain from each version of the model a sample of n and m total costs, respectively. Let us designate the results of these n observations for one version and m for the other $C_{11}, C_{12}, \ldots, C_{1n}$ and $C_{21}, C_{22}, \ldots, C_{2m}$, where the first subscript refers to the version of the model and the second to the observation. The means of the samples, $\bar{C}_1$ and $\bar{C}_2$, are found by

$$\bar{C}_1 = \sum_{i=1}^{n} \frac{C_{1i}}{n} \qquad (9.5)$$

and

$$\bar{C}_2 = \sum_{i=1}^{m} \frac{C_{2i}}{m} \qquad (9.6)$$

Estimates of the variance of total cost for each model, $\hat{\sigma}_1^2$ and $\hat{\sigma}_2^2$, are made by

$$\hat{\sigma}_1^2 = \frac{n}{n-1} s_1^2 \qquad (9.7)$$

and

$$\hat{\sigma}_1^2 = \frac{m}{m-1} s_2^2 \qquad (9.8)$$

where s^2 in each case is the sample variance.

If we are interested in determining simply whether there is any difference between total cost in the two versions of the model, we could test the null hypothesis H_0 that total costs are equal. Letting TC_1 and TC_2 represent total cost, the null hypothesis is $H_0: TC_1 - TC_2 = 0$. By the central limit theorem, the sampling distribution of $\bar{C}_1 - \bar{C}_2$ is approximately normal with zero mean and variance given by

$$\sigma_{\bar{C}_1 - \bar{C}_2}^2 = \frac{\hat{\sigma}_1^2}{n} + \frac{\hat{\sigma}_2^2}{m} \qquad (9.9)$$

If a 0.05 significance level is used, H_0 is rejected if the difference $\bar{C}_1 - \bar{C}_2$ does not fall within the interval $0 \pm 1.96\sigma_{\bar{C}_1 - \bar{C}_2}$.

Simply rejecting the hypothesis of equal total costs for the two versions of the model does not yield any information on how large the difference may be. The same information which was used in the hypothesis testing

---

[17] We will develop this illustration in some detail in this section, since the basic ideas will also be utilized in the next section of the chapter.

procedure can be used to estimate the difference between total costs for the two versions of the model and establish a confidence interval on the estimate. The estimated difference d is the difference between the mean values obtained from each model.

$$d = \bar{C}_1 - \bar{C}_2 \tag{9.10}$$

The 95 per cent confidence limits for this estimate are $d \pm 1.96 \, \sigma_{\bar{C}_1 - \bar{C}_2}$, where $\sigma_{\bar{C}_1 - \bar{C}_2}$ is obtained from Eq. (9.9). When a small sample is employed, as is frequently the case in simulation studies, the central limit theorem does not apply and we might use the t distribution instead of assuming normality as in the preceding discussion. However, the t distribution can be used only if we are willing to assume that the statistics being compared are from normally distributed populations (i.e., in reference to the above example, that the total costs TC_1 and TC_2 are described by normal distributions).

The analyst has available the alternative of employing a nonparametric statistical test. These tests require no assumptions concerning the type of parent distribution from which the test statistics are generated. One of these tests is the rank sum test. In this test hypotheses concern the medians of the parent distributions rather than the means. Construction of the test utilizes the fact that values above and below the median are equally likely when samples are taken. It is often used as a test of the relative location of two distributions when the distributions are assumed to be similar except for location.

Consider the case in which we are testing two policies, A and B, by employing a simulation model. Our standard of comparison is total annual cost. Let n_A be the sample size for policy A (i.e., the number of years independently simulated) and n_B be the sample size for policy B. The two samples are combined and the values are ranked in ascending order (i.e., the rank 1 is assigned to the smallest value, the rank 2 is assigned to the next smallest value, etc.).

The test is based on the following contention: If there is no difference between policy A and policy B, there is no reason to believe that the ranks assigned to the elements of sample A should tend to be larger (or smaller) than those of sample B. If, for example, a disproportionate number of small ranks are assigned to the elements of A, this tends to indicate that they came from a population containing smaller values than did the elements of B. The inference is that policy A has a lower total annual cost.

As an example we will analyze hypotheses related to the above discussion:

H_0:   Median annual costs for policies A and B are the same.

H_1:   The median annual cost for policy A is smaller.

We will assume that policy B is currently employed and that policy A

is a new policy viewed as the "challenger." A level of significance of 0.05 will be used and samples of size three will be used for each policy.

Possible ranks assigned to the elements of sample A range from 1, 2, 3 to 4, 5, 6. W_A is computed by summing the ranks; for example, when the elements of A are ranked 2, 3, 6, W_A is 11. Table 9.2 shows possible values of W_A and the probability of occurrence of each for samples of size three.

Table 9.2 FREQUENCY AND PROBABILITY DISTRIBUTION OF
W_A FOR THE CASE WHERE $n_A = 3$ AND $n_B = 3$

W_A	Frequency	$P(W_A)$
6	1	0.05
7	1	0.05
8	2	0.10
9	3	0.15
10	3	0.15
11	3	0.15
12	3	0.15
13	2	0.10
14	1	0.05
15	1	0.05
Sum	20	1.00

The criterion is established for the rank sum test by noting that a W_A of 6 would occur with probability of 0.05 if the null hypothesis is true. The criterion is: Reject the null hypothesis and accept H_1 if $W_A = 6$.[18]

There are many other possible approaches to statistical planning and analysis of experiments with simulation models. Bonini and Little and Skelton[19] report the use of analysis of variance, and we have previously mentioned the use of the technique jointly to analyze effects of sample size, initial period, and random number seed. Since analysis of variance in conjunction with an appropriate experimental design can be used to investigate the effects of several factors at once, it is useful in simulation studies where the analyst may wish to alter a variety of factors in the model and to determine the ones which have a significant effect on performance of the model. Bonini points out that in his study he wished to examine effects of two different levels of eight factors so that a total of 256 experimental runs would be required to test all combinations. By using a fractional factorial

---

[18]A table of critical values for the rank sum test for other sample sizes may be found in Paul G. Hoel, *Elementary Statistics*, 2nd ed. (New York: John Wiley & Sons, Inc., 1966), Appendix, Table VIII. Also see p. 254 of this reference for further discussion of the interpretation of the test. A slightly different form of the rank sum test is the Mann-Whitney U test, a description of which is found in: Sidney Siegel, *Nonparametric Statistics for the Behavioral Sciences* (New York: McGraw-Hill Book Company, Inc., 1956), pp. 116–127.

[19]Charles P. Bonini, *Simulation of Information and Decision Systems in the Firm* (Englewood Cliffs, N.J.: Prentice-Hall, Inc., 1963), Chap. 7. Jack D. Little and Wayne V. Skelton, *An Example of Man-Machine Simulation in Logistics Research*, P-2050 (Santa Monica, Calif.: The RAND Corporation, August 2, 1960), p. 11.

design, it was possible to obtain desired information with 64 runs of the model. Analysis of variance provides information as to sources of significant variations in the observed behavior of a model. Once the significant sources of variation have been determined, further analysis can be done to estimate the amount of variation caused by each.

Another approach to the problem of investigating the effects of many changes in a simulation model is reported by Cyert and March. Their model simulated the price and output determination process in a two-firm industry. The experimental problem is stated as follows:

> We wish to determine the extent to which behavior in the model is sensitive to variations in various internal parameters. An exhaustive consideration of that question is not really feasible. The number of outputs and the number and combinations of inputs are of an intolerable order of magnitude from the point of view of complete analysis. The model generates a detailed time series of decisions, internal organizational results, goals, and so on for each firm in the industry. As we have already noted, it depends on a rather large number of initial conditions and parameters. To make the analysis we limited attention to a few summary statistics of key output variables and to a sample of parameter inputs. The choice of output to consider and the constraints on the parameter sample were made on the basis of a priori judgments on importance and probable sensitivities. Within those constraints, the specific samples to be considered were determined randomly.[20]

Twelve outputs were obtained from the model for each firm. These outputs were mean values of price, inventory, market share, and profit obtained from periods 26–50, 41–50, and 46–50. Experimentation with the model consisted of varying five initial conditions and 20 internal parameters associated with the firms. This was done by designating one firm as the "fixed" firm and one as the "variable" firm. A sample of size 100 was then drawn by the following procedure.

1. For each parameter we determined a mean value, a range, and a distribution. In each case the mean value was also the value assigned to the fixed firm for the same parameter. The range was designed to restrict possible variations in parameter values to a more or less reasonable extent. The distribution could be either approximately normal or approximately rectangular.
2. From these distributions of parameter values we drew 100 random values for each of the 25 values. In effect, we created 100 different "firms" by a random combination of parameter values.[21]

Experimental runs were then performed with these sets of parameter values to determine the parameters to which the output variables of the

---

[20]Richard M. Cyert and James G. March, *A Behavioral Theory of the Firm* (Englewood Cliffs, N.J.: Prentice-Hall, Inc., 1963), p. 173.
[21]*Ibid.*, p. 176.

"fixed" and "variable" firms were sensitive. The method of analysis is described as follows:

> . . . we have 24 dependent variables. For each of these variables we have 25 independent variables and 100 observations of the model. This situation is repeated in each of the three variations of the model. To these data we apply a multiple regression model to determine (within the linear constraints of the model) the contribution of variations in the parameter values to variations in the output. The multiple regression procedure adds and drops variables systematically (reconsidering the entire set of variables at each stage) according to their contribution to the F-values associated with the regression. It identifies all variables that meet an arbitrary criterion of contribution, the criterion being the same for all 24 regression analyses.[22]

Balderston and Hoggatt describe still another procedure involving a nonparametric test to determine effects of various factors on behavior of a model.[23] And we could cite other examples of different approaches to experimentation with simulation models. It is not our purpose, however, to cover all possible methods of experimentation and analysis. As the examples we have discussed serve to show, methods that may be used depend greatly on the specific form of the simulation model, the purpose of the analysis, and the ingenuity of the analyst.

Optimization in Simulation Studies[24]

Simulation models differ from other mathematical models in that the relevant variables are not related directly through equations in the model. Rather, simulation models represent what happens in a system by tracing simulated transactions and events in the system on a compressed time scale. Statistics regarding the operation of the system are collected while the simulation is run, and conclusions may be drawn as to how well the system works. On successive simulations runs different values of the decision variables can be used and comparisons can be made of the operation of the system with the different values.

In the abstract, a computer simulation program may be viewed as a "black box" with unknown characteristics which responds to various settings of the controls (decision variables) on the box by producing an output value (value of the criterion). We are assuming that multiple outputs of a model can be summarized in some way into a single criterion. Determin-

[22]Richard M. Cyert and James G. March, *A Behavioral Theory of the Firm* (Englewood Cliffs, N.J.: Prentice-Hall, Inc., 1963), pp. 177–178.

[23]Frederick E. Balderston and Austin C. Hoggatt, *Simulation of Market Processes* (Berkeley: Institute of Business and Economic Research, University of California, 1962), p. 119. The model to which the test was applied was discussed previously in Chap. 4.

[24]Some of the material in this section appeared previously in: Robert C. Meier, "The Application of Optimum-Seeking Techniques to Simulation Studies: A Preliminary Evaluation," *Journal of Financial and Quantitative Analysis*, Vol. 2, No. 1 (March, 1967).

istic simulation models produce the same output on successive runs when the same set of initial conditions and same values of the decision variables are used. The output of stochastic models varies randomly on successive runs even when initial conditions and values of the decision variables are held constant.

In simulation models there are no functional relationships that can be manipulated by techniques such as linear programming or calculus to obtain optimum values of the decision variables. Therefore, optimization through experimentation with a simulation model necessitates employment of some sort of search technique. In many cases there is little difficulty in planning the search for an optimum, since there are only a few alternatives to be investigated. But in many other instances, there may be several decision variables and many possible values of each decision variable.

One possible way to conduct a search under these circumstances is to make a series of simulation runs with the model, *predetermined* changes in the decision variables being made from run to run. In other words, the pattern of search is established before the computer runs are made and analysis of the results will yield information as to the combination of values of decision variables which produce the highest value of the criterion. Experimental designs of the sort shown in Fig. 9.1 might be employed, although experimentation would be with values of the decision variables rather than random number seed, length of run, and initialization period as in Fig. 9.1. Another type of search pattern that might be useful for models such as the inventory simulation model in Chap. 1 is a grid or lattice. In the stochastic inventory model, a sample run of which is shown in Fig. 1.5, the relevant decision variables are order point and order quantity. A uniform grid approach to searching for optimum values of these decision variables would involve establishing a grid, as shown schematically in Fig. 9.2, over the region that is thought likely to contain the optimum. Simulation runs would then be made by using the combinations of decision variables indicated by each intersection in the grid. From the results, an approximate optimum order point-order quantity combination might be determined, or further runs might be made to explore regions outside the original grid, or a smaller grid might be used to investigate a promising region within the original grid.

Instead of using a predetermined set of experiments or predetermined search pattern, a somewhat different approach is to perform a sequential search in which the values of the decision variables to be used in each new simulation run are determined by the results of previous runs. A number of techniques, sometimes called optimum-seeking methods, response surface techniques, or techniques of evolutionary operation, have been developed for use in this type of search.[25] It is possible to use such methods as the

---

[25] A complete discussion of these techniques may be found in: Douglass J. Wilde, *Optimum Seeking Methods* (Englewood Cliffs, N.J.: Prentice-Hall, Inc., 1964).

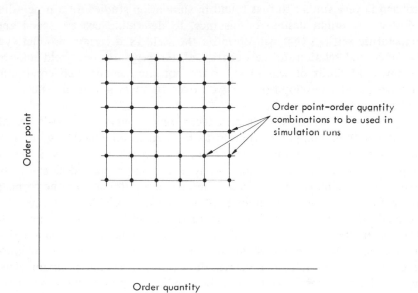

Order point

Order point—order quantity combinations to be used in simulation runs

Order quantity

FIGURE 9.2. Uniform Grid Pattern for Searching for Optimum in Inventory Simulation Model

basis for a manually controlled search or to incorporate an optimum-seeking procedure into a computer program. In a manually controlled search, results of a simulation run are interpreted by the analyst and new values of the decision variables are established by using one of the optimum-seeking procedures that are available. A new run is made, and the analyst repeats the procedure. It is also possible to program the computer to do the work of the analyst so that successive runs are planned and executed automatically without interruption on the computer. We will illustrate the utilization of one optimum-seeking method that might be used in a computer-controlled search procedure.[26]

The technique that we will describe is an adaption of the simplex[27] technique, which has been used in process optimization, where the search

[26]Examples of the application of several other search techniques in simulation studies are found in Maynard M. Hufschmidt, "Simulating the Behavior of a Multi-Unit, Multi-Purpose Water-Resource System," in *Symposium on Simulation Models: Methodology and Applications to the Behavioral Science*, Austin C. Hoggatt and Frederick E. Balderston, eds. (Cincinnati: South-Western Publishing Co., 1963); and Gerald H. Fine and Paul V. McIsaac, "Simulation of a Time-Sharing System," *Management Science*, Vol. 12, No. 6 (February, 1966).

[27]The reader should not confuse this name with the simplex method of linear programming, which also derives its name from the geometric configuration called a simplex. A complete discussion of the simplex method is contained in W. Spendley, G. R. Hext, and F. R. Himsworth, "Sequential Application of Simplex Designs in Optimisation and Evolutionary Operation," *Technometrics*, Vol. 4, No. 4 (November, 1962); and B. H. Carpenter and H. C. Sweeny, "Process Improvement with 'Simplex' Self-Directing Evolutionary Operation," *Chemical Engineering*, July 5, 1965.

problem is very similar to that found in simulation studies. In a processing industry one might desire, for instance, to determine process speed and temperature settings that will optimize the yield of a certain product; yet the functional relationship between speed, temperature, and yield may be unknown. Methods of searching for the optimum under such conditions have been under development for well over 10 years and many successful applications have been made.[28]

We have adapted the simplex technique to serve as a basis for an optimum-seeking computer program to be used in conjunction with computer simulation programs.[29] The computer program (actually a set of subroutines) is a general-purpose optimum-seeking program designed to be used with any simulation program. The program automatically performs a search for the optimum combination of decision variables in terms of a specified criterion variable. For generality, the optimum-seeking program is so constructed that there is a minimum of linkage between the simulation program and the optimum-seeking program. Details of the linkage will not be discussed here, but, in principle, the optimum-seeking program views any simulation program as a "black box" which responds to setting of the controls (decision variables) on the box by producing an output value (value of the criterion). The program is specifically designed to handle the situation in which the output value of the criterion variable on a simulation run is a random function of the settings on the controls.

The automatic search feature is a significant feature of the optimum-seeking program, since it uses the power and speed of the computer to analyze results of the simulation runs that have been made and to determine values of the decision variables to be used in succeeding runs. This does not remove the human analyst completely from the search, since initial conditions, starting points, and certain search parameters must be given to the program, and some judgment must be used in interpreting results after the program has terminated its search. However, much of the search process is carried out automatically and without interruption on the computer, thereby substantially reducing the number of times that results must be interpreted manually and new jobs must be submitted to the computer. The same idea has been suggested in connection with automating physical experiments, as indicated by the following discussion of the possibility of closing the loop between output of results from a physical experiment and input of new control settings for the equipment for the next experiment.

---

[28]For a review of some of the techniques and applications, see William G. Hunter and J. R. Kittrell, "Evolutionary Operation: A Review," *Technometrics*, Vol. 8, No. 3 (August, 1966). Also see William D. Baasel, "Exploring Response Surfaces to Establish Optimum Conditions," *Chemical Engineering*, October 25, 1965.

[29]Development of the optimum-seeking program was supported in part by a grant from the Ford Foundation to the Graduate School of Business Administration, University of Washington.

Clearly, if the scientist can formalize the mental processes he employs in going from results to input commands, those steps can be programmed. If they can be programmed, the data analysis program and the input preparation program can be joined with this "decision-making" program to form a single master program. The master program would accept the data from run i, process them, apply the pre-programmed decision criteria, and, as a result, generate the driving tape for run $i + 1$.[30]

Although the optimum-seeking program that we have developed will theoretically deal with as many decision variables as may be desired, let us consider a case in which there are two decision variables (or controls to set on the "black box"), since this case is easiest to visualize. We will designate the variables y_1 and y_2. Now, suppose that values of y_1 and y_2 are selected and a simulation run is made with these values. From the run, a value of the criterion variable—let us call it Z—is obtained. If a large number of combinations of values of y_1 and y_2 were run and the corresponding values of Z were obtained, we would be able to map the response surface showing the relationship of the criterion variable to the decision variables. In the case of a deterministic simulation, the response surface might appear as sketched in Fig. 9.3 (For ease of illustration, Fig. 9.3 has been drawn as a contour

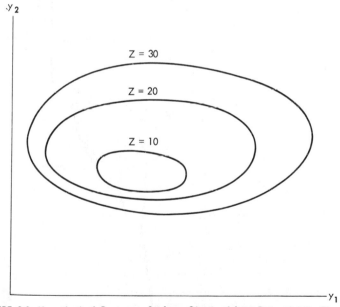

FIGURE 9.3. Hypothetical Response Surface Obtained from Deterministic Simulation Model with Two Decision Variables

[30]R. J. Spinard, "Automation in the Laboratory," *Science*, Vol. 158, No. 3797 (October 6, 1967), p. 56.

map showing points of equal elevation rather than as a three-dimensional figure.)

Although the complete response surface as shown in Fig. 9.3 could be obtained, it is usually not practical to map it out in its entirety, as this would require too many simulation runs. Instead, the simplex method works by starting with three points, or combinations of values of y_1 and y_2. A simulation run is made at each of the points, the value of the criterion variable is obtained for each point, and a new triangle is formed by dropping the highest-valued point (in the case of a minimization problem) and picking a new point on the opposite side of a line between the two remaining points. The procedure is shown in Fig. 9.4. If the initial three points are selected judiciously and if the response surface is reasonably well behaved, repeated application of the procedure will locate the minimum point on the surface quite effectively.[31]

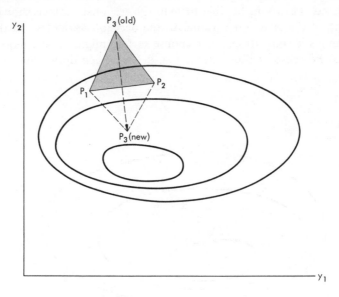

FIGURE 9.4. Basic Simplex Procedure

The optimum-seeking program that we have developed is considerably more complex than the basic procedure outlined above, since it is designed to deal with the case in which the response surface is not a clearly delineated surface but one which might be characterized as "fuzzy" because of the presence of random elements. As a consequence, the value of the criterion variable obtained on successive simulation runs, the same input values

---

[31]A description of the application of the basic simplex procedure to deterministic simulation is contained in Gary F. Healea, "Evolutionary Methods as Applied to Simulation Models," unpublished MBA research report (Seattle: University of Washington, 1965).

being used for the decision variables, is not the same on all runs, but is a
random variable, and the optimum-seeking program has several additional
features for dealing with random variation. It is not difficult to imagine
many ways to handle the problem of random variation, and the present
program is the end product of a substantial amount of evolution as the work
on it proceeded. Also, the program must have automatic termination procedures, and the ones that will be described are the result of experimentation
with several approaches.

One of the modifications that were made in the basic simplex procedure
to deal with the randomness of observed values of the criterion variable
was the addition of a procedure for replication of simulation runs at the
vertices of the simplex (a triangle in the case of a two-decision variable
problem). The minimum number of replications that are to be made at each
vertex is specified as input data together with the level of significance against
which differences in mean values of the criterion variable at the vertices
are to be tested. The program causes additional replications to be performed
if significance is not obtained with the minimum number of replications.
A maximum number of replications is also specified as input data, which
causes the search to terminate if that maximum is reached.[32]

The method used to test for significance of differences between the mean
values of the criterion at the vertices is straightforward (for ease of programing) and, consequently, only approximate. It is assumed that the
variance is the same at all vertices, although the values of the criterion—
$Z_1, Z_2, \ldots, Z_m$—may be different. Mean values $\bar{Z}_1, \bar{Z}_2, \ldots, \bar{Z}_m$ of the
replications made at each of the vertices are used as estimates of $Z_1, Z_2, \ldots,$
Z_m. An estimate $\hat{\sigma}^2$ of the common variance is obtained by

$$\hat{\sigma}^2 = \left(\frac{\bar{R}}{d_2}\right)^2 \tag{9.11}$$

where

$\bar{R}$ = mean of the ranges of the criterion variable at the vertices

d_2 = a factor depending on the number of replications made at
each vertex

Tables of values of d_2 for any number of replications n may be found in
texts on quality control.[33] Inspection of a table of values of d_2 suggests that,
for the number of replications n which the program is likely to be dealing

---

[32]Although Spendley, Hext, and Himsworth (see footnote 27) recommend against
replication to deal with random error, we felt that replication was desirable because of the
decision rules used to reduce the size of the simplex and terminate the search. However,
the program can be run with or without replication.

[33]Eugene L. Grant, *Statistical Quality Control*, 3rd ed. (New York: McGraw-
Hill Book Company, Inc., 1964), Appendix, Table B.

with, say under 15, d_2 may reasonably be approximated simply by $\sqrt{n}$. The estimate of the variance used in the program, accordingly, is

$$\hat{\sigma}^2 = \frac{\bar{R}^2}{n} \qquad (9.12)$$

The program tests, for each pair of vertices, the null hypothesis that there is no difference between the Z's at the vertices. For instance, for vertex one and vertex two, a test would be made of the hypothesis

$$H_0: \quad Z_1 - Z_2 = 0$$

If it is assumed that the sampling distribution of $\bar{Z}_1 - \bar{Z}_2$ is approximately normal, the mean of the sampling distribution when H_0 is true is 0, and the standard deviation is approximated by

$$\sigma_{\bar{Z}_1 - \bar{Z}_2} = \sqrt{\frac{\sigma_{Z_1}^2}{n} + \frac{\sigma_{Z_2}^2}{n}} \qquad (9.13)$$

Since we have assumed that the variance is the same for all vertices and can be approximated by $\bar{R}^2/n$, we have

$$\sigma_{\bar{Z}_1 - \bar{Z}_2} = \sqrt{\frac{\dfrac{\bar{R}^2}{n} + \dfrac{\bar{R}^2}{n}}{n}} = \frac{\bar{R}}{n}\sqrt{2} \qquad (9.14)$$

The specific level at which the significance of differences between vertices is tested is specified as input data to the program. If the level were specified as 2, for example, the difference between $\bar{Z}_1$ and $\bar{Z}_2$ would be considered significant if it were greater than $2(\bar{R}/n)\sqrt{2}$ in absolute value. The entire procedure is, of course, only approximate, but it has the virtue of simplicity from a programing standpoint, an important factor in exploratory work.

The basic simplex procedure has also been modified by the addition of another point, the centroid of the simplex, at which simulation runs are made. The reason for adding this point is to provide a means of testing whether the simplex encloses a possible optimum point in its interior, and the centroid also provides a convenient reference point for forming simplexes, both at the start of the search and as the search progresses. To illustrate how the simplex is formed, the centroid being used as a starting point, let us consider a case in which there are two decision variables y_1 and y_2. The coordinates of the centroid of the initial simplex which we will call c_1 and c_2 are given as input data. Similarly, values that we will call variable increments and designate i_1 and i_2 are given to the program as input data. These variable increments specify the size of the simplex with respect to each of the variables. In a two-decision variable problem, the program constructs a simplex as shown in Fig. 9.5. Figure 9.6 is a sketch of the initial simplex. An analogous

	y_1	y_2
Vertex one	$c_1 - i_1/2$	$c_2 - i_2/3$
Vertex two	$c_1 + i_1/2$	$c_2 - i_2/3$
Vertex three	c_1	$c_2 + 2i_2/3$

FIGURE 9.5. Coordinates of Vertices of Simplex

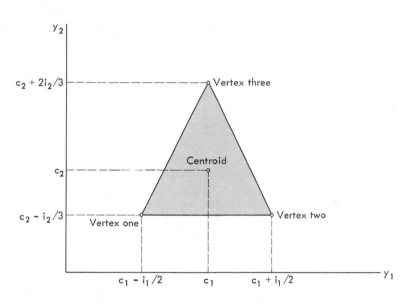

FIGURE 9.6. Construction of Initial Simplex from Input Data in Two Decision
Variable Case

procedure would be followed if more than two decision variables were
involved. As the search proceeds, the simplex is moved as shown previously
in Fig. 9.4, and under certain conditions the size of the simplex is also reduced. The reduction in size is accomplished by reducing the values of i_1 and
i_2 (in the two-variable case) and constructing a new simplex with its centroid
at the centroid of the previous simplex. The program has provision for the
input of both the beginning variable increments and minimum increments
which cause the search to be terminated when they are reached.

As the search proceeds, each simplex is evaluated by the program according to the following decision rules which are expressed in terms of a
minimization problem.

1. If the mean values of the criterion variable at the vertices are not significantly different and if the mean value of the criterion variable at the centroid is not significantly lower than all vertices and if the mean value at the centroid is not significantly higher than the mean at the previous centroid, perform another replication (simulation run) at each vertex and the centroid and evaluate the results again. Terminate the search, however, if the specified maximum number of replications has been reached.

2. If the mean value of the criterion variable is significantly lower at the centroid than at all vertices, decrease the size of the simplex by multiplying all variable increments by the factor [number of replications/(number of replications + 1)]. Form a new simplex, perform the minimum number of replications at the vertices and centroid, and start the evaluation again at step 1.

3. If the mean value of the criterion variable at the centroid is significantly higher than the mean at the centroid of the previous simplex, decrease the size of the simplex by multiplying all variable increments by the factor [number of replications/(number of replications + 1)]. Form a new simplex, perform the minimum number of replications at the vertices and centroid, and start the evaluation again at step 1.

4. If the largest mean value of the criterion variable at a vertex of the simplex is significantly higher than the mean value of at least one of the other vertices and if this vertex with the largest mean value *is* the vertex most recently added, decrease the size of the simplex by multiplying all variable increments by the factor [number of replications/(number of replications + 1)]. Form a new simplex, perform the minimum number of replications at the vertices and centroid, and start the evaluation again at step 1.

5. If the largest mean value of the criterion variable at a vertex of the simplex is significantly higher than the mean value of at least one of the other vertices and if this vertex with the largest mean value *is not* the vertex most recently added, delete the vertex and add a new one on the opposite side of the simplex (see Fig. 9.4). Perform the minimum number of replications at the new vertex and new centroid and start the evaluation again at step 1.

6. If, in decreasing the size of the simplex under the conditions specified in steps 2, 3, and 4, the minimum variable increment is reached, terminate the search.

We will illustrate the operation of the optimum-seeking program, using the inventory simulation program documented in Appendix B. Under normal operation the program takes input data describing the parameters of the inventory system to be simulated, performs the simulation, and prints out the results of the simulation. With the optimum-seeking program added to it, the simulation program operates in general as shown in Fig. 9.7. The program is now a closed loop which continues the search for better values of the decision variables until the search is terminated by one of the decision rules discussed previously. As a test problem, let us consider an inventory system managed on an order point-order quantity basis. The system operates with a restriction that stock level reviews and replenishment order placements can occur only at five-day intervals. Both lead time and demand are random

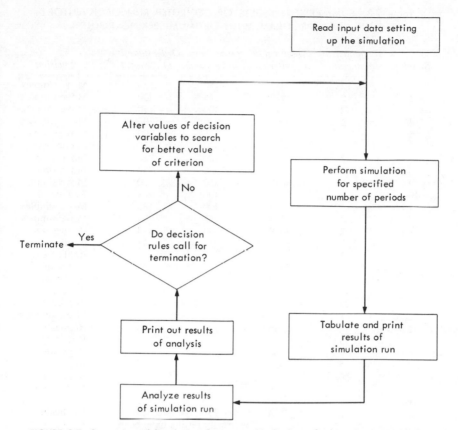

FIGURE 9.7. Operation of Simulation Program with Optimum-Seeking Routine Added

variables, and each simulation run is 1000 periods in length. The relevant decision variables are the order point and order quantity, and the criterion variable is total cost. Data describing this inventory system and parameters to be used in the search were supplied to the combined simulation and optimum-seeking computer programs.[34]

Tabulation of all data generated in the course of the test run on the problem would be too lengthy. Table 9.3 summarizes some essential results.[35] The search was started at an order point-order quantity combination of

[34]A complete description of the input data appears in Robert C. Meier, "The Application of Optimum-Seeking Techniques to Simulation Studies: A Preliminary Evaluation," *Journal of Financial and Quantitative Analysis*, Vol. 2, No. 1 (March, 1967), pp. 44–47.

[35]In addition to the data shown in Table 9.3, the complete printout tabulates location of vertices, individual simulation run results, ranges of criterion at the vertices and centroid, limits of significant differences, and results of tests of significance of differences and application of the decision rules.

Table 9.3   SUMMARIZED RESULTS OF COMPUTER RUN OF INVENTORY
SIMULATION PROGRAM WITH OPTIMUM-SEEKING ROUTINE

Simplex	Number of replications	Mean value of criterion	Order point at centroid	Order quantity at centroid	Decision
1	2	15741	150	150	Move simplex
2	2	8917	225	200	Move simplex
3	2	7779	300	150	Move simplex
4	2	5394	375	200	Move simplex
5	2	4216	375	300	Move simplex
6	2	4085	300	350	Reduce size
7	2	4019	300	350	Move simplex
8	2	3698	350	383	Move simplex
9	2	3619	350	450	Move simplex
10	2	3747	400	483	Reduce size
11	2	3678	400	483	Move simplex
12	2	3527	367	504	Move simplex
13	2	3480	333	483	Reduce size
14	2	3441	333	483	Replicate
	3	3432			Replicate
	4	3481			Replicate
	5	3472			Replicate
	6	3457			Replicate
	7	3446			Replicate
	8	3446			Move simplex
15	2	3466	356	498	Replicate
	3	3454			Replicate
	4	3460			Replicate
	5	3457			Replicate
	6	3488			Replicate
	7	3476			Reduce size
16	2	3510	356	498	Move simplex
17	2	3524	336	511	Replicate
·	·	(For brevity results have been deleted.)			Replicate
·	·				·
	15	3454			Terminate

150–150, which yielded a mean total cost of $15,741 at the centroid of the first simplex. Because of the stochastic nature of the model, input data to the optimum-seeking routine specified that a minimum of two replications were to be made at each vertex and the centroid of the simplex. The optimum-seeking program rather quickly located values of the decision variables far superior to the starting point. By the thirteenth simplex virtually all of the improvement obtained during the search had already taken place. From there on the search continued rather inconclusively until the optimum-seeking program terminated the run on the seventeenth simplex when 15 replications, the maximum number specified in the input data, failed to yield any significant differences between mean values of the criterion at the vertices and centroid.

Examination of the complete printout of all results from the search suggests that the response surface is rather flat in the region around the termination point. This lack of gradient, together with the stochastic nature of the system being simulated, makes it difficult to define the optimum closely. Greater accuracy, however, may not be necessary, since the results have probably already yielded most of the information desired about the particular problem. In retrospect the results also show that an upper limit of five on the number of replications would have terminated the run at the fourteenth simplex with relatively little loss of information. On the basis of this test problem and other test problems, it would appear to be good strategy to start the search with a fairly conservative upper limit on the number of replications required to terminate the search.

As stated earlier, the use of the optimum-seeking program does not guarantee an optimum solution, nor does it eliminate the human element completely from the analysis. On the basis of the results of this first search, the analyst might choose from a number of courses of action, such as restarting the search at the termination point with different search parameters, starting the search at different initial values of the decision variables, or accepting the results as "good enough." There is no firm guide as to what should be done, as this is up to the judgment of the analyst. In this test problem, it was decided to make a second search, starting at a different set of initial values for the decision variables. The second search terminated on the twentieth simplex at an order point of 317 and order quantity of 690 with a mean total cost at the centroid of 3428, very close to the cost at the time of termination of the first search. Examination of the complete output from both searches suggests that the response surface is quite flat for values of the decision variables in the region surrounding the two termination points and in the region surrounding a straight line connecting the termination points. A reasonable conclusion is that the termination points and points on a line connecting them probably represent approximate optimum solutions to the test problem.

We have applied the simplex technique to the test problem primarily as an illustration of the potential for utilizing optimum-seeking methods in simulation studies. Our experience at this time is too limited to permit generalization regarding the efficiency of the method and set of decision rules that were used. Other optimum-seeking methods may be superior; there may be better settings of the search parameters; there may be profitable tradeoffs between length of individual simulation runs and number of replications. The generality of an optimum-seeking program of the type we have discussed is an attractive feature, since its applicability is not determined by the particular form of the problem. As long as a "black box" to represent a problem can be provided in the form of a simulation program with decision variable inputs and a criterion variable output, the optimum seeker can be connected to it.

A similar approach to optimization which uses computer programs to guide the search has been developed by California Analysis Center, Inc.[36] The programs developed at C.A.C.I. involve optimization of a simulation model in three phases using decentralized gradient analysis, followed by linear response surface analysis, followed by quadratic response surface analysis. The decentralized gradient technique is designed to locate the vicinity of the optimum fairly rapidly by examining the elements of the system and making simultaneous changes in the decision variables. When this phase terminates, the linear response surface procedure searches for possible improvement on the current solution by increasing and decreasing decision variables one at a time and rerunning the simulation until no further improvements can be found. The final quadratic response phase attempts to locate further improvements by examining whether simultaneous changes in the decision variables might improve the solution. As yet there is insufficient experience with these techniques or the simplex approach discussed previously to comment on their relative efficiency.

Summary

Simulation models that represent actual systems may be validated by comparing key statistics from the model with those obtained from the actual system. When the model represents a proposed system or one for which no actual statistics are available, the validity of the model can be assured only by exercising care in constructing the model and thoroughly testing its operation. Once a model has been validated, obtaining information through a run of the model presents certain statistical problems in terms of selection of initial conditions, elimination of startup transients, and determination of the nature of an observation or a sample from the simulation run. These factors must be carefully considered in planning simulation runs of the model to avoid biasing results that are obtained.

Experimentation with a simulation model is often done without a formal statistical design in cases where only a limited number of alternatives need to be compared and where results are conclusive. Formal statistical procedures such as hypothesis testing and experimental designs may be required in cases where the interpretation of the results is unclear because of the stochastic nature of the model and when it is necessary to explore many variations in system design, rules of operation, or parameter values.

Although simulation models usually have no inherent capabilities for providing optimum solutions to questions of system operation, they may be used as a vehicle for searching for optimum values of decision variables.

---

[36]Herbert W. Karr, Ernel L. Luther, Harry M. Markowitz, and Edward C. Russell, *SimOptimization Research Phase I* (Santa Monica, Calif.: California Analysis Center, Inc., November 1, 1965); and Ernel L. Luther and Harry M. Markowitz, *SimOptimization Research Phase II* (Santa Monica, Calif.: California Analysis Center, Inc., July 15, 1966).

Search procedures may involve the use of predetermined patterns or may be of a sequential nature in which the nature of each new simulation run is guided by the results of preceding runs. Some experimental computer programs have been developed which guide the search automatically, thereby improving the speed with which a search for an optimum can be carried out.

EXERCISES

9.1 In Exercise 2.2, compare the demand distribution and lead time distribution actually obtained on a simulation run of 30 days with the distributions from which demand and lead time are drawn. What implications do your results have regarding the adequacy of using 30 days as the length of run?

9.2 In Exercise 2.4, determine whether a 30-day simulation run is sufficient to obtain an adequate sample of types of news days and demand on those days.

9.3 Repeat Exercise 2.14 with all values remaining the same except that the firm starts each of the simulated years with a cash balance of $30,000. Analyze the impact of this change of starting conditions on the relative advantage of each of the three strategies.

9.4 Run the model in Appendix C with the following changes in initial conditions. In each case set the sales step SLSTP to 10,000 to eliminate the effect of the step increase in sales. Compare the results obtained in each case.
a. Let initial dealer inventory DINV equal 30,000 units.
b. Let initial dealer inventory DINV equal 60,000 units and warehouse inventory WINV equal 30,000 units.
c. Let initial dealer inventory DINV equal 60,000 units, warehouse inventory WINV equal 30,000 units and factory production ability FPRAB equal 5000 units per week.

9.5 Rerun the model developed in Exercise 3.11 with an initial value for average sales of 5000 units per month. Explain the impact of this change.

9.6 Repeat the simulation in Exercise 4.8 and compare your results with those obtained previously.
a. Begin with the 100 males all employed.
b. Begin with 60 males employed.

9.7 Establish 95 per cent confidence limits on the mean completion time found in Exercise 2.16.

9.8 In Exercise 2.9b, develop and execute a plan for establishing reasonable confidence limits on
a. the average waiting time per student during a one-hour study period.

      b. percentage utilization of the teacher and helper during a one-hour study period.

9.9   Simulate the servicing of 500 customers through the order-taker system described in the section of Chap. 2 dealing with waiting lines. Use the interarrival time distribution shown in Fig. 2.6 and the service time distribution shown in Fig. 2.7. Tabulate the time in system (waiting time plus service time) for the 500 customers.

      a. Compute the mean and standard deviation of time in the system, considering the 500 observations to be independent.

      b. From your results in part *a*. above compute the anticipated distribution of means of samples of five customers.

      c. Treat the 500 customers as 100 consecutive samples of five customers and compute the means of these samples.

      d. Compare the distribution of means found in part *c*. above with the anticipated distribution found in part *b*. and explain your results.

9.10 Using the model developed in Exercise 1.5, carry out a series of experimental runs designed to permit a statistically valid statement as to the method of operation which yields the lowest waiting time for emergency vehicles to arrive.

9.11 Carry out a series of experimental runs, using the model developed in Exercise 2.12 to permit a statistically valid statement as to the maintenance policy that produces lowest cost.

9.12 Carry out a series of experimental runs, using the model developed in Exercise 2.15 to determine the replenishment policy which yields the lowest number of units of lost demand.

9.13 Instead of using a sample size of 50 in Exercise 8.8, devise and test an automatic termination procedure to be used

      a. in conjunction with the rejection method.

      b. in conjunction with the crude Monte Carlo method.

9.14 Devise and test an automatic termination procedure to be used in conjunction with Exercise 2.13b.

9.15 Using the simulation model developed in Exercise 2.12, devise and test a method for finding the optimum time between inspections for repair policies of the same type as policy 2 in the exercise.

BIBLIOGRAPHY

Agin, Norman, "Optimum Seeking with Branch and Bound," *Management Science*, Vol. 13, No. 4 (December, 1966).

Baasel, William D., "Exploring Response Surfaces to Establish Optimum Conditions," *Chemical Engineering*, October 25, 1965.

Balderston, Frederick E. and Austin C. Hoggatt, *Simulation of Market Processes*. Berkeley: Institute of Business and Economic Research, University of California, 1962, Chap. 9.

Bonini, Charles P., *Simulation of Information and Decision Systems in the Firm*. Englewood Cliffs, New Jersey: Prentice-Hall, Inc., 1963, Chap. 7.

Brenner, Michael E., "A Cost Model for Determining the Sample Size in the Simulation of Inventory Systems," *The Journal of Industrial Engineering*, Vol. 17, No. 3 (March, 1966).

————, "A Relation Between Decision Making Penalty and Simulation Sample Size for Inventory Systems," *Operations Research*, Vol. 13, No. 3 (May–June, 1965).

Brooks, Samuel H., "A Comparison of Maximum-Seeking Methods," *Operations Research*, Vol. 7, No. 4 (July-August, 1959).

Bryant, Edward C., *Statistical Analysis*, 2nd ed. New York: McGraw-Hill Book Company, Inc., 1966, Chap. 8.

Carpenter, B. H. and H. C. Sweeny, "Process Improvement with 'Simplex' Self-Directing Evolutionary Operation," *Chemical Engineering*, July 5, 1965.

Clelland, Richard C., John S. deCani, Francis E. Brown, J. Parker Bursk, and Donald S. Murray, *Basic Statistics With Business Applications*. New York: John Wiley & Sons, Inc., 1966, Secs. 9.4–9.8.

Cochran, W. G. and G. M. Cox, *Experimental Designs*. New York: John Wiley & Sons, Inc., 1957.

Cohen, Kalman J. and Richard M. Cyert, "Computer Models in Dynamic Economics," *The Quarterly Journal of Economics*, Vol. 75, No. 1 (February, 1961).

Conway, R. W., "Some Tactical Problems in Digital Simulation," *Management Science*, Vol. 10, No. 1 (October, 1963).

Conway, R. W., B. M. Johnson, and W. L. Maxwell, "Some Problems of Digital Systems Simulation," *Management Science*, Vol. 6, No. 1 (October, 1959).

Cyert, Richard M. and James G. March, *A Behavioral Theory of the Firm*. Englewood Cliffs, New Jersey: Prentice-Hall, Inc., 1963, Chap. 8.

Davies, Owen L., ed., *The Design and Analysis of Industrial Experiments*. London: Oliver & Boyd, 1956, Chap. 11.

Duer, Beverley C., "The Use of Multidimensional Search Techniques in Large Scale Simulation," in *Proceedings on Simulation in Business and Public Health*. First Annual Conference of American Statistical Association (New York Area Chapter) and Public Health Association of New York City, 1966.

Fetter, R. B. and J. D. Thompson, "The Simulation of Hospital Systems," *Operations Research*, Vol. 13, No. 5 (September–October, 1965).

Fine, Gerald H. and Paul V. McIsaac, "Simulation of a Time-Sharing System," *Management Science*, Vol. 12, No. 6 (February, 1966).

Fisher, Ronald A., *The Design of Experiments*, 7th ed. London: Oliver and Boyd, 1960.

Fishman, George S., "The Allocation of Computer Time in Comparing Simulation Experiments," *Operations Research*, Vol. 16, No. 2 (March-April, 1968).

Fishman, George S. and Philip J. Kiviat, "The Analysis of Simulation-Generated Time Series," *Management Science*, Vol. 13, No. 7 (March, 1967).

Freund, John E. and Frank J. Williams, *Elementary Business Statistics: The Modern Approach*. Englewood Cliffs, New Jersey: Prentice-Hall, Inc., 1964, Chap. 9

Gafarian, A. V. and C. J. Ancker, "Mean Value Estimation from Digital Computer Simulation," *Operations Research*, Vol. 14, No. 1 (January–February, 1966).

Geisler, Murray A., "A Test of a Statistical Method for Computing Selected Inventory Model Characteristics by Simulation," *Management Science*, Vol. 10, No. 4 (July, 1964).

————, "The Sizes of Simulation Samples Required to Compute Certain Inventory Characteristics with Stated Precision and Confidence," *Management Science*, Vol. 10, No. 2 (January, 1964).

Healea, Gary F., "Evolutionary Methods as Applied to Simulation Models," Unpublished MBA research report. Seattle: University of Washington, 1966.

Hoggatt, Austin C., "Statistical Techniques for the Computer Analysis of Simulation Models," Appendix A in Lee E. Preston and Norman R. Collins, *Studies in a Simulated Market*. Berkeley: Institute of Business and Economic Research, University of California, 1966.

Hufschmidt, Maynard M., "Simulating the Behavior of a Multi-Unit, Multi-Purpose Water-Resource System," in *Symposium on Simulation Models: Methodology and Applications to the Behavioral Sciences*, Austin C. Haggatt and Frederick E. Balderston, eds. Cincinnati: South-Western Publishing Co., 1963.

Hunter, William G. and J. R. Kittrell, "Evolutionary Operation: A Review," *Technometrics*, Vol. 8, No. 3 (August, 1966).

Jacoby, J. E. and S. Harrison, "Multi-Variable Experimentation and Simulation Models," *Naval Research Logistics Quarterly*, Vol. 9, No. 2 (June, 1962).

Kabak, Irwin W., "Stopping Rules for Queuing Situations," (Letter to the Editor), *Operations Research*, Vol. 16, No. 2 (March-April, 1968).

Karr, Herbert W., Ernel L. Luther, Harry M. Markowitz, and Edward C. Russell, *SimOptimization Research Phase I*. Santa Monica, California: California Analysis Center, Inc., November 1, 1965.

Luther, Ernel L. and Harry M. Markowitz, *SimOptimization Research Phase II*. Santa Monica, California: California Analysis Center, Inc., July 15, 1966.

Meier, Robert C., "The Application of Optimum-Seeking Techniques to Simulation Studies: A Preliminary Evaluation," *Journal of Financial and Quantitative Analysis*, Vol. 2, No. 1 (March, 1967).

Naylor, Thomas H. and Donald S. Burdick, "Design of Computer Simulation Experiments for Industrial Systems," *Communications of the ACM*, Vol. 9, No. 5 (May, 1966).

Naylor, Thomas H., Donald S. Burdick, and W. Earl Sasser, "Computer Simulation Experiments with Economic Systems: The Problem of Experimental Design," *American Statistical Association Journal*, Vol. 62, No. 320 (December, 1967).

Naylor, Thomas H. and J. M. Finger, "Verification of Computer Simulation Models," *Management Science*, Vol. 14, No. 2 (October, 1967).

Nelson, Rosser T., "Labor and Machine Limited Production Systems," *Management Science*, Vol. 13, No. 9 (May, 1967).

Page, E. S., "On Monte Carlo Methods in Congestion Problems," *Operations Research*, Vol. 13, No. 2 (March–April, 1965).

Seaman, P. H., "A Teleprocessing System Design, Part VI: The Role of Digital Simulation," *IBM Systems Journal*, Vol. 5, No. 3 (1966).

Spendley, W., G. R. Hext, and F. R. Himsworth, "Sequential Applications of Simplex Designs in Optimisation and Evolutionary Operation," *Technometrics*, Vol. 4, No. 4 (November, 1962).

Van Slyke, Richard A., "Monte Carlo Methods and the PERT Problem," *Operations Research*, Vol. 11, No. 5 (September–October, 1963).

Wilde, Douglass J., *Optimum Seeking Methods*. Englewood Cliffs, New Jersey: Prentice-Hall, Inc., 1964.

Wilde, Douglass J. and Charles S. Beightler, *Foundations of Optimization*. Englewood Cliffs, New Jersey: Prentice-Hall, Inc., 1967, Chaps. 6 and 7.

Appendices

TABLE A.1 UNIFORMLY DISTRIBUTED RANDOM VARIATES

53076	98356	71012	57081	50378	24782	59604	68503	87115
67675	66328	31868	44108	30976	97286	11185	85146	80501
11682	77634	35669	11988	76536	47230	5101	56004	447
80779	52122	53345	98605	43750	96415	48056	23627	15127
18002	40596	31530	56785	91219	98542	55551	52010	42465
74217	49876	28094	78516	83703	49785	37480	43103	15747
10332	39877	18937	80203	5878	25213	86229	53043	65949
81641	6372	15397	98026	56147	41803	27564	16801	49977
43916	21062	73364	15617	27252	47003	80081	60913	65541
76522	33375	75162	76477	51924	56899	87600	11637	32607
89254	71515	72226	30405	13914	88805	6010	56571	62411
32280	90189	77336	34756	49649	3071	44055	58885	55252
43878	83500	48961	1404	55651	50495	41115	45496	87123
92040	11812	5970	68108	38973	22272	71589	45584	73886
6359	2591	68104	22993	21631	36380	53439	58588	61660
86313	36575	46153	28847	5297	49395	51115	55731	29636
87662	73748	84288	52395	7084	53295	15741	99974	74435
24285	66547	48913	53551	65409	21248	56997	85000	35454
69058	76804	13315	99615	35505	85816	44036	39754	6913
19215	42140	60830	32894	51061	1645	31020	41339	67819
98467	1399	87220	81485	9378	93059	14486	55807	24842
52206	36683	53151	83242	19358	84254	96160	94802	49007
93275	36216	90302	87642	66725	25401	72950	94381	32159
53953	7594	26512	15915	70083	52465	93485	44128	31367
72734	80239	16993	75399	85135	69427	2434	12818	3234
20823	36035	11101	50068	5666	15313	75499	19621	44791
18203	39387	32534	38175	88661	63836	62019	61531	77848
32030	42255	75145	53716	47878	47411	84658	96763	92145
32626	32699	4949	66642	15814	72257	7122	58807	78031
42589	5796	44046	99642	28893	33251	92302	72065	16855
45818	6379	22194	16463	4221	83866	11458	55554	54878
15188	51600	35924	45465	84325	66904	2428	6880	18112
56103	99032	40717	97265	49433	88443	47471	44185	87971
85959	49977	27971	84439	79377	62707	42935	49401	56964
79082	70637	1453	38065	52271	787	80762	35583	63603
22815	10297	4490	44966	31144	64458	78696	88324	29508
62014	56652	42726	37607	42638	54659	67205	259	57143
68594	76822	31362	58100	28842	83207	58900	70070	40103
77866	66073	79150	43637	42600	17149	95556	96339	72246
45063	57832	12466	11314	96443	75026	50885	27642	93890
12734	19579	3176	48602	45393	85057	31695	9856	67375
64837	54064	78104	60400	68663	45096	90193	81828	92087
56683	73431	70175	96677	58275	50851	93630	88019	27138
7263	98095	12841	65134	64661	9645	58195	71850	4143
48058	25821	89441	28807	6601	42032	54674	82623	80138
48051	19019	48678	20914	17274	18822	53466	84952	87683
25867	34598	86636	10061	54130	83161	13024	7262	67539
70560	25520	90985	30384	61363	11016	17455	98874	84514
11130	30614	38973	80797	53708	25215	88232	38211	67251
70042	12020	12248	60797	46160	44691	89594	88327	32170

TABLE A.1 (Cont.)

81220	89905	96270	3623	90920	91528	5124	78102	99305	12198
2014	96843	72247	97374	98257	89117	15199	63100	32723	29380
73567	4564	20262	80530	5760	16541	92486	53998	12614	1070
8847	68279	65016	31205	24808	61308	56989	76232	46886	64975
84935	70822	84952	87846	56112	91074	54363	74277	8944	64363
7043	80474	49962	12441	29898	63879	24339	20601	16021	76895
29407	42824	38890	40494	29968	3065	38387	41567	93671	28325
99049	58423	97500	22786	81410	70815	77952	50940	82326	85601
77766	66495	97116	42433	51279	30837	60086	45643	32648	54973
17725	66003	9927	38545	98164	78503	96499	30562	87855	64955
81120	90401	87452	65591	844	70565	30688	12251	40816	49486
37314	78605	98343	58618	90702	41387	15651	15600	60412	68847
85817	44878	74780	7073	10142	27440	94016	70152	20730	44038
50524	66059	64853	69569	43822	42330	49230	87444	57565	47094
27781	31945	57841	20988	99685	70551	16834	82722	78239	35710
68139	46107	92977	40399	35679	89097	96061	96834	62644	80971
58373	47705	76396	8519	42943	42827	42016	38177	33948	43368
57099	85151	85064	99127	35661	78037	34949	35350	32095	6267
40550	81835	99200	8138	65345	10632	36604	75115	39045	93913
57156	81887	50162	10946	48234	68378	62644	80983	54443	53328
346	45443	34641	29396	31907	48096	63436	65724	32923	27460
20551	66428	30398	24441	21103	13002	85275	7796	26772	31961
13237	18786	17842	81901	64066	73767	4053	17150	96371	4372
85865	56546	37401	64846	62861	33533	31696	11715	9585	99254
95711	50585	29939	70075	44808	61069	19937	57696	77096	2724
5360	11764	58574	46894	72658	290	87552	64119	42070	92144
4992	47278	52559	86678	98174	14897	63431	60280	38274	29566
90597	81910	73621	59393	58848	615	9830	42081	3249	20599
19083	11456	53840	56265	58926	14049	22596	92848	12921	5625
96383	15958	15256	19494	19480	74910	36517	89190	87469	82434
5254	7036	73613	50525	70951	52644	10981	82883	37911	70583
13242	23236	26973	31103	23110	46336	1108	98940	50512	58286
2078	59372	38074	32130	41471	61442	89835	27125	81561	27098
98302	17526	69175	52521	49220	54538	47889	58361	36290	63880
77196	1375	63116	48593	56607	5183	37144	9873	84918	53938
58134	51069	10277	84679	17500	53137	59070	38531	84397	38345
43426	36102	77651	52946	69670	101	116	15814	72050	1696
43107	19419	44704	2231	11132	80806	78995	84566	5640	89349
32610	18515	49308	64825	42509	45466	57749	29870	1691	76404
26610	70580	45769	57831	10834	17156	41694	18903	33120	22320
37474	37018	85106	41007	38652	15310	36791	60364	21221	30898
4539	99115	23110	2108	89143	20156	15174	38180	36639	10213
41476	2827	2481	59144	11743	21120	30667	91562	38376	31092
38167	24378	58748	20093	12822	12344	33373	72754	134	33442
7121	57739	20073	93123	85809	41746	70687	51690	25597	66914
37304	68971	50934	76143	57872	12168	58969	38353	8263	89050
51342	79992	72212	62334	73850	48866	26419	81749	13486	64870
85490	21180	89743	36291	65229	87035	51856	90132	21086	96808
42013	35035	19893	14783	50447	37474	37616	77744	44506	5727
93659	18359	94140	92910	74259	76318	31448	65133	47542	14312

334

TABLE A.2 NORMALLY DISTRIBUTED RANDOM VARIATES, $\mu = 0,\ \sigma = 1$

1.71648	-1.33170	1.07306	1.58042	-1.43516	1.45585	-0.51436	-0.99189	-1.29397	0.77315
-1.73813	-0.54027	0.55555	-0.65354	-0.78132	0.18979	-1.47266	0.11538	-0.35698	-0.24716
-0.74550	0.68742	-0.80876	-0.80876	-0.00360	0.11434	-2.62138	-0.09607	0.16903	-0.01439
-0.55222	-0.02719	1.34539	-0.15431	0.18872	0.40392	1.12159	2.23587	0.11953	-1.01369
1.71438	0.66586	1.50306	1.36644	0.44200	1.05033	-0.56470	-0.46048	0.65293	-0.98963
-1.62146	1.02796	1.21487	-1.98693	1.16107	1.20166	0.23805	0.15671	1.66661	0.79802
-1.85603	-0.61613	-1.13629	-1.82099	0.96172	0.15016	0.87185	-0.24282	-0.29850	0.43202
0.70102	-0.25520	0.73838	-0.05188	1.26263	-0.67420	-0.86111	1.27395	1.42200	0.11800
-0.33179	-1.46614	-1.81486	1.31641	-0.78344	0.45335	1.22713	0.13180	0.18966	-1.89884
-2.46673	-1.72077	0.43004	0.25085	-1.46866	-0.61383	0.76436	0.16811	0.46224	0.45422
-0.40532	0.53820	-0.51448	0.68423	1.19405	-0.01106	-1.22396	-0.62401	-0.32934	1.06287
-0.58156	0.05084	-0.71958	0.39436	0.91565	0.63693	0.66671	-0.12468	0.37895	-0.19138
0.59156	0.14998	-0.11586	-0.30824	-1.32124	0.65388	0.50440	1.18535	1.27921	0.45197
0.63957	0.80327	-0.84253	0.34068	1.23003	-0.11559	-0.52538	-0.41183	-0.14701	1.36110
-1.23876	0.81061	0.54871	-0.97316	0.68939	-1.17361	0.65062	0.33880	-1.32791	-0.31493
1.65689	-0.26334	-1.15926	-0.14205	0.62721	-0.34420	-0.03578	0.49290	-1.60911	0.23506
-1.47786	-0.58648	-0.50586	-0.42965	1.88544	-0.39147	-1.62963	-0.13425	-0.12153	0.89014
0.18468	0.53360	0.56816	-0.12864	-0.21279	-2.66878	-0.64096	-1.03714	-0.06503	-0.41441
0.40964	-0.89723	-0.39989	-0.45845	-0.17572	0.11226	0.11226	0.09291	0.25293	-0.00934
-1.07800	0.50921	0.27916	-1.47693	0.00647	-0.55704	-0.81963	-0.39484	0.54359	-1.76433
-0.56235	0.53449	-0.03781	-0.28263	-0.64709	-1.44950	-1.25988	-0.00070	-0.91045	0.24058
-0.91937	0.33473	-0.24904	-0.85226	-0.47128	-1.25988	-0.31990	2.14058	-0.99917	-0.64906
-0.51845	1.26822	1.01385	0.10038	-0.75033	-1.42594	2.14058	0.31990	0.77307	2.14552
1.22276	0.26882	-0.87242	-0.60597	-0.16689	0.45156	-1.02550	-0.65409	0.87829	0.64778
1.32965	0.12343	0.48868	0.64714	1.41386	0.09315	2.06977	-0.20197	-1.12086	-0.13956
0.06034	0.38254	0.27159	1.34904	1.09384	-0.11881	-2.71249	-1.05718	-0.48185	-0.29956
-1.15365	0.58500	0.65198	0.00561	-0.40296	-0.61314	-0.64784	-0.50026	-1.05718	0.93444
-0.00145	-0.39907	0.69114	-0.24988	0.78550	-2.12662	0.92632	0.87420	0.24453	0.64679
2.71450	-0.91712	-0.09154	0.72329	-0.51683	0.65343	0.68982	-0.41774	-0.37943	0.20260
-0.81069	0.63601	0.02547	-0.49848	-0.52361	0.64708	0.60054	2.31734	0.32482	0.87054
-0.23523	-1.38973	-0.17247	0.05711	0.80017	-1.43786	2.31734	0.67534	-1.59603	0.95059
0.17318	-1.75785	-0.48832	1.84641	1.98579	0.12760	2.54210	-0.79695	1.01304	-0.36977
-0.23868	-0.38919	0.82004	-1.58783	0.43750	0.54207	0.60471	-1.49329	0.47658	-2.47903
-1.51375	-1.02318	-0.51494	0.27593	-1.36099	0.07174	1.20259	-1.41889	1.05664	0.82140
0.66034	0.76606	1.11162	0.29105	-2.09082	-0.50734	-0.48509	0.11868	-0.06955	-0.28581
2.03513	0.31958	-1.54857	-0.11860	-0.86771	-0.55283	-0.50734	0.22218	0.08034	2.28098
2.00286	1.89884	3.53464	0.47706	-1.44733	-0.38721	-0.38721	-1.04392	0.24022	-0.83839
-0.31140	0.12808	1.20514	-2.99727	-0.29095	-0.12799	0.39311	-1.33080	0.89763	0.00647
1.36656	-2.65711	1.20036	0.82757	-0.17167	-1.01621	1.72748	0.83804	0.70392	0.35477
0.71100	3.25985	-1.65150	-0.96652	0.96652	-0.78303	-2.73619	0.85297	0.75580	0.50066
-1.01510	3.11903	-0.40846	-1.38708	0.59376	-1.05153	2.57717	-0.60095	-1.25018	0.38022
-0.46931	-0.72984	-0.13393	-2.14274	-0.98830	2.57717	0.12274	1.65157	-1.42599	-0.37654
1.00445	2.95047	-2.95047	1.73506	-0.26155	0.22127	0.52309	1.10658	0.60699	-0.63870
1.56860	-0.66106	-1.31186	0.40771	0.41669	0.54084	0.17993	0.12235	-0.18684	-1.75149
0.46811	-0.55070	0.44935	1.20738	0.58053	-0.20566	2.78693	1.18820	0.17491	0.71653
0.53914	-0.35390	-1.76717	0.34197	0.97523	0.03749	-0.15529	-0.32184	0.05470	1.35381
0.29653	-0.99160	0.66192	-0.57463	-1.43049	-0.32362	0.22556	0.22556	1.01133	0.72330
0.65728	0.42669	2.32798	0.22118	0.61346	-0.13014	-0.74257	-0.37818	-0.81889	0.40862
0.66385	0.02935	0.63201	0.63201	0.22118	0.22556	-0.24304	-0.14740	0.01680	-0.46821
0.51972	0.73216	-0.97054	-1.01783	-0.57737	1.35574	-0.60971	-0.60971	-0.72372	0.18993

335

TABLE A.2 (*Cont.*)

-0.14848	1.75252	-0.03263	3.43919	-0.99915	0.12627	0.68640	0.29326	0.35213	0.46595
-0.15636	-0.10648	-1.27457	0.12069	-0.08225	-0.44648	0.66616	-0.80657	-0.54292	-1.83306
0.58156	-0.66422	-0.50329	0.73796	0.66946	0.57219	-0.65529	-2.85028	0.10042	0.99701
0.00819	1.51408	-0.56498	0.29161	-0.33635	0.18282	1.40831	0.61286	0.60134	0.51832
0.19934	-0.95310	0.14401	0.42978	0.53175	0.18893	2.02068	-1.39455	0.49320	-0.01742
1.10284	1.07321	1.19672	2.29889	1.72338	0.23924	0.47686	-1.28572	0.40393	0.53300
0.85601	-0.85276	-0.51143	2.02063	-0.88046	1.15101	-0.34864	-1.26227	0.85169	0.43907
0.27800	1.53794	-1.35163	0.83144	-0.03941	1.55847	-0.72474	-0.70350	0.29771	0.62097
0.71740	-1.80814	-2.16080	-0.05749	-0.09406	0.59497	-1.09554	-0.32820	0.86613	0.37624
1.34474	1.34564	-1.12238	0.42935	0.05612	-0.64358	1.45062	1.56206	1.49201	0.64755
-0.08053	0.99529	0.77500	-0.30178	-0.01590	-1.41920	0.77050	0.65045	-0.82900	-0.21432
-0.59544	0.45811	-0.08618	-0.47433	-1.64500	-1.38333	-1.80860	1.89571	-0.02272	-0.03775
1.42078	-0.49120	-0.81857	1.16962	-0.27856	1.62091	0.24770	1.03350	-0.01332	0.95822
-0.77699	-0.80382	-0.55654	0.55348	0.18165	-0.60011	-0.16185	-0.09873	0.33673	-0.19950
0.24106	-1.56620	-1.52166	-0.39409	-0.19363	0.47632	0.92940	-0.36755	-0.61242	0.27181
0.12673	-0.03573	0.47517	-0.03298	0.34510	0.18458	0.03000	-0.59048	0.91512	0.61164
-0.73874	0.14222	1.57630	-1.57864	-0.40500	0.05429	2.46640	0.59480	0.05765	-0.71585
-0.43855	-0.93995	1.81000	2.22071	-0.88681	-1.66458	0.60961	-0.57395	-0.02432	0.70108
-0.40343	0.62771	0.03221	0.26227	-0.92739	1.56073	0.79330	-0.55709	0.09924	0.66378
-0.41509	0.42798	-0.71581	1.58268	-0.04238	0.57122	-0.51721	0.72006	1.05770	-0.61542
0.55899	-0.47756	-1.34493	1.04867	-1.55915	-0.90554	0.02398	0.72066	-0.96183	-1.50333
-1.02417	-0.49121	0.79787	-1.07079	0.90863	1.51932	0.71322	-2.24276	1.25105	-1.41493
0.25974	-0.70065	0.00440	0.89418	0.38600	-1.14269	0.23249	-0.28567	-0.24505	-0.15974
0.58151	1.44704	0.03800	-0.11410	0.05015	-0.30831	0.56627	1.23199	-0.38980	-0.14984
1.03418	0.38325	-0.23394	-0.06229	-0.69203	1.65747	0.26627	1.02901	-2.05391	1.28293
2.33482	1.59516	-0.16381	0.14811	0.58620	0.56073	-0.58605	-0.31083	0.04592	-1.88948
-0.71370	-1.47710	0.34754	-0.75723	-1.45430	0.85793	-1.33153	-0.53305	-0.39816	-1.13852
-0.01617	0.24040	1.05169	-1.00440	0.72108	-1.01425	-0.68148	-0.55305	0.28510	0.85059
0.62591	-0.05534	-0.50306	-1.46431	-1.96500	0.01912	0.42636	-1.12894	1.97402	1.45640
1.61277	0.67942	-0.13743	0.44896	0.60895	1.34324	-1.15417	-0.02538	-0.90192	-0.00952
-0.76405	-1.53378	1.17878	-0.37857	0.23156	0.45605	1.07771	-0.79732	1.22985	-0.22143
0.15565	1.81018	-1.26690	-1.36584	-0.38238	0.02327	0.49131	-1.67404	-0.26794	0.34147
-0.55450	0.08678	-1.29459	0.34984	-0.20697	0.41749	-1.32414	0.10455	0.04290	-2.68806
0.15727	-2.08333	-1.08357	-0.82657	0.77991	-0.21925	0.36623	0.42701	-1.84609	0.19862
-0.74299	0.73995	1.09647	0.00454	0.60641	-0.65527	-0.71020	0.83566	-0.10789	0.00975
0.15018	0.96971	0.19255	0.87070	-0.12082	2.21327	2.21327	-1.20754	0.22396	1.35454
-0.14967	-0.71898	-1.04735	0.87572	0.33465	1.11154	-0.39603	-0.19813	-0.53398	1.18003
1.63417	-0.24130	-0.61632	0.51841	0.51841	1.17202	0.03240	0.50796	-1.23370	-1.00044
-0.77445	-0.46709	1.28394	-1.59233	-1.47252	1.10567	0.23287	-0.08027	-1.02505	-0.17911
-0.61304	0.01925	-0.57606	-0.67866	-0.82380	1.11503	-0.59230	1.02462	0.10949	0.20596
0.53682	-1.44595	0.81188	-0.35529	-1.03544	2.77781	2.77781	-0.69018	1.05155	0.37102
0.10528	1.45176	0.38156	-1.51803	-0.35399	0.05654	0.06245	-0.86536	-0.03704	1.36585
-0.42575	-0.82324	-0.52394	0.70902	-1.11953	0.65121	0.371C8	-1.00054	-0.01421	-0.97299
0.60854	-0.12635	1.27620	-0.07343	-0.01586	0.05443	1.01073	0.56123	0.36768	0.85394
0.66247	-0.32369	1.12995	-0.25964	-0.31616	-0.84910	1.63780	-1.22958	-0.28960	0.98406
0.18366	0.22833	0.09195	0.59561	0.84374	0.33758	0.92063	-0.94988	-2.42044	1.01999
-1.76747	0.14303	-0.52352	0.39594	0.78532	-0.86178	0.65072	0.88388	-0.48011	-0.73430
-0.07944	-0.34117	0.71100	1.68729	-0.52265	-0.35374	2.47852	0.70971	-0.15441	1.17749
-0.45838	0.10739	-0.73481	-0.15865	1.49441	-0.10688	-0.76107	0.26565	2.04714	-1.57069
1.25960	1.16617	0.27897	-1.24673	-0.01148	-0.22633	-1.36324	0.57307	-1.89693	0.06371

Appendix B Inventory Simulation Program

General Description of Program

The program is designed to simulate the operation of an inventory of one product at one stock point. Various options are available with regard to character of lead times for filling replenishment orders, character of demand, and the handling of shortages of inventory. Various output options are also available to permit reporting of each transaction, periodic status reports, and a final summary as desired.

Costs may be assigned to placing replenishment orders, receiving replenishment orders, entering backorders, losing orders because of inventory shortages or excessive time on backorder, and carrying inventory. These costs may be reported as the transactions occur and are summarized at the end of each simulation run. The order quantity and order point are selected at the beginning of each run and stay constant throughout the run.

After the initial data for a run have been entered, the program follows a fixed cycle in handling transactions for each period of time. The cycle is followed for succeeding periods until the specified number of periods for the simulation run have been attained. The sequence of operations in each period is as follows:

1. The file of replenishment orders is checked to determine whether any orders are due in. The oldest order in the replenishment order queue is checked first; if it is due in, the quantity on order is added to inventory and the next oldest order in the queue is checked to see whether it is due in. The checking continues until the queue is exhausted or an order is found which is not due in until a later time period. At this point checking terminates and the orders, if any, remaining in the queue are moved up to any positions which may have been vacated.

2. If one of the two shortage options has been chosen which permits backordering of demand that cannot be filled from inventory, a check is made to see whether any backorders are outstanding. If there are backorders outstanding, these are filled from inventory starting with the oldest backorders until either the inventory is exhausted or all outstanding backorders are filled. If any backorders remain outstanding, these are moved up to any positions that may have been vacated in the backorder queue.

3. Depending on the demand option chosen, demand for the period is obtained either from the next item in a list of demands or by generating a random number and selecting the quantity demanded using the cumulative distribution of demand. Demand for the period is subtracted from inventory on hand.

4. If the inventory on hand is not sufficient to fill the demand for the period, the amount of demand that cannot be filled is either lost or backordered, depending on the shortage option chosen.

337

5. If one of the two shortage options is chosen which permits backorders, the unfilled demand is placed as a single order at the end of the backorder queue. (The program allows for a maximum of 100 orders in the back-order queue at any one time. Should this maximum be reached, subsequent orders are added to the one-hundredth order in the queue.]

6. If the shortage option is chosen which provides for losing backorders from the backorder queue, each backorder, starting with the oldest, is checked to see whether it stays in the queue or drops from the queue. The determination of whether a backorder stays or is dropped is made by comparing a random number with the probability of loss of an order that has been on backorder for the number of periods that the order has been in the backorder queue. If any backorders drop from the queue and if there are backorders remaining, these are moved up to fill any positions that may have been vacated in the backorder queue.

7. The number of periods of time which have elapsed since the inventory level was last checked for possible placement of a replenishment order is compared with the interval between reviews. If the prescribed time between reviews has elapsed, the status of inventory level, replenishment orders outstanding, and backorders outstanding are checked against the order quantity to see whether a replenishment order should be placed (see step 8). If the prescribed time between reviews has not elapsed, the sequence of operations for the period terminates and begins again for the next period.

8. If the inventory on hand plus on order minus the outstanding backorders is not below the order point, the sequence of operations for the period terminates and begins again for the next period. If the inventory on hand plus on order minus the outstanding backorders is below the order point, a replenishment order is generated for the amount of the order quantity and is placed at the end of the replenishment order queue. Depending on the option chosen, the lead time for the replenishment order is obtained either from the next item in a list of lead times or by generating a random number and selecting the lead time by using the cumulative distribution of the lead time. If there are other replenishment orders outstanding, the due-in date of the order being placed is compared with that of the last order in the replenishment queue. If the due-in date of the order being placed is earlier than that of the last order in the replenishment queue, the due-in date of the order being placed is changed to that of the last order in the replenishment queue. If the quantity ordered is not sufficient to bring the inventory on hand plus on order minus backorders above the order point, the quantity of the order being placed is increased in increments of the amount of the order quantity until the on hand plus on order minus backorders are above the order point. (The program allows for a maximum of 100 orders in the replenishment order queue at any one time. Should this maximum be reached, subsequent orders are added to the one-hundredth order in the queue.)

Input for Simulation Run

For each simulation run, the options to be used on the run and the data for the run are entered on cards in the following sequence. The program is so constructed that data for as many separate runs as are desired may be placed one behind the other; the program will continue from run to run until all of the runs for which data are supplied are completed. *Each run requires all of the following cards, except those which are optional.* The program allows complete freedom to change options and data as desired from run to run. *All numbers must* be punched *with the decimal point.* The location of the numbers within the columns indicated is not critical as long as the decimal point is punched.

Card number	Columns	Punching instructions
1	50–70	The program automatically places the title INVENTORY SIMULATION on the output. Further identification of the run is punched in the location shown and will be printed on the following line.
2	1–7	Punch 1.0 if only a printout of the summary of the run is desired.
		Punch 2.0 if a printout of each transaction plus a summary of the run is desired.
		Punch 3.0 if a printout of periodic status reports plus a summary of the run is desired. (The number of periods between the status reports is specified on card #3.)
		Punch 4.0 if a printout of each transaction plus periodic status reports plus a summary of the run is desired. (The number of periods between the status reports is specified on card #3.)
	8–14	Punch 1.0 if it is desired to specify the exact sequence of lead times to be used in the simulation run. [The sequence of lead times is specified on card(s) #5.]
		Punch 2.0 if it is desired that the program should select lead times randomly from the cumulative distribution of lead times. [The cumulative distribution of lead times is specified on card(s) #5.]
	15–21	Punch 1.0 if it is desired to specify the exact sequence of demands to be used in the simulation run. [The sequence of demands is specified on card(s) #6.]
		Punch 2.0 if it is desired that the program should select demands in each period randomly using the cumulative distribution of demand. [The cumulative distribution of demand is specified on cards(s) #6.]
	22–28	Punch 1.0 if it is desired that all demand that cannot be filled immediately from inventory on hand is to be lost. (The cost of losing each unit of demand is specified on card #4.)
		Punch 2.0 if it is desired that all demand that cannot be filled immediately from inventory is backordered until sufficient stock is available to fill the demand.

Card Number	Columns	Punching Instructions
		Punch 3.0 if it is desired that all demand that cannot be filled immediately from inventory is backordered, but that backorders have a specified probability of being lost in the period in which they are placed and in all succeeding periods while they are waiting to be filled. [The cost of losing each unit of demand is specified on card #4. The probability of a backorder being canceled in the period in which it is placed or in any succeeding period is specified on card(s) #7.]
3	1–7	Punch the number of periods in the simulation run.
	8–14	If any of the following options are chosen, the program will be required to generate random numbers:
	15–21	Lead time option 2 (i.e., card #2, cols. 8–14, is punched 2.0). Demand option 2 (i.e., card #2, cols. 15–21, is punched 2.0). Shortage option 3 (i.e., eard #2, cols. 22–28, is punched 3.0).
		When any of these options are chosen, the required random numbers are generated by using a random number generator subroutine from the system library tape. (Note that the FORTRAN program included in this writeup does not include the subroutine itself. If this subroutine is not already on the system library tape where it will be available when the FORTRAN program is compiled, the user must supply the subroutine.)
		If the options chosen require the generation of random numbers, punch any number *larger than* 100.0 in cols. 8–14. Punch any number between zero and 100.0 in cols. 15–21. Punching different numbers in these columns on different simulation runs will produce different sets of random numbers.
		If no random numbers are required because of the options chosen, punch 0.0 in both cols. 8–14 and cols. 15–21.
	22–28	If either output option 3 or 4 is chosen (i.e., card #2, cols. 1–7, is punched 3.0 or 4.0), punch the number of periods which are to elapse between status reports.
		If either output option 1 or 2 is chosen (i.e., card #2, cols. 1–7, is punched 1.0 or 2.0), punch 0.0.
4	1–7	Punch the price or value (in dollars) of a unit of the stock item being simulated.
	8–14	Punch the beginning inventory at the start of the simulation.
	15–21	Punch the order point.
	22–28	Punch the order quantity.
	29–35	Punch the number of periods that are to elapse

Appendix B (*Cont.*)

Card Number	Columns	Punching Instructions
		between reviews of the stock level for possible placement of a replenishment order. If a review is to take place every period, punch 1.0.
	36–42	Punch the cost of placing a replenishment order. This cost is assumed to be independent of the number of units ordered.
	43–49	Punch the cost of receiving a replenishment order. This cost is assumed to be independent of the number of units ordered.
	50–56	If either shortage option 2 or 3 is chosen (i.e., card #2, cols. 22–28, is punched 2.0 or 3.0), punch the cost of entering a backorder. This cost is assumed to be independent of the number of units backordered. If shortage option 1 is chosen (i.e., card #2, cols. 22–28, is punched 1.0), punch 0.0.
	57–63	If either shortage option 1 or 3 is chosen (i.e., card #2, cols. 22–28, is punched 1.0 or 3.0), punch the cost of losing each unit of demand.
		If shortage option 2 is chosen (i.e., card #2, cols. 22–28, is punched 2.0), punch 0.0.
	64–70	Punch the interest rate *per time period*.
5 (Punch as many cards as required up to a maximum of 1000.)	1–7 8–14	If lead time option 1 is chosen (i.e., card #2, cols. 8–14, is punched 1.0), punch the sequence of lead times in cols. 1–7, one lead time per card. The *last card* in the sequence should also have 1.0 punched in cols. 8–14. It is important to estimate the number of lead times that will be required during the simulation run so that a sufficient number are entered.
		If lead time option 2 is chosen (i.e., card #2, cols. 8–14, is punched 2.0), punch the lead time in cols. 1–7 and the corresponding cumulative probability in cols. 8–14, one pair per card. The cards must be arranged in order of increasing cumulative probability, and the last card must have 1.0 as the cumulative probability.
6 (Punch as many cards as required up to a maximum of 1000.)	1–7 8–14	If demand option 1 is chosen (i.e., card #2, cols. 15–21, is punched 1.0), punch the sequence of demands in cols. 1–7, one demand per card. The *last card* in the sequence should also have 1.0 punched in cols. 8–14. The number of demands must be the same as the number of periods in the simulation run as specified on card #3, cols. 1–7.
		If demand option 2 is chosen (i.e., card #2, cols. 15–21, is punched 2.0), punch the demand in cols. 1–7 and the corresponding cumulative probability in cols. 8–14, one pair per card. The cards must be arranged in order of increasing cumulative probability, and the last card must have 1.0 as the cumulative probability.
7	1–7	If shortage option 3 is chosen (i.e., card #2,

341

Card number	Columns	Punching Instructions
(Punch as many cards as required up to a maximum of 100.)	8–14	cols. 22–28, is punched 3.0), punch the probabilities that backorders will be cancelled in the period in which placed and in each succeeding period. The first probability in the sequence of probabilities is the probability that the backorder is cancelled in the period in which the order is placed; the second probability is the probability that the backorder is cancelled in the period after the order is placed, provided that it was not cancelled in the previous period, and so forth. The period (starting with 0.0) is punched in cols. 1–7 and the probability of cancellation is punched in cols. 8–14, one pair per card. The last card must have 1.0 as the probability of cancellation.

If either shortage option 1 or 2 is chosen (i.e., card #2, cols. 22–28, is punched 1.0 or 2.0), this card is not used. *Omit this card completely; do not insert a blank card.* |

FORTRAN VOCABULARY

AVGINV	Average inventory
BKOCST	Cost of entering backorder
BKOSER	Service interval on backorders (average number of periods to fill backorders)
CARCST	Inventory carrying cost
CSTNRC	Cost for receiving n replenishment orders
CSTQLO	Cost of losing n units of demand
CUMDEM(I)	Cumulative probability of ith demand occurring
CUMLDT(I)	Cumulative probability of ith lead time occurring
IDEMND(I) ZDEMND(I)	The ith demand
IDEMOP ZDEMOP	Demand option
IDMAND ZDMAND	Demand in the nth period
IDUEIN(I)	Time at which the ith order in the replenishment queue is due in
ZINTRT	Interest rate per time period
ILDTIM(I) ZLDTIM(I)	The ith lead time
ILDTOP ZLDTOP	Lead time option
ZLOCST	Cost of lost demand per unit
NBOCAN	Number of backorders canceled in any time period
NBOQUE	Number of orders in the backorder queue
NBOSAT	Number of backorders filled in one time period
INDCAY ZNDCAY	Number of periods for which a probability of loss of a backorder is specified
INDEMD ZNDEMD	Number of demands entered either as a sequence of demands or in a cumulative probability distribution

INLDTM	Number of lead times entered either as a sequence of lead
ZNLDTM	times or in a cumulative probability distribution
NRPQUE	Number of orders in the replenishment queue
INPERD	Total number of periods for which simulation will run
ZNPERD	
INRECP	Number of replenishment orders received in one time period
ZNRECP	
ORDCST	Cost of placing a replenishment order
IORDPT	Order point
ZORDPT	
IORDPR	Quantity ordered in any single period
IORDQN	Order quantity
ZORDQN	
IOUTOP	Output option
ZOUTOP	
PRBBOL(I)	Probability of losing backorder on the IPRSBO(I) th day after
	order is placed
IPRSBO(I)	Number of days since backorder was placed associated with
ZPRSBO(I)	ith value of PRBBOL
IPERBO	Number of periods plus one since a backorder was placed
PRICE	Price of item (in dollars)
IPRIOD	Clock time in number of periods since start of simulation
ZPRIOD	
IQLOST	Amount of demand lost on one transaction
ZQLOST	
IQNBKO(I)	Quantity backordered on the ith backorder in the backorder
	queue
IQNINV	Inventory on hand
ZQNINV	
QNINV	
IQNORD(I)	Quantity ordered on the ith replenishment order in the reple-
	nishment order queue
IQNREC	Number of units received in one time period
IQNSHT	Quantity short for one transaction and placed on backorder
RANDOM	Random number
RECCST	Cost of receiving replenishment order
IRPINT	Interval between status reports
ZRPINT	
IRVINT	Interval between reviews
ZRVINT	
SBOCST	Total backordering cost for simulation run
ISBOFL	Cumulative sum of number of units of demand filled after
ZSBOFL	being placed on backorder
ZSDEMD	Cumulative sum of demand
SERFAC	Service factor (fraction of total demand filled)
ISHTOP	Shortage option
ZSHTOP	
ZSINON	Cumulative sum of inventory quantity on hand
SLOCST	Total lost order cost for simulation run
ISLOST	Cumulative sum of demand not filled and lost
ZSLOST	
ISNBKO	Cumulative sum of number of backorders entered
ZSNBKO	

343

ISNORD	Cumulative sum of number of replenishment orders placed
ZSNORD	
ISNREC	Cumulative sum of number of replenishment orders received
ZSNREC	
SORCST	Total ordering cost for simulation run
ISQNBO	Sum of quantity backordered at any time
ZSQNBO	
ISQORD	Sum of quantity on order at any time
SRCCST	Total receiving cost for simulation run
ISUDLY	Product of the number of units of demand backordered times
ZSUDLY	the number of periods on backorder before being filled
ITMBKO(I)	Period in which the ith backorder in the backorder queue was placed
TOTCST	Total cost for simulation run
TOTSER	Service interval on all orders (average number of periods to fill all orders)
X	First number used to start random number sequence
Y	Second number used to start random number sequence

PROGRAM LISTING

```
C
C INVENTORY SIMULATION PROGRAM  -- ISP3
C
C     DIMENSION SUBSCRIPTED VARIABLES
C
      DIMENSION ZLDTIM(1000),  ILDTIM(1000),  CUMLDT(1000),
     1 ZDEMND(1000),  IDEMND(1000),  CUMDEM(1000),
     2 ZPRSBO(100),  IPRSBO(100),  PRBBOL(100),
     3 IDUEIN(100),  IQNORD(100),  ITMBKO(100),  IQNBKO(100)
C
C     INPUT AND OUTPUT FORMAT STATEMENTS
C
  100 FORMAT (1H1 48X,20HINVENTORY SIMULATION )
  101 FORMAT (1H 48X,20H                     )
  102 FORMAT (10F7.2)
  103 FORMAT (1H0 52X,14HRUN INPUT DATA   //)
  104 FORMAT (4H X = F8.2)
  105 FORMAT (4H Y = F8.2)
  106 FORMAT (24H INITIAL RANDOM NUMBER = F10.6)
  107 FORMAT (25H NUMBER OF TIME PERIODS = I4 )
  108 FORMAT (27H INTERVAL BETWEEN REVIEWS = I3)
  109 FORMAT (16H PRICE OF ITEM = F11.2,3X,8HPER UNIT )
  110 FORMAT (22H BEGINNING INVENTORY = I7,3X,5HUNITS)
  111 FORMAT (14H ORDER POINT = I7,3X,5HUNITS )
  112 FORMAT (17H ORDER QUANTITY = I7,3X,5HUNITS )
  113 FORMAT (38H COST OF PLACING REPLENISHMENT ORDER = F9.2 )
  114 FORMAT (40H COST OF RECEIVING REPLENISHMENT ORDER = F9.2)
  115 FORMAT (29H COST OF ENTERING BACKORDER = F9.2)
  116 FORMAT (22H COST OF LOST DEMAND = F9.2,3X,8HPER UNIT )
  117 FORMAT (32H INTEREST COST PER TIME PERIOD = F9.6 )
  118 FORMAT (1H0,5X,9HLEAD TIME,10X,20HCUMULATIVE FREQUENCY/(8X,I3,19X,
     1F7.4))
  119 FORMAT (1H0,6X,6HDEMAND,11X,20HCUMULATIVE FREQUENCY /(7X,I4,19X,
     1F7.4))
  120 FORMAT (20HOPERIODS BACKORDERED,5X,19HPROBABILITY OF LOSS /
     1(8X,I3,19X,F7.4))
  129 FORMAT (7HOPERIOD,7X,7HON HAND,6X,8HON ORDER,5X,8HQUANTITY,6X,
     16HDUE IN//)
  130 FORMAT (7HOPERIOD,7X,7HON HAND,6X,8HON ORDER,6X,7HORDERED,6X,
     16HDUE IN,6X,8HRECEIVED,5X,8HDEMANDED,5X,4HLOST,10X,4HCOST//)
  131 FORMAT (1H I5,I15,I14,31X,I8,29X,F9.2)
  132 FORMAT (1H I5,I15,I14,44X,I8)
  133 FORMAT (1H I5,I15,I14,44X,I8,I10,4X,F11.2)
  134 FORMAT (1H I5,I15,I14,I13,I12,43X,F9.2)
  139 FORMAT (7HOPERIOD,6X,7HON HAND,4X,8HON ORDER,3X,8HQUANTITY,5X,
     16HDUE IN,28X,12HON BACKORDER,6X,8HQUANTITY,3X,6HPERIOD//)
  140 FORMAT (7HOPERIOD,6X,7HON HAND,4X,8HON ORDER,4X,7HORDERED,5X,
     16HDUE IN,5X,8HRECEIVED,4X,8HDEMANDED,3X,12HON BACKORDER,3X,
     211HBACKORDERED,6X,4HCOST//)
  141 FORMAT (1H I5,I14,I12,27X,I8,12X,I15,16X,F9.2)
  142 FORMAT (1H I5,I14,I12,50X,I12)
  143 FORMAT (1H I5,I14,I12,39X,I8,I15)
  144 FORMAT (1H I5,I14,I12,39X,I8,I15,I14,2X,F9.2)
  145 FORMAT (1H I5,I14,I12,I11,I11,56X,F9.2)
  149 FORMAT (7HOPERIOD,4X,7HON HAND,4X,8HON ORDER,3X,8HQUANTITY,4X,
     16HDUE IN,26X,12HON BACKORDER,6X,8HQUANTITY,8X,6HPERIOD//)
  150 FORMAT (7HOPERIOD,4X,7HON HAND,4X,8HON ORDER,4X,7HORDERED,4X,
     16HDUE IN,4X,8HRECEIVED,3X,8HDEMANDED,3X,12HON BACKORDER,3X,
     211HBACKORDERED,3X,4HLOST,6X,4HCOST//)
  151 FORMAT (1H I5,I12,I12,25X,I8,14X,I12,23X,F9.2)
```

```
152 FORMAT (1H I5,I12,I12,47X,I12)
153 FORMAT (1H I5,I12,I12,36X,I8,I15)
154 FORMAT (1H I5,I12,I12,36X,I8,I15,I14,9X,F9.2)
155 FORMAT (1H I5,I12,I12,36X,I8,I15,17X,I4,2X,F9.2)
156 FORMAT (1H I5,I12,I12,47X,I12,14X,I7,2X,F9.2)
157 FORMAT (1H I5,I12,I12,I11,I10,61X,F9.2)
160 FORMAT (1H0,49X,20H    RUN SUMMARY        )
161 FORMAT (15H0TOTAL DEMAND = F10.0)
162 FORMAT (20H AVERAGE INVENTORY = F9.2,31X,19HCARRYING COST      =
   1F11.2)
163 FORMAT (19H NUMBER OF ORDERS = I5,36X,19HORDERING COST      =
   1F11.2)
164 FORMAT (21H NUMBER OF RECEIPTS = I5,34X,19HRECEIVING COST     =
   1F11.2)
165 FORMAT (14H DEMAND LOST = I7,39X,19HLOST DEMAND COST   = F11.2)
166 FORMAT (17H SERVICE FACTOR = F5.2)
167 FORMAT (23H NUMBER OF BACKORDERS = I5,32X,19HBACKORDERING COST =
   1F11.2)
168 FORMAT (47H AVERAGE NUMBER OF PERIODS TO FILL BACKORDERS = F7.2)
169 FORMAT (47H AVERAGE NUMBER OF PERIODS TO FILL ALL ORDERS = F7.2)
170 FORMAT (1H0 59X,19HTOTAL COST           = F11.2)
180 FORMAT (1H0,I5,I15,I14/(40X,I8,I12))
181 FORMAT (1H0,I5,I14,I12,50X,I12)
182 FORMAT (1H ,34X,I8,I11)
183 FORMAT (1H ,99X,I8,I9)
184 FORMAT (1H0,I5,I12,I12,47X,I12)
185 FORMAT (1H ,32X,I8,I10)
186 FORMAT (1H ,94X,I8,I14)
190 FORMAT (1H0,49X,20H    TRANSACTIONS      )
191 FORMAT (1H0,49X,20H    STATUS REPORTS    )
192 FORMAT (1H0,49X,20H    STATUS REPORT     )
195 FORMAT (1H0,5X,47HERROR IN INPUT OF OPTIONS FOR RUN. CHECK CARDS.)
C
C     SET UP RUN HEADING
C
    1 WRITE (6,100)
      READ (5,101)
      WRITE (6,101)
C
C     READ OPTIONS
C
      READ (5,102)ZOUTOP,ZLDTOP,ZDEMOP,ZSHTOP
      IOUTOP = ZOUTOP
      ILDTOP = ZLDTOP
      IDEMOP = ZDEMOP
      ISHTOP = ZSHTOP
C
C     CHECK FOR ILLEGAL OPTIONS
C
      IF(IOUTOP.LT.1.OR.IOUTOP.GT.4) GO TO 998
      IF(ILDTOP.LT.1.OR.ILDTOP.GT.2) GO TO 998
      IF(IDEMOP.LT.1.OR.IDEMOP.GT.2) GO TO 998
      IF(ISHTOP.GE.1.AND.ISHTOP.LE.4) GO TO 13
  998 WRITE (6,195)
      RETURN
C
C     READ AND PRINT OTHER RUN PARAMETERS
C
   13 READ(5,102) ZNPERD, X, Y, ZRPINT
      INPERD = ZNPERD
```

```
      IRPINT = ZRPINT
      WRITE (6,103)
      IF(ILDTOP.EQ.2) GO TO 222
      IF(IDEMOP.EQ.2) GO TO 222
      IF(ISHTOP.LT.3) GO TO 223
  222 RANDOM = RANDM(X)
      WRITE (6,104)X
      WRITE (6,105)Y
      WRITE (6,106)RANDOM
  223 WRITE (6,107)INPERD
      READ (5,102)PRICE,ZQNINV,ZORDPT,ZORDQN,ZRVINT,ORDCST, RECCST,BKOCS
     1T,ZLOCST,ZINTRT
      IQNINV = ZQNINV
      IORDPT = ZORDPT
      IORDQN = ZORDQN
      IRVINT = ZRVINT
      WRITE (6,108)IRVINT
      WRITE (6,109)PRICE
      WRITE (6,110)IQNINV
      WRITE (6,111)IORDPT
      WRITE (6,112)IORDQN
      WRITE (6,113)ORDCST
      WRITE (6,114)RECCST
      IF(ISHTOP.EQ.1) GO TO 3
    2 WRITE (6,115)BKOCST
    3 IF(ISHTOP.EQ.2) GO TO 5
    4 WRITE (6,116)ZLOCST
    5 WRITE (6,117)ZINTRT
C
C     READ LEAD TIMES OR LEAD TIME DISTRIBUTION
C
      I=0
      INLDTM=0
  601 I=I+1
      READ(5,102) ZLDTIM(I), CUMLDT(I)
      INLDTM=I
      IF(CUMLDT(I).EQ.1.) GO TO 602
      GO TO 601
  602 DO 6 I=1,INLDTM
      ILDTIM(I) = ZLDTIM(I)
    6 CONTINUE
      IF(ILDTOP.EQ.1) GO TO 8
      WRITE (6,118)(ILDTIM(I),CUMLDT(I),I = 1,INLDTM)
C
C     READ DEMANDS OR DEMAND DISTRIBUTION
C
    8 I=0
      INDEMD=0
  603 I=I+1
      READ(5,102) ZDEMND(I), CUMDEM(I)
      INDEMD=I
      IF(CUMDEM(I).EQ.1.) GO TO 604
      GO TO 603
  604 DO 9 I=1,INDEMD
      IDEMND(I) = ZDEMND(I)
    9 CONTINUE
      IF(IDEMOP.EQ.1) GO TO 11
      WRITE (6,119)(IDEMND(I),CUMDEM(I),I = 1,INDEMD)
   11 IF(ISHTOP.LT.3) GO TO 14
C
```

```
C     READ ORDER DECAY PROBABILITIES
C
      I=0
      INDCAY=0
  605 I=I+1
      READ(5,102) ZPRSBO(I),PRBBOL(I)
      INDCAY=I
      IF(PRBBOL(I).EQ.1.) GO TO 608
      GO TO 605
  608 DO 607 I=1,INDCAY
      IPRSBO(I)=ZPRSBO(I)
  607 CONTINUE
  606 WRITE(6,120) (IPRSBO(I), PRBBOL(I), I=1, INDCAY)
C
C     SET VALUES TO ZERO
C
   14 ZSINON = 0
      ZSDEMD = 0
      ISNORD = 0
      ISNREC = 0
      ISDMSA = 0
      ISLOST = 0
      ISQORD = 0
      ISNBKO = 0
      ISQNBO = 0
      ISUDLY = 0
      ISBOFL = 0
      NRPQUE = 0
      NBOQUE = 0
      IPRIOD = 0
C
C     SET UP OUTPUT HEADINGS
C
      IF(IOUTOP.EQ.1) GO TO 15
      IF(IOUTOP.EQ.3) GO TO 329
      IF(IOUTOP.EQ.2.OR.IOUTOP.EQ.4) WRITE(6,190)
      IF(ISHTOP.EQ.1) WRITE(6,130)
      IF(ISHTOP.EQ.2) WRITE(6,140)
      IF(ISHTOP.EQ.3) WRITE(6,150)
      GO TO 15
  329 WRITE(6,191)
      IF(ISHTOP.EQ.1) WRITE(6,129)
      IF(ISHTOP.EQ.2) WRITE(6,139)
      IF(ISHTOP.EQ.3) WRITE(6,149)
C
C     SET CLOCKS
C
   15 DO 999 N = 1,INPERD
      IPRIOD = IPRIOD + 1
      IRVINT = IRVINT - 1
      IRPINT = IRPINT - 1
C
C     CHECK FOR ORDERS IN QUEUE
C
      IF(NRPQUE.LT.1) GO TO 16
   17 INRECP = 0
      IQNREC = 0
      DO 18 I = 1,NRPQUE
      IF((IPRIOD-IDUEIN(I)).LT.0) GO TO 20
C
```

```
C     RECEIVE ORDERS
C
   19 INRECP = INRECP + 1
      ISNREC = ISNREC + 1
      ISQORD = ISQORD - IQNORD(I)
      IQNINV = IQNINV + IQNORD(I)
      IQNREC = IQNREC + IQNORD(I)
   18 CONTINUE
   20 IF(INRECP.LT.1) GO TO 16
   21 NRPQUE = NRPQUE - INRECP
      ZNRECP = INRECP
      CSTNRC = RECCST * ZNRECP
      IF(NRPQUE.LT.1) GO TO 24
   22 DO 23 I = 1,NRPQUE
      IN = I + INRECP
      IQNORD(I) = IQNORD(IN)
      IDUEIN(I) = IDUEIN(IN)
   23 CONTINUE
   24 IF(IOUTOP.EQ.1.OR.IOUTOP.EQ.3) GO TO 29
      IF(ISHTOP.EQ.1) WRITE(6,131) IPRIOD,IQNINV,ISQORD,IQNREC,CSTNRC
      IF(ISHTOP.EQ.2) WRITE(6,141) IPRIOD,IQNINV,ISQORD,IQNREC,ISQNBO,
     1CSTNRC
      IF(ISHTOP.EQ.3) WRITE(6,151) IPRIOD,IQNINV,ISQORD,IQNREC,ISQNBO,
     1CSTNRC
   29 IF(ISQNBO.LT.1) GO TO 16
C
C     CHECK STATUS OF BACKORDERS
C
   31 NBOSAT = 0
      DO 32 I = 1,NBOQUE
      IQNINV = IQNINV - IQNBKO(I)
      IF(IQNINV.GE.0) GO TO 34
   33 ISQNBO = ISQNBO - IQNBKO(I) - IQNINV
      ISUDLY = ISUDLY +((IPRIOD - ITMBKO(I)) * (IQNBKO(I)+IQNINV))
      ISBOFL = ISBOFL + IQNBKO(I) + IQNINV
      IQNBKO(I) = -IQNINV
      IQNINV = 0
      GO TO 35
   34 ISQNBO = ISQNBO - IQNBKO(I)
      ISUDLY = ISUDLY + ((IPRIOD - ITMBKO(I)) * IQNBKO(I))
      ISBOFL = ISBOFL + IQNBKO(I)
      NBOSAT = NBOSAT + 1
      IF(IQNINV.LT.1) GO TO 35
   32 CONTINUE
   35 IF(IOUTOP.EQ.1.OR.IOUTOP.EQ.3) GO TO 39
      IF(ISHTOP.EQ.1) GO TO 16
      IF(ISHTOP.EQ.2) WRITE(6,142) IPRIOD,IQNINV,ISQORD,ISQNBO
      IF(ISHTOP.EQ.3) WRITE(6,152) IPRIOD,IQNINV,ISQORD,ISQNBO
   39 IF(NBOSAT.LT.1) GO TO 16
   40 NBOQUE = NBOQUE - NBOSAT
      IF(NBOQUE.LT.1) GO TO 16
   41 DO 42 I = 1,NBOQUE
      IN = I + NBOSAT
      IQNBKO(I) = IQNBKO(IN)
      ITMBKO(I) = ITMBKO(IN)
   42 CONTINUE
   16 IF(IDEMOP.EQ.2) GO TO 44
C
C     DETERMINE CURRENT DEMAND
C
```

PROGRAM LISTING (Cont.)

```
 43  IDMAND = IDEMND(N)
     GO TO 47
 44  RANDOM = RANDM(Y)
     DO 45 I = 1,INDEMD
     IF((RANDOM-CUMDEM(I)).LE.0.) GO TO 46
 45  CONTINUE
 46  IDMAND = IDEMND(I)
 47  IQNINV = IQNINV - IDMAND
     ZDMAND = IDMAND
     ZSDEMD = ZSDEMD + ZDMAND
     IF(IQNINV.LT.0) GO TO 53
 48  QNINV = IQNINV
     ZSINON = ZSINJN + QNINV
     IF(IOUTOP.EQ.1.OR.IOUTOP.EQ.3) GO TO 66
     IF(ISHTOP.EQ.1) WRITE(6,132) IPRIOD,IQNINV,ISQORD,IDMAND
     IF(ISHTOP.EQ.2) WRITE(6,143) IPRIOD,IQNINV,ISQORD,IDMAND,ISQNBO
     IF(ISHTOP.EQ.3) WRITE(6,153) IPRIOD,IQNINV,ISQORD,IDMAND,ISQNBO
     GO TO 66
 53  IF(ISHTOP.EQ.2) GO TO 58
     IF(ISHTOP.EQ.3) GO TO 55
C
C    COMPUTE SHORTAGES
C
 54  IQLOST = -IQNINV
     IQNINV = 0
     ISLOST = ISLOST + IQLOST
     ZQLOST = IQLOST
     CSTQLO = ZQLOST * ZLOCST
     IF(IOUTOP.EQ.1.OR.IOUTOP.EQ.3) GO TO 66
     IF(ISHTOP.EQ.2) GO TO 66
     IF(ISHTOP.EQ.1) WRITE(6,133) IPRIOD,IQNINV,ISQORD,IDMAND,IQLOST,
    1CSTQLO
     IF(ISHTOP.EQ.3) WRITE(6,155) IPRIOD,IQNINV,ISQORD,IDMAND,ISQNBO,
    1IQLOST,CSTQLO
     GO TO 66
 55  RANDOM = RANDM(Y)
     IF (RANDOM - PRBBOL(1)) 54,54,58
 58  ISNBKO = ISNBKO + 1
     ISQNBO = ISQNBO - IQNINV
     IF(NBOQUE.GT.99) GO TO 60
 59  NBOQUE = NBOQUE +1
     IQNBKO(NBOQUE) = -IQNINV
     ITMBKO(NBOQUE) = IPRIOD
     IQNSHT = -IQNINV
     IQNINV = 0
     GO TO 61
 60  IQNBKO(100) = IQNBKO(100) - IQNINV
     IQNSHT = -IQNINV
     IQNINV = 0
 61  IF(IOUTOP.EQ.1.OR.IOUTOP.EQ.3) GO TO 66
     IF(ISHTOP.EQ.1) GO TO 66
     IF(ISHTOP.EQ.2) WRITE(6,144) IPRIOD,IQNINV,ISQORD,IDMAND,ISQNBO,
    1IQNSHT,BKOCST
     IF(ISHTOP.EQ.3) WRITE(6,154) IPRIOD,IQNINV,ISQORD,IDMAND,ISQNBO,
    1IQNSHT,BKOCST
 66  IF(ISHTOP.LT.3) GO TO 70
C
C    DECAY BACKORDERS
C
     IF(NBOQUE.LT.1) GO TO 70
```

350

```
 68 NBOCAN = 0
    DO 69 I = 1,NBOQUE
    IF((IPRIOD-ITMBKO(I)).LT.1) GO TO 69
 71 RANDOM = RANDM(Y)
    IPERBO = IPRIOD - ITMBKO(I) + 1
    IF((RANDOM-PRBBOL(IPERBO)).GT.0.) GO TO 69
 72 NBOCAN = NBOCAN + 1
    ISQNBO = ISQNBO - IQNBKO(I)
    IQLOST = IQNBKO(I)
    ZQLOST = IQLOST
    ISLOST = ISLOST + IQLOST
    CSTQLD = ZLOCST * ZQLOST
    IQNBKO(I) = 0
    IF(IOUTOP.EQ.1.OR.IOUTOP.EQ.3) GO TO 69
 73 WRITE (6,156)IPRIOD,IQNINV,ISQORD,ISQNBO,IQLOST,CSTQLO
 69 CONTINUE
    IF(NBOCAN.LT.1) GO TO 70
    IF((NBOQUE-NBOCAN).LT.1) GO TO 70
 75 DO 79 I = 1,NBOQUE
    IF(IQNBKO(I).GT.0) GO TO 80
 76 L = I + 1
    DO 77 J = L,NBOQUE
    IF(IQNBKO(J).GT.0) GO TO 78
 77 CONTINUE
 78 IQNBKO(I) = IQNBKO(J)
    ITMBKO(I) = ITMBKO(J)
    IQNBKO(J) = 0
 79 CONTINUE
 80 NBOQUE = NBOQUE - NBOCAN
 70 IF(IRVINT.GT.0) GO TO 99
C
C      REVIEW INVENTORY LEVELS
C
 81 IRVINT = ZRVINT
    IORDPR = 0
 82 IF((IQNINV+ISQORD-ISQNBO-IORDPT).GT.0) GO TO 99
C
C      PLACE ORDER
C
 83 ISNORD = ISNORD + 1
    ISQORD = ISQORD + IORDQN
    IORDPR = IORDPR + IORDQN
    IF(NRPQUE.GT.99) GO TO 89
 84 NRPQUE = NRPQUE + 1
    IQNORD(NRPQUE) = IORDQN
    IF(ILDTOP.EQ.2) GO TO 86
C
C      DETERMINE DUE DATE
C
 85 IDUEIN(NRPQUE) = IPRIOD + ILDTIM(ISNORD)
    GO TO 250
 86 RANDOM = RANDM(Y)
    DO 87 I = 1,INLDTM
    IF((RANDOM-CUMLDT(I)).LE.0.) GO TO 88
 87 CONTINUE
 88 IDUEIN(NRPQUE) = IPRIOD + ILDTIM(I)
250 IF((IDUEIN(NRPQUE-1)-IDUEIN(NRPQUE)).LT.1) GO TO 90
251 IDUEIN(NRPQUE) = IDUEIN(NRPQUE - 1)
    GO TO 90
 89 IQNORD(100) = IQNORD(100) + IORDQN
```

```
 90 IF((IQNINV+ISQORD-ISQNBO-IORDPT).GT.0) GO TO 95
510 ISQORD = ISQORD + IORDQN
    IORDPR = IORDPR + IORDQN
    IQNORD(NRPQUE) = IQNORD(NRPQUE) + IORDQN
    GO TO 90
 95 IF(IOUTOP.EQ.1.OR.IOUTOP.EQ.3) GO TO 99
    IF(ISHTOP.EQ.1) WRITE(6,134) IPRIOD,IQNINV,ISQORD,IORDPR,
   1IDUEIN(NRPQUE),ORDCST
    IF(ISHTOP.EQ.2) WRITE(6,145) IPRIOD,IQNINV,ISQORD,IORDPR,
   1IDUEIN(NRPQUE),ORDCST
    IF(ISHTOP.EQ.3) WRITE(6,157) IPRIOD,IQNINV,ISQORD,IORDPR,
   1IDUEIN(NRPQUE),ORDCST
 99 IF(IOUTOP.LT.3) GO TO 999
    IF(IRPINT.GT.0) GO TO 999
310 IRPINT = ZRPINT
    IF(IOUTOP.EQ.3) GO TO 415
    IF(IOUTOP.EQ.4) WRITE(6,192)
    IF(ISHTOP.EQ.1) WRITE(6,129)
    IF(ISHTOP.EQ.2) WRITE(6,139)
    IF(ISHTOP.EQ.3) WRITE(6,149)
415 IF(ISHTOP.EQ.2) GO TO 419
    IF(ISHTOP.EQ.3) GO TO 423
416 IF(NRPQUE.GT.0) GO TO 418
417 WRITE (6,180)IPRIOD,IQNINV,ISQORD
    GO TO 999
418 WRITE (6,180)IPRIOD,IQNINV,ISQORD,(IQNORD(I), IDUEIN(I),I = 1,NRPQ
   1UE)
    GO TO 450
419 WRITE (6,181)IPRIOD,IQNINV,ISQORD,ISQNBO
    IF(NRPQUE.GT.0) WRITE(6,182)(IQNORD(I),IDUEIN(I),I=1,NRPQUE)
    IF(NBOQUE.LT.1) GO TO 450
422 WRITE (6,183)(IQNBKO(I),ITMBKO(I),I = 1,NBOQUE)
    GO TO 450
423 WRITE (6,184)IPRIOD,IQNINV,ISQORD,ISQNBO
    IF(NRPQUE.LT.1) GO TO 425
424 WRITE (6,185)(IQNORD(I),IDUEIN(I), I = 1,NRPQUE)
425 IF(NBOQUE.LT.1) GO TO 450
426 WRITE (6,186)(IQNBKO(I),ITMBKO(I), I = 1,NBOQUE)
450 IF(IOUTOP.LT.4) GO TO 999
451 WRITE (6,190)
    IF(ISHTOP.EQ.1) WRITE(6,130)
    IF(ISHTOP.EQ.2) WRITE(6,140)
    IF(ISHTOP.EQ.3) WRITE(6,150)
999 CONTINUE
C
C   COMPILE SUMMARY STATISTICS AND PRINT SUMMARY
C
    WRITE (6,160)
    ZPRIOD = IPRIOD
    ZSNORD = ISNORD
    ZSNREC = ISNREC
    ZSLOST = ISLOST
    ZSNBKO = ISNBKO
    ZSUDLY = ISUDLY
    ZSBOFL = ISBOFL
    ZSQNBO = ISQNBO
    WRITE (6,161)ZSDEMD
    AVGINV = ZSINON/ZPRIOD
    CARCST = AVGINV * PRICE * ZINTRT * ZPRIOD
    WRITE (6,162)AVGINV,CARCST
```

PROGRAM LISTING *(Cont.)*

```
      SORCST = ZSNORD * ORDCST
      WRITE (6,163)ISNORD,SORCST
      SRCCST = ZSNREC * RECCST
      WRITE (6,164)ISNREC,SRCCST
      IF(ISHTOP.EQ.2) GO TO 97
   96 SLOCST = ZSLOST * ZLOCST
      WRITE (6,165)ISLOST,SLOCST
      SERFAC = (ZSDEMD - ZSLOST)/ZSDEMD
      WRITE (6,166)SERFAC
      IF(ISHTOP.EQ.1) GO TO 98
   97 SBOCST = ZSNBKO * BKOCST
      WRITE (6,167)ISNBKO,SBOCST
      BKOSER = ZSUDLY/ZSBOFL
      WRITE (6,168)BKOSER
      TOTSER = ZSUDLY/(ZSDEMD - ZSLOST - ZSQNBO)
      WRITE (6,169)TOTSER
   98 TOTCST = CARCST + SORCST + SRCCST + SLOCST + SBOCST
      WRITE (6,170)TOTCST
      GO TO 1
      END
```

PROGRAM FLOW DIAGRAM

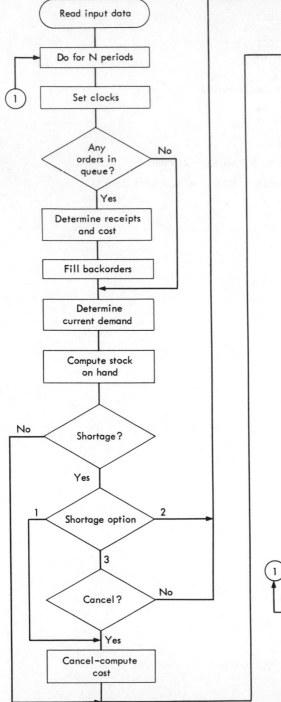

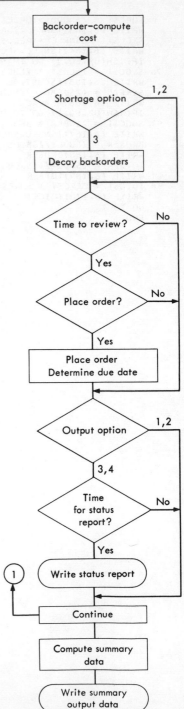

Appendix C Industrial Dynamics Model of Production-
Distribution System Written in DYNAMO


```
*           DYNAMO
RUN
NOTE        MODEL OF PRODUCTION-DISTRIBUTION SYSTEM
SPEC        DT=0.1/LENGTH=52/PRTPER=1/PLTPER=1
PRINT       1)DSLSR/2)DSHPR/3)DINV/4)DORDR/5)WUNOR/6)WSHPR/7)WINV/8)WORDR/9)FO
X1          BKL/10)DEPR/11)FPRR
PLOT        DORDR=C,WORDR=R,FPRR=P,DSLSR=S(8E+C3,16E+03)/DINV=I,WINV=N,FOBKL=B
X1          (0,200E+03)
NOTE
45R         DSLSR.KL=STEP(SLSTP,8)                        DEALER SALES RATE
54R         DSHPR.KL=MIN(DSLSR.JK,DSRLM.K)                DEALER SHIPPING RATE
20A         DSRLM.K=DINV.K/DFDOR                          DLR SHIP RATE LIMIT
1L          DINV.K=DINV.J+(DT)(GRECR.JK-DSHPR.JK)         DEALER INVENTORY
39R         GRECR.KL=DELAY3(WSHPR.JK,TRNDL)               GOODS RECEIVED RATE
7R          DORDR.KL=AVDSL.K+DINAJ.K                      DEALER ORDER RATE
3L          AVDSL.K=AVDSL.J+(DT)(1/TAVDS)(DSLSR.K-AVDSL.J) AV DLR SALES
21A         DINAJ.K=(1/TADIN)(DDINV.K-DINV.K)             DEALER INV ADJUSTMENT
12A         DDINV.K=(DWIND)(AVDSL.K)                      DESIRED DLR INVENTORY
1L          WUNOR.K=WUNOR.J+(DT)(DORDR.JK-WSHPR.JK)       WHSE UNFILLED ORDERS
54R         WSHPR.KL=MIN(WSRLM.K,WNSPR.K)                 WHSE SHIPPING RATE
20A         WSRLM.K=WINV.K/DFWOR                          WHSE SHIP RATE LIMIT
20A         WNSPR.K=WUNOR.K/DFWOR                         WHSE INDICATED SHIP RT
1L          WINV.K=WINV.J+(DT)(FPRR.JK-WSHPR.JK)          WHSE INVENTORY
7R          WORDR.KL=AVWSL.K+WINAJ.K                      WHSE ORDER RATE
3L          AVWSL.K=AVWSL.J+(DT)(1/TAVWS)(DORDR.JK-AVWSL.J) AV WHSE SALES
21A         WINAJ.K=(1/TAWIN)(WDINV.K-WINV.K)             WHSE INV ADJUSTMENT
12A         WDINV.K=(WWIND)(AVWSL.K)                      WHSE DESIRED INVENTORY
1L          FOBKL.K=FOBKL.J+(DT)(WORDR.JK-FPRR.JK)        FACTORY ORDER BACKLOG
20A         INDPR.K=FOBKL.K/WBKLD                         INDICATED PRODUCTION
56A         DEPR.K=MAX(INDPR.K,0)                         DESIRED PRODUCTION
3L          FPRAB.K=FPRAB.J+(DT)(1/TAJPR)(DEPR.J-FPRAB.J)  PRODUCTION ABILITY
6R          FPRR.KL=FPRAB.K                               FACTORY PRODUCTION RATE
NOTE
NOTE        CONSTANTS
NOTE
C           SLSTP=12000  UNITS/WEEK                       SALES STEP
C           DFDOR=1      WEEK                             DELAY IN FILLING ORDER
C           TRNDL=2      WEEKS                            TRANSIT DELAY
C           TAVDS=12     WEEKS                            TIME TO AV DLR SALES
C           TADIN=8      WEEKS                            TIME TO ADJUST DLR INV
C           DWIND=4      WEEKS                            DEALER WEEKS INV DES
C           DFWOR=1      WEEK                             DELAY IN FILLING ORDER
C           TAVWS=8      WEEKS                            TIME TO AV WHSE SALES
C           TAWIN=16     WEEKS                            TIME TO ADJ WHSE INV
C           WWIND=4      WEEKS                            WHSE WEEKS INV DESIRED
C           WBKLD=4      WEEKS                            WEEKS BACKLOG DESIRED
C           TAJPR=4      WEEKS                            TIME TO ADJUST PRODN
NOTE
NOTE        INITIAL VALUES
NOTE
6N          DSLSR=10000  UNITS/WEEK
6N          AVDSL=DSLSR
6N          DINV=DDINV
6N          DORDR=DSLSR
6N          WUNOR=DSLSR
6N          WINV=WDINV
6N          WORDR=DSLSR
6N          AVWSL=DORDR
12N         FOBKL=(DSLSR)(WBKLD)
6N          FPRAB=DEPR
```

Appendix D Flow Charts for Heuristic Program to Play Two Person, Zero Sum Game*

ANALYSIS OF MATRIX ROWS

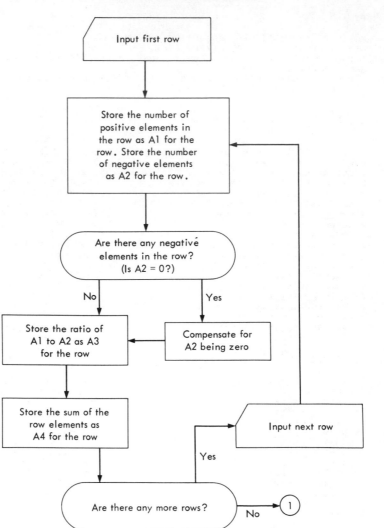

*Adapted from C. Richard Corner, *Simulation of Human Thought: A Study of Decision Making in a Structured, Competitive Environment,* unpublished MBA thesis (Pullman, Washington: Washington State University, 1965).

CREATION OF PLAYER'S (MACHINE'S) PREFERRED ROW LISTS

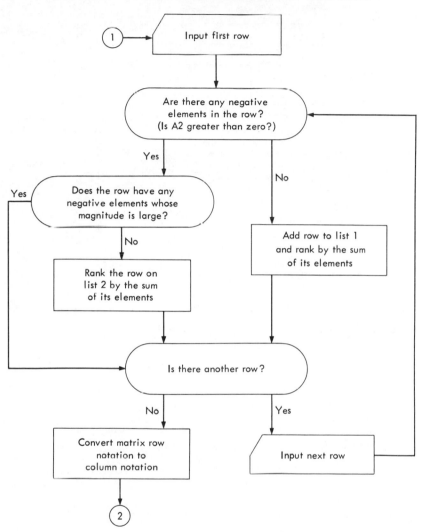

ANALYSIS OF MATRIX COLUMNS

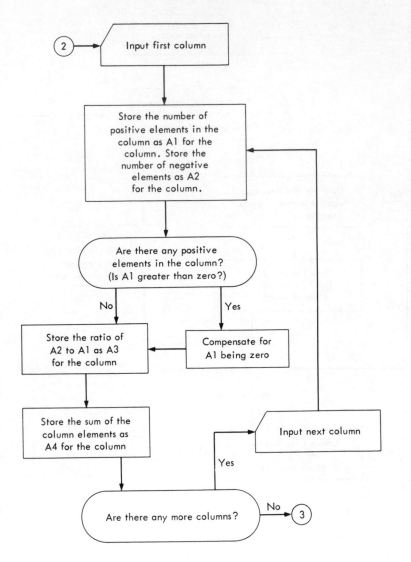

CREATION OF PREFERRED COLUMN LIST FOR OPPONENT

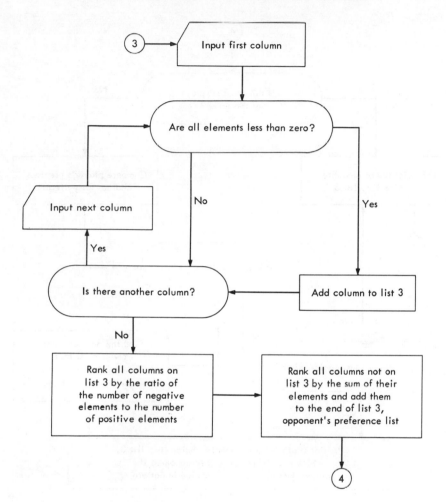

PREDICTION OF OPPONENT'S CHOICE

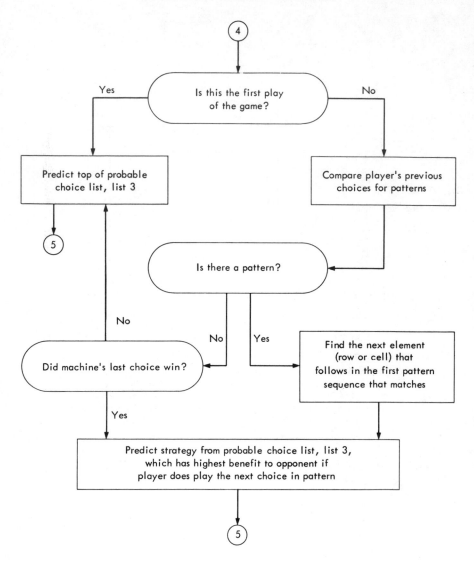

SELECTION OF PLAYER'S CHOICE

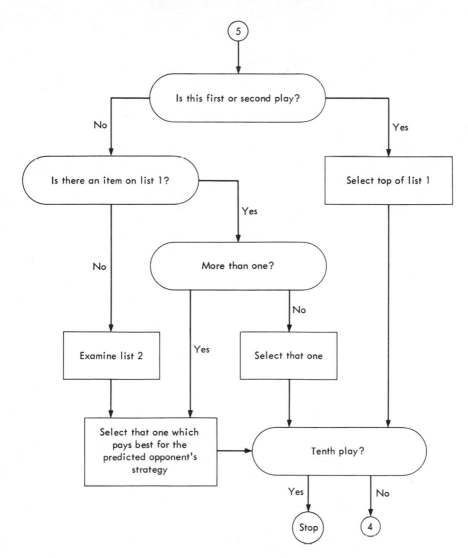

Index

363